TEACHER

POLITICIAN

LAWYER

JOHN M. MWANAKATWE

TEACHER

POLITICIAN

LAWYER

_____

My Autobiography

Bookworld Publishers

Published by Bookworld Publishers
PO Box 32581, Lusaka, Zambia.
2003

ISBN 9982-24-021-8

The author and publishers wish to thank the following for permission to
publish extracts from their publications: Fr Drevensk for extracts from
Challange Magazine No 3, Vol 3, 2001; the editor of the *Daily Mail* for an
extract from the edition of 21/11/83; Robert Molteno and William Tordoff
for a quotation from "Government and Administration" in *Politics in
Zambia*, ed W Tordoff, Manchester University Press, 1974; Peter Snelson
for quotations from *To Independence and Beyond; Memoirs of a Colonial
and Commonwealth Civil Servant*, the Radcliff Press, 1992.

Typesetting by Fergan Limited, Lusaka, Zambia.

Printed by Intrepid Printers (Pty), Ltd
Pietermaritzburg, South Africa.
5350

To my children, Kalelelya,
Mupanga, Chisha and Chipampe
and their children

Also by John M. Mwanakatwe

Growth of Education in Zambia since Independence. Oxford University Press, 1968.

End of Kaunda Era. Multimedia, Zambia, 1994.

CONTENTS

Part Four : 1991-2002

LIST OF ILLUSTRATIONS

P R E F A C E

It is universally accepted that an autobiography is, by definition, a subjective piece of writing. It is equally accepted that a politician or former politician finds the task difficult and daunting. Writing an autobiography is difficult because it is based on the author's own recollections of events, his feelings or opinions. Consequently, readers may sometimes feel that the author is creating the impression that his life was different from the lives of others.

Of course, that is not true. Where an author reveals remarkable successes or failures in his lifetime in an autobiography, there will often be hundreds of other people deserving of praise or sympathy for his or her success or failure. Although I have always worked hard in my life, nevertheless I have always been surrounded by members of my family and many friends whose advice, support and encouragement has been invaluable. Therefore, for all my successes in my teaching career, in politics and law practice I owe gratitude to many friends, fellow workers and colleagues in Zambia and elsewhere. However, for my failures I alone accept responsibility.

In writing this biography, I owe a debt of gratitude to many people. However, I am obliged to thank a variety of individuals whom I owe an enormous debt. A one time colleague of mine in the political arena, Boniface Zulu, was the first person to request me to write my autobiography. His request fell on deaf ears – I was not keen, not least because I knew that it was an arduous and time-consuming exercise. Later, an intimate and trusted friend, the late Andrew Mutemba, similarly requested me to write my autobiography. His request, too, fell on deaf ears. The late Andrew Mutemba then decided to write the biography and seriously embarked on it. Alas, he died before the project was completed.

It was in response to the wishes of Boniface Zulu and the late Andrew Mutemba that I undertook late in 2000 to write this book. I retreated with my wife in September 2001 to River Motel, a quiet place about one hour drive south of Lusaka, the capital city of Zambia. There I chose, in the words of the famous English poet, John Milton, "to scorn delights and live laborious days". I regret that Andrew Mutemba died before the publication of this book. I here record my deep gratitude to Boniface Zulu and the late Andrew Mutemba for sowing the seed. Fortunately, eventually it fell on fertile ground.

My thanks also go to my family who were unfailingly supportive of my efforts throughout. In particular, I thank my wife, Margaret, for her usual patience and for ensuring that my routine requirements of tea and meals at regular intervals were readily available in our home in Lusaka or at River Motel in Kafue. For the services rendered by the efficient staff at the River Motel, I say "thank you".

My eldest son, Mupanga, showed exceptional interest in my book-writing effort. He often undertook to research for me the necessary information when it was not available in my library. He also willingly undertook to proofread some chapters when I was too preoccupied. I shall remain eternally grateful to him for his assistance. Many individuals and publishers of newspapers were very supportive of this exercise and I wish to record my appreciation of their assistance and encouragement. Without doubt, early publication of this book would have been impossible without the assistance I received from the Director of the National Archives of Zambia. I owe to the Director and her staff a debt of gratitude.

Finally, thanks to Dr Fay Gadsden, the Director in Bookworld Publishers Limited, publishers of this book. Without Dr Gadsden's encouragement, completion of this arduous task would not have been achieved at an early stage. Thanks are also due to Mrs Jennifer Mwanza who typed the whole manuscript for this book with remarkable efficiency, patience and dedication.

JM Mwanakatwe, SC, Lusaka, 2003

CHAPTER

1

My Childhood

When I was four years old, I had an unusual encounter with my father. It happened at Mazabuka in the Southern Province where we lived in a compound for African employees of the Public Works Department in Northern Rhodesia, called Zambia today. It was an unforgettable experience.

Just before sunset one afternoon, I became excited when I saw my father walking towards our house in the compound. As usual, I ran to meet him. Unfortunately, I stepped on broken glass while running towards him. Consequently, my left foot was badly injured. I sustained a very deep cut on the sole of my foot which started bleeding profusely. I cried. My father was very annoyed with me when he realised the seriousness of the injury. He told me that I should not have gone running to welcome him outside the house when it was getting dark. For my carelessness or thoughtlessness, he chose to mete out punishment. He gave me a few strokes on my buttocks with a light cane. Meanwhile, my left foot continued to bleed profusely. My mother was not amused by what my father had done. She protested mildly – she was by nature a reserved and quiet person.

Fortunately for me our next door neighbour, Julius Kombe, was a close friend of my father. He was a supervisor of carpenters in the workshop at the Public Works Department. My father was a supervisor in the building section of the department. Our neighbour originally came from Kasama District in the Northern Province whereas my father's original home was in Abercorn

1

(now Mbala) some one hundred miles to the north of Kasama. Mr Kombe acted on that occasion as a good Samaritan. He took me to his house, brought warm water for washing the wound and then covered it with cotton wool after applying iodine to protect it from germs. The wound was neatly bandaged. This routine was repeated several times until the wound was healed completely. However, it left a scar which is still visible today. To the best of my recollection that was the only time I was ever caned by my father or any other person.

In later years, I came to know that although my father was a quiet person, though not as reserved as my mother, he was generally a tough, no-nonsense type of man, the product of a lifetime of working with and surviving the harsh white bosses who believed in those days that the African workmen were generally lazy and incompetent.

In 1940, when I was fourteen years old, I had a second memorable encounter with my father, an encounter of a different nature. One of my father's favourite hobbies was hunting and shooting birds and game of all types, a hobby I was to follow in later years as an adult. We had gone out on a hunting expedition at night not far away from where we lived in Lusaka. He was fond of hunting small animals at night with a very powerful torch tied to the cap on his head. It was quite easy to kill animals at night using torch light which tended to blind them. The hunter was able to get quite close to an animal before shooting it.

One of my father's aides (a man called Luneta who was a labourer employed by the government) had joined us on this particular hunting expedition. Just before midnight, my father shot down a duiker. Later, he shot and killed another duiker. Luneta wanted to carry both duikers on his shoulders tied to a wooden stick, one in front and the other behind him. The suggestion was unacceptable to my father who felt strongly that it was my duty to carry one duiker on my shoulders. Luneta tried unsuccessfully to persuade him that I was too young to bear the burden. However, it was quite clear that a command had been given which Luneta and I were obliged to obey.

Indeed, as predicted by Luneta, the duiker was too heavy for me although I did not complain. When hunting at night, the person having the torch and carrying a gun leads the others by a good distance of some twenty or thirty yards in order to minimise noise so that animals do not run away before a deadly shot is fired. Trailing alone behind Luneta, I stumbled over a tree and fell down. I cried to Luneta for help which I readily received from him. Without my father's approval, he found a suitable dry stick which he used to carry the duikers balancing them on his shoulders.

My father had to wait for us whilst Luneta improvised some way of carrying the duikers. When we caught up with him, it was his turn to rebuke me for being a weakling. What my father failed to appreciate, I instinctively felt, was that there were certain tasks which I could not perform because I was too young – not that I was lazy or merely a weakling. However, as I grew up, I began to appreciate that my father wanted me to grow up with a sense of self-reliance and responsibility. In fact, even in my early childhood, I was expected to keep my room tidy and assist my mother by performing some domestic chores.

I was born a few years before the Great Depression which adversely affected the economies of many countries in the world in the early 1930s. My birthplace was Chinsali boma in the Northern Province. I was born on 1 November 1926, the third child of my parents (Timothy Mwanakatwe and Margaret Namukale Nsongola Mwanakatwe) after my brother Joseph Chisha, who was twelve years older, and my sister Emily Chola, born four years before me. There were other children born before me who did not survive. Fortunately, in later years, I had two younger sisters, Rachel Chisha and Hellen, and a brother, Abel, born after Rachel but before Hellen. My parents always told me that I was an extraordinarily healthy child from the time I was born.

My father gave me two names when I was born, Jonathan and Mupanga, the first a name from the Bible and the second my maternal grandmother's name. In my early childhood, only a few people called me Jonathan. Most people, in fact nearly everyone, simply called me *John*. Apparently, the vast majority of our relatives and friends could not pronounce the name Jonathan. It was much easier for them to call me *John*. That is understandable. My own mother was illiterate. She had never gone to school in her life. In fact, it is probably not an exaggeration to suggest that when I was born very few people in the whole country knew how to read or write. Later, in 1936 when I was baptised into the Methodist Church by Reverend John R. Shaw, the name *John* featured on my baptism certificate. Both my father and mother were present at the simple church service in a classroom at the Central Trades School.

It is by accident that I was born at the boma in Chinsali District. My father's home district was Abercorn in the Northern Province of the then Northern Rhodesia. At the end of the First World War, my father left employment as a supervisor of village schools with the London Missionary Society at Kambole Mission in Abercorn District. He had attended school at Kambole Mission at the beginning of the twentieth century and completed the elementary school course, later qualifying as a certificated teacher responsible for supervision of village schools under the authority of Reverend James A. Ross, the minister-in-charge. While in the employment of the London Missionary Society, my father also acquired building and carpentry skills.

When I was born, my father was already employed by the government in the Public Works Department. He was stationed at Chinsali with the team which was responsible for construction of buildings, such as offices and houses for the government. Later, he had a stint in Fort Rosebery, called Mansa today, on a similar assignment before he was transferred to Mazabuka. There he participated in the construction of the Agricultural Research Station and other structures under Mr Walker, overall supervisor of projects undertaken by the Public Works Department in Mazabuka.

It was during our stay in Mazabuka from 1929 to 1932 that I remember listening to my father's tales about his family's position in the social hierarchy of the Ulungu people of North-East Zambia. These fireside tales were told to us from time to time, even when we became older boys and girls, in order to inculcate in us a sense of pride. We were told that in Ulungu one's name is inherited and transmitted patrilineally as membership of a particular name-category. One such name-category is the royal category – *Kazwe* and another is the former royal category – *Nyangwe*. We learnt that male members of a name-category are distinguished by the prefix *Si-* and female members of a name-category take the prefix *Na-*.

My father inherited the patrilineal name-category of – *Kazwe* when he was born. However, early in his boyhood he adopted the name *Mwanakatwe* for his own identity. To many relatives and friends he remained a *Sikazwe*. My mother, too, was a *Nakazwe* in her own right. I have always regretted that fate never made it possible for me to know my grand-parents from both sides. They had all died before I was born.

I have never been overly conscious of my social status as a member of the *Sikazwe* clan. Of course, whenever I receive unsolicited respect or favours from men and women who know that I belong to the royal category of Sikazwe, their generosity is appreciated. Fortunately, my father brought me up in a home situation which was congenial. By the standards of his time, we lived in comfort largely because he was a hard-working man. In fact, in my early childhood, I saw little of my father. He left home very early every morning in time to check the report of latecomers to work and absentees. My mother was devoted to her life as wife and parent. It centred entirely around her husband and children. Their health and happiness were the sum of her ambition for them.

However, more importantly I grew up in a family where there was harmony. I can hardly remember a time when my father and mother quarrelled in my presence. They were a rather quiet couple who spent most of their leisure time studying the Bible and praying. We were also encouraged as children to study the Bible and to participate in prayers. So my exposure to the

Scriptures was focused and systematic. Every Sunday (unless some extraordinary event made it impossible) we all went to church. It was the day when we all dressed smartly. As a small boy, I remember attending church services regularly at the old Methodist Church near Chibolya Compound in Lusaka. Church services were held in the morning every Sunday. Often, my father carried me to church on a bicycle. Usually, there was a real treat for lunch after the church service. My mother's special meal for the family on Sunday sometimes included fried rice or cooked sweet potatoes mixed with grated groundnuts. My father was also a lay preacher in the Methodist Church until he retired from government service and returned to Mbala in 1946. Looking back, I can say that it was my father's energy, his enthusiasm, his sense of mission that made me look up to him as a role model. Throughout my childhood and adolescence, my main ambition was to live up to his standard and grow up to be like him.

Only one event in the family saddened me as a child. This happened when I was about seven years old. In the early 1930s – I cannot remember the exact year – a team of fortune-tellers toured Northern Rhodesia from the Far East, most likely from China or Japan. It seems that they were qualified and experienced in astrology. When they arrived in Lusaka (which had not yet replaced Livingstone as the country's capital), there was great excitement. Many white men and women of various nationalities flocked to see and consult the strange *wise men from the East*! They claimed ability to foretell the future of any person who went to consult them upon payment of a very small fee. Because white men and women went in large numbers to consult these fortune-tellers, many Africans, perhaps out of curiosity, also went for advice from the strange men from the East.

My mother's health at that time was of grave concern to my father. She was indeed a more sickly person than my father who suffered from asthma from time to time, especially during cold days in winter. So my father decided to take my mother to the astrologers in the tents they had pitched close to the railway line and centre of our then small town – Lusaka. The outcome of the visit of our parents to the astrologers was extremely demoralising. My father's health was diagnosed as good. From the stars they had read clearly that he had a very long life before him. However, their report on the health of my mother was bleak. They informed my father bluntly that they recognised from the stars that her life would be short – very short indeed. No one, they claimed, was able to change the course of the stars in relation to her life.

Because I was very young at that time, neither of my parents wanted me to know the outcome of their visit to the fortune-tellers. However, through my elder sister, I came to know why there was an atmosphere of sadness and gloom in the family. I was greatly disturbed because I was very fond of my dear mother. Because I was a child, I began spreading the news to my friends – small boys I played with from nearby houses. In turn, they also told their parents about the impending demise of my mother. This caused embarrassment both to "dear mother" and "dear daddy".

However, the authority of men (the astrologers in this case) can never surpass the power of God. As years went by, I came to realise that God is the *ultimate* governing authority. It turned out that my mother, after all, had long life – in fact, she eventually outlived my father who died in 1962. My mother died fourteen years later in 1976.

Once or twice since we became adults I have had the pleasure of talking to my boyhood friend whom I told the verdict of the astrologers when his father and my father worked together for the Public Works Department in Lusaka. We lived in Kamwala compound and later went to the same school, Munali Training Centre. There I had many more friends with whom I engaged in all sorts of activities, including hide and seek, tug-of-war and killing birds with catapults or setting traps to catch them. However, I missed hunting with a bow and arrow and fishing because I spent the formative years of my life living in towns with my parents and not in our village called *Chinakila* in the Chisha area of Mbala District.

Fortunately, when I was ten years old, my father went on leave. The government had allowed my father three months leave in 1936 after four years of continuous service. We spent all that time in the village with the relatives of my father who included the chief himself (Henry Lyapa Sikazwe) who was a cousin of my father. In fact, one of the chief's wives was a younger sister of my father (the chief was a polygamist). The entire area of Chief Chinakila was in those days a self-sufficient community where the word hunger was never heard. Rice, maize, finger-millet, fish, bananas, honey and other foodstuffs were plentiful. For me and my new friends in the village, hunting and fishing were not luxury pursuits; they were available at any convenient time.

After three months of absolute fun and enjoyment of rural life, we returned to Lusaka. Fortunately, life changed for me a few years later. In September 1939, I entered the boarding section of Munali Training Centre. I was enrolled in the upper primary section of the school in standard five. That was the beginning of a long, eventful and interesting process of learning and training.

CHAPTER

2

Education and Training

My formal education began when I was about seven years old. That was a very early age for enrolment of an African child in school in those days. It was done, not without difficulties, only because my father was anxious that I should begin my education at an early age.

In 1933, my father left the Public Works Department and joined Frederick Hodgson, a white officer whom the government had appointed to supervise construction of a new institution for training young African men in carpentry, bricklaying, roof-thatching and other crafts, such as leatherwork and tailoring. The new institution was built where David Kaunda Technical Secondary School is situated today. Therefore, my parents were obliged to move houses in Lusaka from Kamwala Compound to a new settlement near the present day Chimbokaila Central Prison. Our new residence was a short walking distance to the site where the new institution was to be built by the government under Frederick Hodgson's supervision. The proposal to build the new institution, later to be called Munali Training Centre, was the brain-child of the governor of Northern Rhodesia, Sir Hubert Young. The objective of the institution's establishment was to train Africans for government departments and the private sector.

Before the construction of Munali Training Centre was completed, schooling facilities for the children of residents of Chimbokaila Compound were non-existent. For me the nearest school was the Methodist primary school which was about three miles away. It was originally established by the Methodist Church at the request of the African Education Department before the government was able to provide educational facilities for African children in Lusaka. Fortunately, my elder sister had already enrolled as a pupil there before we moved from Kamwala Compound to Chimbokaila. We took at least an hour to walk along a dusty road to the primary school. We had, of course, to walk back home after classes. This was part of our school routine from Monday to Friday every week. The company of my sister on the walk to school and back home was a great relief and consolation to me.

I do not recollect the occurrence of any spectacular event during the two years of my scholarship at the Methodist primary school. Nothing happened which I remember as interesting or exciting except involvement in a fight with other boys occasionally. At no time did I ever go home with a bloody nose. There was hardly any mockery of newcomers by old pupils. Perhaps such conduct was not tolerated in a school run by a Church organisation which had already established two notable full primary schools in the country, namely Kafue Mission School for boys and Chipembi, which was then a coeducational school. Both were boarding schools. The picture I have of my first school is that it was built on sandy soil. In fact, the area surrounding the classroom block was stony ground, a condition which made it difficult for the head teacher of the school to involve pupils in school gardening. Gardening was in those days an important part of the school curriculum. I also remember that we were always over-crowded in class and that there were insufficient school desks.

However, it is said that there is always a silver lining in every dark cloud. My mother had a cousin who lived in a nearby compound called Chibolya. His house was less than ten minutes walk from the school. He was a well known and popular shoe repairer in Chibolya and beyond. And, typical of pre-marital arrangements within the family among the people of Ulungu in those days, Samuel Kalekete's wife was a niece of my father!

So during the first two years of my formal education at the Methodist primary school, I always felt at home away from home. My mother advised me to go to Uncle Samuel Kalekete's home if ever I felt ill or hungry and needed some rest or food to eat.

Nonetheless, I was not unhappy when in 1936 I enrolled in standard one in the elementary school section of the primary school at Munali Training Centre. The construction of the new institution had not been completed yet. But good judgement followed a realisation that construction of an elementary school section was an immediate priority. Construction of such a school was one way of stabilising employees who lived in the Munali area, the Regiment, the Hospital Compound and the Governor's Village. They wanted their children to go to school. As a pupil at the elementary school of Munali, it took less than fifteen minutes to walk from our house to my classroom. Both in winter and in summer I had no difficulties in attending school regularly and punctually.

Throughout a period of three years at the elementary school, we had only three teachers who taught three classes in the morning and three others in the afternoon. William Konie was the head teacher assisted by Peter Chombela and another teacher. They were dedicated men who were liked and admired by their pupils. They rarely applied corporal punishment on offending pupils. They were both fatherly and kind to all, although they wanted us to be punctual at all times, clean and tidy and well behaved. Unfortunately, the trio were later forced to separate. William Konie was transferred on promotion to open a new elementary school about fifteen miles from Lusaka on the Great North Road. He well deserved the promotion because he was one of the few highly educated Africans at that time with long experience in teaching. He had attended Tiger Kloof High School in South Africa and obtained a Junior Secondary School Certificate. He knew my parents who liked him as much as I did. So we all regretted his transfer to a new station. However, little did I know that one day old William Konie would act as my *shibukombe* (the man entrusted to negotiate with a girl's parents on behalf of a man intending to marry their daughter). That is exactly what happened fourteen years later!

Peter Chombela was appointed head teacher after William Konie's departure from our school. Jameson Nyirenda arrived from Eastern Province to assist Peter Chombela. The school was never the same after William Konie's departure. The new assistant teacher lacked enthusiasm and he failed to inspire the boys and girls. Fortunately, I passed well in the standard four examinations. Therefore, early in September 1939, I progressed to standard five in the upper primary school. That progression entitled me to a place in a boarding school. I felt that as a boarder at Munali I would no longer be under the care and protection of my parents. I was excited by the prospect of enjoying some form of freedom which I could not really define. Yet my parents were always generous and affectionate towards me. But I do not remember playing with my father or with my mother as I grew up at home. In some societies, it would not be strange for a ten or twelve year old boy to refer to his father as his chum. In our culture that would be taboo. As a boarder, I looked forward to the opportunity of making new friends and growing up to be more independent of my parents.

In some ways, my parents had prepared me for the time when I would fend for myself in life. During school holidays, I usually joined other boys of my age at the Golf Club in Lusaka. There we worked as caddies for golfers intending to play one round of nine holes after a day's work. Golf is known to be an expensive game generally. Therefore, in the late thirties and early forties it was only a white man's game. If a caddie was smartly dressed with a little knowledge of spoken English, the chance of regular earnings from performing the services of a caddie was quite good. A caddie was paid only three or at the most six pennies for a round of nine holes. Yet to my mother that otherwise paltry sum of money was like a ton of gold. She made certain that I saved every penny. Occasionally, she allowed me to draw a few pennies from the savings kept in a tin to buy sweets or scones for myself. Once my father paid the boarding fees, he did not hesitate to give me the full amount of pocket money which he considered adequate for each term. He was satisfied that I was properly prepared to account for the way I spent my pocket money. This is a habit which I have tried over the years to inculcate in my own children.

One hurdle, however, appeared insurmountable to me. Was I going to survive the traditional mockery of newcomers by old students? Because I grew up in the Munali environment, I knew the severity of mockery of new students and the extent of barbarism exhibited by the old students in the process. Were oldcomers likely to inflict on me the worst form of mockery because my own father was a member of staff at the school? I suffered from endless nightmares due to such considerations. My worries in reality came to nothing due to the unexpected intervention of a senior student on my behalf. That student was Abraham Willombe. He was a cousin of my mother and, therefore, an uncle to me. He became my protector.

Munali Training Centre was officially opened in October 1938. The name "Munali", a word meaning master, was one of the names given to Dr David Livingstone, the famous nineteenth century explorer. It was conceived as a "composite institution" to provide "a full Primary Course with Junior Secondary, Teacher Training, Clerical, Interpreters' and Trades Courses superimposed".* The Annual Report describes the educational content and scope of the primary school course as follows:-

The primary school recruits boys from all parts of the Territory and prepares them specifically for entrance to the vocational courses. English and scientific subjects receive special attention and the curriculum has a wider application than is possible at the average village school. While whatever is studied is applied to local conditions, the teaching aims, nevertheless, at developing a European attitude towards methods and processes.

---

* Annual Report 1938: Munali Training Centre: Department of Native Education

13

The school was well staffed and equipped to undertake its mission effectively. The staff at Munali responsible for teaching academic subjects, instructing carpenters and bricklayers were properly qualified and carefully selected. The principal, assistant master, clerical instructor and industrial supervisor were all Europeans. There were sixteen African members of staff.

There was a special relationship between Frederick Hodgson, the principal, and my father. He was among the first Africans from the government's Public Works Department to join Frederick Hodgson's team appointed early in 1934 to set up a new trades school in Lusaka. Apparently, from the first time they met a rapport developed between them. Progressively over the years, Frederick Hodgson entrusted more responsibilities to my father in the administration of the school. He was specifically employed as the thatching instructor. When I became a boarder at the school in September 1939, my father was also performing the boarding master's responsibilities. They involved purchasing all food items such as maize meal, meat, beans and vegetables, keeping records of such purchases and their utilisation. He was responsible, too, for supervision of cooks in the school kitchen and the employment of all casual workers in the school.

These responsibilities kept my father fully occupied. That is why I saw little of him during my early childhood. Casual job seekers always knew that my father's decision to employ or not to employ them was usually final. They nicknamed him *Ba Kabiyeni* which meant literally "Mr Go Away". He used the word *Kabiyeni* to tell jobseekers politely to go away when a job was not available. The principal, too, like most members of staff, had a nickname. He was called "Mr White" by students. Reason? Both during the hot weather and even when the weather was cool he invariably wore a white suit. He was immaculately dressed every day.

Under the principal, Frederick Hodgson, and the head African teacher, ACJ Ramathe, Munali was run like a public school in England. Discipline among students was strictly enforced. All students were expected to rise at 5.30 hours except on Saturdays and Sundays. We began the day immediately with physical training at 6.15 hours followed by breakfast. All students assembled for morning prayers at 6.45 hours and then dispersed to the classrooms and workshops until noon. In the afternoon, academic students were offered practical training in woodwork or in arts and crafts while the trades apprentices occupied the classrooms for instruction in English and arithmetic. Games, scouting activities or out-door work continued until 18.00 hours.

I always developed cold feet for practical lessons in woodwork or in arts and crafts. I lacked both interest and natural ability for these subjects. It was only many years later, while training as a teacher, that I realised the value of arts and crafts in the education process. On the other hand, I enjoyed evening activities which were optional, arranged from time to time by various student groups. The evening activities included debates, plays, concerts and community singing until lights out at 21.00 hours. There was hardly time at Munali for boys to engage in mischievous activities except during week-ends.

The education we received at Munali reflected the importance the school attributed to character development. Education was not merely for the acquisition of knowledge and skills. Character was developed through the system of school and dormitory captains, the scout troop and cub pack, parades with the school band which was trained by the Northern Rhodesia Regiment and regular sessions of physical training under a sergeant seconded from the regiment. We were encouraged not to despise manual labour through weekly inspection of our dormitories on Saturdays. At a very early age, we were taught about the dignity of labour in a practical manner. We enjoyed waiting at table, washing up of dishes after meals, cleaning and sweeping of dormitories and classrooms.

Of all the hobbies and recreational facilities available at Munali, I especially enjoyed participating in the Boy Scouts and organised school debates. Although I played football and table tennis occasionally, my performance was no more than mediocre. I played the games for the love of sport, not for expectation of any glory.

Perhaps for me the real and lasting benefit I derived as a boarder at Munali was the school's encouragement of religious activities among students. Although Munali was a government-controlled institution it was compulsory for all students to attend the daily morning prayers. Secondly, it was also compulsory for all students to attend Scripture lessons which were part of the curriculum. Thirdly, missionaries of various denominations were afforded facilities to hold their Sunday services at Munali. This arrangement enabled me to enrol in a class of catechumens who took lessons for eventual confirmation as full members of the Methodist Church eligible to participate in the Holy Communion.

Mr John Chikungu, one of the instructors in carpentry, was responsible for teaching catechumens and preparing them for confirmation. He was an experienced teacher and supervisor of catechumen classes. I enjoyed attending his class from which I derived a clearer understanding of important passages in the Holy Bible. After attending classes for about six months, we wrote the qualifying examinations. It was a joyful day in April 1941, when I was confirmed by the Reverend James Mulala. He was the minister-in-charge of the Methodist Church in Lusaka with Reverend John R. Shaw as the overall superintendent. My parents were present in Church at my confirmation.

I was about thirteen years old when I entered Munali. I enrolled as a student in standard five for the two-year upper primary course. In those days, the standard six final examinations were notoriously difficult. They were set and marked centrally by officials at the headquarters of the Department of African Education in Mazabuka. A student's success in the examinations opened unlimited opportunities for acceptance to the two-year junior secondary school course at Munali, medical assistants' course at the African Hospital in Lusaka and to teacher training courses elsewhere in the country, apart from opportunities for training in various courses as artisans. Naturally, the standard six certificate in those days was also highly prized by job seekers in government, the mines and native authorities.

However, mere possession of a standard six certificate was not a guarantee for admission to the first year of the junior secondary school course at Munali. It was the only officially recognized junior secondary school in the country at that time. Competition for the few places available in form I each year was really stiff. The night before I was due to leave our house and move into the dormitory where I was allocated a bed, my father summoned me for a lecture in the presence of my mother. He reminded me that I had always performed well at school. He had always been pleased with my school reports which he received from the head teacher of the lower primary school. However, he emphasized that hard work was the secret for success in life, not least in one's quest for a responsible position in society. Even at that very early age, I learnt from my father that struggle or fighting is the essence of life, that if one cannot struggle or fight one cannot win. I, of course, clearly understood that my father, while emphasizing the necessity of struggle or hard work in life, meant also that discipline was important. That night he reminded me that he was on the staff of Munali. He stated bluntly that misconduct or indiscipline on my part would embarrass him.

Academically, my achievements at Munali in both standards five and six were satisfactory. I was certainly not the best student in our class. I always thought Jones Mzaza was the cleverest student. Mando Mtine was especially clever in arithmetic and general science, but Mzaza's all round performance was notable. Consequently, he came first or – quite rarely – second in tests and examinations. He was a year or two older than me. Perhaps I was the youngest student in the class. Fortunately, my house captain was Abraham Willombe. He was interested in my welfare generally and in my progress academically. He always encouraged me to study hard and to behave properly at all times. He was a third year student in the industrial section of Munali taking carpentry and building courses. I owe him a debt of gratitude. He encouraged me at a critical stage in my educational career. Although sometimes playful, throughout the two-year upper primary school course, I maintained a respectable position among the top five in the class in tests and examinations.

At Munali, for the first time I was taught by teachers who had themselves been properly educated. Some of them held university degrees. I especially admired RJ Seal, an Englishman, who taught us science. He had a master's degree from the University of London and was the author of a science textbook which was prescribed for use in upper primary schools in Northern Rhodesia. Kenan Ng'ambi's lessons in arithmetic and Henry Makulu's in English were always interesting. Both were kind, friendly and conscientious teachers. English and arithmetic were key subjects for success in the standard six examinations.

The teacher who was truly my idol was Donald Songishe. He taught our class geography. Like ACJ Ramathe, he was an African expatriate. Donald Songishe was the most versatile and popular teacher in the school. He was a bachelor, a musician, an athlete and a good football player. He sometimes composed songs. He was also a good guitarist. Often I attended his coaching sessions for football players. There was always something to learn from him. I especially admired his spoken English. His accent did not betray the fact that he was a Xhosa from the Union of South Africa. Undoubtedly, Mr Songishe influenced me to opt for a teaching career after completing secondary education more than any other person.

Our class at Munali was very well prepared for the standard six examinations which were held throughout the country in May 1941. After writing the last paper I had no doubt that I had done well in the whole examination. However, there was a rider to my sense of optimism. Had I performed well enough to merit selection for form one at Munali the following school term? Apart from the few places available at Munali, opportunities for secondary school education were non-existent in the country. Consequently, selection for form one was fiercely competitive. The school authorities could offer places in form one to only fifty to sixty boys who obtained the highest marks on a territorial basis in the standard six examinations.

After writing the examinations I spent the first part of my school holidays with my parents at Munali. Later, in the middle of June, I joined my elder brother's family in Livingstone in the Southern Province. While in Livingstone I received a letter from my father. He informed me that I had passed the standard six examinations and because my performance was very good, the school authorities at Munali had offered me a place in form one. An acceptance form was attached to the letter. Successful applicants were required to report to the headmaster of Munali Secondary School at the beginning of September for the Michaelmas term.

My elder brother was employed in government as a civil servant at that time. He was the senior court interpreter in the High Court in Livingstone. Additionally, he worked for the registrar of the High Court as a stenographer and typist. In those days, the post of shorthand/typist was the preserve of English-speaking white women. The majority of African clerical employees were merely copy typists. He had an insatiable appetite for learning and thereby improving his educational qualifications and advancing his skills. Through correspondence studies, he had obtained the junior secondary school certificate from the University of South Africa. Simultaneously, he had also obtained shorthand and typewriting certificates from Pitman's College in London.

With this background he had on his own undertaken to explore the opportunities available for the furtherance of my education at a recognized institution in South Africa. Through contacts with some friends who had previously gone there for education, he had identified Adams College. It was a well known institution for academic courses and teacher-training programmes. It was certainly suitable for furthering my education. The college's prospectus provided information on the level of fees payable before and after enrolment of students and the range of available course programmes. Although the financial implications of sending me to Adams College were serious, by the time I left Munali at the end of May 1941 he had secured provisional admission for me to form one for the beginning of the first term in February, 1942. He was prepared to make sacrifices to educate me at a reputable institution of learning where I would proceed to complete form five without interruption, subject to satisfactory performance in end-of-year examinations.

Of course, I was excited when I received my father's letter and the form of admission to Munali. Little did I know that my elder brother had obtained a place for me in form one provisionally at Adams College. His proposal meant postponing my entry into form one at Munali in September 1941 to February 1942, at Adams College. My father and I were easily persuaded by my elder brother that his option was advantageous. At Munali at that time I was guaranteed secondary education only for two years after completing standard six. On the other hand, my elder brother was prepared to make sacrifices to educate me at a reputable learning institution at least to matriculation level. But his scheme was initially unacceptable to my mother. She maintained that I was too young to be consigned like a parcel to a foreign land far away. She was neither amused nor enthusiastic about my three-day train journey from Livingstone through Bulawayo, Mafeking and Johannesburg to Durban in South Africa. The last lap was a short journey by train from Durban to Amanzimtoti (Sweet Waters), a small town twenty-three miles south of Durban, followed by another short journey by bus to Adams College. To my mother, it was undoubtedly a long and daunting journey for a fifteen-year-old boy. She was reminded, however, that my boyhood friend, Peter Hodgson, the principal's son, travelled frequently from Lusaka to a high school in Cape Town, South Africa. He was only a year or two older than me.

Reluctantly, my mother accepted my elder brother's proposal to send me to South Africa for secondary education and training.

* * *

In the months following the decline of the offer of a place in form one at Munali, I was quite anxious about my future. The standard six examination results had been sent to Adams College. Even as late as October in 1941, the authorities there had not confirmed the acceptance of my application to enrol in form one at the beginning of 1942. My elder brother was an optimist. He expected a positive response to the application eventually. Therefore, he did not consider another option in the event of my application being unsuccessful. In fact, he was more concerned about mobilizing the necessary resources to pay my school fees, the return railway ticket, book allowance and out-of-pocket expenses generally.

The age difference between us was quite big – something like twelve or thirteen years. According to our culture, I treated him like a parent. Indeed, in conversations with our father, my brother had always emphasized his desire to relieve him altogether from responsibility for my education and training. He wanted me to receive a good education and my elder brother believed I would develop a sense of self-reliance and responsibility by receiving education far away from my parents. He also believed that it was necessary to expose me to foreign cultures at an early age. In that sense, Adams College, an educational institution in the heart of Zululand, run by a community of black and white Christian scholars, had the right environment.

Luckily, the long expected letter accepting me as a student at Adams College arrived in November 1941. What was like a dream to me suddenly became a reality. At last I was accepted for form one in the junior secondary school at the beginning of February 1942. From what my own brother and others had told me, in terms of advancement in education, the sky was the limit.

Luckily, too, my elder brother had mobilized the necessary funds for the realization of his ambition. Before the end of the year, the necessary student's travel documents had arrived.

I had not returned to Lusaka to see my parents since I had left for Livingstone in June. Therefore, it was necessary to go to Lusaka to say goodbye before leaving the country for South Africa for at least one year. My elder brother had advised me to forget the luxury of returning home twice in one year for holidays. To allow me to spend my holiday at home once a year was a real financial burden on him. For two weeks, I was running around in Lusaka bidding farewell to my relatives and friends.

Then the day of reckoning came at the beginning of February in 1942 – departure from Livingstone by train to Johannesburg, Durban and Amanzimtoti. I cannot remember exactly the date and time when I left for South Africa. It was late in the evening when the South Down so-called express train left the station in Livingstone for Johannesburg. My elder brother, my sister-in-law and some of their friends came to the railway station to see me off. Leaving home and saying goodbye to relatives and friends was an emotional experience for me. Somehow, the cheerfulness of my elder brother especially gave me comfort, although I confess that I did shed a few tears as I said goodbye to him. He was proud that he had achieved his ambition. He was proud that I was travelling that evening to South Africa by train in second class at a time when that class was virtually a monopoly of white travellers!

It happened that by God's providence the journey from Livingstone to Amanzimtoti was trouble-free. In fact, the journey was enjoyable and an unforgettable experience. Where we changed trains – Bulawayo, Johannesburg and Durban – a few more students joined us with, of course, ordinary passengers. I felt a sense of relief to see some students wearing the Adams College green blazer with the motto "Arise and Shine" on the badge. In the event of any difficulty, I knew that one or more of them would help me or render the necessary guidance. However, the sense of loneliness persisted because I was unable to engage freely in conversation with young men and women whom I did not know. Buses were waiting for us at the Amanzimtoti railway station to take us and our luggage to Adams College only a few miles away. After a journey of about three days, I arrived eventually at my new *alma mater*. My elder brother's wish was accomplished – I had arrived at an educational institution far away from home; an institution where he expected me to develop a sense of self-reliance and responsibility.

Tired after a very long journey, I went to bed early and slept soundly. In my deep sleep, I felt as though my elder brother was exhorting me never to disappoint him – as though he was saying to me "you must never disappoint me; you must never fail an examination". I have always remembered those words of exhortation.

The first thing that struck me when I arrived at Adams College was its massive buildings of stone blocks. They were scattered all over a large area of the land which belonged to the college. The main buildings included the men's hostel called *Jubilee*, the music hall, the chapel and the dining hall. There were also many small buildings for classrooms and laboratories. The women students had their own residential hostels and ancillary facilities. Not all male students were accommodated in *Jubilee* Hostel. Some senior students lived in small buildings around it. The focal point of all the key buildings was the dining hall which was centrally situated on the campus. It was a unique and imposing structure and it was used for serving meals, for cinema shows and for public lectures and debates.

Adams College was quite a different world from the one I had known at Munali. There were more than five hundred men and women enrolled as students in various departments when I arrived at the college in February 1942, more than treble the population of Munali at the time of my departure! It was quite a spectacle to see streams of students from all directions rushing to the chapel in the morning or to their classrooms. Although at first I felt lost, within only a few days after my arrival I started feeling at home. Actually, I do not remember feeling at all homesick.

I met new students who were also foreigners. They came either from Nyasaland (now Malawi) or from Southern Rhodesia (now Zimbabwe). There was a common factor among us – foreigners from countries far away. Developing friendship with some of them was not difficult. On the other hand, I did not find the average Zulu student friendly to foreigners. In fact, even students from up-country in South Africa thought that Zulu students were unfriendly. But there are always exceptions. After studying at Adams College for seven years, I could count at least two former Zulu-speaking school mates who became life-long friends. In fact, some Zulu students who stayed for many years at Adams College eventually became "detribalised" like their brothers and sisters from up-country areas such as Johannesburg. Once I came to understand their way of life, it was always a joy to be in their company shouting and singing Zulu war songs.

Adams College was a more elitist institution than Munali. Mockery of newcomers was not severe or humiliating, although occasionally seniors treated juniors with haughtiness and disdain. It was established by the American Board of Missions in 1835. Dr Newton Adams was the founder of Adams Mission Station and Adams College. The first college building was completed in 1853. Rev David Rood was the first principal from 1853-1864. By 1942, when I enrolled in form one, the college had been in existence for nearly ninety years. There were four main departments in the college, namely, the high school, the teacher-training, the industrial and music departments. Each department was under a headmaster who controlled his own staff in the department. The overall responsibility for the administration of the institution was vested in the principal. Dr Edgar Brookes was the principal in 1942. The deputy principal was Dr KR Bruekner. He was also responsible for the administration of the industrial department.

Dr Edgar Brookes had at one time served as professor of political science in an Afrikaaner dominated university in South

Africa. Because he had liberal views which were intolerable to many white students, in 1934 he resigned his position as a professor in the university in order to take up the post of principal at Adams College. A few years later he was appointed, with three other whites, to represent the interests of Africans in the Senate (the Upper House) of the South African Parliament. Consequently, Dr Edgar Brookes was usually away from Adams College during term time attending sittings of the Senate in Cape Town. Students usually looked forward to the return of "The Hon Professor Edgar H. Brookes, MP." whose public lectures on political issues in South Africa were always popular among students in the college.

In the first few weeks after completion of the registration formalities, each student was required to obtain two certificates from the bursar, the first confirming the student's compliance with the obligation to surrender his or her cash for safe custody. Only large amounts of money were to be surrendered. A student was free to withdraw funds from time to time for tuckshop purposes and other approved expenditures. The second requirement related to a certificate confirming a student's good health and fitness. At the beginning of each term, a team of medical doctors from the then McCord Zulu Hospital in Durban was invited to examine all students at the college. This process took two or even three days. The objective of the medical examinations was to ensure the good health and fitness of students before commencement of serious work in the college. Where only minor ailments were diagnosed, instructions were given for treatment of the victims in the college's clinic. On the other hand, where the diagnosis revealed that a student was suffering from a serious disease, the authorities were obliged to transfer the student to McCord Zulu Hospital in Durban.

During my first year at the college, I became a victim of the routine medical examination. The doctors found that I had tonsillitis. They recommended my transfer to the hospital in Durban for a "minor" surgical operation to remove the tonsils in the long term interest of my health. Although I was only

25

fifteen years old and had been in college for less than three weeks, I stubbornly resisted the order. The doctors emphasized that removal of tonsils required only a minor operation. However, they also emphasized that it was necessary for a senior member of the college to authorize the hospital authorities to perform the operation. Neither my parents, nor my elder brother as guardian were available to give the necessary authorisation. No senior staff member of the college was willing to authorize the doctors at McCord Zulu Hospital in Durban to perform the operation. That is how I escaped the ordeal of undergoing a surgical operation for removal of tonsils early in 1942. I have lived with them since that time – sixty years ago! During this period I have been hospitalised twice, not due to tonsillitis but due to other ailments.

Classes commenced in earnest within a few days of the arrival of students. On the first day of classes, there was confusion with some students arriving late for lessons or going to the wrong classrooms. There were three form one classes, each having at least twenty students and all of them mixed with boys and girls. It was an exciting experience for me to sit with girls of about my own age and compete with them in class. It became quite clear to me after some time that the brighter boys were often more popular among girls than boys who were less gifted intellectually.

The classrooms were a long distance from the hostels for the men and women. The hostels were linked to the classrooms and the dining hall by roads. The main road from the classrooms to the dining hall was popularly known as Lover's Lane. Girls in the college often liked to invite boys to accompany them along Lover's Lane carrying their books up to the dining hall. The lucky boys always appreciated such invitations. The practice had apparently the tacit approval of the authorities. It was not in any way inconsistent with their desire to inculcate English manners and culture in their students.

Like many other students, I hadn't the slightest idea what subjects were preferable at the high school level in preparation for my occupation in future. When I left Munali, my intention was to train as a teacher in a secondary school. No one was able to assist me. The dilemma was minimized because there was little choice, in any event, among subjects offered to form one students.

There were two distinct groups of students in the high school department at Adams College in 1942. One group consisted of students in forms one, two and three preparing for the junior certificate examinations. The second group consisted of senior students in forms four and five preparing for examinations set by the Joint Matriculation Board of the South African Universities. Candidates for admission to form four were required to have passed previously two promotional examinations; firstly, the form one examinations and, secondly, the form three examinations conducted by the University of South Africa.

In form one in my first year at Adams College, I chose to study English, mathematics, Latin, history, geography, physical science and agricultural science. I was also obliged to learn Afrikaans, which was the second official language in South Africa at that time. Fortunately, there was for foreign students a special course called "Afrikaans for Beginners". It was the only subject of great concern to me during my first year at the college. However, we had a very good teacher for this subject. She was an Afrikaans woman remarkably competent in teaching her mother-tongue. We had also an African arithmetic teacher who was popular with all students in our class. He encouraged me to like his subject. I had always considered myself as poorly endowed in mathematical and science subjects.

There were altogether more than seventy students in form one in 1942. In my own class, it was quite clear that I was not among the top five students. That realization encouraged me to pull my socks up in order to keep pace with the students whose performance in class was enviable. At the end of the year, I passed the promotional examinations and qualified for admission to form two. My elder brother was on the whole

27

satisfied with my performance in form one. However, he encouraged me to work harder in my studies because selection to form four was fiercely competitive. I promised to heed his advice.

Surprisingly, after my slow and undistinguished start in form one, I settled down well in form two in 1943 and maintained a commanding position among the best five students in our class in tests. Through hard work, I was easily the best student in our class in English, Latin and history in the mid-year and promotional tests. There were three reasons for the dramatic improvement in my performance. I was greatly inspired personally by the new teacher for English, the distinguished and much admired scholar, Dr Donald Mthimkulu, the headmaster of the high school department in the college. I rapidly developed an interest in English literature and poetry. I enjoyed memorising poems and long passages in William Shakespeare's plays.

Latin is understandably a difficult language – often described as an irrelevant dead language. In form two, we were given a new teacher for Latin – Professor Max Boxwell. He was requested by the headmaster to accept a part-time teaching appointment after retirement from a university in South Africa. His enthusiasm and novel methods of teaching brought life to a dead language.

I was allowed to abandon one subject I had not liked in form one, namely Afrikaans for Beginners. In form two, we were also allowed to choose for study either mathematics or geography. Although the geography option gave a chance to students manifestly weak in mathematics to abandon it, I resisted the temptation to do so. There was somehow a stigma to the choice of geography – a self-confession of hopelessness in mathematical and science skills! I chose to soldier on with the study of mathematics. The new dispensation reduced the number of subjects for study by two. More importantly, the opportunity to abandon the study of Afrikaans was very welcome. It was a subject on which I had spent many hours burning midnight oil unproductively.

My performance in the form two end-of-year examinations exceeded my expectations. In fact, the results pleasantly surprised my form master, Mr BP Bopela, who taught us mathematics and physical science. I obtained the first position in form two as a whole. A male student in another form two class gained the second position. I was certain that the results would be received by my elder brother with joy and relief. In due course, the college authorities would post the school report to him. Owing to financial constraints, I was unable to go home to Livingstone for the long holiday at Christmas time. The college authorities generously offered to employ me as a casual worker in the library from mid-December to the end of January in 1944.

During the third year, I continued to concentrate on my studies. Throughout the year, I worked hard and with confidence in all subjects. I anticipated passing the junior certificate examination and gaining selection to study in form four at the beginning of 1945. However, in the mid-year examinations in form three, I was not among the top five students. Other students became front-runners to my disappointment. In the year-end examination for the junior certificate, I did not perform as well as I had expected. Fortunately, I was among the few students who became eligible for selection to study for the examination conducted by the Joint Matriculation Board of the South African Universities. Early in January 1945, while in Livingstone on holiday, I received an official notification of my selection to study in form four at Adams College.

The news was received by members of our family and all our friends with joy. To some it was unbelievable that I was offered a place in form four to pursue studies for the Joint Matriculation Board ("JMB") examination. For my elder brother my successful performance in the junior certificate examination constituted the accomplishment of objective number one of my career in education in South Africa. My success two years later in the Joint Matriculation Board examination was no longer a remote possibility.

Whereas more than seventy boys and girls wrote the junior certificate examinations at the end of 1944, our form four class in February 1945 consisted of eighteen students only. Fifteen were male students and three were female students. About one-third of the students in the form four class were new faces altogether. They were students from various secondary schools in South Africa and elsewhere who preferred to study for the Joint Matriculation Board examination at Adams College. Their acceptance was entirely on merit. I remember among the new faces Herbert Chitepo, Tengo Jabavu and Cleopas Khumalo. Herbert Chitepo had recently completed a teacher-training course at Adams College. Previously, he was a student at a well known Anglican school called St. Peter's Secondary School in Rosettenville, Johannesburg. Tengo was the son of Professor Jabavu, professor of Bantu languages at the University College of Fort Hare in the municipality of Alice in the Eastern Cape Province, South Africa. In those days, for the black scholars from Southern, Central and Eastern Africa Fort Hare was like Oxford or Cambridge, Harvard or Yale in terms of prestige. Professor Jabavu also taught Latin, history and anthropology. He had been awarded a degree in English from the University of London.

During our studentship in the fourth and fifth forms, I found that these three men were truly brilliant scholars. It was a real struggle on my part to match their performance in the examinations. Somehow, I kept up with just above average performance. I was not ashamed to claim that I was always among the top five in class although the prospect of ever gaining the first place again in an examination was remote. Herbert Chitepo's spoken and written English was impeccable. However, occasionally I outclassed him in this particular subject and in Latin, a subject which Tengo Jabavu and Cleopas Khumalo avoided.

The most memorable events of my life at Adams College relate to the wider range of extra-curricular activities in which I participated, especially during the period of studentship in forms four and five. At Adams College, participation in extra-curricular activities was not compulsory. However, in the high school department the authorities relied on senior students to encourage junior students to play games such as football, tennis, cricket and netball by example. Before I completed form three tennis was my favourite game. In fact, I became a star in tennis when I was in the junior school. I started playing tennis regularly for the college team in form four. Later, in the teacher-training department, I continued playing competitive games in tennis and assumed the position of captain. Otherwise, I did not distinguish myself as an all-round sportsman, although I played non-competitive football and participated in physical training exercises as a learner boxer.

I particularly enjoyed activities of a social nature, participating in debates and drama. From early childhood, speaking to others has never been a problem for me. I have always enjoyed an argument. In fact, my interest in debates started at Munali before I completed primary school education. My class mates in form four encouraged me to join the college's debating society. As a member, I was privileged to attend lessons in elocution. One cannot be a good debater overnight. Debate is an art which one acquires through practice over time. Although some people have a natural flair for public speaking, training and guidance given by an experienced elocutionist are invaluable. In competitive debates, for example, it is necessary to map out the functions of a team's first speaker and the last speaker. Apart from marshalling facts, I learnt that the way in which the facts are presented – sequence, language and interpretation – is an important consideration to a seasoned debater.

For four years from 1945 to 1948, I was privileged to participate in inter-school debates as a member of the Adams College debating team. Those were very happy years for me. Little did I know at that time that the debating skills I learnt at Adams College would be useful to me in parliamentary debates in Zambia one day. As a government minister in charge of the education portfolio after independence and later, as minister of finance, I found these debating skills useful in defending government policies. An effective debater should rise to the occasion and perform well even at short notice or none at all. Indeed, I also realized later that a lawyer, especially one regularly engaged in court proceedings, requires such skills for effective presentation of arguments.

Fifty two years later in May 2000, I was privileged to visit Adams College in the company of my wife. I was pleasantly surprised that there was still a very active debating society in the college. An interesting report on the activities of the debating society appears in the Adams College magazine for 1999. The debating society's chairperson reported that:

> The debating society members have been working together successfully since last year. As a result we have not lost any of the debates we have had. This year we began by winning against Singnisezwe High School and finally against Sithengile High School.

> We would like to thank our school mates for their support and attendance, Mrs Hlengwa and Mrs Grobler for guiding us and correcting the mistakes we made on the way, not forgetting Mr Hlongwane for organizing everything for us.

My academic work did not suffer significantly from active involvement in the sporting and social activities of the college. In many ways interaction with students in other educational institutions during debates or competitive games such as tennis was of real benefit to me. The exposure broadened my horizons and outlook generally to the environment and people around me. All along my own political consciousness was vague. During sessions of the debating society, I gradually became conscious that black and white relations in South Africa were not altogether harmonious. There was certainly harmony between the white staff and their African counterparts at Adams College. Indeed, as students our own relations with the white staff were no less harmonious than between us and the African members of staff. But gradually I began to see undercurrents of suspicion and even fear between members of staff from different racial groups. Because of my preoccupation with extra-curricular activities, often I had to work long hours to recover lost ground in my academic work. Throughout the two year matriculation course, my ambition was to penetrate the fortress occupied by the three cleverest students – Herbert Chitepo, Tengo Jabavu and Cleopas Khumalo. The group was nick-named the "Triumvirate". On two occasions only in the internal examinations, I succeeded in penetrating the Triumvirate's fortress. Otherwise, the fortress remained intact. All three men were my friends, but Herbert Chitepo was my closest friend. Apart from members of the Triumvirate, Samuel Parirenyatwa was another intimate friend. We enrolled in form one at the same time in 1942. He, too, was a good tennis player.

Latin students in our class often warned each other with the phrase *tempus fugit* which means "time flies". Our mid-year form five examination was held in June in 1946, followed in October by the mock examination. The days of reckoning followed a month later – the examination under the Joint Matriculation Board of the South African Universities. I passed the examination in the second class. Herbert Chitepo, Tengo Jabavu and Cleopas Khumalo passed in the first class. One other student, Andrew Mabaso, passed like me in the second class. Three other students passed the examination in the third class. Out of eighteen final year students at Adams College for the Joint Matriculation Board examination in 1945, eight in all passed and obtained the full certificate. A pass rate of almost fifty per cent in the notoriously difficult examination was as pleasing to the staff of the high school department as it was to the successful students. The pass rate was higher than the recorded pass rates in the previous four years.

Of the remaining ten students, four obtained conditional passes. Such students failed in only one key subject to fulfil the requirements for award of the matriculation certificate. It was a necessary condition, for example, to obtain a pass in English "A" or Afrikaans "A" and in at least one second language such as Sizulu, Xhosa or Latin in order to obtain a full certificate. All students who obtained conditional passes were eligible to sit the supplementary examination in February or March in the subject they failed to pass in the final examination. My friend from Southern Rhodesia, Samuel Parirenyatwa, did not obtain a full certificate in the matriculation examination in 1946. In the supplementary examination in February 1947, he was successful in the subject he had failed previously.

Early in January 1947 after the announcement of the results of the matriculation examination held in 1946, I was informed that the Natal Provincial Education Department had granted me a scholarship to cover my teacher-training fees for two years at Adams College. The award of a scholarship was made on the strength of my second class pass in the matriculation examination. In anticipation of passing the examination, I had completed the application forms for admission to the teacher-training department at the beginning of the new term in 1947. I had not applied for a scholarship because my elder brother had undertaken to see me through the Post-Matriculation Teachers' Diploma course provided I was successful in the examination at the first attempt. Furthermore, as a foreign student, expectation of such a scholarship award from the Natal Provincial Education Department was a remote possibility. Therefore, what happened was a miracle to me and my elder brother. He was relieved from the burden of paying boarding and tuition fees. His responsibility was to provide money for books and pocket money for my personal needs.

Cleopas Khumalo and another student in our class were also awarded scholarships to train as teachers at Adams College. Many students in our class were recruits from other educational institutions in South Africa. Adams College in those years offered a high profile two-year teacher-training course. It was designed to produce teachers who were competent to teach in secondary schools and teacher training institutions. We were taught conventional subjects for trainee teachers. They included education, educational psychology, history of education and methods of teaching. However, the course was unique in one respect. There were two distinct conditions for obtaining the Post-Matriculation Teachers' Diploma. Firstly, a student was required to pass the examinations in all professional subjects. Secondly, it was also a requirement for a student to pass a minimum of four degree courses during the two-year teacher-training programme. At the beginning of the teacher-training programme, every student was registered simultaneously for studies with the correspondence courses department of the University of South Africa.

I pursued my teacher-training course without difficulty during the two-year period from 1947 to the end of 1948. Our lecturers were highly motivated, competent and experienced. Dr Karl H. Wilker, the headmaster of the teacher-training department, was a renowned scholar. Of German origin, he emigrated from Nazi Germany with other Quakers before the Second World War to the United States of America. Later, he offered his knowledge and experience in the service of the American Board Mission which established Adams College in 1853 in Natal, South Africa. He lectured to us in two key subjects – educational psychology and pure psychology. He was a strict disciplinarian. He always emphasized that an educated but indisciplined child was a danger to society. Therefore, he did not discourage corporal punishment to compel wayward school children to behave properly. Yet, as we discovered, he could be warm, approachable and helpful.

At the end of the two-year teacher-training course I passed all the examinations. I received my Teachers' Diploma Certificate in January, 1949. Additionally, over the two-year period I had accumulated six courses for the degree of Bachelor of Arts of the University of South Africa. Under the regulations, I was required to pass at least four courses, including passes in two teaching subjects, English and history to qualify for the award of the Teachers' Diploma Certificate. In fact, with six courses to my credit I required passes in only five more courses to obtain the Bachelor of Arts degree. My English tutor, Raymond Keet, encouraged me to complete studies for the degree as an external student of the University of South Africa. He was a former Rhodes scholar at Oxford University in the 1930s. He gave me the impression that with six courses to my credit passing the remaining five was not impossible provided I continued working hard in preparing for examinations. I did not lose contact with him for many years after leaving Adams College. I feel to this day an immense and irredeemable debt of gratitude to him for his advice and encouragement.

During the long vacation after examinations in December, students were in the habit of re-establishing contacts with old friends. In this way, I succeeded in tracing some of my old friends at Adams College. The chosen careers of many of them were on course. Harry Bwanausi sat the examination for the Joint Matriculation Board of the South African Universities in November and December 1948 while I battled to pass my examinations for the Teachers' Diploma and four courses for the Bachelor of Arts degree of the University of South Africa. He passed the examination in the second class. Consequently, the Nyasaland government offered him a bursary to study at Fort Hare University College for the degree of Bachelor of Science (Hygiene). On successful completion of the first degree, his government undertook to sponsor him for medical studies at Witwatersrand University in Johannesburg. Tengo Jabavu was in the third year in 1949 at Fort Hare University College studying for the degree of Bachelor of Science (Hygiene). He, too, intended to proceed to the Witwatersrand University to study medicine in order to qualify as a medical doctor. Herbert Chitepo was also a third year student at Fort Hare preparing to take the degree of Bachelor of Arts at the end of 1949.

Quite often, I reflected on my future in the light of the achievements of my closest friends at Adams College. I had no doubt that as graduates one day they were destined to be the

36

African elite in their communities. Futhermore, a university degree in those days was truly a passport to financial success. Apart from the advice and encouragement I got from my mentor, Mr Raymond Keet, these considerations strengthened my resolve to complete the five remaining courses for the Bachelor of Arts degree. At that time, records showed that many fine lecturers and students made Adams College famous throughout Southern Africa and the world since its establishment in 1853. I resolved to be a part of its history. I could not have hoped for a better start in life. I remain, to this day, proud of my years at Adams College.

CHAPTER

3

Teaching Career

Before I left Adams College in December 1948, I applied for a job as a teacher in a secondary school or any other suitable educational institution. My application was supported by two good references. The headmaster of the high school department provided one reference. The other was written by Dr Karl Wilker, the headmaster of the teacher-training department. Dr Karl Wilker was particularly emphatic in his reference that I had the ability to be a good teacher. While in Livingstone on holiday, I received a letter from the director of african education confirming my appointment as a teacher at Munali Secondary School. The effective date of my appointment was the first of February 1949. The letter brought relief and joy to my parents and my elder brother and to Ethel his wife. During a period of seven years of my education and training at Adams College, I had passed examinations and gained certificates which qualified me for a teaching position. It was anticipated that my employment was unlikely to be well-paid, at least by prevailing conditions in those days. However, they all readily accepted that their sacrifices during my education and training at Adams College were not in vain.

In any event, I had expected my application for employment to be successful. The majority of teachers in the secondary schools were expatriates at that time. My posting to Munali Secondary School for teaching duties was expected. It was also welcome. It was my old school, after all, where I completed primary education before proceeding to Adams

College for secondary education. I saw Munali, therefore, as the best environment for learning my job as a young and inexperienced teacher. However, a week before the end of January, I received another letter from the headquarters of the Department of African Education informing me that my services as a teacher were required urgently at Chalimbana Teacher Training Centre near Lusaka. The reason for the sudden change of my initial posting to Munali was that the teacher responsible for teaching mathematics to students taking the T2 teachers' course decided suddenly to return to South Africa to complete his studies for the Joint Matriculation Board examinations. When Wesley Nyirenda tendered his resignation from temporary employment at Chalimbana, a vacuum was created. The officials at the headquarters emphasized that my transfer to Chalimbana was only for five months. That was my first disappointment as a newly designated civil servant. One of the regulations in the civil service which I learnt the hard way early in my career was that a civil servant was liable to be posted anywhere at any time according to the exigencies of the service. Although I was given the reason for the change of my original posting to Munali, that was merely a courteous consideration. I accepted the temporary transfer to Chalimbana as a challenge. I resolved to demonstrate at Chalimbana my ability to assist students to pass examinations and gain certificates.

The provincial education officer in Livingstone was instructed to make arrangements for my journey to Chalimbana at the end of January. I was expected to travel by train to Lusaka and by road transport to Chalimbana. Early in the morning on the last Friday of the month of January, I boarded the train to Lusaka. As a student, I always travelled from Livingstone to Durban in second class. As an African civil servant in the 'B' salary scale, I was not entitled to a second class ticket when travelling by train on duty. Yet on arrival at the railway station in Lusaka a few minutes after midnight, I was met unexpectedly by two white men. From the train I saw them walking up and down and I suspected that they had come to the station to meet me. My guess was correct. After disembarking from the train, I followed them and said, "Gentlemen, John Mwanakatwe is my name. Are you looking for me?" They were not puzzled. They confirmed that they came to the railway station to meet me. The Reverend Maxwell Robertson introduced himself as the principal of Chalimbana Teacher Training Centre. He then looked at his companion and said "Meet Mr Clifford Little, the principal of Munali Training Centre". Although I put on a brave face after the introductions, in reality the encounter frightened me. "Were they bogus men or truly genuine?" I wondered. It appeared unusual to me that two elderly men would forego the comfort of their homes in order to meet a young man of twenty-two years at a railway station at midnight. As I reflected silently, we were on our way to the station master's office to collect my luggage.

From the railway station, we drove to Clifford Little's home at Munali Secondary School where Reverend Maxwell Robertson and I spent the night. In the morning after breakfast, Reverend Maxwell Robertson and I drove in his car to Chalimbana Teacher Training Centre about thirty-five miles east of Lusaka on the Great East Road. However, before our departure, Clifford Little reminded me that I was merely on a temporary assignment to the teacher training institution. He then said "I expect you to join the staff at Munali in five months' time". It was a welcome confirmation of the news I had received previously from the headquarters of the Department of African Education.

Alport Phiri, a teacher at Chalimbana Teacher Training Centre, greeted me on my arrival. Fortunately, he was not a stranger to me. He was a student in the junior secondary school at Munali when I was a student in the primary school. He had offered to accommodate me in his house because he, too, was a bachelor. I welcomed the arrangement. It had two main advantages for me and my host. Firstly, it was an arrangement which was likely to minimize the cost of maintaining the house. Secondly, it was likely to reduce boredom and loneliness. I have been a music lover all my life, but Alport was not fond of music. I liked to play tennis or even football in which the standard of my performance was below average, but Alport had little or no interest at all in sports. However, Alport and I both liked reading Shakespeare's plays. He liked to recite poems written in English, especially Alfred Tennyson's and William Wordsworth's poems. This strengthened our friendship when we were living together in his house at Chalimbana. We were both devoted Christians and regular churchgoers. Apart from reading Shakespeare's plays together or reciting poems, Alport and I occasionally read and discussed passages in the Bible. These sessions enriched me spiritually. So Alport and I coexisted happily under one roof for five months before I moved out to go to Munali. We often wrote to each other after I went to Munali. It was a way, perhaps, of maintaining our passion for English literature.

Alport Phiri was a product of Makerere College in Kampala, Uganda, the forerunner of Makerere University. Makerere College was in the early 1940s the mecca for ambitious students who wanted to advance their education beyond school certificate level. The founding father of the United Republic of Tanzania, Mwalimu Dr Julius K Nyerere, was a student at Makerere College in the 1940s. Alport Phiri, after completing his academic studies at Munali, received a scholarship to study for four years at Makerere College in order to qualify for the diploma in education. His spoken English was envied by many of our countrymen. Over the years, he developed into an accomplished English language tutor at the teacher training institution at Chalimbana.

Teaching was my primary responsibility at Chalimbana. I had no difficulty in teaching mathematics to students enrolled for the T2 teacher training course. Teaching civics and history in the primary school was equally straightforward and more enjoyable. When I encountered a teaching problem, Alport was at hand to guide or assist me. Miss Mary Pike took an interest in my teaching career. She was the head of the English language department. Often, to my pleasure, in spite of an increase in the workload, Miss Pike co-opted me to teach English when the substantive teacher was not available. The discussions with her and her guidance in the methodology of teaching languages were helpful to me. I have remained eternally grateful to her.

Activities in sports at Chalimbana were virtually non-existent. However, football was the most popular game among students. Some students played football with skill and enthusiasm. The "A" team had a good record of victories in football matches. The "B" team was not so successful. When news spread that I was on the staff of the institution, representatives of the football players invited me to accept appointment as honorary coach. The invitation was accepted although I had neither training, skill nor experience for such an appointment. Nonetheless, in the course of time my usefulness to the footballers was recognized and appreciated. I acted more as a friend and adviser of the fraternity of footballers at the institution. I encouraged the footballers to observe a number of universal practices for success in a sporting activity. Among such practices, I emphasized the importance of training individually and as a team to achieve physical fitness; the importance of self-discipline by each football player at all times; and the necessity of promoting team spirit in their activities. Many years later, two members of the "A" team won accolades as outstanding footballers in Northern Rhodesia. That they received their colours and played football for the Northern Rhodesia team caused me much satisfaction. I had the feeling that although I was not a trained football coach, my efforts to encourage the young players at Chalimbana were not in vain.

Alport and I did not employ a domestic servant to perform such chores as cooking, cleaning our house and washing and ironing our clothes. We chose to perform these domestic functions ourselves. It was amazing how quickly I adapted myself to performance of these chores because of the way we were brought up by our mother at home. However, before I joined him, Alport had selected a young man to assist him from time to time with cooking food and cleaning the house. Dennis

Sichombo, the young boy selected to help him in the house, was a student in the primary school. He was a humble, quiet spoken and trustworthy boy.

Late in June in 1949, I arrived at Munali Training Centre to take up my appointment as a secondary school teacher. My journey with the driver of a government Landrover was short. On my arrival at the school, I reported to the headmaster, Wesley Matsie, who confirmed that accommodation was available for me immediately. I was allocated a house in the residential area for African teachers and instructors. The house had most of the requirements for a bachelor, including a bed and mattress, basic hardwood furniture for the dining room and sitting room and a stove for the kitchen, the kind of stove for use with dry firewood.

The geography of Munali had remained largely unchanged during the years I was in South Africa. However, here and there I saw new buildings used as classrooms or laboratories. It was still the best secondary school in the country in those days.

I soon settled down to study in the library and prepare for teaching responsibilities. The new Michaelmas term was due to start in September. I was expected to start teaching history, mathematics and religious knowledge. I had also special qualifications in physical training and music. My workload was heavy, but I was happy to teach both history and mathematics, the subjects of my preference, to various classes in the junior secondary school. The syllabus for each subject did not present me with any problems. With carefully prepared schemes of work for teaching each subject, completion of syllabuses was not an impossibility. I had been trained to aim for completion of the set syllabus for any subject some time before the examinations. That approach allowed sufficient time for revision work and assisting slow learners to prepare for examinations effectively. A senior teacher was appointed by the principal to coordinate teachers' work in each subject and provide guidance where it was required. After several weeks of attending to formalities, I felt confident that I was ready to contribute effectively to the education of young boys who were privileged to come to Munali.

I was always conscious of the nobility of the teaching profession.

During the period of settling down at Munali, I attended a few briefing sessions with the principal of the school, Clifford Little. He explained his idea of a good teacher. A good teacher was one whose responsibilities in a boarding school were not confined to work in the classroom only. His philosophy was that a teacher was always on duty – he was on duty twenty-four hours a day. Clifford Little also encouraged self-discipline among students. Wesley Matsie, the school's headmaster, worked very closely with the principal in running the school. He was an African expatriate from the Protectorate of Basutoland and a graduate of Fort Hare. These two men were in the forefront of the school's successes in all fields of students' endeavours. Over the years at Munali, I grew to rely on their friendship and willingness to support my efforts as a member of the teaching staff.

I was a great admirer of Clifford Little. He was truly a great scholar, an excellent administrator and a benevolent human being. I do not recall meeting any man or woman who ever made an unkind remark about him. He came from an upper middle class family in England. His early education was at Rugby a well known public school. Later, he went to Oxford University where he obtained a first class honours degree in history. He had first come to Northern Rhodesia before the 1939-45 war as a young education officer. After the war, he was appointed principal of Munali. He held this post until 1955, when he was promoted to the top job of director of African education by the Colonial Office. His promotion to the most senior position in the education sector of the colonial administration was a recognition of his exceptional administrative abilities.

Clifford Little ran Munali on the lines of a British public school. Consequently, Munali became one of the leading educational institutions in East and Central Africa. Grace Keith is the author of a book entitled *The Fading Colour Bar*. The book is a critique on social, political and economic development issues after the independence of Zambia in 1964. She wrote:

> Munali is a secondary boarding school for African boys, outside Lusaka, where many of Zambia's new leaders – including the President himself – received their education. Its annual examination results have always compared most favourably with those of European secondary school and its university entrance record has recently been very high.

Maintenance of high academic standards and a disciplined student population were the main goals of the staff of Munali. The organisation of the school on the lines of a British public school paid dividends. It introduced an alien way of life for many students and, indeed, to some teachers. With the passing of time, the system became institutionalised. It became a way of life for new and old students and the staff. Peter Snelson, a former education officer in Northern Rhodesia from 1954 and in Zambia after independence from 1964 to 1968, is the author of a book entitled *To Independence and Beyond*. On the effective manner in which Munali was run under Clifford Little, he wrote:

> He ran Munali on the lines of a British public school: academic standards were high; the house system flourished; service to others was encouraged; discipline was strict; a muscular form of Christianity prevailed. Clifford would cheerfully cane offenders and then pray for the miscreants. He was held in high esteem by the boys. They knew him as "he who never sleeps" because of his habit of walking his dog around the dormitory area late at night and again at first light. He knew each boy by name, knew how to make them work and how to make them laugh. A bachelor, he gave all his time and energy to the school.

There were five education officers in the secondary school who were designated as expatriate civil servants. Wesley Matsie and Ezra Mogwe were expatriate African teachers. Six Africans qualified to teach in the secondary school were designated as masters to teach in the secondary school at Munali. Seven

Africans were designated as instructors qualified to teach in the industrial section of the school. The staff was multinational, classified generally into two categories, local and expatriate. The majority of expatriate staff came from the United Kingdom. During the 1948 session the total number of students enrolled in the secondary school section was 123. Six years later, following the school's move to a new site off the Great East Road in Lusaka in January, 1952, the enrolment of students increased from 123 to more than 340.

Munali had a very strong tradition of promoting sports among students. Football was the most popular sport. Inter-house football competitions were encouraged. After receiving the time-table for my teaching load each week, I was assigned the responsibility of assistant housemaster for Maybin House. The housemaster requested me to assist the house football team to ensure the retention of the inter-house football shield won by Maybin House in 1948. In this matter, the housemaster was pushing an open door. I had enjoyed the experience of assisting the "A" and "B" football teams at Chalimbana. The Maybin House team won the shield because the players were skilful and well motivated. After watching their performance during football practices, I was convinced that the Maybin house football team was good. However, to maintain its superiority, it was necessary for players to change their attitude. Too many of them tended to show off instead of playing as members of a team. Throughout the year, I warned them about the danger of the football team's complacency. They were encouraged to continue practising the game hard and to develop a spirit of sportsmanship.

Maybin house also had a strong team in athletics. It was not an activity in which I was able to assist the students effectively. The school's tennis court was constructed a few months before I joined the staff of Munali. I was ready to coach students who were prepared to learn how to play tennis. Some expatriate members of staff played tennis regularly at the school. In particular David Bell, head of the history department, was an outstanding tennis player. It was always a joy to play a game of singles with him. At one time, he won the men's singles tennis championship at the whites only tennis club in Lusaka.

Outside of sporting activities, my interest was in promoting constructive programmes for the Munali branch of the Students' Christian Association. I succeeded Mr Safeli Chileshe early in 1950 as chairman of the SCA. Its membership was small but their activities were remarkably impressive in the community. Members of the Munali branch of the SCA held meetings regularly. They organized Sunday School classes for children at Munali itself and at the African suburb now called Chilenje township. As a student in the primary school at Munali, I had joined the literary and debating society. When I returned to Munali as a teacher eight years later, the society was still flourishing. Debates were held regularly. Over the years, I observed, there had been some improvement in the standard of debates. It was always a pleasure to attend debates organized by the society and to guide and encourage them.

Gradually within a few months my circle of friends widened. I cultivated friendship with ordinary men and women, civil servants and non-civil servants, whom I met outside the school grounds. In those days, the colour bar was firmly entrenched in Northern Rhodesia. Conditions of service for civil servants were categorized purely on racial grounds. The white civil servants were given preferential salaries, housing and schooling facilities for their children. They enjoyed these privileges not because of their superior abilities but simply because of the colour of their skin. That was, perhaps, why the African civil servants had organized for themselves a strong body, the African Civil Servants Association, whose senior members solicited my support and encouragement. I registered as a member of the association in 1950. Two years later, I was elected vice-president. The doyen of the African Civil Servants Association was Franklin Temba. As its president he was greatly respected and his voice carried weight in government circles when he spoke on behalf of African civil servants. The association's main preoccupation through its executive council was to fight the colour bar in terms of salaries and conditions of service generally.

I was free to participate in the activities of the African Civil Servants Association. It was a recognized body with an approved constitution. However, as civil servants, we were under orders not to get involved in politics. The colonial government had transplanted to Northern Rhodesia the age-old custom of a civil servant's neutrality in political affairs. Yet circumstances in Great Britain were totally different from those prevailing in Northern Rhodesia. For example, the fight against the colour bar in Northern Rhodesia was essentially a political issue in which it was virtually impossible to expect African civil servants to take a neutral position. Therefore, the imposition of the rule relating to the neutrality of African civil servants in politics was virtually impossible to observe. It was observed more in breach by the African Civil Servants than subservience to it.

Outside the fraternity of African civil servants I found that the business community had a reservoir of talented men and women. Once I was well settled at Munali, I started interacting with some of them. That is how I met many men who became lifelong friends, among them Lewis Changufu, Emmanuel Chalabesah, James Mapoma and Nason Tembo. Through one of my newly found friends, I learnt in mid-1951 that a fiery young African politician, Harry Nkumbula, was billed to address leaders of the African National Congress and members of the public in the welfare hall in Kabwata, Lusaka, on the issue of the proposal by white settlers in Southern Rhodesia, Northern Rhodesia and Nyasaland to form a federation of the two British protectorates and Southern Rhodesia, which was a self-governing territory. The Africans in the two protectorates opposed the proposal vehemently because it was perceived as a strategy by the white settlers to frustrate their hopes of achieving self-government and independence. Two years earlier, Nkumbula and Dr Hastings Banda had prepared a memorandum in London against the proposed federation. Printed copies of the memorandum were distributed widely in the United Kingdom. It was the first time I was going to attend a meeting organized by a political party in Northern Rhodesia. It was a great inspiration for me to listen to Harry Nkumbula's fiery speech. His oratory was of the highest order and in the style of the most celebrated English orator of all time, Sir Winston Churchill.

During the general discussion of the issue of the proposed federation after Nkumbula's fiery speech, many speakers condemned it as a wicked and unacceptable ploy. I, too, in my contribution supported the viewpoint that the proposal was intended primarily to frustrate the hopes of the black majority to achieve self-government and independence rapidly. Like speakers before me, I maintained that the black majority were entitled to protection from the political machinations of the white settlers who were in the minority, although they had at that time both political and economic power. I appealed to the British government to heed the demand of the majority of the African people who were opposed to the proposal for a federation of Northern Rhodesia, Southern Rhodesia and Nyasaland. I implored the British government metaphorically "to drop the idea of federation like a hot brick". That metaphor apparently stirred the anti-federation feelings of many people in the audience judging by their applause when I sat down.

In the urban areas in the 1930s, Africans lacked institutionalised means of expressing their grievances to the administration in the districts. On the other hand, native authorities performed this function on behalf of Africans living in rural areas. Early in the 1940s, the government established urban advisory councils to represent the interests of Africans working in towns. Later, provincial councils were created embracing both urban and rural areas to which the urban local councils sent representatives. Ultimately, the provincial councils nominated representatives to the African Representative Council. Its first meeting was held in 1946. Members of the African Representative Council then held meetings in Lusaka at least once a year. Their main function was to inform the government of African opinion, especially on such matters as housing conditions, racial discrimination, lack of educational opportunities and inadequate representation of Africans in the Legislative Council of Northern Rhodesia.

When I was a teacher at Munali, I rarely missed attending sessions of the African Representative Council which were held during the school holidays. It was fascinating to listen to the debates on important subjects of great concern to the African majority. Unfortunately, the African Representative Council had no executive powers. Like the lower organizations, the local and provincial councils, the African Representative Council was merely an advisory body. It was like a toothless bulldog. However, the council's resolutions were often taken seriously by the government. It became a Frankenstein monster in the course of its existence. Members of the African Representative Council were provided, fortuitously, with an official platform for expressing African opposition to the proposal for a federation of Northern Rhodesia with Southern Rhodesia and Nyasaland. It became also a convenient training ground in parliamentary procedures and practices for African politicians. They were destined, in any event, to increase in number in the Legislative Council in response to the demands of the Africans.

Two members of the African Representative Council were prominent, namely Dauti Yamba and Paskale Sokota. In 1952, they were both members of the Legislative Council, elected by members of the African Representative Council to represent the interests of Africans. I also met the veteran politician, Donald Siwale, who was in his seventies and the most respected member of the African Representative Council. The first generation of well known politicians I met at Munali were Mr Amos Walubita, Nelson Nalumango, Knox Kaniki and Chief Mwase Lundazi.

I recall the courage of these men as they debated political, social and development issues during meetings of the African Representative Council at Munali. Their enthusiasm and their sense of mission greatly inspired me as a young teacher in my mid-twenties. I can say that to a large extent this first generation of politicians influenced my willingness twelve years later to opt for a short political career.

At Munali life was more interesting than at Chalimbana. With a growing circle of friends and increasing responsibilities, life gradually became hectic. However, I was conscious all the time that I had only five more examinations in five courses to pass in order to complete the requirements of a BA degree from the University of South Africa. I had hastily re-registered with the correspondence courses department early in 1949, after receiving notification of my success in the examinations at the end of 1948. It was always clear to me that the coveted university degree was well within my grasp provided I worked hard in my studies. My resolve was constantly to remember the words of the poet John Milton "… to scorn delight and live laborious days" in the sonnet *On His Blindness*. It was a virtue to burn the midnight oil for this purpose; it earned me respect and admiration among my fellow teachers. It was not an easy road to follow, but I believed that obtaining a university degree was undoubtedly a passport to financial success and, more importantly, to a position of leadership in the community.

For two years from 1949 to 1950, my priorities were fixed: firstly, to teach my subjects at Munali to the best of my abilities; and, secondly, to concentrate on my studies. Other activities were of secondary importance. The reward for hard work was in the encouraging remarks of my principal tutors in English and history after marking my assignments. I remember only one unfortunate outcome of reduced hours of sleep due to my studies at night. After lunch one day, I relaxed on the couch in my house and fell asleep. Yet I had a class to teach immediately after lunch. Consequently, I arrived in the classroom late by about ten minutes. The principal of the school, Clifford Little, had apparently seen me going late into the classroom. Unexpectedly, he followed me and sat at the back. He remained in the classroom until a few minutes before the end of the lesson. I taught the lesson adequately and with confidence. I was not rebuked or questioned on my late arrival in the classroom. I learnt a lesson, however, on that day – never to take a siesta on a working day!

Early in January 1951, I received a notification from the registrar of the University of South Africa that I had passed the examination in the remaining courses for the BA degree. The news was exciting for me and all my colleagues at Munali. Clifford Little reported the news to the headquarters of the African Education Department. My achievement was also widely published in the local newspapers. For me personally, my life's ambition had been achieved. Otherwise, life had to go on as before with maximum dedication to the teaching profession. By the end of February in 1951, I had acquired my academic dress (gown, hood and cap) in readiness for the graduation ceremony at Fort Hare University College.

I travelled to Alice in the Eastern Cape Province on my way to Fort Hare. Fortunately, I was not a complete stranger there. I met old friends from Adams College who were now students at Fort Hare. A sizeable group of about five Northern Rhodesians were students at Fort Hare studying for various degrees. Under the leadership of Belemu Mudenda, they organized a small reception to celebrate my graduation. They were proud that their fellow countryman had acquired a university degree for the first time in the history of Northern Rhodesia. Their generosity was appreciated.

A few days after the graduation ceremony, I returned to Lusaka and resumed my teaching responsibilities. I somehow became more conscious that even with a university degree, there was much that I did not know. I appreciated more the fact that the process of learning does not end in life. It is true, indeed, that "we learn from the cradle to the grave". Quite rightly, many of my countrymen thought that I made a very good start in life with the completion of a university degree at twenty-four. In reality, I knew that I was not extra-ordinary. But I knew also that I was a diligent worker. That enabled me to achieve more than the less diligent worker. I was no longer haunted by the possibility of failing an examination. When I returned to Munali after the graduation ceremony at Fort Hare, I was anxious to succeed in my work as a teacher. For at least two years after my graduation, I was the only Northern Rhodesian African graduate teacher at Munali Secondary School. The rest of the graduates were expatriates, mainly from the United Kingdom. That realization strengthened my determination to succeed as a teacher; and I knew, of course, that success is achieved through hard work.

At the end of 1951, the year of my graduation, the secondary school section of Munali Training Centre was moved to a new site about five miles from the town center on the Great East Road. The new Munali at its new site was officially called *Munali Secondary School.* Two years earlier, the government decided to separate the academic section at the old Munali from the industrial section of the school. In 1949, Munali at its old site was the only institution providing a full academic course for students. Therefore, a new site was required for the school's expansion to accommodate more students and thereby increase opportunities in the country for secondary education. It was decided to leave the old site for students pursuing industrial courses such as carpentry, building, thatching and tailoring.

The move to the new site presented its own problems to teachers and students alike. They were merely teething problems, such as problems of transport for teachers attending medical treatment at the hospital in town. Such difficulties were outweighed by many advantages. The new school was planned to at least double the secondary school intake to about 400 students at the new site. The dormitories for students and houses for staff were well designed and properly constructed. More facilities were provided for extra-curricular activities. Apart from football and athletics, facilities were available for playing cricket, hockey and tennis. A very large school hall was built with a modern stage suitable for concerts and production of plays. The school's prestige was enhanced. Boys were proud to be students at Munali. I was quite happy to be a teacher at

Munali. All teachers and their families felt that the new environment was conducive to the possibility of giving the best education to boys who were destined to be the African elite in Northern Rhodesia.

The students who went to Munali from 1952 were fortunate in many ways. The school was very well organized. When I joined the staff, Clifford Little, the principal, was assisted by Evan G Goddard, the vice principal, and Wesley Matsie the headmaster. In the absence of the principal, the vice principal assumed responsibility for the administration of the school on an acting basis. As a staff member at Munali, I held the post of *master* applicable to all African teachers whether they were university graduates or not. As a civil servant, ultimately I was responsible to the principal for the performance of my duties and for my activities generally. In addition, apart from clerical staff, we had two other posts of boarding master and instructor in handicrafts. None of the European staff held the post of master. They held the more senior position of *education officer* although practically all of them were occupied with teaching responsibilities only at Munali. The European teaching staff outnumbered the African teachers by a ratio of about three to one in 1952. However, in subsequent years the number of African teachers at Munali increased progressively. For each subject, an education officer or a master was appointed head of the department to coordinate the work of teachers. Most of the expatriate education officers appointed to teach at Munali were young and inexperienced.

Another important responsibility in the school was that of *housemaster*. Nearly all housemasters were African teachers. Some education officers were appointed assistant housemaster to support the housemaster and act for him from time to time. There were six houses altogether when the school was moved from the old to the new site. At the old site there were only four houses because the enrolment of students was low. I was the housemaster of Maybin House. Peter Whitworth, the Latin scholar, was for some time my assistant housemaster at new

Munali. Peter Whitworth was a man of few words but action-oriented. Apart from the annual school magazine, each house was expected to publish its own house magazine annually. With his flair for languages, I assigned him the responsibility of supervising the editorial committee for the production of the Maybin House Magazine. It was produced each year on time and with articles which showed the literary talent of many students. For some time, Sikota Wina was the editor of the magazine. We had observed from the time he went into the third year of schooling at Munali that he was a gifted writer in English. Therefore, he was given the responsibility of editing the Maybin House Magazine at a very early age – in fact, at a time when more senior students would have readily accepted the challenge of editing our house magazine. I owed a debt of gratitude to Peter Whitworth for the outstanding success of the editorial team of the Maybin House Magazine.

Unfortunately, Sikota Wina's last production was a disaster not in terms of lack of quality articles from students but due to his failure to adhere to the prescribed time-table for its production. I did not hesitate in a meeting to put the blame squarely on the assistant housemaster whom I had appointed to guide and assist the editorial committee. In turn, Peter Whitworth queried Sikota Wina who had apparently received draft articles from students but failed to pass them to members of the editorial committee for editing. For the first time, the quiet Peter Whitworth exploded with anger. I have never forgotten the manner in which he conveyed his disappointment to Sikota Wina. His rhetorical question was: "Why did you sit on the articles like a hen sits on eggs to hatch chickens?" Sikota Wina did not reply. Later, the Maybin House Magazine was published. Six years later, Sikota Wina became a successful, well known and respected journalist in Northern Rhodesia!

I enjoyed teaching history and English, and I also always took my responsibilities seriously as a housemaster. Housemasters were *in loco parentis* in a boarding school. Some students entered form one at Munali when they were very young.

At the tender age of twelve or thirteen years, their need for parental guidance was unquestionable. Even older students required guidance or help from time to time, be it on financial problems or problems concerning studies. A housemaster who made himself readily accessible to students was likely to be more effective in counselling them in disciplinary matters than one who was aloof all the time. Today, some forty-five years since I left Munali Secondary School, some of my closest and most reliable friends are men I was privileged to teach at the school. Some are men of great reputation holding important positions in local and international organizations, in the central government and in commerce and industry.

The staff of Munali was multi-national from the time of its establishment in 1939 until independence in 1964 and for many years after independence. The relations between staff of different races were generally cordial in a country which was rife before independence with racial discrimination. Munali was, of-course, an African secondary school. It was established for African children and that fact was readily accepted by all. But the colour bar was firmly entrenched in the country. It was to a large extent institutionalised. At Munali itself teachers lived in separate housing areas – an area where better houses were built for the occupation of education officers who were invariably white men and women; and an area of inferior houses for the occupation of non-European teachers and the clerical staff. The whites enjoyed privileges not because of their superior abilities or qualifications but simply because of the colour of their skin. Throughout Northern Rhodesia in those days racial discrimination was rampant in terms of schooling, hospitals, salaries and entertainment amenities. Because both the European and African teachers belonged to the well educated class in society none suffered from the complex of inferiority. At Munali, I had some good friends among fellow African teachers and good friends among the European teachers. My inclination to develop friendship with someone depended much more on the existence of common interests.

However, because the colour bar was institutionalised by the government itself in some vital areas of human existence, mutual confidence and absolute cordiality between the black and white members of staff at Munali was impossible to achieve. For example, in accordance with the recommendations of the 1952 Follows Report on civil service salaries, the salary of an African teacher was pegged at three-fifths of the salary of a European teacher, even when their academic and professional qualifications were equal. I decided with Joseph Mwemba, another indigenous African graduate also teaching at Munali Secondary School, to challenge what was to us a blatant example of racial discrimination in the civil service. We wrote on 8 November 1952 a private circular as civil servants protesting to the government for its perpetuation of racial discrimination in the civil service. In the circular we stated:

> It is now over fifty years since the Europeans came to live with us here in Northern Rhodesia; and during these years the theory has been held that Africans do not deserve high wages because they are not highly educated and their standard of living is low. That argument is probably true, but we do not believe that an African graduate can be said to be living at a standard lower than that of an average European.... What makes the difference that people holding the same qualifications, doing the same job, are paid differently? We are baffled and finally constrained to think that it is nothing but colour.

Richard Hall referred to our circular in his book on Zambia as one of the milestones in the development of Zambian nationalism.

In the overall prevailing conditions in Northern Rhodesia at that time, tension between black and white teachers at Munali was inevitable. Both the racial groups were in a sense victims of circumstances. The cordial relations between black and white members of staff at Munali were in reality superficial. There were deep cultural differences between African teachers on the one hand and European teachers on the other, differences in

57

attitudes, background, tastes and political opinions. At mid-morning break for tea, the white teachers tended to group together in one corner and the black teachers in another corner of the staff room. During weekends, we often met with our families in our homes in the African residential area to play indoor games like monopoly, snakes and ladders and chess. These occasions provided opportunities for some gossip about current social and political events. On the other hand, our white colleagues at Munali met separately in their homes or went for picnics at selected beauty spots in Lusaka which were exclusively for use by Europeans.

In terms of black and white relations at Munali, I had a unique experience in 1955. In that year at the end of June, Wesley Matsie went to Basutoland on leave for three months. I was appointed by Clifford Little to act as headmaster until Wesley Matsie's return from leave. In carrying out my duties, I received complete cooperation from all white teachers. Similarly, the African teachers, with one exception, supported my efforts beyond expectation. The African teacher who did not support my acting appointment claimed that the principal should have considered the factor of age before making the appointment. He deserved the acting appointment because he was senior in terms of length of service and much older. These claims were quite correct. However, he forgot one other important consideration – his academic qualifications were inferior to mine. This fact was brought to his attention one day by students he was teaching in the classroom. He had apparently digressed during the lesson to complain about the principal's bias by ignoring his eligibility for appointment to act as headmaster. One student stood up in class and asked whether he was a university graduate. The teacher was embarrassed. He remained silent for a moment. Then, he retorted in IciBemba: "Bushikubumo bakamona apo icula cipasa umulilo!" (One day they will see how a frog puts off a burning fire!). The student immediately retorted: "Suppose it is electricity and not charcoal fire?" The teacher made no further comment. He continued teaching his lesson. Later, one of the students told me about this incident. I did not hold any grudge or ill-will against the teacher. I continued to give him the respect he deserved by virtue of his age.

Many expatriate teachers at Munali believed that the boys' interest in education was merely to pass examinations in order to gain certificates and later qualify for well-paid employment. It was to some extent true that the remunerative motive existed in their quest for good education. However in my experience of teaching in secondary schools for many years, many boys showed initiative, interest and talent in the classroom. Their ultimate goal was to pass examinations. However, many of them used education to broaden their minds and extend their horizons. That was my experience as a history teacher and teacher of current affairs or civics at Munali.

Some boys at Munali were innovative and exceptionally witty. I used to wonder if anyone would have found a more amusing and meaningful nickname for my assistant housemaster, Peter Whitworth. He used to stammer a little when speaking. However, under provocation he had an uncontrollable temper. When he became annoyed, it was difficult to understand him because of the speed of his speech and sarcasm of his language. In Maybin House and throughout the school, he was fondly called 'Mr Spitfire'. What an appropriate nickname! Our principal, Clifford Little, was given two nicknames. Sometimes he was called *Ba Kanono* (Mr Little). The word 'kanono' in IciBemba means 'little'. He was also nicknamed *Springbok* after the South African fast running animal. Its ability to leap gracefully when running is greatly admired. During the Second World War, Clifford Little suffered a minor injury to one of his legs while fighting with the British army in the Far East. A tall, well built and handsome man, he limped slightly when walking. Apparently his style of walking was admired by nick-naming him *Springbok*.

Outside the boundaries of Munali Secondary School the activities of African teachers were limited. Firstly, there was the transport constraint. The school's vanette was available to take one or two teachers to town when extra seats were available. Otherwise, African teachers used their own bicycles to go to town for shopping or visiting friends in the townships. On the other hand the majority of their European counterparts owned their own cars. Motor vehicles were not easily affordable to African teachers whose salaries and conditions of service were less competitive. However, to overcome my own transport problem, I bought an old car from Mr Safeli Chileshe, a prominent businessman in Lusaka. It was a Chevrolet five-seater saloon car 1939 model. The car's body was not particularly attractive but its engine was good. Because Mr Safeli Chileshe had known me as a young boy in the primary school section at the old Munali, he asked for payment of a price which was not exploitative - only fifty pounds. I offered to pay a small deposit on the purchase price and the balance in monthly instalments. He readily accepted my offer. In retrospect, I acknowledge now that the sum of fifty pounds in those days was good money. However, the car served my transport needs satisfactorily from 1952 to 1955.

I was always happy to offer lifts to the teachers undertaking shopping errands in town. Students at Munali were quick to realize that free transport to town on Saturday morning was no longer a remote possibility. Not unexpectedly, students walking to town along the Great East Road on Saturday morning were particularly alert to ask for lifts in my car if room was available. Since I was driving an old car it was impossible to guarantee that it would never break down on the road. In that event, I would rely on my passengers to assist in pushing the car to a safe place. I could not guess what was in their thoughts all the time. Later, I learnt that my car was nicknamed the *Munali Bus!* About mid-June in 1955, I sold the old Chevrolet saloon. A new car – British make – called Standard Eight was introduced onto the market at that time in Northern Rhodesia. It was a small and attractive car. The price for a new car was affordable. I was never disappointed at any time with its performance until

I sold it in 1960 for a slightly bigger and more comfortable new car – the Hilman Minx.

The solution of the problem of transport early in my teaching career at Munali was necessary. Although the staff at Munali were usually preoccupied with teaching and other responsibilities, it was generally appreciated that they were members of a larger community which embraced men and women outside the boundaries of Munali. Without reliable means of transport, teachers felt isolated from the wider community which also required their services, albeit to a much lesser extent. As civil servants, African teachers were under orders not to get involved in politics. In reality the policy was unworkable. With the discrimination which existed against all Africans based purely on colour, Africans were bound to participate in partisan politics. Liberal-minded Europeans in very senior positions sympathized with the African civil servants' dilemma. Some turned a blind eye to breaches of orders forbidding participation in politics. Others actually encouraged educated African civil servants to follow political developments and to provide leadership where possible. Clifford Little was one such liberal-minded European senior civil servant. He was aware that Joseph Mwemba and I were occasionally visited at Munali by African members of the Legislative Council for consultation on major political problems in our country. The consultations were made to ensure that their representations in the Legislative Council truly reflected the interests of a broad spectrum of the African population. Joseph Mwemba and I truly appreciated the confidence reposed in us, especially by Mr Paskale Sokota and Mr Robinson Nabulyato. The visits of these eminent persons to Munali to seek advice from us marked the end of splendid isolation even in the world of politics.

In the early 1950s, at the peak of African opposition to the proposal for closer association of Northern Rhodesia and Nyasaland with Southern Rhodesia, the African National Congress in Northern Rhodesia successfully lobbied some Labour MPs in the United Kingdom to rally behind nationalists' opposition to the imposition of the Federation of the two protectorates and the territory of Southern Rhodesia. Kenneth Kaunda, the secretary-general of the African National Congress, was charged with the responsibility of raising funds to enable a member of the Labour Party to visit Northern Rhodesia to assess the extent of African opposition to the imposition of Federation. Kenneth Kaunda wrote a letter to me and Joseph Mwemba asking us to donate generously to what he called "a noble cause". His emissary for the delivery of the letter was Titus Mukupo, assistant secretary of the African National Congress in the headquarters in Chilenje in Lusaka. We obliged.

It was early in 1954 when I realized that Clifford Little accepted that Joseph Mwemba and I quietly sympathized with the African nationalists who were in the forefront in the struggle for freedom and independence. In retrospect, I realize that Clifford Little, as an outstanding scholar, must have known that freedom and independence for Africans in Northern Rhodesia was inevitable after the Second World War. I surmise that early in the 1950s he had observed the rapidly changing political scene in Northern Rhodesia. For this reason, he adopted a pragmatic approach to the orientation of new education officers recruited from the United Kingdom to teach in Northern Rhodesia.

For example, in January 1954, a new education officer, Peter Snelson, arrived at Munali Secondary School as a teacher of history and English. Clifford Little requested me and Joseph Mwemba to brief him generally about life in Northern Rhodesia and about political developments in particular. This was arranged to enable the newcomer to settle down in his work quickly and satisfactorily. In order to assist Peter Snelson, Joseph Mwemba and I chose to speak frankly on the political situation in the country. Forty years later, Peter Snelson wrote a book entitled *To Independence and Beyond* published by the Radcliffe Press. He recalled the briefing session with us as follows:-

There were thirty or so of us on the Munali staff, giving a generous staffing ratio for the four hundred boys in the school.

Most of us were from Britain, there being very few African graduates in the country. Wesley Matsie was the headmaster and worked closely with Clifford Little in running the school. Next to him in seniority were John Mwanakatwe, the first African from Northern Rhodesia to obtain a university degree, and Joseph Mwemba. Both were friendly and helped me, a newcomer, to settle in, but they would say little about African hopes for political advancement. They made no secret, however, that they strongly resented the imposition, as they saw it, of the Central African Federation which had come into operation in October 1953, despite the bitter opposition of African political opinion.... In common with nearly all Africans, John and Joe were totally opposed to the Federation; they were sure it would entrench the power of the European settlers, particularly those in Southern Rhodesia, and would wreck any chance there might have been for Northern Rhodesia to achieve its own independence under black majority rule.

As they gave me their views in the staff room, none of us could guess that within ten years the Federation would have been dismantled, Zambia would be an independent republic, John Mwanakatwe would be minister of education in President Kaunda's government and Joe Mwemba would be Zambia's permanent representative at the United Nations. Clifford Little lived to see that day, although he did not, alas, survive for long after independence. Even he was surprised at the speed at which the changes he accurately predicted actually took place.

Our interest in political activities was stimulated by a number of liberal-minded white men who established an interracial club in the Kabulonga area in Lusaka. Kabulonga was a low density area exclusively for European businessmen and civil servants. Father Patrick Walsh SJ of the Roman Catholic Church and Harry Franklin were responsible for the establishment of the club. Harry Franklin was a journalist and a member of the Northern Rhodesian Executive Council representing African interests. The interracial club provided the only place in Lusaka in the years between 1953 and 1962 where

Africans and Europeans could meet and talk. Joseph Mwemba and I joined the club where we frequently met some members of the African National Congress and independent-minded businessmen, both black and white.

In the midst of teaching responsibilities at Munali and socializing occasionally with friends outside the school, I had time to teach adults in evening classes at Kabwata Primary School. The classes were organized by the adult education officer at the headquarters of the African Education Department. They were organized in selected areas for adults willing to attend night schools in order to improve their educational qualifications. They enabled many serious minded men and women to upgrade their academic qualifications. My interest in teaching adults in night schools was especially to assist able men and women to qualify for promotion to senior positions in government, commerce and industry after passing the standard six or form one examinations. An allowance was paid to night school teachers. It was too small and inconsequential to motivate teachers. What was rewarding was to see some of their students passing examinations well and gaining promotion in their employment afterwards. In my own case, an adult student to whom I taught history and civics in form one and form two eventually passed the Cambridge School Certificate Examinations. On the basis of his academic qualifications, he was among the first Africans promoted to the position of assistant commissioner of police following attainment of independence in October 1964.

Life at Munali became more interesting and more challenging from year to year. I had no crystal ball to determine the future pattern of my life. In mid May 1957, Hedley Roberts, who had succeeded Clifford Little as principal, handed a letter to me from the director of African education. He had summoned me to his office for what he called "a short interview". It had been decided to transfer me to Kasama Secondary School in the Northern Province. I was appointed headmaster of the school to take over from Peter Whitworth, who was transferred to

64

Chiwala Secondary School. The principal congratulated me on the appointment. I said "thank you". The promotion took me completely by surprise. It was necessary to reflect on its implications and, of course, to consult my wife. She reminded me that my transfer from Munali to Kasama Secondary School was a promotion which would involve all the advantages of occupying a supervisory position in government. In further consultations with Joseph, my elder brother, my promotion was welcomed. In particular, he emphasized that the government was satisfied that I was suitable for the appointment on the basis of my performance of duties and responsibilities in the past.

Four weeks later, I arrived in Kasama. My wife remained in Lusaka for one month. She was expecting our second child to be born early in July. I had made arrangements for her to join me later in Kasama. For her own and the convenience of our children, I arranged air transport on a Central African Airways flight from Lusaka to Kasama. My journey to Kasama was by road in our car in the company of George Chipampata, my wife's younger brother. Settling in was not difficult. The principal's house was quite large and well furnished. It was built on a small hill near the classroom block and students' dormitories. A domestic servant was at hand for employment. I hasten to say, though, that not much could be done to make the house completely habitable until my wife's arrival from Lusaka a month later. She was able then to get the house fitted with curtains and cushions. In any case, our heavy baggage had been consigned to us in Kasama via Thatcher and Hobson, the private company engaged in the business of transportation of goods by road to various parts of the country. Delivery was expected two or three weeks later.

Kasama Secondary School was situated about two miles away from the centre of Kasama township off the road to Malole Catholic Secondary School. It was the only government secondary school in the Northern Province. At the time of my arrival at the school, it was only a single stream male secondary school. For the year September 1957 to May 1958, I was authorized to increase the intake of boys in form one to at least sixty for two streams. The plan was to provide within three years sufficient places for at least one hundred and eighty boys in the school with three streams in form one and three streams in form two. With such a full-fledged junior secondary school, the government might consider upgrading it to a senior secondary school.

The provincial education officer, Evan Goddard, was responsible for the supervision of the functions and responsibilities of the Department of African Education in the Northern Province. He was based in Kasama, the provincial capital. He was assisted by an education officer and a woman education officer. He was also assisted by an education officer based in Chinsali and responsible specifically for Mpika, Chinsali and Isoka Districts. Other senior staff at the provincial headquarters included the secretary for the Local Education Authority, the building foreman and an assistant master. All holders of these posts were expatriates except Mr Nathan Chellah, the assistant master. Evan Goddard did not hesitate to emphasise that I had been appointed to a senior position in the African Education Department. He was optimistic that I would perform well in my duties. I was quick to inform him that I was prepared to work hard but expected support and encouragement from him personally and the staff in his office in Kasama.

Evan Goddard once taught at Munali Secondary School before he was drafted into the administrative wing of the African Education Department. A holder of an MA degree from Bristol University, he taught history and English. He was remembered as a strict disciplinarian who exhorted students to develop a culture of punctuality and smartness. Most important of all to me, Evan Goddard was brought up in the same mould as the English scholars I admired during my teaching career at Munali – liberal-minded, friendly and helpful. That was the background of the man I was destined to work with as my immediate boss in the Provincial Education Office in Kasama.

On the other hand, although I felt comfortable working

with Evan Goddard, I was rather apprehensive about the attitude of other expatriates. The more senior civil servants in other government departments were unlikely to resent my appointment or collaboration with them. However, I had serious reservations about the attitude of the less educated white clerical officers and businessmen. Such white men and women enjoyed privileges – salaries, housing and social amenities not because of their superior abilities or qualifications, but simply because of the colour of their skin. Social life in Kasama for white expatriates centred on their local club where they played golf, danced and dined and played billiards and other games. Their activities at the local club were of little interest to me. My concern was to be given a chance to run Kasama Secondary School satisfactorily, for example, to receive cooperation from suppliers of foodstuffs services. It was in this context that my appointment was a great challenge to me. Many people of all races regarded my appointment as principal of Kasama Secondary School as a test case. They were anxious to see if an African principal of a secondary school would demonstrate the necessary qualities of leadership, supervisory capabilities, honesty, integrity and ability to deliver. I was prepared to work hard and determined to succeed. But I accepted that success in running a secondary boarding school – indeed any school – was a cooperative effort. The head should share with members of the teaching staff and its administration the same goals for the school. Initially, my school's teaching staff was small. For two form one streams and one form two stream, I had three teachers to support me, apart from ancillary staff responsible for cooking meals and maintenance of school grounds. In addition, a part-time clerk was available for service in my office. Severin Njelesani, a graduate of Fort Hare University College was responsible for teaching science and mathematics with Cyrus Chellah, a holder of a teacher's diploma. Cyrus Chellah also taught geography and civics. Dancewell Bowa was another graduate teacher from Fort Hare University College with a BA in English.

In those days, French was not commonly taught in secondary schools. Apart from English which was a compulsory subject, Latin was the more commonly taught second language even when a local language such as ChiTonga, CiNyanja, IciBemba or SiLozi was also taught. However, not many secondary school teachers were qualified to teach Latin. I was qualified to teach Latin and my favourite subjects, English and history. With our combined efforts, the teaching load for each teacher was reasonable. I also had responsibility for the day to day administration of the school. For me each day started early in the morning at about 5.00 am and ended at 10.00 pm when I retired to bed after dinner. The programme for each weekend was not heavy and Sundays in particular were reserved for church, family visits and picnics with my wife and children. Otherwise, as the school's principal, I realized it was my responsibility to set standards both for the teachers and the students. I believed that it was better to educate people by example than by precept. I had learnt at Adams College that a businessman's days are a continuous fight with hours and a struggle with time. After some years of teaching, I came to realize that a teacher's days are a continuous struggle with time.

Throughout my stewardship of the school, harmony prevailed among the staff and between the staff and students. Even when there was turmoil and confusion in many secondary schools in Northern Rhodesia between 1957 and 1960, Kasama Secondary School was a haven of peace. Many educators believe today, as indeed in those days, that our world is too full of men and women and systems whose way of dealing with boys and girls is to make them feel small. However, there are others who endeavour to make even small men as well as boys and girls feel great, thus starting in them their growth toward greatness. That was my approach in moulding the character of boys at Kasama Secondary School. Each boy was encouraged to feel that he was valued and trusted whether he came from a poor or rich family, whether he was exceptionally bright or not so bright. Each had the desire to reciprocate such trust by behaving

68

properly and responsibly at all times. The good discipline of our students and their excellent pass rate each year in final examinations gained a good reputation for the school.

We had only one football field at the school in July 1957. For a school with a small enrolment of students it was adequate. The students were encouraged to play football after classes in the afternoon. They played inter-house football matches from time to time in order to promote the spirit of friendly competition. Occasionally, our team played football against Malole Secondary School. Our school's football team rarely defeated the Malole School. It had a larger enrolment of students and the Malole football team consisted of much bigger and heavier players.

Facilities for other forms of sport like tennis or boxing did not exist. A few students showed an interest in athletics, but no teacher was available to coach them. In terms of extra-curricular activities, our students were interested in the activities of the literary and debating society. Membership of this society was compulsory. Teachers were encouraged to attend some of the debates organized by the committee of officials of the society. From time to time lectures were given by staff members or invited guests. Participation in debates was encouraged as one way of improving the standard of spoken English among the students. Such participation in debates was also a way of identifying students with a talent for public speaking.

In my English classes, I encouraged play acting by students in the classroom. I was always amazed in those days how much the students loved to act plays of their own composition. That is how I discovered a talent for drama among some of our students. That encouraged the staff and students later to stage a play towards the end of 1958 entitled *The Bishop's Candlesticks*. Although I had difficulties during preparations with helpers – stage management, lighting, costumes – the production was very successful. As producer, I had concentrated on speech training and scenery. The successful production of the play to a mixed audience of black and white men and women enhanced our school's reputation. Evan Goddard sent a congratulatory letter, through me, to all the staff and students in the school.

Officials of high rank in government rarely visited our school due undoubtedly to its remoteness from Lusaka. However, in November 1959, Gabriel Musumbulwa, the minister of African education, decided to visit some parts of the Northern Province. In 1958 the Northern Province had been rocked with serious political disturbances. Some schools were burnt down by African nationalists in protests against the Federation. We were informed that the minister intended to visit our school when he arrived in Kasama. He was known to sympathise with a white dominated political party, the United Federal Party, which in fact he later joined. This fact posed a problem for the staff and students of our school. We were not keen to welcome Musumbulwa to the school as our honoured guest.

The option of a boycott of Musumbulwa's visit was considered seriously. We decided against it. It was considered unwise to cause embarrassment to the provincial education officer with whom our school had a good rapport. One teacher remarked wittily that we were entitled to accept the existence of the office of minister of African education but to refuse to accept Gabriel Musumbulwa as a suitable person for that office. He came and visited the school and left. There was not any excitement, cheering or ululation!

Throughout my three year period of stewardship of Kasama Secondary School, we had a steady stream of ordinary visitors. Most of them were school inspectors, education officers, district officers, medical officers, auditors, chiefs and many others, well-wishers or government officers on duty. I have never forgotten the visit to our school of a young white man employed in Kasama by the Post and Telegraph Department. He came to the school one day to rectify a fault on the telephone line to the office with an extension to my house about one hundred yards from the classroom block. He was a technician with two African handymen to assist him. When the technician and his men arrived, I was in my office and the door was wide open. He suspected that the fault might have been with telephone wires in the office so he walked into the office. I was marking exercise books. He told me that he wanted to talk to the *Bwana*. In those days, *Bwana* was a word of respect for a white man – originally a Swahili word for a gentleman. Therefore, I told him that I was the *Bwana*. However, he insisted that he wanted to talk to the *Bwana* who was in-charge of the school. It was quite clear to me at that stage that I was speaking to a pathological racist. In the circumstances, I felt that firmness was totally justified. I then shouted at the top of my voice, "Look young man, I am the *Bwana* here. I am in-charge of this school". To my surprise, the technician walked out of my office. His African helpers outside the office during the altercation joined the technician and they drove away. The telephone line was not repaired.

At the first opportunity on the following day, I reported to Evan Goddard the intolerable attitude of the technician. As I expected, he was not amused by the technician's blatant display of racialism. I requested him to intervene on my behalf to get the telephone line restored to facilitate the school's operations. His response was positive. To my surprise the technician returned to the school that same day to work on the telephone line with his team. He looked tame like a person who had just been carpeted. However, true to his character, he merely walked into my office and started working on the telephone line. We did not exchange greetings. On this occasion he did not ask to meet the *Bwana* before doing his work. About an hour later he came to me and said, "Now the telephone is working", and he went away with his men. I learnt something about the incorrigible nature of hard-core racists. They are unrepentant. Although the technician was of no real consequence to me, nevertheless I learnt the obvious lesson that in every race there are good people and bad people. Generalisation about humankind can be misleading and even dangerous at times.

Derek White was the first principal of our school. His tenure of office was short – only one year. He was transferred to another province to perform the duties of an education officer.

Peter Whitworth was the school's second principal from 1955 to 1957, when I assumed principalship of the school in July. The school's budget was controlled by Arthur Smith, the secretary of the Local Education Authority, in the office of the provincial education officer. As principal of Kasama Secondary School, I was responsible only for maintaining the school's accounts for monies collected from students for boarding fees and school uniforms. Auditors were expected to examine and check the accounts kept by the head teacher at least once a year. However, no such audit of the school's accounts had been carried out since September 1954, when the school was opened for admission of students to form one.

I had been warned about the principal's accounting responsibilities. Before I left Munali, it occurred to me that I needed guidance on how to keep books of accounts in a simple manner that would satisfy auditors. Isaac Lewanika was the senior African clerk with the knowledge and experience of what I wanted to know. He devised for me a simple method of recording our income and expenditure on opposite pages supported with appropriate receipts. Later, I was glad I had obtained guidance from Isaac Lewanika in keeping accounts.

In December 1957 before the Christmas break, two white men arrived unexpectedly at our school. They introduced themselves as members of the staff of the Auditor-General's Office in Lusaka. They also told me that they were touring the Northern Province in order to conduct audits of some government departments and institutions, including Kasama Secondary School. They were friendly and courteous. For the first time I learnt that auditors, as a rule, did not announce in advance their intention to visit an institution in order to carry out an audit. They had not visited the school previously to conduct an audit. However, that did not worry me. For the period I was responsible for the school's management I had done my best to keep up-to-date records of monies received and monies paid out (almost all of it to the government from boarding fees and cost of school uniforms).

The auditors took two days only to complete their work. They were methodical and thorough. However, although the duo were friendly at all times, they kept me and my staff at arms length. Each day my domestic servant brought tea to my office at tea-break about mid-morning. I always felt obliged to ask the auditors to join me for a cup of tea. Each time, one of them quickly reminded me that they always carried their own tea in flasks. It dawned on me eventually that this was a good habit. It was, I thought, a necessary precaution for people who performed delicate functions and responsibilities. However, the result of the auditors' work was of more concern and interest to me. The auditors found the school's record of accounts in order. The auditors informed me that they intended to submit a favourable report on the audit to the authorities.

Quite understandably, Evan Goddard used to monitor various reports and comments by visitors and school inspectors on our performance at Kasama Secondary School. Early in 1958, Mr AE Arro visited our school. He was the supervisor of physical training at the headquarters of the Department of African Education in Lusaka. Fortunately, I had taken a special interest in physical education in my teacher-training course at Adams College and had been active in giving physical training lessons to students at Munali Secondary School. My interest in physical training was undiminished at Kasama. At the end of the visit, Mr Arro submitted a glowing report to the PEO in Kasama. He hastily conveyed to me Mr Arro's favourable report with his own compliments. The PEO informed me that he was anxious also to improve the standard of physical education in primary schools in the Northern Province.

Later in the first half of 1958, with the PEO's approval, I arranged a programme of visits to a few selected upper primary schools in Mporokoso District of the Northern Province. Apart from interviewing standard six boys who had applied for a place in form one at Kasama, I intended also to assess the standard of physical education in primary schools. For my official visits to selected upper primary schools in Mporokoso District, I was provided with a Landrover, a driver, a requisition book for the purchase of fuel and petty cash for out-of-pocket expenses. Accommodation was arranged for me in the government's guest house in Mporokoso for five days.

Unfortunately, my tour of schools started with an unpleasant incident – the kind of incident which later caused laughter and which I have never forgotten. I arrived early in the evening on a Sunday before the start of my tour programme the following day. The driver knew the geography of Mporokoso township well. So he drove the vehicle directly to the government guest house. After a long and tedious journey, I chose to rest in the lounge, leaving the driver to offload my luggage and consult the caretaker on the arrangements for my accommodation. Actually, on our arrival I saw that the guest house was a large building with a spacious lounge and large open veranda with wire-gauze for protection against flies and mosquitoes. Later, I saw that there were two large bedrooms and three small ones.

After some time a distraught-looking driver came into the lounge to see me. He was apologetic for disturbing my short rest. Then he dropped a bombshell. He told me that the caretaker of the guest house refused to allocate a room to me because only European officers were allowed to spend nights in the guest house. I then retorted: "Didn't you tell the caretaker that I am a gazetted officer?" The driver replied "I told him, sir, that you are an officer, that you run a school previously headed by Mr Peter Whitworth and that you live in the house in which he lived before he was transferred to Ndola. But he still refused to give you a room in the guest house". I then said to the driver, rather impatiently, "Tell the caretaker to come and see me immediately".

A few minutes later, the caretaker came to the lounge with the driver. He was an elderly man, dark with wrinkles on his face. His English was poor. Therefore, he preferred to speak in his own language, IciBemba, a language spoken in the Northern Province in which I was quite fluent. He told me bluntly that he

74

had worked as a caretaker of the guest house for many years but he had never known an African civil servant who was allowed to sleep there. The rooms were reserved for occupation by *abasungu* only. The word *abasungu* in IciBemba means Europeans. He told me that he was certain of instant dismissal from employment if I occupied a room with his consent. It was evident that further argument with the caretaker was pointless. At his age, with hardly any education and living in a remote part of the country, it was unlikely that he knew about the limited social and political changes which were taking place in favour of the Africans. I decided to go to the district commissioner's house to solicit his intervention. I knew that course of action implied disturbing his peace. The district commissioner was out of the station. Therefore, I drove to the district officer's house to ask for assistance.

The district officer, a young man who was probably in his late twenties, was embarrassed by the caretaker's refusal to allocate a room to me. The Provincial Education Office had notified the district commissioner of Mporokoso about my official visit to the district and the desirability of reserving accommodation for me at the government guest house. For these reasons he apologized to me profusely for the caretaker's failure to comply with the instructions he had been given. Apparently, he believed that the instruction related to reservation of accommodation for a white officer. Indeed, old habits die hard!

To settle the problem, the district officer came with me to the guest house to give instructions to the caretaker in my presence. The district officer spoke to the caretaker in IciBemba, although he was not entirely fluent. He told the caretaker that his office's instruction related to preparation of a room for me for occupation for five days. Suddenly, the caretaker beamed and smiled. He became excited. He started speaking to himself loudly in our presence. He remarked: "*Eya lelo incito yawama ukubomba; eya lelo incito yawama ukubomba*" (he was saying literally that "Today work will be enjoyable; today work will be enjoyable"). We all understood the elderly caretaker to imply

75

that having the opportunity to serve a fellow black man in the guest house was exceptionally gratifying to him. Later in the evening, as I sat alone at the table in the dining room, like a possessed person he kept repeating his affirmation of joy at the opportunity of serving a non-white person for the first time. That evening I felt that in preparing and serving the meal he did everything possible to give me complete satisfaction.

Over a period of five days I worked long hours and interviewed many standard six students who had applied for entrance to form one at our school in Kasama at the beginning of the new school year in September 1958. Selection to form one depended largely on a student's performance in the standard six examinations and performance in the special paper which was designed to measure the student's intelligence. Additionally, in selecting applicants reference to the head teacher's report on each student was useful. Visits to a number of upper primary schools for this purpose were worthwhile.

I had the responsibility of meeting many well-wishers and government officials at our school. Sometimes, it was necessary to provide such visitors with accommodation and hospitality. Toward the end of 1958 and in 1959, Margaret and I became more and more involved in receiving at the school victims of political disturbances in the country. A state of emergency was declared by the governor of Northern Rhodesia early in March 1959, followed by widespread arrests of leaders of the Zambia African National Congress which the governor, Sir Arthur Benson, had banned. Many political leaders were rounded-up in the early hours of 12 March 1959 and thereafter restricted to their home areas or to other remote parts of the country. It was in Kasama where I first met Andrew Mutemba during the period of his rustication to his village. He later became a life-long friend. Often he was able to sneak out from his restriction area to visit us at Lukashya where our secondary school was built. In the evening I would drive him back to his place of restriction. In the same way I linked up with an old friend, Emmanuel Chalabesah, whom I met for the first time in Lusaka during my teaching days at old Munali.

Our happiest surprise was Sikota Wina's visit. He had been restricted to Luwingu District in the Northern Province far away from Kasama. When he was released from restriction he honoured us by his unexpected visit before returning to his base in Chingola to pursue his career as a journalist.

Throughout my tenure of office at Kasama Secondary School, life was hectic and interesting – never a dull moment. In discharging my duties and responsibilities as principal, I registered some successes and failures. Fortunately, in the most important area positive results were recognized. In the form two final examinations, all the concerned parties – the staff, students and their parents – had cause for satisfaction. In three successive years our final year students obtained over ninety six per cent pass rate. Good results were achieved because the staff and students worked harmoniously as a team to achieve set goals; and I consider myself fortunate that I had dedicated staff and responsible and hardworking students. I left the school in June 1960 without misgivings to take up my new duties as an education officer in Livingstone in the Southern Province.

CHAPTER

4

My Wife and Partner

I spent five years in the high school department at Adams College. Later, I was a student in the teacher training department for two years. In these departments, all classes had boys and girls learning or training together. Some of the girls were very clever indeed, others were just beautiful and attractive. Yet in all the years I spent at Adams College, I never made any advance to a girl suggesting the possibility of a husband and wife relationship in future. In those years, I was too preoccupied with my studies. I was more determined to achieve my ambition than to pursue any goal unrelated to it. Of course, like many grown up students, I sometimes indulged in flirtations with girls without any intention of serious marital considerations in future. Therefore, I left Adams College in December 1948 without commitment to any woman.

In December 1949, for the first time in my life I met a young woman in Broken Hill, now known as Kabwe, who swept me off my feet. She was just over fifteen years old. I was nearly tempted to pop the usual question for a man anxious to register his feelings towards a woman with whom he envisages a permanent love relationship. But the circumstances did not permit me to make a proposal to the young woman who was introduced to me as Margaret Chipampata. She was the young sister of Mr Samuel Makungu's wife, Felicity. I had been advised by a fellow teacher at Chalimbana Teacher Training College to ask for assistance from Samuel Makungu if I ever encountered any difficulty in Broken Hill on my journey to Mbala. I wrote a letter asking him to accommodate me for two days in Broken Hill on my journey to Mbala by bus in December. His reply was prompt and favourable. Margaret was a form one student at Chipembi Girls' Secondary School. She had chosen to spend the Christmas holidays with her elder sister in Kabwe. That is how we met.

I stayed with the family for two days only before I took a Northern Province bound bus to Mbala run by a reputable company popularly known as Thatcher and Hobson. I did not see much of Samuel Makungu during the day time. He was the head teacher of Broken Hill Senior School, a government school. However, in the evenings we discussed many issues relating to African education. The discussions were interesting and enjoyable. In the day time, I was rather lonely because Margaret was often involved in household chores, especially with preparation of meals. Most of the time her elder sister was busy nursing her three month old baby.

Occasionally, however, Margaret found time to join me in the sitting room. My first impression of Margaret was that she was a quiet and reserved person. She answered questions intelligently but appeared shy. Most of the time, she kept me company by playing her favourite songs on the gramophone. I remember that she liked playing for me one of Jim Rogers' songs, popularly known as the "Yodelling Cowboy". In later years, when she was already my wife, I used to reflect on some of the words in that song. I wondered if it was intentionally chosen in order to convey a special message to me. It included these lines: "Be honest with me dear, whatever you do; if you really love me, be honest with me". Notwithstanding the words of this song I had already made up my mind to be a well behaved and responsible guest in the home of Mr and Mrs Makungu. If necessary, I was prepared to follow up the establishment of a love relationship between us at a later stage. However, on arrival in Mbala and certainly before proceeding to our village twelve miles away, I sent a Christmas card to Margaret by post. Of course, I thought it was good diplomacy also to send another card to "Mr and Mrs Makungu".

I stayed with my parents for about ten days in our village not far from Chief Tafuna's palace in Isoka. Deliberately I avoided breaking the news of my interest in Margaret to my parents. It would have been premature to announce such news at that time. On my way back to Munali, I had no time to revisit Samuel Makungu and his family in Broken Hill. It was necessary to report on time to Clifford Little. He had been kind to allow me to take leave for ten days in order to visit my parents in Mbala, even before my completion of a year of service in government, a condition for eligibility to what was called local leave. But I did not forget the young woman who had swept me off my feet at first sight with her composure and dignity. Margaret had already grown into a beautiful young woman. I occasionally visited Chipembi before she completed form two in May 1951, if only to impress on her that she had not been forgotten. There is a belief among some people that once "out of sight" then "out of mind" also. Through occasional visits to Chipembi Girls' Secondary School, I maintained a personal relationship with Margaret. Fortunately, my young sister, Rachel, was a staff member at the school. The visits to Chipembi were arranged on the pretext that I had a sister there whom I wanted to see from time to time.

In those days, travelling to Chipembi from Lusaka was difficult. I found it more convenient, although tedious, to travel by train from Lusaka to Chisamba railway station. Thereafter I rode my own bicycle to Chipembi, a journey of about eighteen miles. It meant that I had a similar journey to Chisamba by bicycle and then by train back to Lusaka. But this arrangement actually increased the expenses for the trips to Chipembi. I had to pay a small fee for putting my bicycle on the train. Margaret knew what was involved in the escapades. The extent of her appreciation of my efforts to maintain contact with her after the original encounter in Kabwe was expressed many years later as follows:

I recall one incident which pleased me a lot. At one time my future husband decided to come to Chipembi to see me. He was a teacher at Munali Secondary School in Lusaka. First, he took a train from Lusaka to Chisamba. Then he travelled from Chisamba to Chipembi, some eighteen miles away. Then after visiting us at Chipembi he cycled back to Chisamba and got on the train back to Lusaka putting his bicycle on the train. His effort to come to Chipembi under difficult circumstances pleased me a lot.

Due to my occasional visits to Chipembi, Rachel was the first member of our family to know that I had a very strong love relationship with Margaret. Apparently, without my knowledge, she had planned to interest me in a possible marriage with Betty Nakazwe, who was also a teacher at the same school. She was closely related to us as our cousin. Her father, Reverend John Sikazwe, was a minister of religion. Like our father, Reverend Sikazwe had deep roots at Kambole Mission. From my occasional visits to Chipembi, my young sister realized that my relationship with Margaret was serious and irrevocable. Eventually, realities were accepted. Strong bonds of cousinship continued between Rachel and Betty and later with Margaret their sister-in-law.

In May 1951, Margaret completed her education at Chipembi. Her performance in the junior secondary school examination was very good. She was awarded a scholarship by the Northern Rhodesian government to proceed to Tiger Kloof in South Africa to complete secondary education there. Two other girls in her class also performed well in the examinations, namely Hannah Chibelu and Mary Shancolesha. At that time educational facilities beyond form two were not available for girls in Northern Rhodesia. Margaret declined the offer of a scholarship to Tiger Kloof. However, Hannah Chibelu and Mary Shancolesha both accepted the scholarships.

Margaret opted to return to Mindolo Girls' Boarding School where she had previously completed the standard six primary school course. She preferred to undertake a one year course in domestic science rather than continue with academic studies after form two. The one year domestic science course included lessons in cookery, housekeeping, embroidery and dressmaking. A suitable course, indeed, for a young woman looking forward to the day she would be obliged to manage her own house and care for her husband and children! Therefore, I did not regret her choice of undertaking a one-year course in domestic science rather than the furtherance of her academic education beyond form two.

Early in June 1952, I received a letter from Margaret in which she announced proudly that she had completed her domestic science course successfully. It was clear to me from her letter that she was anxious to know if I would now consider arranging a date for our wedding. In fact, in this regard, she was pushing an open door. Our courtship started in 1950 during my first visit to Chipembi. But I was conscious of the fact that I had not seriously informed Margaret that I wanted to marry her. Secondly, it was also necessary to break the news to her parents, if only to gain their support and encouragement on a matter which was basically our concern. On careful reflection, I decided to deal with one issue at a time. Firstly, I asked Margaret if she was willing to marry me. Her reply to my letter was prompt and positive. At that stage, I realized that proposing to a woman was easy. Under the culture of the Lungu people, breaking the news to her parents should be done in a formal way with a procedure that was elaborate. Therefore, I relied on guidance from my father particularly and other relatives.

My father's inquiries on the background of the prospective bride's parents yielded favourable results. Her father had been a well known resident at Mbereshi Mission in Kawambwa District for many years. My parents were particularly pleased that her father, Mr Jacob Chipampata, was originally a Lungu-speaking man from Chief Chitimbwa's area in Mbala District. He left Kambole Mission with his elder sister, who was married to Shitima Sinkala, when the latter moved with the missionaries to Mbereshi. Both Kambole and Mbereshi were mission stations established by the London Mission Society. My father followed up the positive result of his inquiries. Tradition obliged me to find a trustworthy elderly and respected person who was willing to be the "go-between" and break the news to Margaret's parents about my wish to marry her. My father chose for me an old friend, Mr William Konie, to perform this important function. Our family was well known to him. He accepted the responsibility. He had been my teacher in the Lower Primary School at Munali, and I was quite comfortable with his nomination. I was confident that he would protect my interests properly. First he delivered the betrothal token and later the bride-price to Margaret's parents. Subsequently, we were given the green light to make wedding arrangements.

After consultations with all stakeholders, the 20th of December 1952 was chosen as the date for our wedding. Only my father travelled from Mbala to attend the wedding in Kawambwa. Fortunately, there were two civil servants in Kawambwa who originally came from Mbala. Mr Matthew Kasanga and Mr Pearson Simfukwe with their families teamed up with my father on the wedding day to give me moral support and encouragement.

A week after the wedding, Margaret and I bade farewell to her parents. We were ready to go to Lusaka to start a new life at Munali as husband and wife. Their blessings before departure were greatly valued. We travelled by bus to Mufulira and Ndola. We stayed in Ndola for two nights with my uncle, Abraham Willombe, who was employed as an industrial instructor in the African Education Department. He was particularly happy that I had grown up into a responsible young man teaching in the leading educational institution at that time. Apparently, he knew Margaret when she was a young girl living with her cousin, the wife of a school teacher, Zebron Sikazwe, at Fiwale Hills Mission School in Ndola-Rural.

The last lap of our journey was short; it was by train from Ndola to Lusaka. We were met at the railway station by my elder brother and Mr Victor Manda. He was a close friend of my elder brother, a kind of David and Jonathan relationship. They trusted each other. Before I left Lusaka to go to Kawambwa for the wedding, I had entrusted my old Chevrolet car to Victor Manda's care. At that time, my elder brother did not know how to drive a car. Although Victor Manda had given me lessons in driving, I was not yet competent. I owned a car although I had no driving licence. In these circumstances, it was reasonable to leave my car with Victor Manda.

The big old American Chevrolet was Margaret's big surprise when we arrived at the railway station in Lusaka. During the journey, I told her casually that I owned an old, but mechanically sound, motor vehicle. I, therefore, expected my elder brother and Victor Manda to meet us on arrival at the railway station and to take us to our home at Munali in our own car. She received the news with disbelief. Perhaps it was too good to be true. In less than an hour after our arrival at the railway station, we reached our home safely at Munali and received a warm welcome from friends and neighbours.

The motor vehicle was usually kept by Victor Manda at his house in Chilenje township. From time to time, he was available to supervise my driving practices. I was a holder of a mere learner's licence. Fortunately, by the time of our marriage, I was a reasonably competent driver of a motor vehicle, although I required more practice before submitting myself to a driving test. As far as I can remember, in 1952 there were probably not more than five or six Africans who owned motor vehicles in Lusaka. I had bought my car from a prominent African businessman, Mr Safeli Chileshe. We were all very proud that his wife, Martha, was the first African woman in Lusaka to possess a licence for driving a motor car.

Within days, news spread quickly among the students that their twenty-six-year-old teacher was no longer a bachelor. I had remained single for more than three years from the time I joined the staff at Munali Secondary School. That was to many people an unusually long time for a young man in employment to remain a bachelor. Therefore, many students were curious to

84

know if, indeed, the news was true. If it was true, they wanted to know whether my wife was literate or just an ordinary village girl. Whatever stories went around, the more courageous students chose to come to our house on one pretext or another to see the new bride. Suddenly, our house became popular with boys asking for piecework in the garden at home or chopping firewood for our kitchen stove. In those days, electric stoves were not common. Many years later, in fact more than forty years later, I learnt why our house suddenly became popular among students looking ostensibly for piecework. Emmanuel Kasonde, now a close friend, who was a student at Munali at that time, explained that the students coming to our house in large numbers were more than mere job seekers – they wanted to find out if my wife was beautiful and if she understood and spoke English fluently. What was important to me was that by the time of our wedding in December 1952, Margaret was a beautiful young woman of eighteen!

Margaret and I did not take long to adapt ourselves to life as a married couple. We hardly experienced any agony or strain in having to live together. My own experience was that for the first time in my life I was no longer the active go-ahead person I had been since childhood. Throughout my life, I enjoyed tackling problems "head-on". Sometimes I took ill-considered decisions which I regretted afterwards. Early in our married life I learnt that I was no longer the individual I had been before. I had a partner who was equally affected by difficulties or problems confronting me. She was entitled to participate in finding solutions to them. Therefore, slowly the impetuous tendency to personalization of issues was tempered by a more mature attitude of discussing problems with my wife. Sometimes, I concluded that it was adequate to hold on to an obvious answer until after consultation with my wife.

On the other hand, my wife had not changed from the person I knew when I met her for the first time in Samuel Makungu's house in December 1949. She appeared to me then as a quiet and reserved woman. She remained rather quiet and reserved long after our marriage. Although she appreciated being consulted, almost invariably she would ask for my opinion in any given situation. Often she was prepared to go along with my opinion. If I had none, she would insist that I had an obligation to find a solution and that she was willing to accept my decision. Over the years I have realized that her approach to the husband and wife relationship is deeply rooted in the culture of the Lungu people. The husband among the Lungu is invariably the head of the family. There are ways in which a woman can exercise influence on her husband but she makes every effort that outwardly he is seen to be the leader in the home. It should be remembered that disadvantageous cultural norms have sometimes their trade-off values. On many occasions when things have not gone well in our family, my wife has been quick to remind me that I was solely responsible for the wrong decision. Such a reminder becomes an irrefutable statement of fact. She might be told at some stage that she had not seized the opportunity to suggest a better solution to the particular problem. Nonetheless, such a rejoinder would be merely an exercise in futility.

Throughout my teaching years at Munali and later at Kasama Secondary School, Margaret's role was that of a housewife with children to look after. She was always concerned about my habit of working long hours throughout the year. Occasionally, I would take leave of about a month or two weeks only. When I was not lucky, I would work continuously for two or three years without a break, a habit which close friends and relatives openly discouraged. When I was a young man in my late forties and early fifties, my constitution could stand this kind of strenuous work. However, as I advanced in age, the strain of such work style was no longer bearable. Some habits indeed die hard. Today, I still work for at least ten or even twelve hours a day. I work for such long hours a day not so much for financial gain nowadays but for the joy of keeping myself occupied. An abrupt or drastic change in my style of work might lead to catastrophic consequences.

I have always appreciated Margaret's important role in bringing up our children. In this regard, I owe her an immense debt of gratitude. As a school teacher, a politician and, later, a busy corporate lawyer, I rarely found time to assist her in the up-bringing of our children. The role of parents is vital in the early years of a child's development. Margaret devoted all her time and energy to the promotion of my own and the health and happiness of our children. I played an important role as the family's breadwinner. All our children's needs were provided to their satisfaction. Margaret, nonetheless, took the responsibility of their up-bringing with little or no assistance from me. I was rarely at home from very early in the morning until late at night. Occasionally, I used my situation in the home to instil in our children a life-long abhorrence of mediocrity. I emphasized that if one accepted to do something it had to be done to the best of one's ability. They were encouraged to remember always that: "if anything is worth doing at all, then do it well".

Margaret has never relented from discouraging me from overworking. A few years ago, in an effort to solicit assistance from one of my closest friends, she told him that:

> It is a pity that at sixty-eight years of age John still works so hard. As a professional lawyer, he hardly has time to have three square meals a day. I make every effort to prepare breakfast, lunch and dinner for him every day, but I am lucky if he is available for at least two meals. My only comfort is that he skips some of his meals because he enjoys his work.

As an educationist, I did not believe in sending our children to boarding schools when they were too young. I have always valued the role of parents during a child's formative years. Therefore, all our children went to boarding schools after the age of twelve. Eventually, one by one they left to set up their own homes and establish their own families. Gradually, Margaret's role as a parent diminished. Fortunately, she cultivated a new habit of reading books avidly. She also started passing time solving crossword puzzles and reading newspapers. Today, she has become remarkably knowledgeable on world affairs generally and local politics in particular. It is true, as they say, that practice makes perfect. She hardly relies on me now to solve difficult crossword puzzles. Her vocabulary in English has improved considerably in recent years.

At the end of 1978, the president of Zambia, Dr Kenneth Kaunda, allowed me to retire completely from active politics after a second stint as minister of finance from May 1976 to December 1978. I joined other lawyers to form a law firm called MMW and Company. I intended to concentrate on practising law after retirement from active politics. All other types of business were inconsequential and of no interest to me. However, early in the second half of 1979, I read an interesting advertisement in a local daily newspaper – the *Times of Zambia*. A farmer in Chisamba farming area, about forty miles from Lusaka, wanted to sell his farm. Chisamba was well known as a good farming area. Mr Van de Venter's farm was not too large, but it could support both cattle rearing and crop production. The land was fertile. It was in extent about seven hundred and fifty hectares or two thousand acres.

Although we did not know the price of the farm, I persuaded my wife to show an interest in it. In our discussions I conjured up all sorts of exciting ventures we would undertake if we decided to buy the farm. The idea of owning a farm just outside Lusaka where we could spend week-ends in peace and tranquillity was quite exciting. It was a place to which I would retreat with her to prepare legal opinions or draft complicated legal documents. So a visit to the farm was hastily arranged. Our inspection of the farm was encouraging. We observed that the whole farm was fenced and there was an abundant water supply from two boreholes. There were two dip tanks. Electricity was available from a diesel generator. There were also two running tractors. The farm and equipment were on sale for fifty thousand Kwacha. Unfortunately, we did not have that amount of money.

Margaret was particularly excited by the prospect of being called a "farmer's wife". Over the years, she had become disenchanted with my involvement in politics. I always thought that her over-reaction to being called a "politician's wife" was unreasonable. She believed that it was used with disdain or contempt. "Even if you work very hard", she would say from time to time, "nobody will appreciate your efforts". She desperately wanted us to buy the farm. But she was quick to suggest the necessity of a professional evaluation to determine if the price was reasonable. We selected a trusted valuation surveyor who produced a favourable report. The price which included farm equipment was considered reasonable. With the valuation surveyor's report, our application for a loan from the First Permanent Building Society to finance a portion of the purchase price was approved. The farm itself was mortgaged to the Permanent Building Society as security for the advance.

Because we bought the farm as a going concern, within a few weeks we were able to plant our first crop just before the onset of heavy rain in November 1979. The majority of farm workers chose to remain on the farm and work for us. Apart from our crop of maize, we also grew vegetables successfully. However, to ensure effective management we were obliged to visit the farm every weekend. That is how we monitored operations closely. In farming actual supervision of workers is necessary from time to time, especially if you do not live on the farm. The partnership we forged to run the farm was successful. In less than five years, we paid off the loan we had obtained from the building society. Our initial stock of two bulls and fifty heifers had increased to more than two hundred and fifty cows and more than forty steers in less than ten years. Obviously, the farming venture we started as a pastime, not as a serious business enterprise, proved profitable. We were given two bulls by George Cornhill. A close friend of our family, he wanted this venture to succeed. He was an expert and experienced large-scale cattle farmer in the Southern Province.

Margaret was becoming increasingly active in a variety

of farming activities, such as poultry keeping and growing vegetables, which we found quite profitable. During the first ten years she was a very active partner of Katula Family Enterprises (a subsidiary company of Mbala Holdings Limited). She was supported by a devoted, well trained farm manager. Unfortunately, he eventually resigned his position. We knew for some time that he was looking for greener pastures elsewhere. A prospective employer offered him a monthly salary and conditions of service which our new company was unable to match. Not long after his departure there was a rapid deterioration in the management of the farm. Thefts of farm produce and our cattle had become a way of life. The farm was surrounded by villages whose inhabitants survived mainly on food items stolen from neighbouring commercial farmers. Three years after the departure of the manager we had come to trust, we chose to abandon farming altogether. Rampant thefts of cattle made the venture no longer viable economically. We wasted many hours accompanying policemen in fruitless journeys to trace suspected thieves.

Fortunately, it was a sellers market when we took the decision to sell the farm and equipment. We sold our cattle separately before the farm was sold. Over a period of fifteen years, Margaret was more involved than I was in overseeing operations on our farm in Chisamba. She had previously demonstrated her unique qualities as a wife and as a mother. The Chisamba farming venture demonstrated beyond doubt that, though quiet and reserved, Margaret had the potential to be a good business partner. I must admit that previously my thoughts about her business acumen were entirely different! Since my farming experience in Chisamba, I considered myself even more fortunate to have Margaret for my wife.

On many occasions, people have asked me this difficult question, "What is the secret of a happy marriage?" Obviously, a universal answer to such a question is impossible. In my opinion, it is necessary first of all to accept that "it takes two to tango". No husband and wife relationship can be harmonious unless

unless both are willing from time to time to accommodate the other's feelings or desires. Disagreements or even quarrels between husband and wife are inevitable from time to time. On such occasions the husband or wife should be ready to relent and allow the other to gain the upper hand. More importantly, a harmonious husband and wife relationship will tend to sour where one or the other refuses to accept that he or she can make a mistake. A harmonious marriage will survive vicissitudes in life when the offended spouse is willing to accept the apology tendered by the offending spouse. The secret of success in any marriage is that each partner should endeavour to cultivate and encourage the spirit of give and take.

I recall an incident more than forty three years ago when I offended Margaret while teaching her how to drive a motor car. She was extremely upset. In 1958 during the school holidays, I offered to give her driving lessons. Our second child was one year old. We agreed that at that age we could leave him safely in the care of our house servant. The lessons started well and gradually Margaret was making progress in driving our small car, a British-made "Standard Eight" which was virtually new. All her manipulations of the car were satisfactory except that she had a problem with jerking the car when changing gears. Her coordination of clutch and gear lever operations continued to be poor. Eventually, my patience was exhausted during one of the driving lessons when she failed to achieve a smooth change of gear. I exclaimed at the top of my voice that the problem was with her left leg. The thigh of her left leg was too heavy. My outburst was accompanied by one or two hard slaps on her thigh with my right hand. She drove the car slowly and stopped it beside the road. She gave me the key for the car with the words I shall never forget: "Please drive the car home safely. I shall walk home alone. It is not far away". On a previous occasion when she drove the car incompetently I accused her of dullness. She did not complain on that occasion. There was no doubt in my mind that she was unmoved. My plea to her to return to the car and go back home with me fell on deaf ears.

Later that evening I apologized to her again for my unreasonable outburst and I requested her to forgive me. She was generous to forgive me there and then.

The reconciliation would not have been so easily achieved if I had not accepted that I had treated my wife unfairly and unreasonably. More importantly, after admitting perpetration of an unjust act against my wife, I apologised to her unreservedly.

Within a few days, the husband and wife relations were normalized again. Later she resumed her driving lessons. The incident also taught me another lesson – that husbands are probably not the best people to teach their wives how to drive motor vehicles! But my wife soldiered on with driving lessons as though nothing near catastrophe had occurred before.

Testing learner drivers who applied for driving licences was entrusted to John Green for the Kasama area in 1958. He was the proprietor of a garage and petrol filling station in Kasama. In November 1958 Margaret took her test. She passed on her first attempt. That is how she made her own history as the first African woman to hold a driving licence for a motor vehicle in Kasama. In spite of the hardships she endured learning to drive, Margaret felt amply rewarded with receipt of a driving certificate from the district commissioner's office.

C H A P T E R

5

Education Officer

There were many key posts for the professional, technical and executive staff of the Department of African Education in 1958. All these, at the headquarters of the department, in various provinces and territorial institutions, were held by white expatriates. In Northern Rhodesia, largely due to the negative influence of the white settlers, the appointment of Africans to senior positions in the civil service was painfully slow, indeed non-existent, until towards the end of the 1950s.

The post of education officer was advertised early in 1958 for the purpose of filling vacancies. Applications were invited from civil servants of all races. I applied for the post because I had the necessary qualifications and experience. Subsequently, I was interviewed with other applicants by members of the Public Service Commission.

I was the only successful applicant. The news of my appointment to the post of education officer was unexpectedly sensational. It brought hope and encouragement to local men and women that senior positions in the civil service would henceforth be open to all. Such senior positions would not continue to be reserved for white men and women only. I received congratulatory messages from a broad spectrum of black and white well wishers. A touching congratulatory message came from an elderly man – Belemu Mudenda – who held the post of master at Chalimbana Training College. A graduate of Fort Hare with a Diploma in Education from London University, Belemu Mudenda had also applied and was

93

interviewed for the post. His letter was warm and encouraging. He urged me to remember all the time that I was destined to "blaze the trail" for my fellow Africans. It is a message I have always remembered. It was a timely reminder that I was destined to be a pace-setter.

The appointment of an African to the post of education officer was significant. It was indeed overdue. At a time of considerable disillusionment among Africans with perpetual racial discrimination in the public service and the private sector, my appointment to the post of education officer was over-publicised. In his book on Zambia, Richard Hall commented that "considerable publicity was given to the fact" that I was the first African placed on the full education officer scale.

The majority of education officers in 1958 were engaged in teaching duties in secondary schools and teacher training institutions. However, their main function was administration of the education system. At that time, except for education officers posted to the headquarters of the Department of African Education, they were assigned one or more districts in which they worked as manager of schools, as inspector and as education planner. It was a delicate responsibility which required patience and tact. In many ways the work of an education officer was very demanding, especially in districts with a large number of schools managed by missionaries. Such schools required an inspection by an education officer at least once a year. In the urban areas, the district education officer's responsibilities were less onerous. However, in rural areas where some schools were almost inaccessible due to poor roads in the rainy season, the burden of responsibility was very heavy. That was the kind of work I was expected to perform as an education officer involved not in teaching but in the work of administration.

When I arrived at Kasama Secondary School in the middle of 1957, the government embarked on a programme of expansion of the school in order to increase student numbers. The site for the new school (later called Mungwi Secondary School) was chosen almost half way to Paramount Chief

Chitimukulu's palace. During the construction of the new school, I was regularly consulted by both the contractor and the staff in the Provincial Education Office in Kasama. The new school's construction was completed early in 1960. The intention was to upgrade our school to the status of a senior secondary school. Early in 1960, I was informed that a more senior officer was earmarked to assume principalship of the new school at Mungwi. Later, before the end of the school year in May 1960, the provincial education officer sent me a letter about my posting to Livingstone in the Southern Province. I was expected to replace an expatriate education officer who was due to proceed on leave to the United Kingdom. At first, the impending transfer to Livingstone did not excite me. I had all along anticipated moving on with my staff and our students to the beautiful new school at Mungwi and to assume the responsibility of running a senior secondary school. Instead, the authorities chose Donald Martin as my successor.

When I left Munali to go to Kasama Secondary School, Donald Martin was already an education officer. He was the head of the science department responsible for teaching physics in form six. My wife was disappointed by the news of my impending transfer. However, after more careful reflection, it was quite clear to us that since the interests of our children were paramount, the impending transfer to Livingstone was a blessing in disguise. Better facilities were more likely to be available for the education of our children in Livingstone than in the Mungwi area. With this expectation, we felt that the move to Livingstone would have its valuable compensation. And we looked forward cheerfully to our journey to Livingstone at the end of September 1960.

However, I was entitled to go on long leave at the end of June 1960. For several months, I had given thought to the question of how to spend my leave. There was so much I wanted to do, so many countries I wanted to see in Africa and elsewhere. But my leave was for three months only. I was expected to report to the provincial education officer in Livingstone on 1 October

1960. There was also the financial constraint – the resources at my disposal for holiday expenses were limited. Apart from my own needs, I was obliged to give some financial assistance to my elder sister, Emily. She had offered my wife and children accommodation during my planned visits to foreign countries. She was a senior teacher at a primary school in Abercorn District.

With these considerations, I opted to visit only a few countries. Firstly, I decided to visit only two countries in Africa, namely Congo Kinshasa (now called Congo DR) and Ghana. Congo Kinshasa became independent on 30 June 1960, with Patrice Lumumba as its first prime minister. Before independence, he led the Congo National Movement which had won more seats than other parties, but not a majority. He was one of the most charismatic political leaders on the African continent at the beginning of 1960. Although Joseph Kasavubu was the head of state the limelight was on Patrice Lumumba. The constitution the Belgian government gave to the new Republic of Congo Kinshasa was of considerable interest to many scholars of political science. It provided for six provincial governments, each with more or less the same powers as the central government. In June 1949, Dr Kwame Nkhrumah had founded the Convention People's Party (CPP) which pioneered the struggle for the independence of the Gold Coast (later known as Ghana). Kwame Nkhrumah became a household name in many countries, more especially after the country gained independence from Great Britain on 6 March 1957. Ghana became a republic on 1 July 1960. To me in June 1960, Ghana was like Mecca to a Moslem. For my own inspiration and my further education on political developments in Africa, leaving out Ghana from my itinerary was unthinkable.

The ultimate destination of my month long journey out of Northern Rhodesia was London. For many years I had worked alongside British men and women, especially in schools and colleges in Northern Rhodesia. Some intimate friends had at one time visited places in the United Kingdom or gone there to study in colleges or universities. I had heard interesting stories from them about life in the United Kingdom. Therefore, quite naturally I was keen to visit London not merely as a holidaymaker but as a person determined to broaden his horizons. I would have liked a longer visit to the United Kingdom but this was not possible. The visit to London was self-sponsored. It was for three weeks and not more. I was also fascinated by political developments in Tanganyika under Mwalimu Julius Nyerere, leader of Tanganyika African National Union (TANU). He was working hard to popularise the slogan *uhuru na kazi*. Before I left for my visits to Congo Kinshasa, Ghana and London, I had decided on my way back to visit Dar es Salaam in Tanganyika if possible.

Once I made up my mind on where to go, there was another hurdle. Without previous experience, it was difficult to arrange the itinerary. I was advised to see the British Council representative in Ndola, who was competent and experienced in providing such advice and assistance. Before any advice was provided, I was requested to submit my detailed curriculum vitae with particular emphasis on my educational background and areas of interest during the proposed journey. With typical British efficiency, the British Council's office in Ndola confirmed the travel arrangements to Congo Leopoldville and Ghana. A tour programme for my ten-days visit to London was also confirmed. In less than a month, reservations of accommodation in hotels and air travel bookings were also confirmed. My role was merely to pay for the air tickets. In Leopoldville and London, a British Council official was at the airport to meet me on arrival.

I stayed in Congo Leopoldville for three days only. My centre of interest was in institutions of higher learning. I spent two days visiting what was at that time known as the Université Lovanium. It was founded in 1954 by the Catholic University of Louvain in collaboration with the government. I also visited the Institute for Economic and Social Research. Both institutions were well organized and impressive. I was particularly struck by the fact that there in the land of pygmies – right in the heart of Central Africa – the Catholic University of Louvain had built a modern nuclear reactor for study and research purposes. I viewed the demonstrations with awe. Of course, to me as a person not schooled in the sciences, the demonstrations were beyond my understanding. Nonetheless I was impressed, conscious that in my own country even a university was non-existent.

During my short visit to Leopoldville, I observed an uneasy calm in the city. My contacts were restricted to a few people who were conversant with the English language. People did not disguise their concern that a political conflict might arise at any time between supporters of rival political parties. Ironically, a month later as I drove my car with my wife and children from Abercorn to Livingstone, we saw endless convoys of motor cars with men, women and children who were fleeing from Congo Leopoldvile into our country. Some people were driving not motor cars but other types of vehicles. They were all fleeing from civil war.

I had no official escort during my visit to Accra in Ghana. When I arrived in Accra, I made frantic efforts to contact George Chaane. Before taking up a teaching post in Ghana, he was a master at Chalimbana Teachers' College in Northern Rhodesia. In reply to my letter some months before I travelled to Ghana, he gave me his contact address and promised to show me some places of interest in Accra. During my short visit to Accra, I failed to contact him. The visit to Ghana was largely disappointing. However, I managed to visit the University of Ghana, Legon. I also intended to visit the University of Science and Technology, Kumasi, but I was unsuccessful.

Eventually, I arrived in London to a warm welcome from an official from the British Council head office in London. The programme I was given did not allow me much time to rest. That was not important. I was just too excited. I was pleased that the British Council arranged accommodation for me in central London in Sussex Gardens. The room was a bed sit with breakfast provided at a reasonable rent payable on a weekly basis. The programme included a visit to Wales to observe teaching methods in two schools, a primary school and a comprehensive school in a rural setting. At each school, I was privileged to address an audience of students and teachers about life in Northern Rhodesia generally and conditions in schools particularly. During my visit to the schools in Wales, I noted that many boys and girls had never seen a black man before. They were exceptionally anxious to come close to me just to look at me with a sense of curiosity. That was forty years ago. At that time, even in Metropolitan London there were not as many black people as there are today. The friendliness of the Welsh people I met during my visit to Wales was unforgettable. My visit to Cardiff was followed by two long journeys on consecutive days to Oxford and Cambridge Universities, world famous universities each with its own traditions. The visits were well arranged and I derived maximum benefit and enjoyment from them. On each occasion, I was taken to lunch where I met people interested in the affairs of my country.

Once the official programme arranged by the British Council was completed, I had time to attend to matters of personal interest. More particularly, I was interested in beginning the routine of "keeping terms" by eating each year the required number of dinners at Lincoln's Inn in London. At that time, admission to the Bar was firstly dependent on passing the prescribed examinations conducted by the Council of Legal Education. Secondly, call to the Bar in England depended on eating the prescribed number of dinners. While at Kasama Secondary School, I applied for membership of Lincoln's Inn on the basis of my qualifications and a testimonial of good character. Such a testimonial of good character could be accepted only from a person of high standing in society. Mr Lakement Ng'andu was a member of the Legislative Council at that time. The testimonial he gave me in 1958 was accepted by the benchers of Lincoln's Inn and I enrolled immediately as a member of Lincoln's Inn. In September 1960, I started the process of eating dinners. Mr Lakement Ng'andu is today the paramount chief of the Bemba people in the Northern Province of Zambia. Without his support and encouragement, it would not have been possible for me to qualify for membership of Lincoln's Inn in 1958. I have always felt deeply indebted to Paramount Chief Chitimukulu Chitapankwa II.

Dining at one's Inn of Court before one's call to the Bar in England and Wales is not unique to Lincoln's Inn. It is an age-old custom which is common to the other three Inns of Court, namely Gray's Inn, the Inner Temple and the Middle Temple, from which men and women eventually qualify as barristers-at-law in England and Wales. It is considered today to be an archaic custom. Yet the tradition has its own usefulness which is not easily recognized by lay men and women. It is believed, and is to a very large extent true, that the dinners offer unique opportunities to would-be lawyers to imbibe from the experienced successful lawyers (among them judges of the High Court and the Court of Appeal) the virtues of dignity, integrity and diligence. To this day some of the interesting tales I heard from senior lawyers at the Bar while dining at Lincoln's Inn have never been forgotten. They related to a variety of experiences of lawyers in practice such as exposure to risks, marital problems – the list is endless. The spirit of brotherhood (and sisterhood) fostered among the upcoming lawyers and seasoned ones is the most important benefit of perpetuating the tradition of "eating dinners".

After three weeks away from home, it was time to go back. By the last week in December, I had confirmed my flight to Abercorn in Northern Rhodesia via Dar es Salaam in Tanganyika. Naturally, I arranged my return home after visiting famous places of interest in London – Trafalgar Square, Hyde Park Corner, Madame Tussaud, the London Zoo and Piccadilly Circus. Towards the end of my visit to London, I accidentally met Mainza Chona, a fellow countryman. He was a final year student when I joined the staff of Munali. The government of Northern Rhodesia gave him a scholarship to study law at Gray's Inn and he became the first African from Northern Rhodesia entitled to practise law in English courts. Our reunion was a welcome opportunity for reminiscing about the good old days. He made my first visit to London especially interesting by taking me out one evening to an opera at Covent Garden followed by a dinner. A day or two later, I flew from Heathrow Airport to Dar es Salaam. After two days there I returned to Northern Rhodesia.

I drove my wife and our children from Abercorn to Livingstone in two days, with a stopover in Lusaka where we spent a night with my elder brother, Joseph, and his family. My Standard Eight saloon car was still in good condition although it was already five years old in 1960. I had bought it brand new in Lusaka before I was transferred from Munali to Kasama. The standard of car maintenance in John Green's garage in Kasama was excellent. So it never let me down. I expected it to carry us faithfully and reliably from Abercorn to Livingstone over all manner of roads, a distance of just under one thousand miles. As anticipated, at the beginning of October 1960, we arrived in Livingstone from Abercorn the northernmost town to Livingstone the southernmost town in Northern Rhodesia. As a solo driver of the car over a very long distance covered in only two days, it would have been reasonable to ask for a day or two "off" in order to rest and settle down before getting myself involved in the education officer's onerous duties and responsibilities. But I was only too anxious to put my hands to the plough immediately. Meanwhile, we were booked into a comfortable guest house for three nights.

David Bell was the provincial education officer and, therefore, my new boss in Livingstone. I had previously worked with him at Munali, both at its old and new sites. David Bell and I were both history teachers and he became head of the history department when we moved to the new site. More importantly, however, David Bell and I had one common interest – playing tennis. He was a better tennis player than I, but we both contributed much to the popularisation of the game among students at Munali. So, by good fortune some four or five years after this quiet, friendly and courteous Englishman and I parted company at Munali, I joined his team of education officers in Livingstone in the Southern Province. I had no anxiety whatsoever about support and encouragement from my new boss in performing my duties and responsibilities. When I arrived in Livingstone, TDT Carter and Ian Cruickshank were education officers under David Bell. My posting to Livingstone restored the full complement of staff at the level of education officer in the Southern Province. CT Woodbridge also occupied a key position in the PEO's office. He was the secretary for the Local Education Authority in the Southern Province. Practically all support staff, the clerks, typists, drivers and office messengers, were Africans. Within a period of one week working with the men and women in our office in Livingstone, I had a feeling that I was welcome in their midst. Clearly, under David Bell's leadership all members of staff, black and white, worked harmoniously to achieve maximum efficiency in the administration of the education system in the Southern Province.

I settled in within a week and managed to read relevant files and to get to know the staff well. In particular, I found discussions with David Bell and with fellow education officers quite informative and useful in understanding the problems which confronted administrators of the education system in the province. The provincial education officer was responsible for overall supervision of the operations of the African Education Department in the province. In this regard, the implementation of government policies was his primary responsibility. The education system comprised of government-controlled schools, colleges and institutions on the one hand and schools and colleges administered by missionaries with financial support from the government on the other hand. Such schools and colleges were referred to as "grant-aided" schools and colleges. It was the provincial education officer's duty to supervise and control the expenditure of government funds in both government and grant-aided educational institutions.

These were onerous responsibilities which the provincial education officer was not able to perform satisfactorily without assistance. Education officers were personally responsible for supervision of schools and colleges which they were required to visit in person at least once a year. Furthermore, they were responsible also for the inspection of schools generally and teachers' work in particular. Without an adequate number of education officers in each province, the maintenance of uniformity in the standard of education in government and grant-aided schools would have been virtually impossible. In addition the education officer was the official representative of the provincial education officer at meetings of the Local Education Authorities at provincial and district levels. These were composed of representatives of government, native authorities and mission agencies. They were responsible for the supervision of education in their areas, execution of development programmes, financial management and maintenance of acceptable standards of education in Local Education Authority schools. In short, an education officer was "a manager of schools, an inspector and education planner".

From the nature of his duties and responsibilities, an education officer was mainly a field worker – always out of the office inspecting schools (classrooms, domestic science rooms, laboratories and teachers' houses). The education officer also spent much of his time out of the office attending Local Education Authorities meetings at the district level. Southern Province was a very large province comprising at that time six districts all together. Even with three education officers in the PEO's office in Livingstone, each person's burden was still heavy. Within three weeks, my first tour programme was arranged for inspection of schools in Choma and the remote Namwala District. We used a Landrover for the tour with a driver and an office orderly who was the handyman to take care of our luggage and assist with preparation of meals or accommodation if there was necessity to do so. Even in the dry season – in fact, October was generally dry and hot in the Southern Province – we were advised to sleep under a mosquito net and to use repellents in order to avoid the risk of getting malaria. I was also advised during such tours to take some reading material.

It was fashionable for officers on duty touring rural areas to wear light clothing, usually shorts rather than trousers and a short-sleeved shirt. It was a contrast to the kind of dressing to which I was accustomed as a teacher at Munali and later Kasama Secondary School. I was told while training as a teacher to be properly dressed, in fact smartly dressed, in front of students at all times. This meant to me and other teacher-trainees that wearing a pair of long trousers, with a shirt, tie and jacket, was the proper form of dress for a teacher. In schools everywhere in the world, students were encouraged to be clean and properly dressed at all times. It was quite logical to inculcate such habits among students by the teachers' own example. I bought my new attire for tours to the districts from a retail shop in Livingstone – it was much cheaper than the conventional school teacher's attire. In fact, it was comfortable and convenient for the work of inspecting schools and colleges as an education officer.

Ian Cruickshank knew all the districts in the Southern Province well. He had toured the districts many times on previous occasions. Therefore, he knew many of the head teachers of the schools and college principals in the area. Even more importantly, he was familiar with the intractable problems of certain schools which required attention. During the short period of our interaction in our office in Livingstone, a period of about three weeks, I came to like him. He was friendly, helpful and genuinely anxious that I settled down well in my new job. In terms of length of service in government I was senior to him, a fact which he often brought to my attention. He showed no trace of racialism. It was my good fortune to know Ian Cruickshank for many years. Our first meeting was in Livingstone at the beginning of October 1960. He remained colour blind and was very much liked by his African colleagues. Of all the Scotsmen I have ever met, Ian has remained the most witty, friendly and dedicated worker in promoting advancement of education in our country. In Choma and Namwala districts we inspected many lower and upper primary schools both government-owned and grant-aided schools controlled by missionary agencies. As expected we found that some schools were properly managed and run efficiently. In such schools, class enrolment was satisfactory with, in fact, over-enrolment in some classes. In well-run schools, pupil attendance on a weekly or monthly basis was high. Of course, a one hundred per cent pupil attendance was rare due understandably to some unavoidable factors such as illness or funerals in families. On the other hand, some schools were poorly managed and inefficient. In such schools, the desks were usually in disrepair or inadequate for the needs of the number of pupils.

After an inspection tour the responsible officer was expected to prepare a report based on guidelines in a circular issued to all provincial officers under the Department of African Education. They included statements on enrolment of pupils in various classes in the school, attendance figures for pupils, number of teachers in employment and their qualifications, condition of school buildings and state of the school garden, if any. Ian Cruickshank had warned me to prepare myself for this task. I did not anticipate any difficulty in writing a tour report because similar reports were available on files for guidance. Furthermore, Ian Cruickshank was always ready to assist me.

On our journey back to Livingstone, while driving between Choma and Livingstone we made a stopover at Kalomo, a small rural township about forty miles from Livingstone. We arrived in Kalomo just before sunset. It was a convenient place for refreshment in the form of tea or soft drinks. Ian Cruickshank led me to a club near the main road which he had always patronized. Apparently, the bar owner at the clubhouse was a white man. We experienced an ugly incident which embarrassed my colleague. When we entered the clubhouse, the white men who were chatting heartily suddenly became quiet. There was total silence as Ian Cruickshank asked the bar-owner for tea for me and a glass of beer for himself. After a pause, the bar-owner replied: "You can sit down and drink your beer but the African chap can't sit and drink tea here". "We are together; he is my friend", retorted Ian Cruickshank in a strong voice and with confidence.

"Look, I don't care whether he is your friend or not; he's an African; he's not allowed here", growled the bar-owner at the top of his voice. Meanwhile, the white men merely looked on with an air of apparent approval of the stand taken by the bar-owner. I then chose to intervene. Quite audibly to all who were in the bar, I said to Ian Cruickshank, "Look! You should remain here and have your drink. Meanwhile, I shall wait for you in the landrover".

Ian Cruickshank told the bar-owner that he was in the company of a person who was more educated than the majority of white men who patronized his club. I was unhappy with the acrimonious tone of Ian Cruickshank's remarks. I thought his mini-lecture to die-hard racialists was a sheer waste of time. As we left the bar, he continued to complain about the evils of the colour bar. He told me that the incident had embarrassed him. He apologized profusely. I reminded him that as a black man I had been humiliated before and abhorred racial discrimination as one of the worst evils in society.

My report of our tour of schools in the Choma and Namwala districts was well received by the provincial education officer. He sent a copy to the headquarters of the Department of African Education in the usual way. With his encouragement, more tours were undertaken to various districts for routine supervision of activities in both government and grant-aided schools and inspection of teachers' work in classrooms. In the course of time, I began to enjoy work in my tour programmes more than the routine work of processing files in the office in Livingstone. By the end of December 1960, I had inspected many schools in various districts in the Southern Province. Therefore, at the beginning of the new year I had a good idea of areas for concentration in the government's efforts to improve the standard of education in the country. In districts where the Roman Catholic Church controlled most grant-aided schools, the level of education in primary and secondary schools was quite high. During my tours I made lasting friendships with some outstanding Jesuits who were responsible for teaching Catholic students at Canisius College and managing their own grant-aided schools. Wherever I visited Roman Catholic schools in the Southern Province, the hospitality I received was exceptional.

I had an unforgettable experience of an unusual kind of hospitality at a Roman Catholic primary school I visited in the Monze area. In the morning, I attended classes for a period of forty minutes in each class to assess the lessons taught by the various teachers. The morning programme was completed satisfactorily. During morning lessons the head teacher had indicated in advance that it was his family's wish to lunch with me in their house and the invitation was gratefully accepted. After a short prayer at the table, the bowls with the food the housewife had cooked were uncovered. I saw that she had prepared our traditional food for lunch consisting of thick porridge, boiled chicken and vegetables. The menu looked delicious and appetizing. However, suddenly the head teacher ordered his wife to take away the food. She took away the food. I wondered what had actually gone wrong. Without saying a word to me, he followed his wife and I remained alone in the dining room completely puzzled. A few minutes later, he re-entered the house and apologized with a sincerity which was quite transparent. He told me that his wife had not prepared the proper meal for that occasion. She had not understood his instructions correctly.

While we waited for food to be prepared again, the gong was sounded for the beginning of afternoon classes. I decided to carry on with my observation of lessons. Later, after completion of afternoon classes, I was again invited to "lunch". Alas! The food was the same boiled chicken and vegetables with one exception – the thick porridge known to the local people as *insima* was left out altogether. In place of *insima* she brought rice which was served with the boiled chicken and vegetables.

I was reliably informed that the irate head teacher almost applied corporal punishment on his wife for misunderstanding his instructions in the first instance. He had apparently told her that I was an education officer different from other Africans she had seen visiting the school for other purposes, such as delivery of text books and exercise books or school desks. If I had left the school with the impression that the staff did not appreciate my status as an education officer it would have been her fault. It was wrong to give me the kind of food usually given to African visitors to the school. Ironically, four years later, while visiting my parliamentary constituency in Kawambwa District, I had a similar experience. As minister of education, my entourage included government officers and political party activists. Our host at Nchelenge Boma was rebuked for preparing a Zambian dish for our meal. Our host should have excluded thick porridge, called *ubwali* in that part of the country, from the menu. Yet I know many highly educated men and women who love their *insima* or *ubwali* even if they have travelled widely in this world or lived in foreign countries for a long time. Perhaps, these were the kind of painful experiences Mr Belemu Mudenda anticipated when he wished me well in "blazing the trail" after my promotion to the post of education officer by the Colonial Office in 1958.

At the height of the rainy season from January to the end of March, all education officers were preoccupied mainly with routine office work. This included preparation of year end reports for submission to the provincial education officer, setting papers for internal examinations for primary schools and conducting oral English examinations. It was the period when education officers spent more time with their families. I enjoyed taking my family to the Zambezi riverside during weekends. The breeze on the bank of the mighty Victoria Falls was always refreshing and invigorating. Livingstone town itself has rather hot weather which can be unbearable in the months from August to the end of the year. As a family, we have always been churchgoers wherever we have settled. By attending church services regularly on Sunday, we made friends whose company we enjoyed at home or in their homes. Our house was in town quite near the North Western Hotel and the railway line from Livingstone to the north. I do not remember any other African couple who lived in the vicinity of our residence. We lived in a government house. It was an old building, quite comfortable but not attractive. Most of our neighbours were Indian families who lived in houses close to their shops. The location of our residence was quite convenient. The house was only a stone's throw from the Indian shops and the main street in town.

I was transferred to Livingstone at the height of vehement African opposition to the Federation which the British government had imposed in 1953 on the people of Northern Rhodesia. Like other civil servants, I was under an obligation not to get involved in politics. However, to our people, although I was a civil servant who held a senior gazetted post in the government, nonetheless I was an African who was as much a victim of racial discrimination and political deprivation as any other African. Both the African National Congress (ANC) and the United National Independence Party (UNIP) were well organized and active political parties in Livingstone. However, UNIP was more proactive than the ANC. Not long after our arrival in Livingstone from Kasama two senior officials of UNIP visited our home for the purpose of canvassing our sympathy for their party's cause and support for their fundraising efforts. I assured them that we espoused their cause. They showed interest and appreciation to know that in 1959 I used to teach Zambia African National Congress (ZANC) inmates at Milima Prison in Kasama in my spare time at their request. They had a vision of an independent Northern Rhodesia one day in which they hoped to be active participants in the development process. The officer-in-charge of the prison approved their request for my voluntary services, which I willingly offered. However, I stated categorically that although I was willing to support their noble cause when it was justified, I was a civil servant in a senior position. I was not prepared to get involved actively in politics.

Before the end of 1960, Mr Kenneth Kaunda as president of UNIP was expected to arrive in Livingstone to evaluate his party's activities and consult with its local officials. The senior officials relayed to me the news of his visit. They invited me to meet with him in Livingstone at a time and place mutually convenient. The courteous manner in which I was invited to meet Mr Kenneth Kaunda and the fact that the opportunity to meet him was unique made acceptance inevitable. Joe Mwemba and I had hoped to meet him at Munali Secondary School when he was fundraising for an ANC sponsored visit of a British Labour Party MP to Northern Rhodesia to collect evidence of African opposition to Federation. He was then the general secretary of the African National Congress led by Mr Harry Nkumbula. Instead, he sent Titus Mukupo, the deputy general secretary, with a letter asking for financial support to which we responded favourably.

Gradually the number of our friends in Livingstone increased. We had made friends with fellow Africans, with men and women of Asian origin and with a few white people. However, we missed the company of our relatives who were far away in Lusaka and further in the north of the country. I often toyed with the idea of driving to Lusaka with my wife and children, during the long holidays at Christmas or Easter time. However, a distance of about three hundred miles from Livingstone to Lusaka was daunting, especially when the turnaround was over a period of three or four days only. The dream was never realized. This thought, however, triggered off my desire to buy a more sturdy and larger car to replace the Standard Eight. Over a period of four years, the Standard Eight never let us down. It was still in good condition. It had carried us faithfully and reliably over dirt roads and in every kind of weather between Lusaka and Abercorn. We found a more robust and slightly bigger car which we liked. It was a Hillman Minx which a garage was selling at only five hundred pounds brand new! That was an investment which I never regretted in later years when I joined politics. The garage proprietor agreed on trade-off terms and early in 1961 we bought a new Hillman Minx. The purchase of a new car was done with the belief that it was a necessary asset for making trips to Lusaka and even to Abercorn where my parents lived. My parents-in-law lived in Kawambwa in another remote part of our country.

Little did I know about an impending change in my fortunes. After the Easter holidays, the provincial education officer received a circular from the Establishment Division in which African civil servants were invited to apply for appointment to fill a newly created post of assistant to the commissioner for the Northern Rhodesian Office in London. The job description stressed experience in education and ability to guide and assist Northern Rhodesian students sponsored by the government to study in colleges and universities in the United Kingdom and elsewhere in Europe. I did not hesitate to show an interest in the position. I requested for a more detailed job description. Effectively, if a suitable applicant was available to fill the new post, his responsibilities included performance of such administrative functions as the commissioner chose to assign to him. In the absence of the commissioner, the assistant assumed responsibility for the administration of the office.

Over the years from the end of the Second World War in 1945, the Colonial Office was responsible for providing services to students sent to the United Kingdom for studies or training. A students branch was set up in the Colonial Office for this purpose. The colonial governments (including, of course, protectorates such as Northern Rhodesia) were encouraged to set up their own students units in their offices in London which were responsible for liasing with the head of the students branch in the Colonial Office. The colonial governments were required to pay a subsidy to the Colonial Office for the services provided by the students branch. By 1956, most colonial governments had established their own students units but some, including Northern Rhodesia, had not. In an effort to encourage all colonial governments to establish their own students units in London, the secretary of state for the colonies issued Circular 982/56 dated 12 September 1956 on "The work of the Colonial Office for students from Colonial Territories in the United Kingdom and Republic of Ireland". In essence the circular obliged the territories which had not yet set up their own units to send all applications to the head of the students branch in the Colonial Office.

Five years later in July 1961, the Office of the Northern Rhodesia Commission in London established a students unit. I was selected to take the position of assistant to the commissioner and to assume responsibility for student affairs in the Commissioner's Office at 57 Haymarket Street, a few minutes walk from Piccadilly Circus in central London. That appointment meant more pioneering and more challenges which proved to be as interesting as the previous ones had been.

Before taking up my appointment as assistant to the commissioner in the Northern Rhodesia Office in London, I had assumed that mine was an important but senior position that did not require much work. That proved later to be a misconception. There were many students in universities and colleges in the United Kingdom whose welfare became my responsibility. Some students studying in universities and colleges elsewhere in Europe considered themselves eligible to obtain assistance or advice from the students unit by virtue of holding a Northern Rhodesian passport. In spite of the burden of my responsibilities, I found the variety of problems for settlement on a day to day basis interesting and worthwhile.

Mr James Murray was in charge of our office. He was an amiable and friendly old man who had retired honourably from the colonial service. He held the post of senior provincial commissioner for what was then called the Copperbelt Province. It was known to be the most volatile province politically before independence in 1964. Indeed, it was the most important province in economic terms as well. His appointment as commissioner for the Northern Rhodesia Office in London was a kind of reward for his success in the administration of the

Copperbelt Province at a time of intense political activity. In discharging my duties, Mr James Murray left me to work freely without any interference. When I chose to seek his advice, often he preferred to know my own thoughts or ideas first of all before giving me his own advice. He was truly a remarkable man. Later, I learnt that he had an outstanding record of scholarship at Oxford University before he joined the Colonial Overseas Civil Service. To the best of my recollection, apart from Clifford Little (another outstanding Oxonian), James Murray was the best senior colonial officer I ever had the pleasure of working with before independence.

It was in the United Kingdom, while I worked in the Office of the Northern Rhodesia Commissioner, that I met men who later became prominent in independent Zambia. Andrew Kashita was at that time a student due to complete a degree in mechanical engineering at Leeds University. In 1961, he married June Rose Spalton at a wedding ceremony which I attended in Leeds. He was the first Zambian to qualify as a mechanical engineer. In 1964 he became a senior mechanical engineer and he was permanent secretary in the Ministry of Transport, Power and Communications from 1967 to 1968. At the political level, he later held many portfolios, including that of minister of mines and industry. I was also privileged to meet Valentine Musakanya and his wife Flavia. Both were at Cambridge University where Valentine was undergoing specialized training at postgraduate level in administration. It was the first time the Colonial Office had allowed Africans from Northern Rhodesia to pursue the prestigious course for senior officers in administration. He was a livewire intellectual who left a great impression wherever he made an appearance as a representative of Zambia. After independence he was the first African to serve in the top civil service post as secretary to the cabinet.

During our stay in England, we lived in Thornton Heath, Surrey, not very far from Croydon in South England. Thornton Heath was not more than thirty to forty minutes by train from Victoria Station. Therefore, our house in Leander Road was easily accessible to many friends and countrymen and women from home, especially during weekends. It became a place for reunion with some of our friends and relatives involved in the political struggle for our country's freedom. We met and developed friendship with Fitzpatrick Chuula and his English wife, Rosemary. They lived in Croydon with Rosemary's parents. Fitzpatrick was reading law and was called to the Bar in England in February, 1962. He was an active member of UNIP in London. Chikako Kamalondo was the official representative of UNIP in London. He, too, was a law student. He was called to the Bar in England in November 1964. I was regularly in contact with Fitzpatrick Chuula and Chikako Kamalondo to keep abreast of political developments in our country.

Two of our children enrolled at Gonville Primary School which was less than fifteen minutes walk from our house. It was a good modern school run by the London County Council. At the beginning of July in 1961, our son, Mupanga, was four years old. Yet in early August, a woman school inspector came to our home unexpectedly to check whether, as new arrivals in the neighbourhood, we had children of school-going age. On the inspector's insistence, our seven year old daughter and four year old son were both enrolled in classes at Gonville Primary School at the beginning of September 1961. Our second daughter, Chitalu, was only two years old. She was not affected by the compulsory school attendance regulations. She provided the company my wife needed to escape from loneliness and boredom during weekdays. In the course of time, we made friends with some churchgoers at the Norbury Methodist Church. Some of my wife's associates at Church became her lifelong friends. On 27 May 1962, Chisha, our second son, was born at home. A midwife was arranged by the superintendent of Croydon Hospital to attend on my wife at the birth of our child. Croydon Hospital was a public health institution.

Dining at Lincoln's Inn was an unexpected advantage of my posting to London. Requirements for call to the Bar are set out in the consolidated regulations of the four Inns of Court.

Apart from passing examinations a student cannot be called to the Bar unless he has kept a certain number of terms. Terms are kept by dining in the hall of the Inn of which the student is a member on not less than three occasions in each of twelve dining terms. I started dining in the hall of Lincoln's Inn during the Michaelmas term in September 1960, during my first visit to London on holiday. While in London performing my duties in the Commissioner's Office, I embarked on keeping terms at Lincoln's Inn. This convenient arrangement for keeping terms came to an end a year later – actually at the end of June 1962 – due to political developments in Northern Rhodesia.

These political developments had their origin in a new phase of nationalist-colonialist conflict in 1958. The conflict was led by Mr Kenneth Kaunda who broke away with other leaders in that year to form their own party. The new party was formed to wage a more militant struggle and to break the Central African Federation in order to accelerate the freedom and independence of Northern Rhodesia. The mounting of the Cha Cha Cha campaign thereafter had forced the British government in early 1962 to propose a new constitution for Zambia which was not wholly acceptable to either UNIP or ANC. But the provisions of the proposed constitution were tolerable. The UNIP and ANC leaders agreed to participate in the elections at the end of 1962 for seats in the Legislative Council against the United Federal Party (UFP) led by the white settlers. In 1962, Queen Elizabeth II issued the Northern Rhodesia Order-in-Council which established a constitution with three voters rolls:-

I)   The Upper Roll was for the whites to elect fifteen members;

II)   The Lower Roll was for the blacks to elect fifteen members; and

III)   The National Roll was for *both* racial groups to elect fifteen members provided:-

        a)   for a white man to be elected, he had to get a

majority of white votes and ten per cent of the total votes cast by the Africans in the constituency.

b) for an African to be elected, he had to get the majority of the African votes and ten per cent of the votes cast by the whites in the constituency.

c) to be elected to a reserved seat, a candidate must be of Asian origin voted in by the Asian community.

Although both UNIP and ANC agreed to participate in what came to be known as the 15-15-15 Constitution, it was fraught with grave risks, for none of the political parties was likely to win an outright majority in the elections at the end of October 1962. Each political party was anxious, therefore, to field the best available candidates in an effort to win as many seats as possible. The strategy of the Colonial Office was obvious. Firstly, the new constitution did not provide universal adult suffrage which would have guaranteed African majority rule. The Colonial Office opted for a constitution that would provide a transitional period before African majority rule. Therefore, the constitution had fifteen seats for mainly white voters and fifteen other seats for mainly African voters designated as upper roll seats and lower roll seats respectively. However, winning any seat on the national roll (except the one seat specifically reserved for a candidate of Asian origin) was made difficult. To win a national seat a candidate was required to get a majority of the African votes (if an African) and at least ten per cent of the white votes or a majority of the white votes (if a white person) and at least ten per cent of the African votes. Secondly, the constitution also provided for the retention of five senior colonial civil servants on the Executive Council and the Legislative Council as members.

Early in 1962, UNIP agreed to contest the elections at the end of the year on the basis of the 15-15-15 Constitution. In scouting for candidates to participate in the election, the UNIP leaders were anxious to gain the confidence of the whole electorate – the black and white voters alike. They were particularly concerned to select suitable candidates to contest difficult seats. The seats on the lower roll were safe seats for African candidates in the elections. On the other hand, seats on the upper roll were safe for white candidates. Candidates contesting seats on the upper roll on either the UNIP or the ANC ticket had an almost impossible task. The seats on the national roll were made difficult to win by any party which decided to field candidates in the elections. It is in this context that messages filtered through the UNIP structures to inquire if I was prepared to join UNIP's campaign in the 1962 elections. In the early part of 1962, I received requests from many friends to return home in order to support UNIP at a critical hour in the political history of our country. I did not take the requests seriously. Later, I received an official request from the UNIP headquarters through Chikako Kamalondo, the representative of UNIP in London. At the same time, I was informed that a number of notable African civil servants had been invited to join UNIP's election campaign later in the year.

At first I was not enthusiastic about accepting the request to join politics. The risks were too many. The advantages for me and my family in the short term were virtually nonexistent. However, purely on the basis of national interests, a positive response was sensible and necessary. On that basis, therefore, other considerations became irrelevant.

At the end of March 1962, I submitted my letter of resignation to the chief establishment officer through the Ministry of Education. I gave three months' notice to the government. My last day of duty as a civil servant was 30 June 1962. That date marked the end of my career as a civil servant in the Northern Rhodesian government.

C H A P T E R

6

Candidate for Northern Rural Constituency

In June 1962, I flew from London with my wife and children to Lusaka. Chikako Kamalondo, the UNIP representative based in London, came to Heathrow Airport to wish me and my family a safe journey to Lusaka. He was also at the airport to assist us as might be necessary before departure. I observed that he was particularly happy that I had agreed to leave a good job in London to enter the unknown world of politics in Northern Rhodesia.

I remember that the weather was glorious when we left London in mid-summer. None of my children, not even the baby boy who was three weeks old, were uncomfortable at the airport. However, during the flight the baby, Chisha, was miserable. He was crying most of the time in the aircraft. My wife had virtually no rest during the flight. Unfortunately, I was not able to assist her. I have always been fond of nursing little children, but only when they are at least three months old. Fortunately, due to God's providence, we all arrived at Lusaka Airport safely the following day.

At Lusaka Airport, my elder brother, Joseph, was there to meet us. I had alerted him not only to meet us but also to arrange accommodation for us. His good friend, Victor Manda, had driven to the airport in the Hillman Minx, the faithful motorcar which I bought the previous year in Livingstone.

My wish when we left London was to stay for only two or three days in Lusaka before proceeding by car with my family to Mbala. With the enthusiasm and energy of a young man in the late thirties, rest for only two or three days was sufficient. Indeed, as I anticipated, my discussion with officials in the Establishment Division was short. They informed me that I was not entitled to receive a pension or gratuity because I had not served for a minimum of twenty years in the civil service. However, I did not regret forfeiting pension and gratuity benefits for joining the political struggle for the freedom and independence of our country. The officials informed me that I was entitled to cash payment for the leave days I had earned. That was, of course, a paltry sum. At the same time, the officials assured me of their willingness to provide transport for our household goods which had been stored in crates at the Government Stores during my term of office in London.

Throughout the discussion at the Establishment Division, the department officials responsible for the administration of the civil service, were polite and helpful. However, I observed that they were conspicuously reserved regarding the decision I had made to resign from the civil service in order to join politics. In retrospect, I often wondered whether they were of the view that I had made a good decision. Senior positions in the civil service were occupied by Europeans. Their attitude may well have been different from mine – that I was privileged to join fellow countrymen in the fight for freedom and independence. That, obviously, required personal sacrifice from as many Africans from all walks of life as possible.

I also met senior UNIP officials in Freedom House in Lusaka to report my arrival from London. In contrast with the cold reception I received from officials in the Establishment Division at Kent House, my "comrades" in Freedom House received me warmly and enthusiastically. It was a remarkable welcome with remarks such as "he has arrived" and "he is with us" from junior and senior officials alike. Without exception, they were smiling and cheerful that I had chosen to join the struggle for freedom and independence, albeit in its last phase.

To my surprise, the UNIP officials informed me that I was expected to join the UNIP president's tour of the Copperbelt towns at the beginning of July. I had expected the bureaucrats in Freedom House to allow me some time to make adequate arrangements for settling my wife and children in Mbala before embarking on political campaigns. In any event, I had no choice but to accept participation in UNIP's presidential campaign visits to various towns on the Copperbelt.

Before the end of June, I arrived in Mbala with my wife and children. God's hand was upon me and all members of the family. We travelled to Mbala safely without any hitch although a long stretch of the road from Kapiri-Mposhi to Mbala was not tarred. Fortunately, my young brother had made all necessary arrangements for accommodating my family in Mbala. Abel was in business with our father. After completing junior secondary school at Munali, he returned home determined to work with our father to improve the family business. At that time, he was among the most prosperous local businessmen in Mbala. Because I wanted to avoid serious disruption of the education of our eldest daughter, Kalelelya, and eldest son, Mupanga, Mbala was a better place for the family to live than Isoko village. In the village, the children would have been obliged to travel a long distance to school from Katula homestead to the primary school in Isoko village. Indeed, medical facilities at Isoko village were limited. On the other hand, in the event of serious illness, the Mbala District Hospital was well equipped for providing the necessary treatment.

After staying with Father for three days, I bade him farewell. I told him about my resignation from employment in the government. As I expected, he was not amused at all. His view was that I had made a wrong decision. He believed that politics was an occupation more suitable for retired people who had achieved success either in the field of business or a profession. For the first time, Father told me that he had been proud of my steady progress in the civil service from the time of my appointment as a school teacher to the time of my promotion to the post of education officer. I remember the exact words he used in our language – *ichilungu*, referring to what his peers often said in and around the village. They would say *wemo umwanako umuzungusile* which means "as for your son, he is a European". At the time of bidding farewell to my father, he revealed a fact I did not know. He told me that he knew Kenneth Kaunda when he was a student at Munali Secondary School. He had a vivid recollection of how Kenneth Kaunda with other students led a protest against the school's authorities for sometimes providing poorly prepared meals for students. From that incident, he believed that Kenneth Kaunda possessed leadership qualities. He was not surprised that he had become the leader of the most popular political party for Africans in Northern Rhodesia. He blessed me as I was about to leave our house at Katula. Alas, little did I know that it would be my last time to see him alive.

From discussions with UNIP leaders at Freedom House, it was quite obvious that my services in the 1962 elections were definitely required. UNIP, like its rival African political party, namely the African National Congress, found it absolutely necessary to attract European supporters in the elections. The new constitution for Northern Rhodesia was devised in such a way that for any political party to obtain a majority of seats in the Legislative Council it had to win support from both Africans and Europeans in the elections. Indeed, the electoral provisions of the constitution were unusual and difficult to implement. The February 1961 Constitution which was drawn up when Iain MacLeod was secretary of state for the colonies was modified on 1 March 1962. Under the February 1961 Constitution, the Legislative Council was to consist of forty five elected members and up to six official members nominated by the governor on instructions from the British government. Of those members elected, fifteen would be returned from single member constituencies by upper roll voters, fifteen from single member constituencies by lower roll voters and fifteen from national constituencies by voters on both rolls voting together. In order to qualify for election in national constituencies, a candidate was required to obtain the same prescribed minimum percentage of votes cast on each roll. Therefore, a candidate's overall support would be expressed as a percentage figure, calculated by averaging together their respective proportion of votes on the upper roll and the lower roll.

Because a candidate required a minimum of twelve and a half per cent of support from voters on each roll, the possibility of success in a national constituency by any candidate whether black or white was virtually nil. However, there was in the Constitution a subtle provision which favoured European candidates. If they failed to obtain a minimum of twelve and a half per cent of the votes actually cast on the lower roll, they would succeed if they received a minimum of four hundred votes on the lower roll. That provision existed also for African candidates standing in a national constituency if they obtained four hundred votes on the upper roll, but failed to obtain a minimum of twelve and a half per cent of the votes. However, it would be very difficult for candidates sponsored by UNIP or ANC to obtain even half of the four hundred votes cast on the upper roll.

Consequently, Kenneth Kaunda fought vigorously against MacLeod's constitutional proposals of February 1961. He launched a master plan of civil disobedience throughout the country which was meant to be a non-violent, positive action campaign. However, in the course of time, it led to untold racial strife, chaos and bitterness. Therefore, the British government's subsequent compromise constitutional proposals for Northern Rhodesia contained two important changes to the 1961 Constitution. Firstly, a candidate for the national constituency required only ten per cent of votes on the roll meant for the other racial group. Secondly, the four hundred vote option which favoured the UFP was eliminated. Both Harry Nkumbula for the ANC and Kenneth Kaunda for UNIP reluctantly accepted the new constitutional proposals for Northern Rhodesia. The UFP also reluctantly accepted the new constitutional proposals.

It was a landmark in the political history of Northern Rhodesia when the main political stakeholders accepted the

March 1962 Constitution. For both UNIP and ANC, the most difficult or, perhaps, mischievous part of the constitution related to the requirements for winning a seat on the national roll, especially for UNIP which was considered as a terrorist political organisation by the Europeans. Whether their candidates for national seats would obtain a minimum of ten per cent support from largely white voters on the upper roll was questionable. Nevertheless, Kenneth Kaunda was determined to woo the white voters on the upper roll for their support to win seats on the national roll for UNIP. He realised that more than sixty per cent of the white settlers were resident on the Copperbelt. Therefore his strategy, which had the approval of the Party Central Committee, was to campaign very vigorously on the Copperbelt in order to solicit support from the white settlers for UNIP's candidates on the upper roll and on the national roll.

It is these considerations which prompted UNIP's Central Committee to concentrate initially on recruiting Africans and Europeans to join UNIP as members – that is Africans and Europeans who commanded respect and admiration among Europeans throughout Northern Rhodesia. Fortunately, there was enormous goodwill towards UNIP and Kenneth Kaunda in particular among the African intelligentsia. Presumably, that explains the consistent appeals to me to join UNIP's political campaign after the announcement of the proposals for Northern Rhodesia by the colonial secretary, Reginald Maudling, on 1 March 1962. Within three to four months following the announcement of a new constitution for Northern Rhodesia, many African intellectuals and technocrats agreed to support UNIP's cause for the final phase of the struggle for freedom and independence.

The group of political newcomers in UNIP became known as the party's new men. Within a short period, Kenneth Kaunda had managed to present a highly qualified team of candidates. Mulford, author of *The Northern Rhodesia General Election 1962* states in his book that "Europeans showed considerable interest in the new personalities" and that the party's new team played a highly important role in Kenneth Kaunda's efforts to woo European support for UNIP. The new men Kenneth Kaunda included on the list of UNIP's candidates for elections in October 1962 are described as follows:

> Well over half of UNIP's candidates were not closely associated by Europeans with UNIP's past; only seven were party officials and none were drawn from below the party's Central Committee level. Among the most outstanding new men were: John Mwanakatwe, Northern Rhodesia's first African university graduate and the first African principal of an African secondary school who resigned his post in the office of the Commissioner for Northern Rhodesia in London (then one of the highest posts in the civil service held by an African) stood for UNIP in Northern Rural; Reverend Isaac Mumpenshya (Luangwa), newly appointed lecturer at Mindolo Ecumenical Centre, who had recently returned from Oxford University; Elijah Mudenda (BSc, MA Cambridge) (Midlands), son of a senior chief and author of two Tonga publications, who resigned his research position with the government; Robinson Puta (Lower Kafue), president of the Northern Rhodesia African Traders' Association, Mubiana Nalilungwe (BA Hons, MA, BEd) (Barotseland East), who resigned from teaching economics at Munali Secondary School; Dr Mashekwa Nalumango (Southern Rural); Joseph Shaw (Western Rural), a European candidate and former secretary of the Bancroft Chamber of Commerce; and two senior councillors of native authorities – HE Habanyama (Southern) of the Gwembe Native Authority; and Samuel Mbilishi (North-Western) of the Lunda Native Authority.

In the remaining days of June 1962, I started my political activities for UNIP. I joined Kenneth Kaunda on the Copperbelt where a programme of addressing indoor meetings was arranged. These meetings were attended by men and women drawn from various sections of the Copperbelt community. We held two meetings in Ndola and one meeting in Kitwe, which were all quite successful. The meetings were well attended by European businessmen, European civil servants and the rank and file of the white communities in these towns. The white men and women who attended these meetings asked questions about the ability of Africans to run a government efficiently, to maintain the required standards in health and educational institutions and to maintain law and order. Most of their questions revealed naivety and manifest prejudice against the capabilities of the African people. With my background in elocution, answering questions at these meetings was a pleasure. I spoke candidly, without any emotion, about the urgency of racial reconciliation. The message during my interventions at these meetings was that African majority rule was inevitable. It was merely a question of time. From personal knowledge, I testified to the fact that students at Munali Secondary School performed well in examinations and often better than students at prestigious schools for white students only, such as Gilbert Rennie Secondary School for Boys and Lady Rennie Secondary School for Girls in Kabulonga, Lusaka.

At these meetings, the president of UNIP, Kenneth Kaunda, always excelled at confirming that it was in the interest of all races for an African government to maintain law and order. Indeed, it was in the interest of the country as a whole. Many Europeans who attended the meetings left with the impression that Kenneth Kaunda was an honest and sincere political leader who was not inclined to make wild promises.

The impact we made at these meetings with the support of selected local party officials was considerable. However, we learnt the bitter lesson that attitudes and habits really die hard. The white men and women and the Asians who attended our meetings on the Copperbelt did not actually believe that a multi-racial society was possible in a country where the white minority dominated the African majority. Somehow, they suffered from a kind of phobia that chaos would prevail with the attainment of African majority rule; indeed, they believed that it might take one thousand years before Africans would be ready to run an efficient administration.

Less than seven days after joining Kenneth Kaunda's political campaign on the Copperbelt, my father died at Katula homestead in Isoko village. My young brother in Mbala relayed the news of Father's death to Freedom House. The news was in turn relayed from Freedom House to the president of UNIP in Chingola. He was in bed in Aaron Milner's house in Chingola suffering from flu. Aaron Milner was among the first Euro-Africans to join UNIP in support of the struggle for freedom and independence. At that time, the colonial government tacitly practised the game of divide and rule. It sought to weaken the African struggle by encouraging the Euro-Africans to think that they were more privileged than the Africans.

Throughout our political campaign on the Copperbelt, I was privileged to live with Timothy Kankasa and his wife Bessie Kankasa. Both were very strong members of UNIP who held senior positions at the district level in Ndola. They lived in an African township called Twapia. Their hospitality was excellent. Timothy Kankasa received a message from Kenneth Kaunda requesting me to travel to Chingola immediately to meet him. I responded quickly and drove in my car, the Hillman Minx, to Chingola. When I arrived he divulged the sad news which he had received from Freedom House in Lusaka and conveyed his condolences to me on the untimely death of my father. The news shocked me completely. It took more than fifteen minutes to recover from the shock and to react to Kenneth Kaunda's condolences and kind words of encouragement.

After recovering from the shock of my father's sudden death, I asked the UNIP president to excuse me from participating in the remaining meetings with the white community on the Copperbelt. His response was positive. For the first time I observed his innate feelings and kindness to his fellow men and women. Firstly, he offered his own driver to accompany me to Mbala. He believed that, having lost my father suddenly, it was dangerous to drive my car alone over a distance of more than six hundred miles. That was a gesture of kindness from Kenneth Kaunda which I shall never forget. In addition,

126

he put his hand in the pocket of his trousers and brought out five pounds in bank notes. He asked me to accept the money as a token of his sympathy on my bereavement in accordance with our culture. That touched my heart even more than allowing his driver to accompany me to Mbala. In those days, that amount was almost sufficient for buying fuel for the motor car for the entire journey to Mbala.

He came out of Aaron Milner's house to see me off and to wish me a safe journey. He remarked that he had appreciated my contribution during the meetings we held with representatives of the white community on the Copperbelt. He asked me to return to Lusaka as quickly as possible after mourning the death of my father. With Kenneth Kaunda's blessings, we had a trouble-free safe journey to Mbala. Although we arrived late in the afternoon the following day, I chose not to spend a night in Mbala. We continued our journey to the village about fifteen miles from Mbala Township. After a week of mourning, we returned to Lusaka to join our comrades in Freedom House in order to carry on with the political campaign.

I invariably stayed with my elder brother and his family in a new residential area near Kabwata, where the government had built modern houses for African civil servants. It was always a pleasure to be in my elder brother's company. He had been my mentor since my boyhood. Unfortunately, on this occasion, I stayed with my elder brother's family in Lusaka for only a few days. While visiting my comrades in Freedom House one day, I was given a programme of touring three districts in the Northern Province. At that time, the Northern Province included what is now called Luapula Province. In particular, we were required to visit Kasama, Mporokoso and Kawambwa Districts, holding meetings with UNIP party officials, meeting chiefs and holding open air meetings with the general public. The programme was for approximately two weeks.

The tour programme had been arranged as a second phase of my familiarisation with our party's organisation and activities in the Northern Province. The objective of the tour was to introduce me to senior and junior party officials in those districts. Aaron Milner, as a senior and trusted member of the UNIP political hierarchy, was chosen to lead our two-man delegation. He was responsible for introducing me to the party officials. This particular tour was not completely successful. We held meetings with party officials and met chiefs in Kasama District as originally planned. However, after meeting with party officials and others for only two days in Mporokoso District, Milner fell ill. In fact, he was so ill that medical treatment became necessary. We returned to Kasama where he was treated. Therefore, although the campaign programme for Kasama was completed successfully, it was only partly completed in Mporokoso. Subsequently, we returned to Lusaka without holding further meetings in Mporokoso. It was also not possible to proceed to Kawambwa. Nevertheless the tour was not entirely unproductive. I had met senior party officials in both Kasama and Mporokoso who would be useful contacts in the event of my nomination as a candidate in a constituency including those districts. Throughout our tour of Kasama and Mporokoso Districts we were guests of the UNIP officials who extended excellent hospitality to us. The spirit of comradeship in UNIP in those days was fantastic. Although their financial means were understandably limited, we were rarely asked to give them gifts. Often, they were on the alert to find out what they could do for us.

It was quite interesting to learn that the senior officials in UNIP Central Committee were extremely happy with the way I had been integrated into the party's political system. In particular, one member of the powerful Central Committee hinted privately to me that they were certain that I had no outrageous political ambitions. Apparently, some members of the Central Committee suspected that some of the new men entertained ambitions of ascending to senior positions in the UNIP hierarchy. Obviously, Aaron Milner kept a watchful eye on all my activities during our short visit to the Northern Province.

Late in August, a general conference of UNIP was

convened in Monze. It was attended by more than one thousand delegates from various UNIP regions in the seven provinces of Northern Rhodesia. Delegates at the conference included party officials at the branch, constituency and regional levels of UNIP throughout the country. The new men were also invited to attend the mammoth General Conference. Briefing the party functionaries on arrangements for the 1962 general elections for the Legislative Council was the most important item on the agenda. Secondly, it also provided the Central Committee with the opportunity to introduce the new men to the party officials countrywide. The third important subject on the agenda of the General Conference was notification of candidates selected to stand on the UNIP tickets in various constituencies in the October 1962 general elections. It was announced at the conference that I was selected to stand as the UNIP candidate for the Northern Rural Constituency.

I was among a few of the new men who were selected to address the General Conference on any subject of their own choice. For the first time, I felt greatly inspired by the determination of the rank and file of the party membership to make sacrifices to ensure UNIP's success in the general elections. Otherwise, the camp site for the General Conference in Monze was rough and far from comfortable. We lived in small grass-thatched shelters, three or four men in each such shelter. Yet life was quite interesting and enjoyable. Groups of choirs of men and women spent time singing at the camp site till the early hours of the morning every day. There was also much gossip and fun, day and night. The spirit of selfishness was simply not there. Instead, the spirit of sacrifice and patriotism was conspicuous in practically all the men and women at the camp holding various positions or attending the General Conference merely as party members.

After about five days at the UNIP General Conference, all delegates dispersed and returned to their homes. I returned to Lusaka determined to visualize the best strategy for me to adopt in preparing for the general elections in October 1962.

Quite clearly, I was selected by the Central Committee to contest a seat which was definitely unsafe. The Northern Rural Constituency was a constituency on the upper roll. It was not a safe seat because about three quarters of the voters on the upper roll were white men and women with their racial inclinations and fear of UNIP. They were unlikely to cast their votes in favour of an African candidate. Moreover, it was in geographical terms the largest constituency of all fifteen upper roll constituencies. To campaign by visiting voters personally in all the districts was impossible. Therefore, it occurred to me that the best way of campaigning was by addressing a circular letter setting out my personal credentials and a brochure describing my priorities for improving the lives of voters in the constituency. That was the strategy I envisaged for the election campaign on my return to Mbala.

To my surprise the Central Committee had devised a tour programme for me and Arthur Wina to tour the Eastern Province at the end of the General Conference in Monze. The Central Committee had a progressive policy of deliberately exposing leaders to party officials in various parts of the country outside their own home provinces. It sent me and Arthur Wina to join Humphrey Mulemba, the UNIP official in-charge of the Eastern Province, on a tour of the Eastern Province. The ten day visit was educative. It became apparent to us during the tour that Humphrey Mulemba was an articulate, progressive and enlightened UNIP leader whose capabilities were unsurpassed. He had vast knowledge of political problems in the province in relation to competition with the ANC. In a short time, the intended lesson was clearly understood – there were competent men among the old guards in UNIP. In terms of hospitality, party officials looked after me and Arthur Wina quite well. In fact, we hardly spent any money for our upkeep. It was there that Arthur Wina got a great shock. I had been away from my wife and children for more than three weeks. It was unlikely that I would join them until after another week. Therefore, he accompanied me to the post office in Fort Jameson (now known as Chipata) to send some money to my wife. I instructed the post master to send five pounds by telegraphic order to her in Mbala. Arthur Wina thought that I was not serious. He regarded my action as a joke; yet that was all the money I had to spare for their maintenance.

Ten days later, I arrived in Mbala to plan my strategy of campaigning as UNIP candidate for the Northern Rural Constituency. In mid September 1962, Freedom House officials arranged yet another tour programme for me of visits to Mpika, Chinsali and Isoka Districts. A veteran politician who was UNIP's national secretary was selected to introduce me to party officials in the districts. He was Mainza Chona. The tour programme was intended to enable me to campaign for votes among prosperous Africans, teachers, senior clerical officers and missionaries and other Europeans enrolled on the upper roll in the Northern Rural Constituency. Mainza Chona was the first African from Northern Rhodesia to train as a lawyer in London. He was prominent in UNIP circles because he voluntarily surrendered his leadership of UNIP to Kenneth Kaunda after the latter's release from detention in Kabompo in 1959. Indeed he was a patriot par excellence. Throughout our one week tour, I enjoyed every minute of the time I spent with Mainza Chona. He was extremely popular with party officials because of his sense of humour. At least I was comforted that some effort was made to campaign, albeit covering only a small part of the large constituency, for support for me in Northern Rural.

UNIP's plan to build a railway line from Kapiri-Mposhi through Mpika and Nakonde to Dar es Salaam in Tanganyka, now known as Tanzania, was disclosed for the first time by a senior official at an open air political meeting at Mpika. At that time, the people who attended that meeting regarded UNIP's promise to build a railway line from Kapiri-Mposhi to Dar es Salaam as a pipedream. Yet only eight years later, the Chinese had completed building it (Tan-zam Railway). This proposal was Mainza Chona's favourite subject at all the meetings we addressed. The tour programme was successful.

I returned later to Mbala encouraged that I was likely to command considerable support among African voters on the upper roll in the Northern Rural Constituency. Shortly after my return to Mbala, the UNIP Central Committee gave all candidates the green light to campaign vigorously with the support of party officials in readiness for the general elections at the end of October. We had in Mbala at that time a printing company called the Lake Press. It was a small family enterprise which produced a local newsletter for white settlers in Mbala District in particular. The European proprietor of the Lake Press was personally known to me. In fact, I had a cordial relationship with him.

Time for posting campaign newsletters and posters was running out. However, good fortune was definitely with me. He willingly undertook to print several copies of a brochure I prepared for circulation to the voters in the constituency. The brochure contained an account of my background in education and in administration both in Northern Rhodesia and abroad as a civil servant. The brochure also contained an account of what I intended to do for the people in the Northern Rural Constituency if elected to the Legislative Council. In particular, I emphasized my determination to improve feeder roads, agriculture and education. Both agriculture and education would be accorded priority in the development programmes.

The distribution of the brochure was deliberately arranged to follow the circulation of the newsletter to voters, both African and European, in the constituency. In the newsletter, an attempt was made to describe the aims of UNIP as contained in its manifesto in the event that UNIP won the elections and formed the government before the end of the year.

Eventually, the day of reckoning arrived – 31 October 1962. Both the African and European voters turned out in very large numbers to cast their votes at polling stations scattered all over the country. As stated already, the system of voting adopted for the first general election involving Africans was extremely complex. Consequently, the voting was not conclusive because neither African nor European candidates were able to secure the ten per cent votes required from voters of the opposite race in national roll constituencies. In the event, none of the main political parties which took part in that election succeeded in winning a majority of seats in the Legislative Council.

Efforts by various political parties to win seats on the national roll in a subsequent election rerun in December 1962 were completely futile. Consequently, after considerable horse-trading between the UFP and ANC, eventually UNIP and ANC agreed to form a coalition in order to obtain a majority of seats in the Legislative Council. UNIP and ANC together had eighteen seats against sixteen for the UFP. Consequently, UNIP and ANC formed a government in December 1962.

It was for me significant and a source of pride that I was the only UNIP candidate to win a seat on the upper roll. The UFP, the white-led political party, won thirteen seats plus one seat reserved for Asians only on the upper roll. I fought in that election in the Northern Rural Constituency two stalwarts. The Liberal Party fielded Unwin Moffat as its candidate. He was a brother of Sir John Moffat, both descendants of a well-known pioneer missionary in Northern Rhodesia. The Liberal Party was a small and newly formed political party. The ANC fielded Viviane Shone who was a well-known European businessman in Kasama to whom the UFP lent its full support. In spite of the formidable difficulty of appealing for support from European and African voters in a vast constituency, nevertheless I succeeded in winning the Northern Rural Constituency for UNIP. The significance of my victory is demonstrated by the wide margin between the number of votes I won and the votes won by my nearest rival in the elections. UNIP received 1,172 votes, the ANC got 297 and the Liberal Party 140. In his book, *The Northern Rhodesia General Elections 1962*, Mulford observed as follows:

In Northern Rural, the UFP believed that the upper roll

133

Africans, having been alienated from UNIP by the disturbances of the previous year, would support a moderate party like ANC. Instead of nominating its own candidate the UFP lent one of its European supporters in Kasama, VA Shone, to stand for ANC. Shone was well known to the constituency's five hundred European voters and if thirty per cent of the Africans chose the more moderate African party, UNIP would be defeated.

However, UNIP placed one of its most outstanding candidates, John Mwanakatwe, in Northern Rural Constituency. Mwanakatwe, whose home district was Abercorn (now Mbala), had a distinguished record with the government .... Apart from Kaunda, Mwanakatwe was UNIP's most widely respected candidate among Europeans, particularly those in the provincial administration. The UFP's plan was further frustrated by the entry of a third candidate, the Liberal's Unwin Moffat, a brother of Sir John Moffat. In the end, Mwanakatwe demonstrated UNIP's upper roll African solidarity in the North and won a few European votes as well. Shone won slightly over half the constituency's European votes, and Moffat lost his deposit.

There was also a possibility of success in the Southern Rural Constituency where UNIP fielded Dr Mashekwa Nalumango as its candidate. It was also an upper roll constituency in which the majority of voters were white settlers. The voters were mainly railway men, farmers and businessmen in the Southern and Western Provinces. Dr Mashekwa Nalumango fought tenaciously as UNIP's candidate. He produced the closest contest of the election on the upper roll, although he lost. To a certain extent, Kaunda's concern to appeal vigorously to European voters for their support during the campaign was vindicated by UNIP's success in the Northern Rural Constituency and the strong competition it provided in the Southern Rural Constituency. Otherwise, on the whole, Europeans did not believe that Kaunda truly wanted to build a non-racial society in Northern Rhodesia.

Early in December 1962, UNIP acceded to Nkumbula's demand for a minimum of three portfolios in the coalition government, including the portfolio of African Education. Consequently, on 15 December, the governor announced Northern Rhodesia's first African government. The governor's appointments were as follows:

Ministers

Kaunda, KD	(UNIP)	Local Government and Social Welfare
Nkumbula, HM	(ANC)	African Education
Kapwepwe, SM	(UNIP)	African Agriculture
Kamanga, RC	(UNIP)	Labour and Mines
Stubbs, FN	(ANC)	Transport and Works
Cousins, CE	(ANC)	Land and Natural Resources

Parliamentary Secretaries

Zulu, AG	(UNIP)	Local Government and Social Welfare
Banda, FJA	(ANC)	African Education
Mudenda, EK	(UNIP)	African Agriculture
Mwanakatwe, JM	(UNIP)	Labour and Mines
Chembe, FB	(ANC)	Transport and Works
Michello, JEM	(ANC)	Land and Natural Resources
Wina, ANL	(UNIP)	Finance

Chief Whip

Wina, S	(UNIP)

A few days after the appointment of ministers and parliamentary secretaries by the governor, I was instructed to travel to Lusaka in order to report to the chief secretary for official accreditation as parliamentary secretary in the Ministry of Labour and Mines. Before the end of December, Reuben Kamanga and I were properly settled in our offices in the Ministry of Labour and Mines. I was particularly happy to work under Reuben Kamanga, a highly respected and senior political activist who was on many occasions imprisoned by the colonial government for advocating the cause of freedom and independence in Northern Rhodesia. He was a quiet spoken but a clear-minded colleague from whom I learnt much about the game of politics. It was particularly pleasing that he always respected my views and advice. In the course of time, we became life-long friends.

Our permanent secretary in the Ministry of Labour and Mines was Roy Philport. It was also a happy coincidence that Roy Philport was not a stranger to me. He knew Joseph, my elder brother, very well indeed. They had at one time worked together in the High Court in Livingstone in the late 1940s. Like most of the senior officers in the government, Roy Philport was sympathetic to the difficulties confronting ministers in a coalition government. Because of his wisdom and experience, his guidance and advice were invaluable at all times. He worked out a pragmatic system of consultation between me as junior minister and Reuben Kamanga as cabinet minister which enabled us to share responsibilities and the burden of political activities fairly. We held joint meetings every fortnight with Roy Philport which senior officers attended by invitation. In the course of time, I learnt that other junior ministers were underutilised. In fact, some had open quarrels with ministers or senior civil servants in their ministries.

Early in 1963, I realized that it was opportune to reunite with my wife and family in Lusaka. As a junior minister in the new coalition government, I was obliged to live in Lusaka. Therefore, it became necessary to move my wife and children from Mbala to Lusaka. Hitherto, it had not been possible regularly to commute between Lusaka and Mbala. It was no longer convenient to continue the practice. However, finding suitable accommodation to rent at an affordable charge was a problem. Luckily, I eventually found a three bedroom flat for rent in the Emmasdale area quite near the city centre. It was about five hundred yards away from the Emmasdale police station. In terms of security, the location of the flat was ideal. The rent was affordable. Consequently, I seized the opportunity of concluding the lease agreement quickly. By the end of February 1963, my wife and children had arrived and were living with me in Lusaka.

I made one major contribution as a junior minister to the operations of the Ministry of Labour and Mines during the period January to December 1963. In that period, I conceived the idea of establishing an institution within Zambia for training labour leaders in the country. It occurred to me in the course of 1963 that the expectations of workers in the mines and industry generally were high with the formation of the first African government of Northern Rhodesia. Often, they advocated causes which were noble and worthwhile. However, they often failed to achieve them. This was due to lack of knowledge and understanding of the basic principles of trade unionism. When my ideas were discussed extensively in our ministry, support was sought from the chief secretary's office to initiate donor funding for the establishment of such an institution. The idea was critically examined in the chief secretary's office and was accepted in principle. However, the chief secretary decided that re-examination of the proposal was necessary. An inter-ministerial committee was set up for this purpose.

Although the idea of establishing such an institution was mooted prior to the attainment of independence, it was not until 1972 that the President's Citizenship College was established by an Act of Parliament. After observing that there were many areas and fields in which the country needed to train personnel, the government decided that the scope of the college should, apart from labour studies, include cooperative education, economic and social development, as well as general management. It was felt that there was a need for an institution where leaders from all walks of life would go for courses, seminars, symposia and conferences to enable them understand and appreciate their various roles, as well as government policies and plans for national development. This institution was important and crucial due to the limited number of qualified and experienced Zambians to steer the new nation in its development process. Therefore, the 1972 Act establishing the college encompassed and reflected these concerns. In 1994, the President's Citizenship College Act was amended by an Act of Parliament. This amendment established the National College for Management and Development Studies.

Unfortunately, at the beginning of 1963 reports of widespread disturbances on the Copperbelt were received by almost all district commissioners. There were many causes of the unprecedented unrest. For example, figures given by the police showed that in the first six months of 1963 there was a total of 1,331 offences with a known political motive or significance as compared with 283 similar offences for the same period in 1962. Of these offences with political significance, a high proportion were assaults and wounding, malicious damage to property, threatening violence and the unlawful demanding of political documents. The background to these incidents was apparently political between the United National Independence Party on the one hand and the African National Congress on the other.

The government was concerned about widespread unrest in the urban areas of the Western Province*. The governor appointed me to sit on a commission of inquiry. I appreciated the gravity of the task we were called upon to perform. More importantly, it occurred to me that UNIP's leader, Kenneth Kaunda, had considerable confidence in my ability to serve on the commission with diligence, bearing in mind principles of justice and the overall interests of our country.

The governor of Northern Rhodesia appointed a commission of inquiry on 25 June 1963, with the specific terms of reference:

---

* The Copperbelt was in 1963 part of what was called the Western Province.

Having regard to such causes of unrest in the urban areas of the Western Province as may be ascertained to make recommendations that would bring this unrest to an end and, ensure that an atmosphere would be created in which a constructive approach could be made to the problems of the area.

The commission was ordered to submit a report promptly. I was privileged to be appointed as a commissioner with Mr Justice FT Whelan as chairman. Other members were FB Chembe, JEM Michello, AG Zulu and PGD Clark. The governor attached great importance to the task he had assigned to the Commission of Inquiry. Firstly, a High Court judge was appointed as chairman. Secondly, he allowed the ANC and UNIP equal representation and appointed a senior civil servant with vast experience in administration to sit on the Commission of Inquiry. FB Chembe and JEM Michello were members of the Legislative Council elected on the ANC ticket. AG Zulu and I were members of the Legislative Council elected on the UNIP ticket.

1962 had been a relatively peaceful year. In previous years, conflict was rampant between the two main African political parties, ANC and UNIP, especially on the Copperbelt. The Copperbelt was the melting pot of political activities where ANC and UNIP supporters struggled to promote their parties' dominance. Often such struggles culminated in disturbances and riots. The second half of 1962 had been comparatively free from incidents of violence because the majority of the people, as in other parts of the country, had been busily occupied with the preliminaries to the general election in October. They had been encouraged by their political leaders to register as voters and to exercise their votes. The election itself was peaceful.

The Commission of Inquiry began public hearings to take evidence from 2 July in the OB Bennett Hall at Kitwe and completed its public sessions on 1 August again at the OB Bennett Hall. Final submissions were heard on that date from the counsel who appeared before it on behalf of various interested parties. The commission received abundant evidence that incidents began to take place between supporters of the two parties governing the coalition. This culminated in the tragic riots at Chingola on 16 June in which seven people died. In our report to the governor of Northern Rhodesia, we emphasized that " ... the background to these incidents was neither racial nor tribal, but political as between members of the United National Independence Party on the one hand and the African National Congress on the other". Among many causes of unrest in the urban areas of the Western Province, we included political party rivalry, political identification, unemployment, inadequate housing and inadequate educational facilities. To overcome all these problems, we made one important recommendation apart from numerous minor ones. In paragraph 38 of our report we recommended:

.... that a new constitution be granted to the territory and that the date for a general election be announced as soon as possible. These steps would without doubt reduce the present unrest to a considerable degree but we appreciate that party political activity would continue and, in our opinion, it is equally necessary that certain additional remedial measures be taken at one and the same time to ensure that an election campaign is conducted in a peaceful and tolerant manner.

All the recommendations in our report were positive and constructive. We avoided witch hunting and the tendency to apportion blame to one or the other political party whose supporters were usually involved in disturbances. I found my legal background especially useful in assessing the evidence contained in written and oral submissions of witnesses or counsel on their behalf. Participation in the work of the Commission of Inquiry into Unrest on the Copperbelt from July to August 1963 was an enjoyable and worthwhile experience.

The year 1963 ended on a happy note. My good friend, Reuben Kamanga, married Edna in December at a short civil ceremony at the boma in Kitwe. She was the daughter of Oliver Kabungo, a well known businessman. My wife and I were present at the simple ceremony attended by their relatives and a few guests.

C H A P T E R

7

Desegregation of Schools

The United National Independence Party led by Kenneth Kaunda won a landslide victory in the presidential and general elections in January 1964. The elections were heavily contested by two other prominent political parties, namely the African National Congress and the United Federal Party. These two parties were led by Harry Nkumbula and John Roberts respectively. The presidential and general elections were based on universal adult suffrage. The government of Northern Rhodesia appointed Kenneth Kaunda prime minister because he won a majority of seats in the Legislative Council. He was requested to form a new government.

Before the elections, I was the UNIP member of the Legislative Council for the Northern Rural Constituency. In the presidential and general elections held in January 1964, I stood as UNIP candidate in the Mweru Constituency. I won the seat with an overwhelming majority. Because I entered politics without any serious political ambitions in the sense of holding high office, my appointment by Kenneth Kaunda as minister of education came as a surprise. I knew that some of my colleagues, in the course of politicking throughout 1963, had hoped to assume the office of minister of education in the first UNIP government. Although I was humbled by the appointment, nevertheless I had confidence that with my qualifications and experience in the field of education, it would be possible to make a valuable contribution to the effectiveness of the new government. However, later I came to realize that politics was a very difficult game indeed. Some of my colleagues continued to lobby for my removal from the post of minister of education. They made attempts to incite some teachers in Matero township in Lusaka to cause problems by way of industrial unrest. A member of the intelligence service was officially instructed to warn me about that situation. Nonetheless, I was advised not to be alarmed.

In less than four weeks, I realized for the first time that going into politics had altered the course of my life at that point in time. The thought of a powerful ministerial job had never been a dream to me. Yet by the end of February 1964 it was a reality.

I remember very clearly my first day at the headquarters of the Ministry of Education. When I arrived I was an object of attraction; perhaps my presence actually aroused curiosity rather than attraction. Many young African men and women serving as clerical officers left their offices to see me coming out of my car to go into my office on the first floor of the headquarters building. What they discussed later among themselves I shall never know. I guess that to some extent my fellow Africans were happy to see me occupying the highest political office in the Ministry of Education. In fact, I was not the first political person to assume the mantle of political leadership in the ministry. During the coalition government, Harry Nkumbula was the minister of African education from December 1962 to early January 1964. When the United Federal Party was the leader of the white settlers with Colonial Office representatives in the Legislative Council, Gabriel Musumbulwa served as minister of African education. Obviously times had changed. A lot of water had gone under the bridge. The majority of Africans wanted to see a strong African government led by Kenneth Kaunda succeed in its programmes of development.

On that first day I met Major WAR Gorman. He was the permanent secretary in the Ministry of Education. A graduate of Oxford University, he had served as a provincial education officer for many years before he was transferred to the headquarters of the ministry as under secretary. Like other senior officers at headquarters, Bill Gorman welcomed me enthusiastically. He introduced me to the key officers at the headquarters who were all white expatriates. Even my own personal secretary, Valerie Lampry, was an expatriate. Only two fellow Africans were close to me – my official driver and the messenger who was responsible for cleaning my office. Anyway, I had learnt as parliamentary secretary in the Ministry of Labour and Social Services that in politics you do not sulk. In a political position, one can influence the course of events as long as one uses correct procedures to effect change.

During my orientation regarding the organization of the ministry and the education structure throughout the country, the permanent secretary gave me a comprehensive brief to study. The brief was prepared in a scholarly manner. It was a useful critique on the problems facing the ministry at the time and recommended priorities for the achievement of the desired goals in education. After careful study of the brief, I discussed some problems in it with the appropriate officers in order to obtain a clear understanding of ways and means of overcoming the difficulties. My study of relevant papers on education was supplemented by visits to secondary schools and teacher training colleges both in urban and rural areas. By the end of February, I was in a position to formulate policy guidelines for the reform of the education system for approval of the cabinet.

Any policy guidelines for cabinet's consideration had to take into account the UNIP manifesto on education. The UNIP manifesto contained three important reforms. The first related to the need to accord education priority in all development programmes. The second was to place maximum emphasis on expansion of educational facilities both at the primary and the secondary school levels. Thirdly, racialism in all its forms, whether in hospitals or schools, was to be abolished. In terms of the people's expectations, the need for additional places in primary and secondary schools was very urgent indeed. However, my own clear perception was to do first things first, but with the qualification that there was wisdom in prioritising priorities themselves. My perception was that it required time to build new primary and secondary schools. On the other hand, segregation in schools was something that could be eliminated more rapidly. The abolition of racial segregation in schools merely required a political decision followed by the adoption of a correct legal framework for its implementation.

The Northern Rhodesian government had assumed responsibility for education in the territory in 1925. Records show that in that year the new colonial government of Northern Rhodesia inherited from the Chartered Company the supervision of the Barotse National School. It was a small school founded in 1906 for the provision of education for African children. A small school for the children of white settlers was also established. At that time, outside the government's direct control there were some two thousand mission schools with a nominal enrolment estimated at eighty nine thousand and an attendance of about two thirds of that number. In 1921, the Chartered Company had issued the Native Proclamation Number 28 which gave the Chartered Company some control over the registration and inspection of mission schools and the quality of their African teachers. In the years from 1924, the Northern Rhodesian government administered a dual structure of education, one for the education of Europeans and the other for the education of Africans. In fact, the administration of the education of Africans was originally a sub department of the native affairs department. Between 1930 and 1940, two attempts were made by the colonial government to merge the two departments without success. Consequently, the dual system of education continued in Northern Rhodesia until the eve of independence. An amalgamation of the two departments was achieved for the first time in January 1964 when I became the minister responsible for education.

However, over a period of about forty years, the educational facilities available to the European community were far superior to the facilities available for the African community.

145

Of course, the European educational system had its own difficulties, but they were minute compared with the difficulties which faced the Ministry of African Education just before independence.

Before I assumed responsibility for education, the Federation had been dissolved. Following the dissolution of the Federation, Northern Rhodesia had regained control over the education of all its children. It was my responsibility to transform the dual system of education into an integrated education system. Peter Snelson, in his book *To Independence and Beyond* recorded his personal experience of the transformation in the following words:

> John Mwanakatwe's appointment as Minister of Education was especially significant. While the Federation was in existence, the education of Africans was a responsibility of each of the three territories. The education of European, Asian and Coloured children, on the other hand, was a responsibility of the Federal Government. Now, with the Federation dead, Northern Rhodesia had regained control over the education of all its children. As John Mwanakatwe tried to fashion a single, integrated education system, major changes were certain. Nowhere would these changes be more difficult or more bitterly contested than on the Copperbelt.

> Within ten days of Mwanakatwe taking up his appointment I learned that I was to be transferred immediately to Ndola, capital of the Copperbelt.

The programme for the desegregation of schools was undertaken in three phases. To achieve full integration of the African and European education systems overnight merely by a stroke of the pen was virtually impossible. Because the issue of racial integration in schools was a highly emotive subject, a comprehensive cabinet memorandum was prepared for consideration. Major changes which I proposed to implement both in the short and the long term were all carefully analysed in the cabinet memorandum.

An analysis of major differences between the African and non-African education systems just before independence was necessary. Teachers in European and African primary and secondary schools followed different syllabuses. Secondly, European children were enrolled in school in the first year at a much earlier age than African children. The age of entry in non-African primary schools was generally five to five and a half years. Yet in African primary schools the entry to the first year was between seven to eight years. Thirdly, not all African children were able to find a place in grade one when they reached the age of seven or eight. On the other hand there was virtually universal entry to non-African primary schools when children reached the age of five. Fourthly, European children automatically proceeded to form one at the end of the primary segment of education. However, in African schools admission to form one was based on a highly competitive examination. Usually, only about a quarter of African children who completed their primary segment of education were able to proceed to form one for further education. Lastly, during the first four years of education, the African children were obliged to learn in at least two languages – in a vernacular language and in English as well.

It is obvious that the education system for European schools was more favourable than the system which prevailed for African education before independence. Consequently, the idea of integration of schools under consideration in 1964 was vehemently opposed by a majority of white settlers. They believed that racial integration of schools would ultimately lead to the lowering of the quality of education in once European schools. For this and other reasons, they strongly opposed any idea of racial integration in schools. They were particularly concerned about the negative effect of the proposal to end the privilege of European children, including Asian and Coloured children, previously enrolled in former federal schools, to progress automatically from primary to secondary schools. The opposition of Europeans to the proposed racial integration in schools at the beginning of 1964 was succinctly stated by Grace Keith in her book *The Fading Colour Bar* as follows:

> The very mention of the subject conjured up in their minds all sorts of ghastly prospects; educational standards would drop; classes would be too big; bright white pupils would be held back by duller black ones; dull white pupils would be suppressed by clever black pupils – unthinkable situations. Good European teachers would leave and be replaced by less efficient black ones (Would you like your child to be taught by a native?); African children would pass on to European children all kinds of unpleasant habits not to mention fleas, bugs, lice and other unhygienic horrors. Another more terrifying thought exercised the minds of these white parents. This was that their own well-brought-up children might one day have to share school accommodation with African boys and girls who were well known to be sexually precocious. Not only do African children tend to be earlier developers, physically, than European children, but it was common knowledge that due to their starting school at a later age than white youngsters, they could be anything from two to six years older than the average white child in the same form. The outlook was fraught with danger. Multi-racial education – so far as Europeans were concerned – was a non-starter.

Ironically, there were also many Africans who doubted the desirability of multi-racial education. They believed that integration of schools was unlikely to benefit African children. Their belief was that European teachers would deliberately discourage African children who enrolled in previously European schools. They also feared that the introduction of English as a medium of instruction in the first year of schooling would be disadvantageous to the African children. Above all, the fears of many African parents were derived from an inbuilt complex that poor parents' children would be objects of ridicule.

How to reconcile diametrically opposed viewpoints and prejudices was the most difficult task we had to resolve in the Ministry of Education in 1964. It was simply unthinkable that the new African government would tolerate any form of colour bar in schools. Even more importantly, the new African government was obliged to ensure that children of all races were given equal opportunities for education. For example, classes in African schools at both the primary and secondary school levels were overcrowded. On the other hand, classes in hitherto European primary and secondary schools were not crowded. In fact, there were many unfilled places for children in various classes in European schools. The challenge had to be accepted to integrate schools in such a way that the standard of education was not lowered in hitherto European schools. A phased programme of racial integration in schools was adopted for the purpose of maintaining both national stability and the integrity of the political leadership. The achievement of integration of schools in Zambia after only four years became an enviable record.

Over the four year period from the beginning of 1964 to the end of 1967, the integration of former federal primary and secondary schools into the formal African education system proceeded satisfactorily. Firstly, in 1964 and 1965 parents were obliged to pay a small amount for tuition fees for each child enrolled in schools which were previously for Europeans only. This had the advantage of avoiding a flood of applications for places in hitherto European primary and secondary schools. Schools in which payment of tuition fees was required were designated as scheduled schools. The rest of the schools in the country were designated as non-scheduled schools. An important factor in the first strategy was that the tuition fee of K24 per child was affordable for primary schools. Equally, the figure of K40 per child for secondary school pupils was affordable. Consequently, by the end of 1967 nearly all places in both primary and secondary schools were filled. Secondly, the policy decision was taken in 1969 to abolish tuition fees altogether in both scheduled primary and secondary schools. Thus the designation of schools as scheduled or non-scheduled became irrelevant. Thereafter, all schools in Zambia were designated simply as government schools. This differentiated them from aided-schools which were controlled by missionary and other agencies with partial support from the government.

The success of the programme of integration of schools is recorded in *The Fading Colour Bar* as follows:

> None of the Zambians in fee paying schools had ever been in serious clashes of a racial nature. One case I heard of was of a girl who had the habit of shouting "shut-up Kaffir" to any African who was making too much noise. She was reported by a prefect and warned that if she continued to use the word "Kaffir" she would have to leave school. It is a sad but simple truth that even the most vehement Negrophobe can be "tolerant" when he knows he is on the losing side. School children are no exception.

But that is to comment on the negative aspect of multi-racial education in Zambia. The same author deals with the positive aspect of the successful programme of racial integration in schools after independence. She also observed on this important issue as follows:

> But on the whole, when one remembers how European parents fought against the idea of multi-racial schools for so long European children have reacted to the sudden change in their lives with remarkable calm. One girl who found herself the only white girl in the dormitory of all black ones was not quite surprisingly taken away from school and sent elsewhere. Several parents had written to their children's teachers and asked for them to be excused swimming lessons, reasons not stated but understood. And occasionally a disgruntled parent can be heard complaining that a child never got ringworm until he had to sit next to Africans in classes.

Although figures do not tell the full success story of multi-racial education in Zambia, they at least reflect the attitude of different parents towards former European schools – primary and secondary. During the first four years of multi-racial education, there was a sharp fall in the number of European children who continued to enrol in schools previously reserved for white children only. Three reasons encouraged this trend. First, the government made efforts after independence to achieve a unified system of secondary education. Soon after independence, the 'A' and 'M' level courses offered previously in ex-federal schools were eliminated progressively from the curriculum. They were provided exclusively for non-African school children during the Federation. This was an unpopular decision among the European community whose children were required under the new dispensation to sit the Junior Secondary School Leaving Examination and the Cambridge School Certificate Examination subsequently.

Secondly, even the few "liberal" European parents who were happy to allow their children to continue schooling in inter-racial secondary schools received little encouragement with the award of generous education allowances by big industrial groups to their employees for the education of their children outside Zambia. Naturally, they took advantage of the generous allowances to send their children outside Zambia for secondary education.

Thirdly, at first some African parents' efforts to enrol their children in ex-federal schools were frustrated by the prohibitive cost of school uniform for their children. This problem tended to retard the pace of racial integration in schools. Some reactionary European headmasters formulated harsh regulations which enabled them to exclude mainly African children who were not able to buy expensive items of school uniform at the time of enrolment. In order to remove a practice which tended to discourage enrolment of Africans in schools which were previously for whites only the Ministry of Education issued Circular Minute No. 3 of 1967 on the subject of school uniforms. The solution to the problem of school uniforms was couched in these words:

Educational privilege based on race has now been eliminated

151

from our schools and will not be replaced by an obnoxious form of privilege which would confine educational opportunity to the children of parents who were able to afford to buy school uniforms. No child in Zambia is to be denied a place in school because he or she cannot produce a pair of shoes or even a shirt. It follows that Heads must not penalize a child who is not equipped with school uniform. Heads may use reasonable powers to *encourage* parents to provide their children with uniforms, but they cannot *compel* them to do so. They must not refuse to enrol, and neither must they punish, children who lack uniforms.

The desegregation of schools was achieved satisfactorily in less than four years. It was one of the most notable achievements of Dr Kenneth Kaunda's first government after independence. Six years after completion of the process of desegregation of schools, in a book titled *Growth of Education in Zambia Since Independence*, I described what I had always considered to be the most important objective of the exercise. I stated that:

In any multi-racial society, education opportunities should be equal for all children irrespective of their race. The second equally important issue concerns the broad nature and purpose of the education which we seek to offer to our children in schools. We seek primarily to develop the individual personalities of our pupils in schools, to encourage imagination and not memory, and to teach the fundamentals of knowledge and the interdependence of members of a community. It follows that after independence educational apartheid became intolerable. The policy of the government in Zambia is to build a non-racial society and to forge from diverse elements in it a single nation. Multi-racial schools, therefore, provide opportunities for instilling mutual understanding and respect among children of all races in Zambia.

The Copperbelt Province had the largest number of scheduled schools which were previously for white children only. That was the area of potential resistance against racial integration in schools. With the firmness which our ministry adopted in schools and the full support of our field staff, the process was successful. Gradually some white parents began to concede that their children were quite happy at school. Some were proud that their children had good friends among the African pupils. The myth had been exploded that harmony was impossible among pupils in desegregated schools. It is so true, indeed, that negative racial attitudes are implanted by adults into the minds of innocent children!

CHAPTER

8

Power and Politics

The successful implementation of the programme for multi-racial education in the first two years of the UNIP government surprised many people, both Europeans and Africans. Many Africans did not believe that it was possible to achieve multi-racial education in their lifetime. On the other hand, most Europeans abhorred the idea of racial integration in schools. Yet by the stroke of a pen, legalized racialism in schools was brought to an end in 1964. In *The Fading Colour Bar*, Grace Keith observed on the multi-racial programme of education after independence that:

> By and large, the first year of school integration passed without too many difficulties. There were many small incidents which could be chalked up on the credit side of the experiment: a tough Afrikaans boy, with a history of anti-African sentiment, saying to his schoolmaster one day, "Some of these African blokes are quite nice when you get to know them". By the end of 1964 the consensus of opinion among white and black parents was that multi-racial education was not half so bad as they feared it might be.

I have often tried to find the best definition of the word politics, but my efforts have been in vain. However, the *Little Oxford Dictionary* gives a definition which I have found useful. It is defined as "the art and science of government; political life, affairs, principles, etc." Furthermore, the word politics means "activities relating to pursuit of power, status, etc." In

154

practical terms, the majority of men and women go into politics in order to acquire power or status or both usually with a purpose in mind of exercising power to introduce their policies. Similarly, political organizations are formed primarily for the purpose of gaining power and influence in society. Sponsors may use such organizations to promote changes in society. It is the political power gained by UNIP after its landslide victory in the elections in January 1964 which facilitated the programme of multi-racial education in Zambia.

Racial segregation was only one out of many disadvantages suffered by African children under the education system which prevailed before independence. African schools were pathetically neglected by the colonial government. There was an uneven distribution of education facilities throughout the country. In 1964, when I assumed the portfolio of education, there were nearly two thousand lower primary schools scattered over the whole country. They provided four years of education only. In rural areas, after the fourth year, there was a form of selection which enabled about fifty per cent of pupils to go on to the fifth and sixth years of education. In the urban areas, provision was nearly one hundred per cent for children who reached the school going age to enrol in the first year in lower primary schools. In rural areas, only seventy per cent were receiving any education at all in the first year of the lower primary course. After the sixth year, half the children in school were selected to complete the seventh and eighth years of education.

The system of education in 1964 resulted in a pyramid tapering rapidly towards the top. Therefore, a very small proportion of African children accepted for the first year of the lower primary course had a chance of completing the full primary course, especially in rural areas. Furthermore, because of neglect in the past by the colonial government, African schools were generally inferior to schools provided for children of Europeans, Asians and Coloureds. The four years of education which were available to children who enrolled in lower primary schools was not considered long enough to make it useful to the recipients and the country. Therefore, it was desirable to make provision after independence for an increasing number of children in primary schools to complete a full primary course.

Unfortunately, at independence the rate of progression of pupils from primary schools to secondary schools was unsatisfactory. There were very few secondary schools in the country at that time because the colonial government had neglected secondary education. Consequently, at independence Zambia faced a serious shortage of trained manpower. There were practically no indigenous engineers or dentists, no veterinary surgeons or architects either in the civil service or private practice. However, there were a few local graduates in law, medicine, agriculture and general science, arts and economics. The largest proportion of educated people were graduate teachers employed by the government and missions in secondary schools. Because the country seriously lacked educated and trained manpower, the provision of additional facilities for secondary education was given priority in post-independence development programmes.

On my appointment to the education portfolio in January 1964, I was confronted by formidable problems. The most difficult of these problems was to devise a programme for the rapid expansion of primary and secondary schools throughout the country in order to meet people's expectations. It was my responsibility to ensure the new government's positive response to the popular demands for more primary and secondary schools. The challenge was undoubtedly daunting but it was accepted nonetheless. The process of "delivering the goods" to the people involved a cross-section of stakeholders such as the Ministry of Finance, responsible for the provision of funds for the construction of primary and secondary schools, and the Ministry of Transport and Works, which had to review progress on the implementation of the approved development programme. My permanent secretary and I attached importance to the review meetings which we attended in person or by a senior proxy.

Such meetings facilitated completion of projects satisfactorily. I spent many sleepless nights in the months after independence studying draft memoranda for submission to the cabinet for consideration on proposals for rapid expansion of both primary and secondary education. It required dogged determination to persuade my cabinet colleagues to approve costly development programmes for education. Approval of my proposals had the effect of reducing capital expenditure available for projects in other ministries. But both in terms of UNIP's election manifesto of 1962 and purely economic considerations, the development of our human resources was at that time an unquestionable priority. For effective overall national development, educated and trained manpower was essential. Common sense prevailed both on economic and political grounds.

The approved development plan for primary school expansion envisaged more than 120,000 new places in primary schools during the period 1965 and 1966 under the Transitional Development Plan (TDP). This was followed by the First National Development Plan (FNDP) which allocated nearly K80,000,000 to education. It was to be spent on the expansion of primary and secondary education, teacher training, technical education, bursaries, the University of Zambia and on projects such as educational broadcasting and the Library Service. Under the FNDP, secondary school expansion was dramatic. The enrolment of pupils in government and aided secondary schools in forms I, II, III, IV and V was 16,843 in 1966. By 1970 the actual enrolment figure in all the forms was 50,785, slightly below the figure of 54,580 provided for in the plan.

In his book entitled *To Independence and Beyond*, Peter Snelson has described the impact of the education development programme from 1966 to 1970. He outlines the difficulties we encountered in formulating the programme for expansion of secondary education. Much of the opposition to our proposals came from expatriate economists in the Office of National Development Planning under the vice president. Peter Snelson

157

states:

> By any standards, the rate at which Zambia's secondary
> education system expanded in the years immediately following
> independence was very impressive. Much of the credit for this
> must go to John Mwanakatwe whose determination and
> enthusiasm overcame all opposition. It was he who persuaded
> cabinet to agree that the secondary school population should
> increase from nearly 17,000 in 1966 to more than 54,000 in
> 1970. He achieved this in the face of strong arguments from
> the Office of National Development and Planning. The ONDP,
> as it was called, was staffed by economists, mainly expatriates.
> They were responsible for manpower planning and
> development, among other things. It was clear to ONDP that
> Zambia was seriously short of educated people at independence.
> It was equally clear to them that the shortfall could be made up
> within a few years after which the employment market would
> soon reach saturation point. Thus the ONDP challenged both
> the scale and pace at which John Mwanakatwe proposed to
> expand the education system. "By building all these schools",
> they argued, "you are swallowing up resources which are
> needed elsewhere. Moreover, you are educating people for
> unemployment".

However, the response of the Ministry of Education to
this challenge is described by Peter Snelson thus:-

> There were those in the ministry who sympathized with the
> ONDP case. They included the minister's adviser on
> development, Alan Chorlton, director of education for
> Oxfordshire whose services were made available by UNESCO.
> Alan's main task was to advise on the setting up of a planning
> unit within the Ministry. It was a formidable task, made no
> easier for Alan by the minister's reluctance to consult him
> regularly. After the tremendous expansion of facilities which
> had taken place at independence, Chorlton urged that there
> should be a breathing space, a period of consolidation, before
> the programme of rapid growth was resumed. John
> Mwanakatwe would have none of this. Politically and on
> grounds of social justice, he had a strong case. For his cabinet

colleagues, education, like motherhood and apple pie, was a good thing.

They readily accepted his policy formulation which would ensure that one third of primary school leavers would proceed to Form 1; that two thirds of the output from Form 2 would go on to senior secondary: and boarding fees in non-scheduled secondary schools should be abolished.

With the government's policy of rapid expansion of education facilities after independence, the demand for more properly trained primary school teachers was inevitable. Similarly, the expansion of secondary education also accelerated the need to recruit more expatriate teachers. Therefore, when planning the expansion of primary and secondary schools, arrangements were made for the reorganization of the system of training teachers in Zambia. The existing teacher training colleges were not expected to produce the required number of teachers for primary schools. Yet the education planners designed the expansion programme on the assumption that existing standards could be maintained in schools. Two new teacher training colleges were under construction in 1965. However, they were not expected to increase the supply of primary school teachers significantly.

Unlike in many countries in Africa, reliance on unqualified teachers to teach in Zambian primary schools was minimal at independence. For example, in 1962 as many as 11,766 teachers in a teaching force of 24,384 in primary schools in Ghana had received no training at all. In the Eastern Region of Nigeria in that year, 13,393 were trained and 26,273 were untrained teachers. Tanganyika's profile in this respect was excellent. All teachers (10,273) serving in primary schools in 1962 were trained. Northern Rhodesia's profile was very good, too, in 1962. In that year, out of a total teaching force of 6,027 only 174 were untrained.[*]

---

[*] See DG Burns, *African Education: An Introductory Survey of Education in Commonwealth Countries*, London, OUP, 1965, p. 149.

159

The anticipated shortage of teachers for primary and secondary schools was addressed in three ways. Firstly, the government decided to offer a one year residential course to students entering teacher training colleges at the beginning of 1965, followed by one year in schools as "student teachers". This novel scheme of training teachers for primary schools was necessary to meet the anticipated shortage of teachers without employing too many untrained men and women and consequently lowering the standard of teaching in primary schools. The scheme worked satisfactorily. Following the accelerated programme of primary school expansion in 1965, nearly 1,000 additional teachers were required to staff both new and old primary schools at the beginning of 1966. The supply of teachers at the beginning of the first term in 1966 was adequate. A crisis was averted in that year and in subsequent years.

However, the one year residential course was not intended to be a permanent form of training teachers in Zambia. It was only an interim scheme for providing qualified or, at least, semi-qualified teachers for primary schools during the period of rapid expansion of primary education and while the expansion of facilities for training teachers was taking place.

At independence it was estimated that the number of Zambian African graduates was at not more than one hundred. The number of Africans with the Ordinary Level School Certificates was less than one thousand. Personnel possessing other professional qualifications were likewise scarce. Zambia at independence had a critical shortage of educated and trained manpower. With the government poised to initiate ambitious development programmes, the critical shortage of high level manpower was of great concern. Before independence, successful secondary school leavers proceeded to the University of Rhodesia and Nyasaland in Southern Rhodesia (now Zimbabwe) for higher education on government scholarships. Others proceeded to Makerere University in Uganda or to universities elsewhere in Africa or overseas on government scholarships. Following the dissolution of the Federation of Rhodesia and Nyasaland, it was impossible to guarantee places at the university in Southern Rhodesia for African students from Zambia. Therefore, after 31 December 1963, the need to explore the possibility of establishing a university became urgent. Kenneth Kaunda became the first prime minister in Zambia on 23 January 1964. As minister of education in the new government, I included this subject among my priorities for consideration. In February 1964, I submitted to the government the main recommendations of a commission, headed by Sir John Lockwood, a former vice chancellor of London University. In the report, the commission recommended the establishment of a university locally as soon as possible. The commission further recommended a four year first degree course with an entrance qualification based on O level passes. It also recommended that the proposed university would be fully fledged and not affiliated to another university. Therefore, the commission recommended the establishment of a university of full degree awarding status.

At first, it was difficult to persuade ministers to accept all the recommendations of the commission headed by Sir John Lockwood. Some ministers, supported by conservative bureaucrats, opposed vehemently the lowering of entrance qualification to the proposed university, notwithstanding that a four year first degree course was to be introduced at the same time. However, the proposal was accepted once they realized that some universities in western countries accepted O level passes as a suitable qualification for the four year degree courses. The entrance qualification to British universities for the three year degree courses based on A level passes was by no means universal. The Lockwood recommendations meant that the new university would start with the advantage of offering its own degrees and diplomas, working out its own curricula and syllabuses. In the view of the commission, international recognition for its courses and degrees solely depended in the final analysis upon the quality of its products; the depth of the degree courses and the width of the teaching and the quality of the graduates themselves. Lockwood's real objectives were that the new university should be organized to meet the real needs of the nation.

The University of Zambia opened its doors to students early in 1966. It was officially inaugurated in March when its first chancellor, Dr Kenneth Kaunda, president of the Republic of Zambia, was installed at a colourful ceremony. The installation of Dr Kenneth Kaunda as chancellor of the University of Zambia was attended by Mwalimu Julius K Nyerere, president of the United Republic of Tanzania. Thirty five years down the road, the University of Zambia can be said to have achieved its mission as "a seat of learning, a treasure house of knowledge, and a creative centre of research".[*]

The University of Zambia was built over the years with funds provided by the government. However, initially the government undertook to provide half the capital costs. The United Kingdom government made a contribution of one million pounds to the cost of building the new university and small amounts came from other countries. Contributions were received from men and women of goodwill from all walks of life in Zambia who appreciated the value of the new university to the country. A successful fundraising campaign was headed at the national level by Clifford Little, formerly the principal of Munali Secondary School and subsequently permanent secretary in the Ministry of African Education before his retirement. School children with their teachers organised fundraising campaigns. The funds raised through the appeal demonstrated the goodwill of the children and their parents to work with the new university. Peter Snelson described graphically in his book *To Independence and Beyond* the part played by school children in raising funds for the construction of the university:

> The appeal, which raised half a million pounds, reached the smallest village in the most remote part of the country. Thousands of school children played their parts by holding

---

[*] Report on the Development of a University in Northern Rhodesia 1963.

concerts, organizing flag days and selling badges. The minister used his speeches to thank the children and their parents for the contribution they were making to the appeal.

Historically, the establishment of the university was an event of great significance to the nation, for it was the university which would ultimately make Zambia self-sufficient in high level manpower. Zambia would no longer be able to look to universities such as Fort Hare, Makerere and Roma for training of its professional men and women.

I have always looked back with satisfaction at the efforts we made to establish a university in the early years of the independence of our country. The government's decision to accord priority to the construction of a university was justified. During the first six years, the growth of the University of Zambia was spectacular. Indeed, few universities in Africa surpassed at that time the rate of expansion of physical facilities for staff and students which was achieved at the University of Zambia. A steady increase in the enrolment of fulltime and part-time students was maintained. To sustain such a rapid rate of development, the government was obliged to provide more funds each year at considerable sacrifice to other services such as health and agriculture. Of course, some informed observers questioned the project's high cost to the nation. It was a criticism which I was always comfortable to rebut effectively both in Parliament and outside.

In June 1971, five years after the first academic session was opened, the academic staff of the university numbered 268. It was composed of some 29 different nationalities. Only 23 or 8.6 per cent of the academic staff were Zambians. The rest came from other parts of the world. From its inception, a very high standard in the qualifications of the university's teaching force was maintained. Among the different nationalities represented on the academic staff were Indians, South Africans, New Zealanders, Canadians, British and Americans. In 1967, I undertook a goodwill mission to the Soviet Union to prepare for recruitment of suitable lecturers for the university. I insisted in discussions with officials in the Ministry of Higher Education in Moscow that it was desirable for an applicant to have sufficient experience and knowledge to teach effectively and also to be sufficiently proficient in both spoken and written English. Otherwise, an applicant who was unable to satisfy these conditions would fail the selection test. I parried insinuations that I had been influenced by advisers with a colonial mentality. Yet I was accompanied by Francis Jere during the discussions in Moscow. He was the under-secretary in the Ministry of Education responsible for administration generally and staff recruitment in particular. To us it was obvious that a lecturer from the Soviet Union would not teach students effectively, whatever his or her qualifications and experience, unless the lecturer was sufficiently competent in both spoken and written English. That condition was not negotiable. The lecturers we recruited in subsequent years from the Soviet Union fulfilled this condition satisfactorily.

In 1968, speaking at the opening of the academic year, the first vice chancellor of the University of Zambia, Professor Douglas Anglin, expressed satisfaction with the high standard in the qualifications of the university's teaching force. He expressed his satisfaction thus:

> The students of the university can regard themselves as fortunate indeed in the lecturers who are teaching them. As a body the staff of the University of Zambia is one in which any university would be justly proud. This is a point that many have been slow to appreciate.

About twenty five years later, the university had grown tremendously in terms of the number of students enrolled for undergraduate studies, the size of the teaching staff and the number of research personnel. In 1994, without including part-time undergraduates, the student enrolment was 3,784 comprising 2,943 male full-time undergraduates and 841 female undergraduate full-time students. Yet the first intake of

164

undergraduate full-time students was only 300 in 1966. In spite of the financial difficulties the university began to experience from the early 1980s, the staffing of the university continued to be satisfactory. As minister of education, I was instrumental in persuading a renowned Zambian scholar, Dr Lameck Goma, to take up a senior position in the University of Zambia after its establishment in 1965. A graduate of Fort Hare University in South Africa, Cambridge University and University of London, he was a lecturer at the University of Ghana, Legon, when the University of Zambia opened its doors for the first intake of undergraduate students in March 1966. His response, through the chairman of the Council of the University of Zambia, was positive. He was appointed deputy vice chancellor subsequently. In 1969, he launched a plan for accelerated Zambianisation of the university staff with the approval of the Council. The Staff Development Programme was intended primarily for promising young Zambian graduates with a first degree to proceed for postgraduate studies overseas after training at the university for at least one year. This programme was an outstanding success.

At independence in 1964, the majority of teachers in secondary schools were expatriates recruited mainly from the United Kingdom. It was recognized that the establishment of a fully-fledged local university would contribute substantially to the production of graduates to teach in secondary schools. Following the post-independence expansion of facilities for secondary education, the demand for graduate teachers increased considerably. Therefore, in planning the development of education in the early years, the establishment of the School of Education was accorded the priority it deserved. Consequently, in 1994 there were 799 full-time students enrolled as undergraduates in the School of Education, second only to the School of Humanities and Social Sciences with 917 fulltime undergraduate students. The School of Natural Sciences was the third with a total of 731 full-time undergraduate students. The 1994 enrolment figures for full-time undergraduate students show that the vision of the founding fathers of our nation to establish a local university was not trivial or empty. By 1994 the university was widely recognized. In that year, it had links with several universities worldwide including the University of Cape Town in Southern Africa, Royal Institute of Technology in Sweden, University of Dar es Salaam, Constance University in Germany and Universities of Leeds, Manchester, Bristol, Birmingham and a few others in the United Kingdom.

Undoubtedly, the establishment of the University of Zambia after independence was one of the greatest achievements of Dr Kenneth Kaunda's administration during the First Republic. It was the culmination of several years of eager expectation on the part of the people of Zambia to found their own higher educational establishment which would function as the peak of the educational ladder for their sons and daughters. At his installation in 1966 as chancellor of the University of Zambia, Dr Kenneth Kaunda, expressed his feelings in these words:

> For years I have looked forward to the day when a university would emerge in this country .... But the creation of the university is much more than a matter of sentiment with me. Many of our hopes for the future of our land are wrapped up in this institution. Without it, we cannot hope to become the nation we want to be.

I feel proud to have participated in the establishment of this successful institution of higher learning in our country.

During one of many meetings with officials in my ministry about proposals we had received from the planning office for changes to the education programme, the permanent secretary requested me to allow him to take an urgent call in his office. Later, he reported that there was serious unrest among teachers in the Copperbelt Province. In fact, reports of unrest had filtered through to us in the ministry from other parts of the country. However, from the report received from the provincial education officer, the situation was volatile in the Copperbelt Province. There the teachers were already flexing their muscles for a showdown with the government. That was something we abhorred in the ministry, especially at a time when we longed for the peace and stability necessary to effect meaningful development. Our officials on the ground felt that my presence there was required to meet the teachers before any harm was done. I accepted the invitation to visit the Copperbelt Province. In fact, some teachers had already begun canvassing leaders of the Zambia National Union of Teachers to organize countrywide elections if their demands were rejected by the government.

I had no doubt whatsoever that teachers countrywide had genuine grievances. UNIP's landslide victory in the presidential and parliamentary elections in January 1964 was gained on a wave of promises contained in its manifesto. Teachers were among the most ardent supporters of UNIP. UNIP undertook generally once it came to power to abolish racial discrimination, increase job opportunities, improve wages, provide more and better schools, more hospitals and cheaper food. During the political campaign for the 1964 elections, people's expectations were aroused for better living conditions after independence. Therefore they looked forward to big salary increases and better teachers' houses. When new salary scales were introduced, they did not equal their expectations and teachers were bitterly disappointed. The new salary scales for African teachers did not narrow the differential between existing salaries for European teachers and salaries for African teachers with equal qualifications. Yet the erstwhile education systems for blacks and whites were integrated. The teachers were made to believe by some people, probably my rivals who had expected appointment to the education portfolio, that I was responsible for their plight – in short, that I was indifferent and that I had chosen to neglect them.

In these circumstances Peter Snelson, the provincial education officer, invited me to meet representatives of the Zambia National Union of Teachers in Ndola to state the government's position. I devised a simple strategy for the meeting. Firstly, I was prepared to concede that some of the grievances of the African teachers were genuine. For example, no one in government denied the fact that teachers' salaries were still too low. Secondly, there were other government employees, such as civil servants, whose salaries also required upward revision because they were too low. Thirdly, although the government sympathized with teachers, funds were not available immediately to redress their grievances. I intended to appeal to representatives of the teachers union to remember that Rome was not built in a day! In any event, I also had an obligation to emphasise that the government was not prepared to tolerate indiscipline among teachers who were expected to set a good example.

As I anticipated, on the basis of the strategy I had devised for the meeting in Ndola with representatives of the teachers union, the meeting was successful. Peter Snelson attended the meeting. The representatives of the Zambia National Union of Teachers undertook to advise their members to remain patient and avoid misconduct which might put the reputation of the teachers union into disrepute. In *To Independence and Beyond*, Peter Snelson recollects the events leading to that meeting as follows:

> The National Union of Teachers began to talk of a strike. When I met their provincial committee they made it clear that they had no quarrel with me. They accepted that it was government which had determined the new salary scales and that it was the minister who had decided to allot comparatively small sums of money for teachers' housing. At my request, John Mwanakatwe came to Ndola to meet the teachers' representatives. He could speak to them in a way in which I would not have dared. Always polite and moderate in tone, he nevertheless left no one in any doubt that Kenneth Kaunda's government would not put up with any nonsense. All sections of the community were required to make sacrifices, he said. Teachers were fortunate to be employed and to be so well paid. When resources permitted, teachers' houses would be improved. In the meantime, other requirements merited higher

priority. He wished to hear no more talk of possible strike action which he would regard as sabotage and which would result in serious consequences.

For the time being, at least, the teachers accepted defeat .... (but) A little more carrot and a little less stick was the best way of securing their cooperation.

At independence Kenneth Kaunda's new government chose One Zambia One Nation as the motto of our country. It was chosen in order to promote national unity in the land. Zambia was always a multi-tribal, multi-cultural country. Therefore, after independence the government attached great importance to the task of promoting national consciousness throughout the country. It was in the schools where the ideals of national consciousness and national identity would be inculcated among school children. It was accepted among educators that one of the most important and effective ways of promoting national consciousness was the use of the national anthem in all types of schools and institutions. Therefore, in all our schools students were encouraged to sing the national anthem and to relate the anthem to the national hopes and ideals. In the same way, without the institution of the national flag, the ideal of a united and coherent nation would be completely frustrated for there would be no basis for common outlook. The national flag occupies an important role in building a sense of unity and a sense of loyalty to the nation.

Accordingly, appropriate instructions were given to schools and relevant institutions on the rules and regulations for singing the national anthem and saluting the national flag. It was not the intention of the government that singing the national anthem and saluting the national flag should have a religious significance, the government was concerned only with the promotion of national consciousness and national unity. It was expected that all those objectives were acceptable to reasonable parents of school children. I attached importance as a politician to my role in discouraging tribalism in the country. When I was privileged to address an audience on school speech days, often I chose the theme of national unity. On such occasions, I made efforts to encourage children in the presence of their parents to think in national terms rather than in provincial or tribal terms. In the early years after independence, a number of primary school leavers from each province were sent to other provinces for their secondary education. Although this scheme did not benefit many students, nonetheless it demonstrated the government's determination to promote national consciousness and national unity among students in our schools and learning institutions.

Unfortunately, children of members of the Jehovah's Witnesses sect were not allowed by their parents to sing the national anthem or salute the national flag. They took a firm stand because their religion forbade participation in singing the national anthem and saluting the national flag. Eventually, protests of members of the Jehovah's Witnesses sect were brought to my attention for consideration. I took the view that since education was not compulsory, parents were free to withdraw their children from school if they did not like what was taught. Otherwise, I took a firm stand on the basis of the law which allowed the government to prescribe what was to be taught. Therefore, the school authorities were free to expel children of the Jehovah's Witnesses sect who refused to obey the school rules and regulations. Many Watch Tower children chose to obey their parents rather than their teachers. Consequently, first they were suspended from school. Later, without any proof of penitence, they were expelled for refusing to comply with the regulations on the anthem and the flag.

Members of the Watch Tower sect, as they were sometimes called, were dissatisfied with the expulsion of their children from school. They brought a test case to the High Court by way of a petition protesting against one of the expulsions. In the petition, the petitioner maintained that his expulsion infringed his constitutional right of freedom of religion and freedom of conscience. Such expulsion was null and void. On the other hand the respondent argued that the government did not attach a religious significance to either of the two actions, singing of the national anthem or saluting the national flag; and that the government was concerned only with the promotion of national consciousness and national unity.

The petition was heard in the High Court. The chief justice ruled that the regulations were reasonable. His ruling in favour of the respondent, namely the attorney-general of Zambia, was received with great relief and satisfaction in the Ministry of Education. The favourable ruling would enable us to continue with the most important nation building effort after independence in 1964 – the promotion of national consciousness and national unity among boys and girls in our schools. It was important to encourage children at an early age to think in national, rather than provincial or tribal terms. I had personally participated in drafting the Education (Primary and Secondary Schools) Regulations of 1966 which were promulgated under the Education Act of 1966. The minister was conferred with legal power to require children to sing the national anthem and to salute the national flag. It was gratifying to me personally and officials in the Ministry of Education that the High Court's ruling absolved us from blame that the constitutional rights of the children of the Watch Tower sect expelled from schools were infringed.

It has been said quite often and not without justification that in African political life, the disruptive influence of tribalism is rarely far from the surface. The inter-tribal conflicts which rocked UNIP in 1967 and in years thereafter undoubtedly retarded the rate of development which started in January 1964. The post independence struggle for political power in UNIP started early in 1967. The Central Committee, the National Council and the General Conference were the three most important organs of UNIP under the 1967 constitution. Under the constitution, the triennial conference of the party was due to be held in August 1967 at Mulungushi near Kabwe for the election of eight key members of the Central Committee. Kaunda himself had been returned unopposed. Of the seven contested seats, three were particularly important – those of the national vice president, the national secretary and the national treasurer. In the past, members of the Central Committee ran for office on a balanced team ticket which was endorsed by the conference. For the 1967 party elections, Kaunda had announced that all Central Committee posts would be contested on an individual basis.

The president's decision was in line with the process of democratisation of all party organs. Unfortunately, this decision to allow free competition for Central Committee posts – the most powerful party organ – produced intense and bitter inter-tribal rivalry. There had been tribalistic tendencies among some members from the time UNIP was formed. However, factionalism and divisions based on tribal lines were accentuated after the party elections in August, 1967. Two main groups were involved in the elections. One camp was a primarily Bemba-Tonga-speaking alliance which was ostensibly led by Simon Kapwepwe. He was the foreign minister in the government and the incumbent UNIP national treasurer. The other camp was ostensibly led by Reuben Kamanga, the national vice-president and the incumbent vice president of the party. The Kamanga-led camp was primarily a Lozi-Nyanja-speaking alliance. During the months preceding the General Conference, the activists in each engaged in a bitter campaign against their opponents. UNIP was almost torn apart by the intense sectionalism of the leaders and their followers. They indulged in rumour mongering and false accusations in order to discredit their opponents. For example, the Kapwepwe group accused their opponents of being merely intellectuals and CIA agents. On the other hand, the Kamanga group responded by accusing the Bemba-Tonga alliance of being puppets of the communists.

At first, I was completely unaware of the existence of these two main tribal factions which were in existence for several months before the elections. All my political friends and enemies knew that I abhorred tribalism in my life and in all my activities. That was probably the explanation of the fact that although I am a northerner by origin, no one had tried to canvass my support for the Bemba-Tonga-speaking alliance for I would have rebuffed such an appeal with scorn. In fact, some of the more irresponsible activists in the Bemba-Tonga-speaking alliance spread a false rumour that my sympathy in the battle of the giant tribal groups for power was with the Lozi-Nyanja-speaking alliance. It was a figment of their imagination that I supported the Lozi-Nyanja-speaking alliance because its leader, Reuben Kamanga, was my personal friend. The rumour spread like wildfire at the General Conference at Mulungushi. It became a cause of concern to me in terms of my own safety and my integrity. The party president instituted inquiries which revealed the identity of the rumour-monger. He was summoned to a meeting which was attended by both Kapwepwe and Kamanga and chaired by the party president. I was present at the meeting as the complainant. The mischievous activist from the Bemba-Tonga alliance apologized to me and to the party president for his misbehaviour. He also apologized to Mr Kapwepwe whom he had not consulted when he embarked on rumour-mongering expecting to gain sympathy and support for his group from party activists at the General Conference.

When the results of the Central Committee elections were announced at Mulungushi, the Kapwepwe group had won all the contested seats except one. The Lozi-Nyanja alliance was infuriated by the results. The members of the Lozi-Nyanja alliance cried foul. They thought that such ignominious election results showed that their rivals had rigged the elections. They also claimed unfairness on the ground that the basis of representation at the General Conference gave an inbuilt advantage to the Bemba-Tonga alliance. When the delegates to the conference returned to their respective stations, the split within UNIP was serious. The party's operations were adversely affected because the Central Committee lacked material unity. Its effectiveness was reduced. To avert a crisis, President Kaunda appointed a committee of enquiry into the allegations of serious irregularities in the party elections at Mulungushi. The chief

173

justice was the chairman of the committee of enquiry assisted by at least two independent observers. He conducted the enquiry expeditiously and reported his findings to President Kaunda. He stated in the report that a recount of the votes showed that the votes had been miscounted at Mulungushi but that the successful candidates had in fact received the most votes.

Consequently, President Kaunda was faced with a very difficult and delicate situation. Was he going to side with the losers in the elections who demanded nullification of the results completely or accept the election results which the chief justice had confirmed following a recount of votes? The party president decided to accept the election results. He then proceeded to reshuffle his entire cabinet following the appointment of Kapwepwe as his new deputy in UNIP. Kapwepwe became vice president of Zambia. Other cabinet appointments reflected his respect for the elective principle, as expressed at Mulungushi. After according senior posts in the cabinet to suitable newly elected members of the Central Committee, Kaunda applied his skill in balancing the various factions within the party in making other appointments to the Central Committee and the cabinet.

The factional wounds evident at Mulungushi during the party elections were too deep to heal rapidly. In fact, incidents of personal recriminations with tribal and provincial overtones increased considerably. These open quarrels among leaders became a cause of embarrassment and concern to the party's leadership. The Central Committee called a meeting of the National Council to be held in Lusaka in February 1968. Members of the National Council hardly concentrated on the business of the meetings. Those who belonged to tribal or factional groups seized every opportunity to cast aspersions on their opponents without provocation or justification. Consequently, Kaunda became disgusted. When the die-hard tribalists refused to heed his appeal for calm and restraint in their utterances, a disgusted Kaunda announced his resignation and took all participants in the meeting by surprise. The announcement sent shock waves to everyone in the hall in Chilenje township. Both men and women started wailing uncontrollably after President Kaunda stormed out of the hall accompanied by his aides. Then the lights went off. Few men and women dared to leave the hall in darkness, afraid that they might step on the toes of someone with his dagger already drawn. That was Kaunda's instinctive reaction to a power struggle within UNIP which had been waged viciously along tribal, racial and provincial lines. He had been shocked to observe the "spate of hate" among his colleagues.

Fortunately, Kaunda did not immediately follow up the announcement with the constitutional step of submitting his resignation in writing to the chief justice. That night, the 15th February 1968, when the country was technically without a national president, several prominent religious and secular leaders called on President Kaunda at State House to persuade him to withdraw his resignation. He agreed. It is probably this unexpected and shocking act of Kaunda at the National Council in February 1968 which sobered the hardcore tribalists to restrain themselves in their activities. After that episode, Kaunda managed to reunite UNIP behind him in preparation for the first general election after independence. For me the episode had a special lesson – that there was some truth in the proverbial saying that politics was a dirty game! My wife always reminded me that it was also a thankless job!

In the reshuffle of the cabinet after the controversial UNIP elections, I was moved to the Ministry of Lands and Mines. Many people thought that I was demoted by Kaunda because I had no political base, although the good work I had done in the Ministry of Education was widely acknowledged. However, although the Lands and Mines portfolio was less prestigious, I nonetheless looked forward enthusiastically to the challenge of monitoring and guiding the operations of the copper mines which were privately owned by world renowned mining companies. I did not hesitate to confess that I was going to miss ministerial responsibility for education. Even more importantly that I was

175

going to miss colleagues I had worked with happily and successfully as my junior ministers, namely William Nkhanza and Henry Thornicroft and, of course, both senior and junior civil servants. But it was my sincere belief that a period of about four continuous years in a ministry in a political position was long enough to see the fruits of one's labour. Therefore, I was ready to face new challenges in the Ministry of Lands and Mines.

On the other hand, my successor was unhappy to be moved from the undoubtedly prestigious Ministry of Finance to the Ministry of Education. Consequently, he was not enthusiastic at first to accept the new portfolio. Arthur Wina had teamed up with Reuben Kamanga who led the Lozi-Tonga-speaking alliance in the party elections at the Mulungushi general conference in August 1967. He was a Lozi and the party's treasurer. He lost in the election to Elijah Mudenda, who was a prominent member of the Kapwepwe-led Bemba-Tonga-speaking alliance. Mudenda was moved in the reshuffle to the Ministry of Finance and Wina was consequently moved to the Ministry of Education. It is said Wina was deeply hurt by his move from Finance to Education. After a period of about ten days, Arthur Wina reported at the Ministry of Education for duty, a comfortable, relaxed figure, keen and intelligent and with a rich sense of humour. In the reshuffle of the cabinet, Reuben Kamanga of the Eastern Province, who had lost his position of national vice president and party vice-president to Kapwepwe, accepted the Ministry of Foreign Affairs portfolio.

Within a few weeks after the reshuffle of the cabinet and before I settled down completely in the Ministry of Lands and Mines, I decided to join a local golf club – the Chainama Golf Club – in order to learn how to play golf. The golf club was only ten minutes' drive from our residence in Kabulonga. While in the Ministry of Education, I occasionally played tennis with friends at State House. However, the games were played infrequently. It was not always convenient to arrange a game of tennis. In reality there was a special reason why I was anxious to join the Chainama Golf Club. Yes, I was forty one years old in 1967 and I was getting anxious to find a suitable game to play which was less strenuous than tennis. The tribal conflicts which had characterized the party elections at Mulungushi in August 1967 left me completely disillusioned about finding happiness in a political career. Joining the golf club at Chainama provided an opportunity of fraternizing with political and non-political fellow men drawn from various walks of life – the professions, business, diplomacy and the civil service. To my surprise some of my former students at Munali were prominent golf players at Chainama when I joined the club in 1967. Among them I recall Edward Shamwana, Ephraim Chibwe and Bruce Munyama. As months went by my standard of playing golf improved – thanks to my former students at Chainama who were always ready to coach me without charging fees.

The word soon went around that a minister in Kaunda's government was a regular golf player at Chainama. I was later joined by another cabinet minister – Grey Zulu – not just as a member or spectator but as an active golf player. Zulu was a respected veteran politician whom Kaunda had appointed with me to sit on the Judge Whelan Commission of Inquiry into the Unrest on the Copperbelt in 1963. A quiet spoken and dignified gentleman, I had always known him as balanced and trustworthy. He had impressed me as a person whose interest in life was to render service to our people rather than the pomp and trappings of political power. That was the reason why Kaunda trusted him. Often at Chainama during golf competitions, Zulu and I partnered. We sometimes won prizes. Apart from the relaxation derived from playing golf, it was also a good form of exercise, especially when we were able to play eighteen holes in one day, sometimes a total of thirty six holes over the weekend.

Subsequently, President Kaunda heard about our exploits at Chainama Golf Club. In less than two years after joining the golf club at Chainama, Grey Zulu and I were also playing golf at State House. Kaunda had organized the construction of a golf course of nine holes. It was, of course, more convenient for him to play golf within State House grounds when he had time –

which was rare – to relax from his heavy responsibilities as head of state. Grey Zulu and I were among a few privileged ministers in his cabinet who were occasionally invited to play golf with him.

At the beginning of September 1967, I moved to my office in the Ministry of Lands and Mines quite anxious and ready to face new ministerial challenges. I took over responsibility for the portfolio from Grey Zulu, one of my closest friends in the cabinet. This special relationship between us had an advantage. Outside the minister's office and in an informal way, he briefed me on the staff situation and on matters which required urgent attention. He also described a relationship which he had established with the chief executives of the privately owned mining companies. With the written brief the permanent secretary gave me to study, followed by discussions with officials responsible for key departments, I felt quite comfortable that I understood the ministry's role in the government. With the background I was given, it was easy for me to determine my own priorities in the context of our party's manifesto. My first appointment as a full cabinet minister was in the Ministry of Education where I was not a stranger from day one – in terms of knowing the role of the ministry in the government and its programmes and priorities. As an educationist, I readily understood the language of the officials and their advisors. In the Ministry of Lands and Mines I was a complete stranger. Therefore, I did not hesitate to follow the words of advice I was given by an experienced politician on my appointment as a junior minister in 1962. He advised: "whatever you do in the first few days, always do something – preferably something against the advice offered to you; make yourself a nuisance". He then concluded: "the message will soon get round that you are not there to be taken for granted".

Experience shows that civil servants rarely give ill-conceived advice to their ministers. That is why they are often right. Such advice is useful to a person who takes his decisions with care knowing that the instructions he gives are carefully recorded for any subsequent inquiry when things go wrong. For the first time, I was obliged to work with some civil servants whose performance was unsatisfactory and a disgrace to the public service. While I could tolerate civil servants whose ability to express themselves clearly and accurately in English was limited, the story was different when indecision was their weakness. That I was not prepared to tolerate. The permanent secretary and senior civil servants were expected to make decisions followed up with appropriate action. A civil servant's decision might be totally wrong and unacceptable on a given issue. Nonetheless, such a civil servant's performance would be well above the pass mark provided he had carefully considered the issues involved in the matter followed by a recommendation, if necessary, for determination by the final arbiter.

Failure to make decisions was not a weakness of civil servants only. It was a weakness at the political level also. I recall on many occasions during my political career reading files which revealed failure by ministers to make decisions on recommendations received from civil servants. However difficult or sensitive an issue might be, a decision has to be made in order to determine the way forward. For example, a civil servant may, after analysis of an issue, set out in a recommendation three options for the way forward. If in the minute on the file the civil servant requests a minister to state in writing the option preferred, it would be unsatisfactory for the minister to write on the file "any of these options is acceptable". A minister will be equally guilty of indecision to invite the civil servant concerned to his office for a discussion and record on the file later: "proceed on the basis of our discussion of your recommendation". In the event of any variation to the civil servant's original recommendation, the minister is obliged to write a minute recording his final decision after the discussion.

At the Ministry of Education, on the whole I had a capable team of officers at the headquarters. in addition, through the

179

good offices of UNESCO, the team included Alan Chorlton as the minister's adviser especially on matters relating to development and the setting up of the planning unit within the ministry. My predecessor had initiated successful negotiations for the employment of an adviser to the minister in the Ministry of Lands and Mines. Professor John Mars held this position when I assumed the portfolio of Lands and Mines. An economist with many years of experience in advisory positions at the Economic Commission for Africa (ECA) headquarters in Addis Ababa and State House in Lusaka, he was eminently suitable for this position. Above all, he was a hard worker. His briefs were comprehensive and well researched. After reading a brief written by Professor Mars for a meeting with the hard-nosed representatives of the privately owned giant copper mines, I was always confident of successful discussions from the government's point of view. Furthermore, Professor Mars was a prolific writer whose papers senior officials had a tendency to disregard as irrelevant. He had leftwing views and betrayed in most of his arguments a suspicion of the motives of capitalists. My confidence in the efforts of Professor Mars increased and I enjoyed working with him immensely.

When I assumed responsibility for the new ministry, the first priority was to intensify efforts to increase production of coal locally. To maintain copper production on the Copperbelt, the availability of petroleum products and coal was essential. On 11 November 1965, Ian Smith, prime minister of Southern Rhodesia, had unilaterally declared his country to be independent from Britain. Consequently, Smith's UDI dealt a devastating blow to the Zambian economy. At the time of UDI, Zambia imported 90 per cent of her supplies of petrol, oil and lubricants via Rhodesia. Zambian coal consumption at that time was approximately 110 short tons per month. About 50 per cent was used by the copper industry and about 30 per cent by the railways. Nearly all the coal supplies for consumption in Zambia was railed from Wankie colliery in Southern Rhodesia. The coal mine at Wankie was owned by Anglo American Corporation which also owned mines in Zambia.

After UDI the reliability of coal supplies from Southern Rhodesia for use in Zambia, especially in the Copperbelt mines became questionable. Throughout my term of office in the Ministry of Lands and Mines, we concentrated our efforts on locating new coal deposits in Zambia. The Department of Geological Survey intensified efforts to locate coal where the deposits were large enough to sustain mining operations over a long period. The first coal mining operations in Zambia started in 1965 at Nkandabwe in the Gwembe Valley in Southern Province. Unfortunately, the Nkandabwe coal was inferior to the Wankie coal in quality for use in mining operations. In comparison to its low calorific value and high ash content, Wankie coal was preferable, especially for smelting purposes.

The continued efforts of our geologists produced good results. They discovered a much better and larger coalfield at Maamba in the Gwembe Valley in 1968. Consequently, we concentrated our resources on the development of the Maamba coal mine. It was wholly owned by the Zambian government. It began to produce coal in the same year. We successfully installed a coal washing plant at Maamba with the assistance of the French government in order to improve the quality of coal. By the end of 1970, the quality of coal exported to the mines on the Copperbelt from Maamba was almost as good as coal imported from Wankie. By 1972, through proper planning and timely implementation, the production of coal from Maamba colliery was actually greater than domestic consumption. Our ministry ensured the survival of our country in the event of an attempt by the Smith regime in Southern Rhodesia to destroy the economy of Zambia.

At independence Zambia possessed a great economic asset, namely its giant copper mining industry. It accounted for twelve per cent of world production. Between 1964 and 1968, the copper mining industry alone contributed about ninety three per cent of the total value of Zambian exports, about sixty per cent of central government revenues and approximately forty four per cent of net domestic products. Quite clearly, the mining industry was the life blood of the nation. It was absolutely essential to the country's economic survival. This important industry was controlled by two giant mining companies – Anglo American Corporation of South Africa Ltd. and the Roan Selection Trust group – until 1970 when the Zambian government acquired a fifty one per cent interest in the ownership of all the operating mines. Before 1970 these two foreign groups were in complete control of the policies and management of their companies without interference from the government and its agents. On my assumption of the portfolio of Lands and Mines, I attached urgency to a study of ways and means of promoting cooperation with the foreign mining companies to enable the government to know at all times the problems or difficulties confronting them and suggesting solutions where possible. The focus of the study would be on finding mutually convenient ways and means for the government's participation in the formulation of major policies by the mining companies.

Eventually, we successfully established a useful rapport between the chief executives of Anglo American Corporation of South Africa and the Roan Selection Trust group. Meetings were held regularly with them to discuss management and other problems related to mining operations. In this way, for the first time since independence, the government was regularly informed about activities in the copper mining industry. James Reed was the chief executive of the Roan Selection Trust group and Murray Hofmeyer the chief executive of Anglo American Corporation of South Africa Ltd. Throughout my tenure of office as cabinet minister responsible for the portfolio from August 1967 to December 1968, my relationship with them was so cordial that we always spoke to each other on first name basis. However, I recall once having a brush with one of them – James Reed who was the more elderly of the two men.

Early in 1968, I received a report from my officials on the lack of forward linkages in respect of copper produced in

Zambia. I attached urgency to the need to explore a suitable method of using some of the copper we produced as an input for domestic industries. After studying the report, I invited at short notice the chief executives of the two leading mining companies to attend a meeting in my office to discuss the report. Apparently, James Reed had taken exception to the short notice I gave them to attend the meeting in my office. On their arrival at the ministry's headquarters, we exchanged greetings in the usual way. Before the meeting started, he made a joke I did not like. He asked: "Is the minister entitled to act like a schoolmaster who summons students to his office at any time?" "Very well", I said. "If you think that I have acted unreasonably, feel free to go away now. I will continue the meeting without you". He thought for a moment or two before speaking. He then said "I'll stay and attend the meeting. After all, mine was not a serious remark. It was only a joke". We eventually settled down and held the consultative meeting in a cordial atmosphere. That was the first and last occasion I felt obliged to assert my ministerial authority in a rather harsh and unpleasant manner. In my dealings later with the chief executives of the two giant mining companies, the Roan Selection Trust group and Anglo American Corporation of Southern Africa, none of them indulged in making jokes in my presence!

In our discussion, it was agreed that the absence of a metal fabricating industry in Zambia at independence was unfortunate although quite understandable. In the past, the mining companies were content with the export of copper in blister or refined form only. No serious thought was given before independence to the use of copper as an input for domestic industries. In the discussions at this and subsequent meetings, it was agreed that the formulation of a metal fabricating company to produce electrical wire in Zambia was desirable. Simultaneously, it was also necessary to explore the development of an export market within the neighbouring countries for the products of such a company. The absence of a fabricating industry which would have added value to the extraction, smelting and refining stages of copper had constrained the development of positive effects from mining after independence. We held the view in our ministry that the setting up of a metal fabricating industry would increase employment opportunities and save foreign exchange by reducing imports of fabricated copper requirements. Further studies undertaken by the mining companies confirmed the feasibility of establishing a metal fabricating company in Zambia. That is the historical background to the establishment of a company we call *Metal Fabricators of Zambia Limited* today.

At the end of the year 2000, the company was a subsidiary of Phelps Dodge Wire Cable Group which in turn was a subsidiary of Phelps Dodge Corporation. Both companies were incorporated in the United States of America. For the year ended December 2000, the company's trading and profit and loss account reflected its viability even under difficult conditions. It made a profit before tax of twenty three billion Kwacha, nearly double the amount for the previous year. In that year, the average monthly number of persons the company had in employment was 236 and the average remuneration to employees was K500,000.00 per month. The company's donations to worthy charitable causes amounted to nearly K15,000,000. The confidence we had in the recommendation contained in our ministry's study on the feasibility of setting up a local metal fabricating industry was amply justified by the profitability of the operations of *Metal Fabricators of Zambia Limited* from 1962 to 2000. During the ten year period, losses were incurred in 1997 and 1998 only.

During my term of office at the Ministry of Lands and Mines, I discovered that lack of adequate and reliable information made it difficult for my officials to carry out studies on various subjects. Often they relied on information from interested parties such as Anglo American Corporation or Roan Selection Trust. This problem was considered at a conference held in Lusaka in 1967 before my appointment as minister responsible for Lands and Mines. The conference was attended by representatives from four copper producing countries, namely Chile, Peru, Zaire (now the Democratic Republic of Congo) and Zambia. The delegates to this conference decided to establish an organization they called "Inter-Governmental Council of Copper Exporting Countries" (CIPEC). It was formed specifically to coordinate the copper mining policies of the four founding members and to encourage cooperation, thereby reducing the possibility of their exploitation by the more developed copper producing countries such as Canada, the United States of America and the Soviet Union. It was agreed at the inaugural meeting in Lusaka to locate the organisation's headquarters in Paris. It was also agreed to set up the Copper Information Bureau as a wing of CIPEC. Other aims of CIPEC were agreed as follows:-

(a) To harmonise marketing practices among member countries.

(b) To monitor and exchange technological developments in copper mining and processing and to exchange technical know how.

(c) To encourage member countries to add as much value as possible to their copper before exporting the metal.

(d) To encourage the consumption of copper through research and development.

(e) To encourage good relations between copper producing countries and their customers to foster realization of their mutual dependence.

There was some doubt if the private owners of giant mining companies, not only in Zambia but others elsewhere in Chile, Peru or Zaire, were comfortable with the long term objectives of the governments which promoted the formation of CIPEC. The government leaders in CIPEC countries believed that if copper producing countries in the third world failed to harmonise marketing practices, for example, their exploitation was inevitable. Therefore, I was not surprised by the interest taken by one member of parliament when my ministry's estimates of expenditure were debated in the Committee of Supply of the House in March, 1968. Rodney Malcomson, the independent member of parliament for Copperbelt South took a special interest in the proposal to establish the Copper Information Bureau as part of CIPEC with its headquarters in Paris. When he stood up to speak on my ministry's vote during the debate in the Committee of Supply, he claimed that the Copper Information Bureau was unnecessary. He argued that for Zambia in particular all the information on copper production and export of copper that the government might require from time to time was readily available from the copper industry in Zambia. Therefore, it was a waste of the taxpayer's money for Zambia to contribute financially to the setting up of the Copper Information Bureau. His remarks were quite sarcastic. He concluded his argument as follows:-

We have got a copper industry here in Zambia with all the information that the government could possibly need at any time on copper and development of new mines, copper mines and so forth, and why there should be duplication on the part of government, I do not know. Unless it is the mere fact that they are just pursuing and determined to pursue the idea they have in their minds, that time and money grows on trees in this country, and that they are determined to spend that time and money as fast as they can just to show what a powerful and responsible government they are.

There must be hundreds of thousands of pages of information on copper investigation and metal and mineral development in this country. Why not take advantage of them, why not trust the people who know much more than government know about the subject and let the government for a change save themselves some money. However, that may be quite diametrically opposite to their policy and their way of thinking. However, I do think it is a shame and I, as a taxpayer, would ask them to try to use outside sources, the private sources of information sometimes, instead of squandering our money.

In my reply, I chose to wave an olive branch to the member for Copperbelt South. He was a dentist by profession and I had a soft spot for him not least because he was David Bell's father-in-law. David Bell was my superior officer in Livingstone and previously we had played tennis together at Munali. Nevertheless, I had a duty to expose Rodney Malcomson's unjustified prejudice and set the record straight. After all, he was the member for Copperbelt South, a constituency which included white miners and their managers and chief executives who might have given him a biased view of the need to set up the Copper Information Bureau. My contribution to the debate on this subject was as follows:

> First of all, the Metals and Minerals Development Unit is a unit which functions in the ministry at headquarters. Its overall responsibility is to advise the ministry on the policy for the development of minerals and metals throughout the Republic of Zambia. The hon. member is aware that the two copper mining companies have a vested interest, mainly in those areas where they have been allowed to prospect, and to carry out development.

> But the hon. member for Copperbelt South (Mr Malcomson) should also be aware that there are other parts of Zambia which do not fall under the jurisdiction of our two copper mining groups. It is the duty of the government to see and examine very carefully the extent of mineral dispersion in the country and to study possibilities of effective exploitation of our mineral resources.

> In particular, I have been and I am extremely interested in the possibility of encouraging cooperatives in undertaking small mining in the Republic of Zambia. And so, that is the function then of the Metals and Minerals Development Unit. I would add that it is important for the government, anyway, to have its own machinery which it can use to determine and to assess the

work which is being carried out by mining companies.

Now, with regard to the second point, Sir, the Copper Information Bureau is not in my ministry. This is where, perhaps, the hon. member has misunderstood the position. I would agree that if we had a Copper Information Bureau in addition to a Metals and Minerals Development Unit there might be a slight duplication between the two.

The Copper Information Bureau will be set up as part of a CIPEC organization in Paris. CIPEC is the organization that was formed last year following the conference in Lusaka of four copper producing countries. And one wing of CIPEC in Paris will be a Copper Information Bureau.

That reply was sufficient to silence the member who raised the issue hoping to stir a storm in a teacup.

On the occasion of the debate of my ministry's vote in the Committee of Supply, I had a relatively easy time. Most members in the House did not ask difficult questions; nor did they request for information which I was not able to provide on the spot. However, the member for Choma, Edward Nyanga, asked about the government's policy on land repossession in some parts of the country. He referred particularly to the land acquired for white settlers from Africans in the Southern Province without compensation in colonial days. It was a sensitive subject. As a member of the opposition in the House, the debate on my ministry's vote gave him, of course, a golden opportunity to ask difficult questions on the acquisition and distribution of land to landless people in Choma District in particular and the Southern Province generally. He wanted to know if my ministry had any plans to return such land to the people concerned. Of course, his ulterior motive was to embarrass the government, not merely to obtain information about the government's plans for land redistribution in future. His question was phrased as follows:

Mr Nyanga (Choma): Mr Chairman, Sir, I would like to know

from the hon and learned minister of lands and mines, whether he has anything in his plan on the land which was taken off from people during the colonial rule. Because when these people came, the colonialists...

Interruptions
Mr Nyanga: Well I am still going on. They drove some people off from some of this land which they called Crown Land and so forth. Then when we were fighting for our independence we were fighting in order to regain this land back.

Interruptions
Mr Nyanga: Now, are there any plans made that such land will be returned to those who were driven onto some other land when these colonialists came in?

And then further on, Mr Chairman, when we gained our independence, it was said that some of these vacant farms would be divided into plots whereby people could buy and then develop into farms but nothing has been done yet... I do not know whether they have and learned minister of lands and mines was anything in his plans on this? Thank you, Mr Chairman.

I was given the floor by the chairman to reply. I informed the House that the government had appointed the land commissioner specifically to inquire into the problem of vacant or unutilised land and to make appropriate recommendations. At that stage, I was not in a position to anticipate the government's decision on the report of the Land Commission although I assured the House its policy on the issue would be made known to the public at the appropriate time. I then challenged the hon. member to substantiate his statement "about people having been driven away from land" and "to give me examples of the places he had in mind because I was not prepared to answer 'vague' or 'hypothetical' questions". He fell, as I expected, into a trap! He rose and informed the House that "...there were people in Magoye, Choma and other places along the line of rail, who were driven into the hilly parts of the land". He forgot, or did not know, that the white settlers had encroached on land occupied by Africans in other parts of the country far away from the line of rail.

However, before I was given the floor by the chairman to proceed with my reply, another minister rose to his feet to question Edward Nyanga's opposition party, the African National Congress, which had raised more than £300,000 "for what they called the Land Case which they were going to use to fight for land taken away from the Africans and that they would carry the battle right up to the Privy Council". Then he concluded his statement sarcastically thus: "Now, I do not hold any brief for the ANC, but I would be extremely interested to know what happened to that amount of money". His remark was applauded by one hon. member with shouts of "Hear, hear!". The minister of local government and housing, Sikota Wina, inflicted a heavy blow on the hon member for Choma who was apparently unable to explain what happened to the £300,000 collected for the land case. Edward Nyanga was silenced completely.

Nevertheless, I rose again to complete my reply to the question on the land issue. Mr Nyanga had deliberately or inadvertently given the impression that the land issue problem was unique to the Southern Province and in particular to Choma and Magoye districts and other places along the line of rail. I informed the House that it was not only in the Southern Province where colonialists took away the land from Africans. I stated the government's position on the land issue as follows:-

> I want the hon. members to note that it is not only in the Southern Province, where the colonialists took away the land from our people. In Chipata, formerly called Fort Jameson, the same thing was done, in the Northern Province in Mbala District, which I know very well, the same thing was done, and in other parts of Zambia....

> I am not in a position this morning to declare to the country precisely what we shall do in the Southern Province in terms

190

of reclamation of land from which our people were previously driven away by the colonialists. What we do for the Southern Province we must do in the Eastern Province, we must do in the Northern Province and in other parts of Zambia.

Eventually, the Land Commission submitted its report to the government. The Land Commission recommended *inter alia*, the introduction of a new law to make provision for the compulsory acquisition of land and other property in order to settle fairly and effectively the problem of vacant farms and unutilised land. The government accepted the recommendation. In February 1970, the Lands Acquisition Act was included in our country's statute book. The Act has three essential features. Firstly, the power to acquire property compulsorily is vested in the president only "whenever he is of the opinion that it is desirable or in the interest of the Republic so to do". Secondly, under section 5 of the Act, notice in the prescribed form must be given to announce the government's intention to acquire property compulsorily. Thirdly, the provisions of the statute were carefully prepared to ensure that they do not conflict with the provisions of the constitution which enshrine the protection of private property. Therefore, under section 10 of the Act, where property is acquired by the president compulsorily the minister *shall* pay compensation on behalf of the government. However, the Act prohibits payment of compensation for compulsory acquisition of 'undeveloped land or unutilised land' as defined in the Act.

The land problem raised in Parliament by the member for Choma in March 1968 was resolved subsequently in a proper manner. It was resolved without causing injustice or unnecessary legal or constitutional difficulties. At a very early stage in my career I learnt that in administration, like in life generally, the saying *festina lente* (hasten slowly) should be borne in mind at all times. It is advisable to study any given problem carefully before trying to find a suitable solution to it.

I had an effective department which dealt with land issues. At a time when emphasis was on development in the post-independence development programmes, the staff of the Lands Department worked under pressure all the time. During the debate on my vote in the Committee of Supply, Richard Farmer, the member for Copperbelt Central Constituency, complained that the staff of the Lands Department were too slow in processing the issue of title deeds and related documents. He remarked further that he had raised the question before with the attorney-general "…but the delays are still going on". He then asked specifically "…if the hon. and learned minister of lands and mines could do something I should be very grateful". It was my responsibility to ensure that the performance of departments in my ministry was satisfactory at all times. However, it was also my responsibility to protect civil servants in my ministry who were unable to defend themselves in the House. I replied briefly as follows:

> In regard to the second question, Sir, I must admit that there has been widespread disappointment with my Registry Division in the Department of Lands in regard to the execution of their business.
>
> About six weeks ago, Sir, the president of the Law Society of Zambia addressed a letter to me in which he set out *in extenso* the difficulties which a number of people are experiencing. Ten days ago I addressed a letter to the president of the Law Society of Zambia in which I set out in full the remedial measures which my officials intend to take in order to improve the situation.
>
> But I would like hon. members to note that no fault really can be rightly placed upon the shoulders of my staff. They are an overworked staff in the Registry Department who really deserve to be congratulated for a fine job of work. Nonetheless, it is our responsibility to see that we make our system as efficient as possible and I am satisfied with the measures which we have taken for the time being.

Although routine issues in my ministry quite

understandably engaged my attention throughout a period of sixteen months, my concern was always with problems of copper production, copper prices and copper exports. For example, our studies showed that gradually the large copper consuming countries such as USA, Japan, Germany and France became large producers of recycled copper. For many users, the recycled copper was as good as virgin metal from the CIPEC members. Of course, such recycled copper exerted enormous pressure on world copper prices to the disadvantage of copper exports. There were also other problems such as the substitution of copper in many applications and in those applications which required the use of copper, there were improvements in design. Such improvements caused a dramatic reduction in the amount of copper actually used per appliance. Those factors led to a downward trend in copper prices, a trend which the copper industry continued to suffer throughout the twentieth century.

In my opinion, the role of CIPEC was crucial for the preservation of the interests of its founding members, Chile, Peru, Congo and Zambia. I sincerely believed that producer unity was essential to meet the challenges facing the CIPEC members. For these reasons, with the approval of President Kaunda, I was enthusiastic to lead the Zambian team to the first conference of ministers from CIPEC countries held in mid 1968 in Lima, Peru. I led a powerful delegation of experts and senior officials in government, including Andrew Sardanis who was in charge of the Ministry of State Participation. The first CIPEC conference in Lima was successful. It demonstrated to the world that the copper exporting countries from the developing world were determined to cooperate in order to protect their economic interests.

After the conference, I became a self appointed advocate of the advantages of the establishment of CIPEC to its members. I did not know at that time that the existence of CIPEC would be short lived. Although Zambia and Chile were the largest producers of copper at the beginning of the nineteen seventies, twenty years later the position changed dramatically. By the end of the twentieth century, Chile had increased its production of copper to about two million tons per year. Peru's annual copper production had increased too during this period. On the other hand, Zambia's production had declined to less than four hundred thousand tons. Congo's copper production did not increase either. The poor performance of Congo and Zambia in the post 1970 years was due to relatively high costs of copper production. On the other hand, Chile and Peru had relatively low costs of production. Due to these developments the dream of CIPEC faded away towards the end of the twentieth century. In less than twenty five years after its establishment these developments on both the production and consumption side of the copper industry meant that the interests of Chile and Peru on the one hand and Zambia and Congo on the other hand, were no longer wholly aligned. Rodney Malcomson would readily say today that CIPEC's formation in 1967 was an exercise in futility and a complete waste of the taxpayer's money in Zambia. I would still say today that it was a courageous and worthwhile venture which served the promoting countries well while their interests remained aligned. For it is said that where there is no vision men perish!

In the latter part of 1968, like other ministers my time was divided between attending cabinet meetings in Lusaka and visiting my constituents in the Mweru Constituency in Nchelenge District, Luapula Province. For under the Republican Constitution new elections for the president and members of parliament were due at the end of the year. The Central Committee of UNIP was responsible for the selection of its candidates to contest seats in various constituencies countrywide. However, after selecting candidates, the Central Committee often sought consensus with local party officials in the parliamentary constituency to ensure the success of its candidates in the elections. The Central Committee adopted me as UNIP's candidate for the Kawambwa Constituency. My selection as the UNIP candidate for Kawambwa was received with enthusiasm by party officials. On nomination day in

December 1968, we celebrated my election unopposed as member of parliament for the Kawambwa Constituency. I felt happy with the support I received from party officials and from voters generally in the constituency.

Often people say that politics is a thankless job. On the occasion of being returned unopposed in December 1968, my feelings were different. During my term of office in the Ministry of Education as a cabinet minister, the government implemented a phenomenal programme of development in education. In a period of four years only, the government's contribution to the growth of education at the primary and secondary levels throughout the country was tremendous. The people of Kawambwa were beneficiaries of these developments with their countrymen and women in other party of the country. I was the instrument of the government's success in the implementation of the education expansion programme. I believe that the people of Kawambwa appreciated my contribution and they felt that I deserved a pat on the back. I thanked the party officials for their support. I undertook to work closely with them in the development of Kawambwa District.

In the reorganisation of the government following the elections, President Kaunda transferred me to the Cabinet Office as secretary general to the government. It was a new post which had not existed before. He had decided to upgrade the existing post of secretary to the cabinet in order to enable the new appointee to the office of secretary general to the government not only to deal with civil service problems but also with problems of inter-relations of ministers and civil servants.

In order to effect the change, an amendment of the Constitution of Zambia was necessary to remove the office of secretary to the cabinet and to substitute the new office of secretary general. President Kaunda and his advisers believed that having served as a senior civil servant in colonial days and a cabinet minister after independence, I was capable of harmonizing working relations of ministers and civil servants. There was a tendency among some ministers after independence to disregard the good advice of their civil servants which they dismissed as a reflection of the colonial mentality of civil servants. President Kaunda knew, of course, that there was some degree of intolerance of politicians among civil servants and vice versa. However, before I was in a position to take up the challenge of my new appointment, it was necessary for the National Assembly to accept the proposed amendment to the Constitution of Zambia. Meanwhile Valentine Musakanya was allowed to continue performing the functions of secretary to the cabinet. He was an exceptionally brilliant and competent civil servant. He, too, in colonial days occupied a senior position in the administration of Northern Rhodesia. With his educational background and experience in administration, he was selected by the Public Service Commission in 1965 to succeed an expatriate as secretary to the cabinet.

The creation of the post of secretary general to the government was controversial in many quarters. Some people were convinced that I had been demoted by President Kaunda to an inferior position in the cabinet. This viewpoint was supported by the fact that my name was lower in the 1969 order of precedence. It dropped from number twelve in January 1968, to number eighteen in January 1969. Yet some politicians suspected that President Kaunda had a hidden motive for appointing me to supervise and control the public services in Zambia. They thought he was probably grooming me for a higher political office. Yet my intimate friends knew that I had no intention of advancing my political career. After witnessing the inter-tribal conflicts during the UNIP elections at Mulungushi in 1967, I was anxiously looking forward to the day when I would establish my roots as a professional lawyer. In that context, matters of precedence in Parliament or in the cabinet were inconsequential to me.

One serious matter dogged me while I waited to take over responsibility for the Cabinet Office from Valentine Musakanya. A number of senior civil servants were disappointed by President Kaunda's decision to appoint a politician as the overall supervisor of the civil service and in charge of Cabinet Office. Apparently, they directed their hostility to President Kaunda. They feared that he intended to enforce wholesale politicisation of the civil service. I received information from reliable sources that some senior civil servants intended to resign sooner rather than later. Undoubtedly, they were afraid of the unknown. No one had indicated to me a plan for wholesale politicisation of the civil service.

The vice president, Simon Kapwepwe, on 29 January 1969, presented the Constitution (Amendment) Bill to the House to be read a second time. One of the two proposed amendments related to replacement of the office of secretary to the government with that of secretary general to the government. In introducing this particular amendment, he informed members that the government had embarked on a reorganisation of the administration in order to accelerate development with people's participation. He said, "Members will appreciate that it is imperative that at the very centre of the government's machinery there should be located a powerful coordinator invested with wide authority if the success of the new system is to be assured". Furthermore, the secretary general to the government was expected to "coordinate the functions of Lusaka based ministers and those for the provinces". In general, members willingly supported the proposal to replace the office of secretary to the cabinet with that of secretary general to the government. However, some members expressed their concern about the danger of entrusting command of the civil service to a secretary general who was at the same time a politician. They argued that there was a danger of the erosion of the principle of political neutrality of civil servants in the new arrangement.

Consequently, in spite of assurances given to opposition members by ministers on the front bench, the House was divided at the end of the debate on the second reading of the Constitution (Amendment) Bill. Sixty five members voted for the motion and eighteen voted against it. The requisite two thirds majority was obtained for validation of the amendment to the constitution.

I did not participate in the debate. Instead, I listened attentively to the members' contributions. More particularly, I attached significance to the vice president's description of the functions of the secretary general to the government as, "The secretary general will combine the functions previously performed by the minister of state for cabinet and the civil service and the secretary to the cabinet". Within three months of performing these functions, I realized that my appointment was not a demotion after all. In fact, it was an office of authority and influence.

In the book entitled *Politics in Zambia*, edited by William Tordoff, the authors analysed the significance of President Kaunda's administrative reforms in January 1969 as follows:-

> The creation of the post of secretary general to the government was particularly important and meant that President Kaunda intended to implement his new policy of making some senior political and administrative posts interchangeable at the very highest level. The secretary general was both head of the civil service (replacing the former secretary to the cabinet on 1 February 1969) and a minister of cabinet rank. He was responsible to the president for securing the general efficiency of the public services, the smooth running of the Cabinet Office, and 'the coordination of the policy formulating and executing functions of both the central and the provincial ministries'. The first person appointed to this post, Mr John Mwanakatwe, had been a senior civil servant before his appointment as parliamentary secretary in 1962; he had been a cabinet minister between 1964 and 1968. The immediate (and private) reaction of many civil servants to this arrangement was unfavourable. They rightly saw it as formalizing the already declining insulation of the civil service from politics. This was in fact intended by Dr Kaunda, who had invited permanent secretaries to attend a meeting of the UNIP National Council in November 1968 and took the initiative in making them formal council members in March 1969. Under Mwanakatwe the Cabinet Office was quickly given a 'new look'.

In August 1970 the Development Division lost its own separate permanent secretary and became merely one of three divisions in an integrated Ministry of Finance and Development, with the director of planning reporting to an under-secretary, who was not himself an economist. Only in 1972 did the division regain its status as a separate ministry, although now linked with the very different function of national guidance to form the Ministry of Development Planning and National Guidance.

Like the preceding, and by contrast, minor, reorganization of January 1967, the 1969 reforms were undertaken on the initiative of Dr Kaunda himself. They were the result of a political decision, tempered by advice from a number of quarters. First, a working party – composed of civil servants and appointed in January 1968 to consider the reorganization of provincial and district government – had underlined the need for reform in an interim report submitted to the secretary to the cabinet in March 1968.

As secretary general responsible for recommending new policy guidelines from the Cabinet Office to the government, I initiated studies to be undertaken by senior desk officers under a permanent secretary's supervision. One such study related to the cost of allocating government motor vehicles to ministers for use while on duty. Members of the public from time to time criticized the government for allocating expensive motor vehicles for use at the taxpayers' cost. And, indeed, quite often some ministers abused the privilege of free transport arrangements – free fuel, free maintenance of motor vehicles driven by chauffeurs whose salaries were paid with taxpayer's money. From experience, it was well known that a fairly large part of recurrent expenditure of the national budget was spent on provision of motor vehicles to ministers and deputy ministers, permanent secretaries and heads of departments and many officers in government service. The study was intended to focus on savings which would be realized to support development programmes if ministers were obliged to use their own vehicles and were instead paid a reasonable transport allowance.

199

Unfortunately, while officials in the Cabinet Office were studying the problem of providing government motor vehicles for free ministerial use, a junior minister raised it in the House during the debate on the motion to approve the confirmation of the declaration of a state of emergency for a further six months from 24 April 1969 in accordance with provisions of the constitution. The motion was moved by Mr Simon Kapwepwe, the vice president. In his maiden speech, Jethro Mutti, member for the Livingstone Constituency, informed the House that if Mercedez Benz cars were withdrawn from ministers and senior government officials "we can make several savings". Members of the opposition supported his proposal with loud shouts of "Hear, hear!" to the embarrassment of ministers sitting on the front benches. Although he was a back-bencher, Jethro Mutti was minister of state for rural development. Therefore, he was *ipso facto* a member of the government. In this matter, he argued in his maiden speech on national security:

> Mr Mutti: Negroes required for service in Vietnam are being collected from the streets in Harlem, a negro slum in New York in the United States. They are then introduced to a machine called a 'jet' for the first time and, in no time, they go and perform wonders. I am still not convinced that it will require all that lengthy period for us to train our pilots. And, therefore, the argument that we will not have pilots to fly them is completely out. If it is the question of money that is lacking, I know, Sir, that we can make several savings elsewhere. I know we have made a lot of wastages for which I personally do not make any apologies. I would really appreciate it if this matter was taken seriously. I did not want to raise it until I myself, Sir, was entitled to a government car. A Mercedes Benz car costs K6,000. I do not know how many of us, living here in Lusaka, go about driving those Mercedes Benzes with our flags waving. All of us can afford, I am sure, to have our own cars. I am advocating therefore, Sir, that apart from ministers living in the provinces, those of us, civilian leaders, ministers, including yourself, Sir, Mr Speaker, the cars that we drive must be withdrawn from us.

Hon. Opposition Members: Hear, hear!

Applause.

Mr Speaker: I did not intend to interfere with the hon. minister of state's maiden speech, but we should keep to the subject before us. Will the hon. minister please continue.

Mr Mutti: Thank you, Sir, I am advocating for the withdrawal of these cars, Sir, because I think if the excuse for our lack of providing security in this country is money ....

Jethro Mutti did not only advocate withdrawal of government Mercedes Benz cars from ministers and public officers. In his contribution to the debate, he also claimed that "holders of public offices in Zambia – permanent secretaries, hon. ministers, civil servants of various ranks are among the most highly paid people in Africa and statistics are there to prove it". These remarks irked UNIP members who called for his blood and resignation from his office in the government. He was prepared to resign but later President Kaunda settled the problem amicably. It was quite clear that the ministers were totally opposed to any scheme varying their conditions of service which entitled them to the use of government owned Mercedes Benz cars for official duties. Consequently, officials in the cabinet office recommended abandonment of the study I had commissioned. I rejected the recommendation. A short time later, the officials submitted the report of their findings to me. The revelations in the report were interesting. The findings revealed that abuse of motor vehicles allocated to ministers was rampant. Some ministers sometimes used them on errands completely unrelated to their official duties and responsibilities such as ferrying friends or relations from Lusaka to their homes in some remote part of the country. The study also revealed wide differences between mileage covered per month by ministers with a conscience and mileage covered by carefree ministers. Some ministers exploited the drivers employed to drive their official motor vehicles. In the light of all these considerations, it was obvious to me that enormous savings in the government's recurrent expenditure could be made if a new scheme was devised for facilitating the transport requirements of ministers and eligible public officers in the course of performing their official duties.

I accepted with modification a proposal by the study group in the Cabinet Office. They recommended the withdrawal of motor vehicles from senior politicians and civil servants. Under existing arrangements, government motor vehicles were allocated to them on a personal to holder basis. Fuel for the motor vehicle was free and the services of a chauffeur employed by the government were available in accordance with instructions contained in the relevant Cabinet Office circular. Under the new scheme, I recommended the withdrawal of allocation of government motor vehicles on a personal to holder basis. Consequently, if my proposal was accepted, each minister or public officer would be obliged to use his/her own motor vehicle to go to work. However, if any minister or public officer requested for a loan to purchase a motor vehicle of their own choice, it would be granted automatically, interest free and repayable over an agreed period. Furthermore, a driver employed by the government would be available to provide any services such a person might require from time to time. This arrangement contained two more important provisions which were in my opinion necessary to make the new scheme reasonable and workable. Obviously, in the event that a minister or public officer was obliged to attend and officiate at a formal ceremony locally, he would be free to obtain a government vehicle from the mechanical services department with the services of a driver. Equally, he would be entitled to a similar privilege when travelling outside Lusaka for official duties. Secondly, the proposed scheme included payment of a fixed monthly allowance for purchasing fuel for the privately owned motor vehicles the ministers and eligible public officers were obliged to use.

The proposed scheme was discussed with officials in the Ministry of Finance who enthusiastically supported it as they considered it would contribute to proper financial management in the long term. At that stage, I was free to submit a memorandum to the cabinet for discussion of my proposals. However, bearing in mind the hostility experienced by Jethro Mutti in Parliament, I decided first of all to sound President Kaunda's views. Moreover, I was aware from consultations with the ministry responsible for Transport and Works that the minister's support of our proposal was lukewarm. On the other hand, President Kaunda discussed the proposal with me at length. He was particularly keen to understand the reality of financial advantages of the proposal to the Treasury. In addition, personally I was anxious to emphasise that the government had a duty to minimize extravagant expenditure of public funds in order to promote some development using our own resources, such as building schools, hospitals and feeder roads in rural areas. It was a happy surprise one day when I found a memorandum on my desk from the president authorizing submission of a cabinet memorandum on new transport arrangements for ministers and public officers. I knew that the dye was cast. If my recommendation in the cabinet memorandum was rejected I might consider resigning from my office as secretary general depending on the degree of hostility shown to me by my ministerial colleagues.

As expected, the presentation of my cabinet memorandum evoked acrimonious discussions. Several ministers failed to control their emotions. Not surprisingly, President Kaunda's unequivocal support of the memorandum influenced its acceptance. As far as I can remember today, never in the whole of my political life have I ever felt so joyful. It was always obvious to me since independence that the government's image was to a certain extent tarnished by some of our comrades who abused the privilege of using motor vehicles allocated to them by the government for official use. On the day of the discussion of my cabinet memorandum, I was furnished with the facts – irrefutable facts – and figures as my ammunition if I was challenged on the grounds advanced for supporting a change of policy. My officials had done their homework. For example, I had a list showing at least six occasions when drivers were intercepted transporting a mistress in a government vehicle at the behest of a minister! Fortunately, I did not need to use such weapons during the discussion of my memorandum in cabinet.

Following implementation of the recommendations, for a while the number of my friends in cabinet dwindled. I did not care. I had more time to play golf at Chainama Hills Golf Club. But one day a young man recently appointed as a cabinet minister surprised me by his honesty, so rare among us mortals. Long after the withdrawal of government motor vehicles from ministers and senior civil servants, Wilson Chakulya commended me for my courage in recommending their withdrawal. He told me that it was his absolute conviction that apart from minimizing extravagance in government spending, politically also the new policy was advantageous. Before the introduction of the new policy, he believed that talking about a people's government was meaningless. He then confessed that he had opposed the new policy because it should have been introduced at independence in 1964. He complained that it was unfair to introduce that kind of policy in less than six months after his appointment as a minister! He put it succinctly in his mother tongue thus: *ndefwaya ukulilapo* (I, too, would like to enjoy the fruits of independence). That was indeed honesty *par excellence*!

In October 1970, more than a year after the introduction of the new policy on restricted use of government motor vehicles, President Kaunda announced a mini reshuffle of the cabinet. In this mini reshuffle, I was assigned a new portfolio, the Ministry of Finance. Within three years after leaving the Ministry of Education where I had probably overstayed, I was moved for the third time to another portfolio, perhaps the most high profile portfolio I had ever held since independence. For the first time

204

and much to my surprise, I received many congratulatory letters from both old friends and many well wishers who were otherwise unknown to me. For the first time also, President Kaunda wrote an unusually long letter to me explaining the heavy responsibility he had chosen to put on my shoulders which, in fact, were not broad. One piece of advice to me was phrased in graphic form, more or less to this effect. He was advising me in his letter to look out for crooks. He was stating the fact that there are in this world both good people and bad people. He was of the view that some of the bad people, the crooks, would endeavour to befriend me. Then the punch line in his letter, which I have never forgotten, read like this: "...even the crooks will be very well dressed when they come to see you. But you should not be deceived merely by their style of dress or what they say." I took his advice seriously. His words of wisdom on that occasion anchored my soul over many years in public life. But exactly why did President Kaunda assign the key portfolio of finance to me early in October 1970? I had at that time no background whatsoever in economics and finance. I was reasonably comfortable in Education, Lands and Mines and the Cabinet Office with my background as a teacher and lawyer. Probably I shall never know. One fact, however, is that he transferred me to the Ministry of Finance in less than a week after my return from New York, where I led the Zambian delegation to the Twenty Fifth Session of the General Conference of the United Nations Organisation.

In less than two years after taking over responsibilities at the Cabinet Office, I was ordered again to take on a new challenge of managing our country's public finances. I had formulated new arrangements for efficient coordination, at least for some time, in the interests of our country. My successor at the Cabinet Office was Aaron Milner an experienced party stalwart who was widely known as one of President Kaunda's men. He was a hard working and dedicated minister. As I expected, he continued with the new administrative reform programmes efficiently. But, not surprisingly, pressure from ministers mounted on the Cabinet Office to change the policy which led to the withdrawal of government motor vehicles from ministers and certain public officers. A few months after my departure from the Cabinet Office, a memorandum was discussed in cabinet on the arrangement which obliged ministers and eligible public officers to drive their own motor vehicles for duty purposes in Lusaka. The recommendation was accepted to revert to the old system.

The composition of my delegation to the United Nations in September 1970 included the best men and women to support me in order to achieve our goal of effectively highlighting the explosive political situation in Southern Africa. After his reorganisation of ministries in January 1969, President Kaunda chose to retain the portfolio of Foreign Affairs under his supervision. He appointed Moto Nkhama as deputy foreign affairs minister in charge of day to day functions at the headquarters in Lusaka and supervision of the operations of our foreign missions abroad. He was a very capable young man who had a reputation as one of the few intellectuals among party activists before independence. Secondly, in our mission in New York, the permanent representative of Zambia to the United Nations was Vernon Johnson Mwaanga. He, too, was a brilliant UNIP activist before independence. Although quite a young man when he was serving at the United Nations from 1968 to 1972, he was well prepared and qualified for this post. He had previously attended courses at the Institute of Commonwealth Studies at Oxford University in the United Kingdom and at Stanford University in the United States of America, where he studied political science and international relations. Another UNIP stalwart in the delegation was Bessie Kankasa, who led the Women's Brigade of the party.

Apart from participation in the deliberations of a number of committees and working groups at the Twenty Fifth Session of the UN General Assembly, my delegation focused attention on the text of our delegations' address to the General Assembly. I started preparing a draft of the address in Lusaka early in

September with the assistance of Moto Nkhama. President Kaunda wanted a person of ministerial rank to lead the delegation. When we arrived in New York, Moto Nkhama together with Vernon Mwaanga concentrated on redrafting and finalising the address because we intended to obtain an early date for its delivery to the General Assembly. I personally spent many hours in the perfection of the draft address and rehearsing its delivery.

The day of reckoning was 24 September 1970, when President Mr Edward Hambro of Norway called on me to deliver the address to the 1848th meeting of the United Nations Assembly. In my address,[*] I emphasised that Zambia strongly condemned the evil policy of apartheid and racial arrogance in South Africa. As a faithful member of the United Nations and the Organisation of African Unity, Zambia had supported and continued to support resolutions passed by the organs of these two bodies at a great cost to the country. Therefore, I called upon these two bodies to render moral and material support to the victims of apartheid.

After delivering the address, I received a standing ovation from members of the General Assembly which I reciprocated with awe and humility. It was the culmination of several weeks of hard work. For our success at the United Nations, I was truly grateful to all my colleagues for their contributions and encouragement. A few days later, I returned to Zambia leaving Moto Nkhama to lead the Zambian delegation. Two weeks later, I was no longer the secretary general to the government, following my appointment as minister of finance. I have always looked back to my speech to the Twenty Fifth Session of the General Assembly of the United Nations as my most valuable contribution to our government's efforts to stir the conscience of the world against the evils of the apartheid system in South Africa.

---

[*] See Appendix 1 for my address to the UN General Assembly.

C H A P T E R

9

Managing Public Finance

President Kaunda put me in the Ministry of Finance in the second week of October in 1970. It was shortly after I had successfully led the Zambian delegation to the Twenty Fifth Session of the General Assembly of the United Nations in New York. Just as I was settling down to work in the Cabinet Office, I received President Kaunda's letter assigning the portfolio of finance to me. Quite frankly, at first I was not amused, not least because I had not been forewarned about the impending transfer when I left Zambia in the middle of September.

On reflection, I realized that it was the prerogative of the president to reshuffle the cabinet at any time - entirely at his pleasure. If one was affected in such a reshuffle it might imply that one was not performing his or her ministerial functions satisfactorily. On the other hand, there might be no reason whatsoever for one's transfer to another ministry. It might be purely accidental. Indeed, there are occasions when a chief executive of the administration will move a competent minister to another portfolio to strengthen the efficiency and improve the overall performance of the government. Indeed, on further reflection, I also realised that in most governments the minister of finance is accorded seniority among cabinet ministers. In fact, in the United Kingdom, a country on which our own government was modelled, the chancellor of the exchequer is traditionally the second to the prime minister in the cabinet. It was regretinstance that President Kaunda decided to move me from the Cabinet Office where I held the office of secretary general to the government. It was an office of considerable authority and influence. Certainly, I would have wished to remain there a little longer in order to complete my programmes. A period of only twenty one months was too short. In spite of all these considerations, many relatives and friends did not regret my new appointment as minister of finance. It was considered to be another office of authority and influence in the government.

Another reason for feeling quite comfortable that my transfer from the Cabinet Office to the Treasury as a minister was not a demotion was the letter President Kaunda wrote to me on my new appointment. It was an unusually long one. I remember clearly that he emphasised to me repeatedly in the letter that he trusted me; that was the reason why he wanted me to succeed another trustworthy colleague whom he had decided to appoint as minister of foreign affairs. As cheerfully as I could, I moved into my new office in the Ministry of Finance before the end of the first fortnight in October 1970.

I remember my first day very clearly at the Ministry of Finance. It was shortly after my arrival at the ministry that I met Emmanuel Kasonde, the permanent secretary. He was expecting me to turn up sooner rather than later after the official announcement of changes in the composition of the cabinet. I, also, was anxious to meet him in the Ministry of Finance because he was an old friend. Emmanuel Kasonde was by divine providence a student at Munali Secondary School during the early fifties when I was a teacher there. Therefore, I knew him from those early years of his studentship at Munali and, of course, more latterly as one of the most capable and experienced permanent secretaries in our government after independence. In my erstwhile position as secretary general to the government in the Cabinet Office it was my responsibility to assess the performance of permanent secretaries annually. So I knew as the ministerial head of the civil service cadre that he was an exceptionally able person. Fortunately, I also already knew some of the other senior officers at the headquarters of the Ministry of Finance, among them Fred Kazunga and Ephraim Chibwe at the Income Tax Department and Francis Walusiku at the Central Statistical Office. One by one the permanent secretary introduced his senior staff to me, followed by a brief discussion on the organisation of their departments, their functions and responsibilities, their achievements and failures. Meanwhile, with remarkable initiative my personal secretary at the Ministry of Finance knew that I worked well, quietly and with a good measure of concentration, when I was given a cup of tea at the right time in the morning and afternoon.

With introductions and brief discussions with senior departmental officers over, I started reading written briefs on files. They were informative and comprehensive on important subjects, many of them related to implementation of cabinet decisions. However, some issues were so involved that I remained uninformed and mystified after reading even a well prepared brief. I did not owe anyone an apology for being in that position. At the time of my appointment, I recall informing President Kaunda that I had the disadvantage of lacking a background in economics. For a minister of finance it was not absolutely necessary but it was helpful to possess knowledge of basic economics. Of course, it is a fact that some of the best known and most successful bearers of the office of chancellor of the exchequer in the United Kingdom have been men and a woman (Mrs Margaret Thatcher – a lawyer by profession) who were not trained economists. That is why humorists sometimes oversimplify the function of a minister of finance to be that of finding reasons why things can't happen rather than with encouraging them to happen.

I have always been a practically-oriented person by nature. I am happy and I feel a sense of achievement when I get things done. Therefore, to overcome my lack of background in economics, I relied heavily on discussing briefs with the civil servants to ensure that I understood them fully. For I have always thought that the role of a minister is not merely to say 'yes' or 'no' to the advice tendered by his officials. I believe that a minister has a sacred duty to encourage the officials not merely to formulate policies but also to implement the policy agenda finally adopted by the cabinet. Without a minister's clear understanding of departmental activities and functions, ensuring the implementation of the agreed policy agenda would be difficult. The Ministry of Finance, in particular, offers the responsible minister an opportunity to influence the direction and pace of a country's development. In addition to the team of officials who gave me briefs, I was fortunate to receive background papers on the economic development of Zambia from Charles Elliott, formerly reader in economics and head of department, University of Zambia. In addition, Emmanuel Kasonde assigned Dr Raj Sharma to me specifically to render advisory services whenever they were required. He came to Zambia on secondment from the Indian Government to the government of the Republic of Zambia. At first he held the post of senior economist but he rose through the ranks to the post of assistant secretary in the Ministry of Finance. I assigned to him responsibility for a broad range of functions, including project appraisal, analysis of economic and financial trends and assessment of the government's performance in terms of revenue collection and control of government expenditure. From time to time, I sought his advice on the impact of foreign borrowings on the national economy.

After exhaustive consultations and careful study of briefs, I felt confident by the end of October 1970 that I was prepared to manage the public finances of our country. In particular, I felt that by reading briefs and holding discussions with various officials I had acquired a good understanding of the basic features of Zambia's economy and the implications of those features for its economic policy.

At independence in 1964, the economic structure of Zambia, like other countries in the region which are rich in mineral resources, was based on the export of raw materials. In 1970, six years after independence, the predominant factor in the Zambian economy was the mining of copper. In 1964, it provided more than ninety five per cent of total export earnings. In 1970, copper was still the major export. Although by far Zambia's most important export, the country also exported a small amount of other minerals, especially zinc, lead and cobalt. The Zambian economy was a classic example of a dual economy in which a highly sophisticated technology existed side by side with a subsistence sector. The high technology sector was centred around the copper mining industry in the Copperbelt Province and it was a largely urbanised money enclave which existed side by side with the much larger low technology and relatively poor subsistence sector. Also, Zambia was one of the most urbanised countries on the African continent. The statistics – though unreliable – showed that the rural population was only marginally higher than the population in towns and cities. The rural sector of the total population was characterised by low output and productivity and poor standards of living.

Furthermore, copper exports constituted the main source of foreign exchange earnings. Within the modern sector, copper mining occupied a predominant position because for a number of years its contribution was thirty to forty per cent of Gross Domestic Product (GDP) and about forty five per cent of government revenue. The mining industry provided the largest number of employees, apart from the government, in the formal sector. The over dependence of the economy on the mining industry made it highly vulnerable to fluctuations in the price of copper on the international market.

Attempts had been made unsuccessfully since independence to reduce the economy's over-dependence on the mining industry. Many obstacles were encountered in efforts to diversify the economy. Some efforts were made, albeit on a small scale, to establish industries for import substitution in the early years after independence. However, it gradually became difficult to continue with diversification of the economy due to scarcity of foreign exchange and for landlocked Zambia, high transport costs to the sea were always a major constraint. Lastly, Zambia was obliged to reroute transport for exports and imports due to its geo-political situation in the volatile Southern African region. This situation necessitated substantial expenditure for rerouting transport and imposed a heavy cost upon the economy.

Notwithstanding these constraints, the manufacturing sector started growing well beyond the stage of infancy it had been in at independence. To a certain extent it showed promise in the early years of contributing to the growth of the economy. This sector recorded an annual rate of growth of about ten per cent between 1965 and 1970. Its contribution to GDP was only seventeen per cent in 1965.

Zambia was also well endowed with natural resources. Its vast agricultural potential has always presented another important area for investment and economic growth. The potential of agriculture to contribute significantly to GDP and foreign exchange earnings was enormous. The tourist traffic to Zambia was still small and insignificant. Tourism was another industry which had tremendous potential for development and contribution to economic growth.

Among the serious economic problems highlighted by officials in the Ministry of Finance was the consequences of the Mufulira Mines disaster of September 1970. Eighty nine men lost their lives. The Mufulira Mines disaster occurred in the second half of the year when the price of copper, our country's main foreign exchange earner, had started to decline. The most serious aspect of the disaster was the negative effect of a reduction in the quantity of the copper available for export, even though the price had declined.

It was quite obvious to me that the economic situation in the country was precarious due to over-dependence on one commodity – copper - for more than ninety per cent of our foreign exchange earnings. The decline of copper in the second half of 1970 would inevitably cause our mineral revenue to fall at the end of 1970. Consequently, it was anticipated that the budget deficits would increase. Therefore, I had no hesitation about determining my priorities for the 1971 budget. The problem areas in our efforts to build the foundation for sustained economic growth related to the government budgetary deficits; the deficit on the balance of payments and the arrears on our external payments. The level of price inflation and the financial problems of the mining industry in Zambia were also problem areas. Furthermore, it was also clear to me that the anticipated decline in the importance of the mining sector underscored the need to develop the agricultural sector rapidly. It also underscored the duty to monitor carefully the expenditure patterns of the government. It was necessary to establish the possibility or reducing subsidies or eventually phasing them out altogether.

In times of economic hardship, the political leaders and their fellow citizens are expected to make sacrifices in the interest of the nation. My goals were clearly set out along these general principles for the budget at the end of January 1971. However, I was of course aware that the annual budget presented to Parliament by the minister of finance reflects the collective will of the government as a whole. In the final phase of the budget's preparation, the minister of finance consults once or twice with the president for guidance and approval of its basic principles. In Zambia and in many countries in the Commonwealth of Nations, the budget is a confidential document. Its contents should never be leaked to unauthorised persons. In the United Kingdom, ministers and their officials are known to have been sacked for allowing the contents of a budget to be leaked.

At the end of December 1970, I felt relieved that practically all the formalities concerning the preparation of the budget for 1971 had been completed satisfactorily. Emmanuel Kasonde, my permanent secretary, was in and out of my office to consult with me on troublesome aspects of the budget preparation process. For this reason, I was obliged not to leave Lusaka on an official or non-official visit to some far away town or village unless my officials were assured that I would be away for not longer than two days. In fact, I recall rushing to Monze, a small town about one hundred and twenty miles south of

Lusaka in the Southern Province. It was in the early part of January in 1972, after I had approved the form and content of my second budget address. There was an urgent matter on which I was anxious to consult my boyhood friend, George Cornhill, a prominent farmer and businessman in Monze. On my second day in Monze, to my complete surprise, a senior officer from the Ministry of Finance arrived at George Cornhill's house with a file bearing a minute to me from the permanent secretary for urgent attention. I wrote my instructions on the file and the exercise probably only took thirty minutes. My peace was certainly disturbed by the civil servant who brought the file to me in Monze. However, his mission was justified and in the national interest.

Friday 29 January 1971, was budget day. My first budget address as minister of finance was due to be delivered to the House at 14.15 hours. However, by tradition in Zambia, I was obliged to present the whole budget address to the cabinet late in the evening on 28 January for approval by ministers in order to ensure collective responsibility. This procedure did not allow the ministers at that stage to propose major changes to the budget in terms of policies or details. The meeting, however, provided an opportunity for ministers to obtain clarification of policy pronouncements contained in the address. The permanent secretary and two senior officers were present throughout the meeting. It was not acrimonious. In fact, it was a cordial meeting, although one had to exercise patience in clarifying policies which had already been accepted at a pre-budget meeting of the cabinet two months earlier. At the end of the meeting, in the early hours of the morning, ministers' remarks were complimentary. I was assured of unequivocal support by members of the front bench if the small but vocal group of members of the opposition in the House launched an onslaught against the proposals contained in the budget address.

In principle, the 1971 budget proposals were intended to lay the foundation for sustained economic growth in subsequent years, more especially in the long term. It appeared to me an exercise in futility to adopt budgets which were perceived to deal each year with specific economic problems – the adoption of the tactics of a fire-fighter. It was necessary to adopt a pragmatic approach whereby budget proposals dealt with long-term solutions to economic problems. If a set of such proposals were included in the budget for 1971, it was most probable that they would be reinforced in later years. However, while I attached exceptional importance to this approach, I was aware that there were many objectives of a budget in our system of administration. They include the desirability of giving members of parliament the opportunity of asking if monies approved previously were actually spent for authorised purposes; and, indeed, if financial discipline was observed in the utilisation of approved funds. Even more importantly, the presentation of a budget for debate enables MPs to consider the desirability of tax proposals to raise revenue for the operations of the government. They have the right on behalf of the people to approve the tax proposals or reject them – a right to which the forefathers of the Americans attached great importance when they asserted that: "Taxation without representation is tyranny" in 1776.

By presenting proposals in the budget to the House for debate, the tenets of democracy are advanced through transparency and accountability. These are all worthy objectives of a budget presented by a minister of finance to the House in Zambia. But in my first budget address, I emphasised the importance of articulating the government's economic policy upon which the 1971 budget was formulated. The point was emphasised in the following words:

> I now turn to considering the economic policy upon which I have formulated this budget. Government expenditure and revenue do, of course, have important re-distributive and social effects, but in the long run it is the economic effect of the budget that enables government to achieve its social objectives. Government expenditure acts directly on the level of demand in the economy and by generating income and employment

mobilises those resources for productive investment which give us economic growth and increase the welfare of all the people.

I informed the House that the government had decided to make rural development the engine of economic growth in Zambia, with particular emphasis on agriculture. In the past much had been talked about encouraging the development of agriculture, but with only limited success. I reminded the House that it had authorised the sum of K8.16 million for importation of maize and famine relief. In the budget before the House I proposed an even higher sum in the estimates again for importation of maize in anticipation of a shortfall in local production. I informed the House that I was of the view that in spite of the negative effects of the climatic factors, our expenditure on the importation of one food item was not justified. Consequently, I reminded the House that in the previous year "the subject of rural development provoked more public debate …. than ever before in the history of this country." Much had been done by the government but with only little success. Some critics had condemned the operations of the government-sponsored Credit Organisation of Zambia for being wasteful of our limited resources and for failing to make a noticeable contribution to agricultural production. Such critics believed that the policy of rural development was wrong. That notion was wrong. It was necessary to dispel it completely. I then advised that:

> …… simply because the Credit Organisation of Zambia did not achieve as much success as we would have liked in the field of agricultural credit, the policy of rural development was not in itself wrong. Such a conclusion is dangerously misleading since it equates policy with execution. The two are different. Failure to execute does not render the policy itself subject to condemnation. It is a misdirection of criticism.

There were many reasons which justified the selection of rural development with emphasis on agriculture as the first priority in the allocation of scarce resources in the 1971 budget. Firstly, the rural sector was manifestly productive and was capable of absorbing the majority of the people who were drifting at that time to the urban areas, in search of work and social amenities. There was a danger of having a large unemployed population in the towns. At that time I was convinced that the dimension of the problems we faced in our urban areas were likely to decrease if the exodus of people from rural areas was reduced. Under the rural development programme, people were encouraged to stay on the land. Simultaneously, the government repeatedly urged unemployed people in urban areas to return to rural areas. Secondly, experience had shown since independence that in a developing country like Zambia the economy would remain unhealthy until agriculture was developed and the importation of foodstuffs was reduced. Our population was growing and the per capita income was increasing too. These two factors together had a tremendous effect on demand for food. Therefore, it was necessary to meet the challenge of growing more food at an early stage in the life of our nation. I informed the House that we had no choice in the matter. Otherwise "... we have only two options, namely to either allow food prices to increase or to rely on imports. I recommend neither." Thirdly, it was well known that agriculture formed an active counterpart to industrial development. The government accepted that in order to develop a balanced and stable economy it was necessary to encourage the rural population to earn enough money to enable them become part of the market for industrial products. Therefore, the policy of rural development was intended to benefit both the rural and urban populations. In the past, rather half-hearted efforts had been made to encourage and support agriculture to grow. Problems in encouraging the development of agriculture existed, but I did not believe that they were insurmountable.

In the budget address, I referred briefly to other vital issues which affected our economy. They, too, required our attention. It was necessary to restrain inflation, promote industrial peace and restrict price increases of major consumer items. However, above all, the main objective of the 1971 budget was to improve the performance of the agricultural sector within the rural development framework. I reminded the House that it was necessary "to change the attitude of our people to agriculture in at least two aspects." It was necessary to revive the respect given to land by our forefathers "and discard completely the false and dangerous idea inherited from the period of colonial rule that work in an office is more important than work on the land." I went on to say that: "Fortunately, we know where the truth lies. A man who was able to feed himself, and others, was always held in high esteem in our traditional society. The position is not different today. On the contrary, the rewards are higher."

Throughout my budget address to the House, I was aware that members were concerned about the difficult days ahead for our country on the economic front. Their anxiety was due, *inter alia*, to the effects of falling prices of copper and the Mufulira Mine disaster. It was necessary to inform members that I shared their anxiety about the economic situation. Yet I sincerely believed that there was hope of economic recovery in future. In order to persuade the nation's political leaders assembled in the House to support the government in the difficult times ahead, I concluded the budget address with these words:

When my colleague presented the last budget to this House he said that he was presenting what was a "painless budget". I agree with him. The position, however, has since changed with the drop in copper prices and the very unfortunate disaster at the Mufulira Mine last year.

With all the problems that I have outlined and the great potential that this country is fortunate to have, let us all unite and go forward, looking back not in satisfaction over our successes, many as these may be, nor in anger over our failures, but in the awareness that the destiny of this young republic is placed in our hands, so that long after we are gone our descendants can safely boast that we left this nation better than it was handed to us.

Over a period of one week the House met to debate the proposals in the budget for 1971. On 29 February I rose to reply to a number of important points raised in the debate. I thanked the members who had spoken on the motion a week earlier and "for their expression of support, qualified or unqualified, for my budget proposals." I accepted that in the course of the debate some members brought up a number of important points. I promised the House that the government intended to take them into account "to the extent that it was possible to implement them." In particular, I was pleased with the members' desire to see government give increased attention to the development of the rural areas where the majority of our people live. I was particularly encouraged that many members in their contributions emphasised that accelerated development of rural areas was "the only way to reduce both the drift to the urban areas and our dependence on other countries for the supply of some of our foodstuffs."

A prominent member of the frontbench, Simon Kapwepwe, who was our minister of provincial and local government and culture, supported the emphasis on rural development in the budget. In a spirited contribution to the motion for the House to resolve into Committee of Supply on the Estimates of Recurrent Expenditure for the year 1971, he argued forcefully that efforts to develop rural areas would be wasted unless people living in villages were encouraged to change their attitude to work. He believed that it was important to encourage people to work hard. He appealed to the government and members of the House "to go to villages and help to change ... to make them see that we can only survive in Zambia if we can change the present attitude where we spend a lot of time sometimes drinking and sometimes just sitting down." In words which became immortal to me later, Simon Kapwepwe told the House on that occasion that:

Mr Deputy Speaker, Sir, beggars are never respected. If a nation will go with a cup or a bowl in its hands from country to country to beg for money, you will never be respected. Not only this respect, but you should also know the policies of that particular country will have to be dictated by the people who give you loans. If that is a point, then definitely it is the duty of all Zambians to start accepting our responsibility.

We come in this House, Mr Deputy Speaker, asking for more roads, we come in this House asking for more schools, we come in this House asking for more hospitals, we come in this House asking for more facilities, that is fair. But while we are asking for these things we should also remember that we have to maintain these things when we build them.

Another well informed contributor to the rural development debate was Alexander Chikwanda, minister of state in the Office of the President. A graduate of Lund University in Sweden, he was a professional economist and an eloquent speaker. He, too, supported the budget proposals. He opened his maiden speech with these flattering remarks:

Mr Speaker, Sir, the budget which was presented to this House by the hon. minister of finance in my opinion is so good that perhaps the only complaint that one can make is that it leaves us with very few complaints.

Government Member: Hear, Hear!

For those of us who have fallen into the habit of over-dramatising issues, ...it puts us certainly in a very awkward position. I can see hon. members on the opposite side feeling very dejected because the hon. minister of finance has just taken the thunder out of them.

Interruptions.

Alexander Chikwanda cautioned members not to assume that imbalances in the rates of development of different areas were avoidable. He maintained that such imbalances occurred because one area might have better arable land than another area; that one area might have a better water supply than another; or that one area was endowed with rich mineral resources whereas another had none. He preferred to call rural areas "depressed areas" of Zambia which could be developed through "meaningful and intelligent planning". He also cautioned members against the popular but erroneous belief that development of the agriculture sector was cheap. It was not cheap. Initially it required enormous capital expenditure even in rural areas. However, with intelligent planning which allowed development in stages the depressed areas of the country were capable of growing more good. Gradually it would be possible to reduce food imports or to avoid them altogether. He was personally not opposed to the provision of modest subsidies to the agriculture sector. Agriculture was subsidised even in the most developed countries in Europe and in Australia and New Zealand.

On the question of inflation which many members raised in the debate, I agreed with Alexander Chikwanda that much of it was not imported inflation. Much of it, he said, was due to mark-up. I agreed with him that if the public were price conscious they would have helped in containing some of the price increases. In my statement for winding up the debate, I appealed to shop-goers in Zambia to be price-conscious when buying day-to-day consumer commodities. Otherwise, they would continue to be victims of unscrupulous businessmen.

In my concluding remarks, I appealed to all the people to work hard in order to build our country which was endowed with tremendous possibilities for development. I was convinced that provided the political leadership was honest and sincere a better tomorrow was assured for our people. I said:

> Let us unite and teach our people how much hard work will play in the future of our country. The hopes of our people for a better tomorrow, in a country with tremendous possibilities

for development, must surely lie in the sincerity and quality of the leadership of the ruling United National Independent Party. It is, therefore, through the leaders of the dynamic party that I make my summons to the people of Zambia to accept the challenge contained in my budget proposals for 1971 and thereby help to construct a solid base for economic and political stability.

I accepted the portfolio of finance at the beginning of October 1970. I worked feverishly over a period of three months to prepare the budget address. My success in presenting to the House a budget which the members received well was due to the hard work and exceptional competence of the staff at the headquarters of the Ministry of Finance. In particular, Emmanuel Kasonde displayed remarkable administrative flair during the preparation of the budget itself and the budget address later. In giving advice to newly appointed ministers, I have advised them always to take the advice offered by civil servants seriously. They are usually right. However, the joy of a ministerial position is that one's decision is final. Therefore, common sense dictates that proposals in a budget, indeed the spirit of it all, should truly reflect policies and programmes which the minister has approved previously. That involves much work for the minister.

I certainly worked hard to prepare the budget for 1971. Because it was my first budget to present to the House, I was happy that it was well received both in the House and in the country generally. At that time, little did I know that by God's providence I was destined to deliver four more budget addresses in the same House in later years. Therefore, it was not in vain that I laboured so hard to prepare the 1971 budget and the budget address with my officials. I gained useful experience for the future.

My term of office in Finance was for only three years. We all expected the dissolution of Parliament after October 1973, in readiness for the presidential and parliamentary elections in December in that same year. After the delivery of my first budget address I expected to present two more budgets to the House –

223

one at the end of January in 1972 and the last one at the end of January in 1973, unless I became a casualty again of another reshuffle of the cabinet. It turned out that I remained at the helm of the Ministry of Finance in the same capacity until mid December 1973 when a new government was formed.

It was our good fortune at the Treasury that the subsequent budget addresses for the years 1972 and 1973 were modelled on the 1971 budget. Basically, the principal policy of encouraging rural development remained unchanged. The government launched the four year Second National Development Plan at the beginning of 1972. In my budget address to the House on 15 January 1972, I informed the House that the government was determined to pursue the policy of rural development vigorously. I restated the government's policy in these words:

> Last year, I devoted a fair part of my speech to the subject of rural development. I can hardly resist the temptation to repeat what I said last year. In my speech I advanced three reasons why rural development is important to our economy. I said that one reason why rural development must continue is that agriculture and general development of our rural districts are capable of absorbing the majority of our people who are currently drifting to urban areas in search of work and amenities. We must bring both work and amenities to them rather than the reverse.

In accordance with the policy of placing emphasis on rural development, a total sum of K24.3 million was allocated to the Ministry of Rural Development for recurrent expenditure. This is an example of how serious the government was about promoting rapid development of rural areas. Otherwise, the budget addresses for 1972 and 1973 dealt with proposals for revenue measures by way of various forms of tax. Without raising additional revenue, especially in the aftermath of falling copper prices and the Mufulira Mine disaster, yearly increases in taxes became unavoidable. They were necessary to raise revenues to meet recurrent expenditure. The decline of copper prices had caused mineral revenue to fall. Consequently, the budget deficits increased. Simultaneously, the balance of payments deteriorated. Therefore, in these circumstances, we were obliged in the Ministry of Finance to consider diversification of the government's revenue sources. When I took command of the Treasury at the end of 1970, I was in the forefront of the defence of our large investments in health and education after independence. We have increased opportunities in education for our children and free access to health services.

However, I argued that the time had come to increase the proportion of resources allocated to infrastructural projects in the agricultural, industrial and mining sectors. Therefore, our position in the Treasury was clear on the main objective of the Second Development Plan. Emphasis in the plan was to be on the diversification of the economy, in particular its export capacity, concentrating on development of rural areas through directly productive projects. To achieve these goals personal and non-governmental initiative and enterprise was necessary. We maintained that private investment was absolutely necessary for the success of the Second National Development Plan. Although the government intended to allow parastatal institutions to continue to operate in a very large area of the economy, emphasis would be placed on the need to run them on commercial lines.

The Second National Development Plan was prepared at a time when net foreign assets were high. They stood at about $450 million in 1970. However, we anticipated a sharp decline in subsequent years. The government anticipated mobilising a large volume of resources from abroad, both in the form of official development assistance – loans, grants and technical assistance – and, of course, direct investment in the economy.

The government decided to send a goodwill mission in the first half of 1972 to selected countries in North America, Europe and the Far East. The mission was expected to sensitise cooperating partners in developed countries on the detail of the

Second National Development Plan as a framework of priority areas for public and private investment. The plan provided opportunities to foreign investors and multilateral organisations to support the government's efforts to accelerate economic growth and development. I was chosen by President Kaunda to lead a ministerial delegation to Canada, Sweden, West Germany, Denmark and the United Kingdom. President Kaunda had also chosen Jasper Soko, the minister of trade and industry, to join the delegation. I was particularly happy with President Kaunda's choice of Jasper Soko. He was a quiet-spoken and intelligent politician. Although he belonged to the class of the old guards who led the struggle for the independence of Zambia, he was always a pragmatist. Often, he laughed at other old guards who preached socialism or other ideologies they did not quite understand. His portfolio had relevance to the objective of the National Development Plan. I had a good rapport with Jasper Soko. He always respected me as his former teacher at Munali Secondary School in the early 1950s. To support the two man ministerial delegation, the permanent secretary appointed Dr Raj Sharma, a senior economist in the Ministry of Finance. The delegation also included junior civil servants. They were selected from the Ministry of Finance, the Office for Development Planning and the Ministry of Trade and Industry. Our delegation was authorised to sensitise governments and relevant organisations about opportunities in Zambia for private investment. The delegation was also authorised to conclude agreements for technical assistance and explore possibilities of raising loans for Zambia in future.

Before our departure from Zambia, Jasper Soko and I met with senior officials to discuss the brief which Dr Raj Sharma had prepared. It was an excellent brief. The success of our delegation was in a large measure due to his competence and hard work. Jasper Soko and I found him throughout these journeys to be dedicated and hard working.

Our reception by the government of the Federal Republic of Germany was extremely cordial and entirely beyond expectation. This observation does not, and should not, mean that our hosts in the countries we visited earlier, namely Canada, Sweden and Denmark, did not welcome us warmly. However, we observed as a fact that the welcome we received from the time of our arrival in the Federal Republic of Germany until our departure was exceptional. Our ambassador, Moto Nkhama, was at the airport with his entourage. But there were also representatives of the German government among the people who came to welcome us. We saw two policemen who were playfully idling their motorcycles close to the cars in which we were expected to travel to Bonn. The mystery was unravelled when we noticed that we had an official escort on our journey by road from Frankfurt to Bonn. It was the first occasion in my life to be provided with two police motorcyclists for protection during an official visit to a foreign country. Indeed, it was the first and last time I was accorded such a privilege. It was a safe and enjoyable journey from Frankfurt to our hotel in Bonn.

When we started meetings and consultations in Bonn, the administrative city of the Federal Republic of Germany, Jasper and I observed that Moto Nkhama seemed to enjoy great respect and the confidence of officials from the Foreign Office. Evidently, he had made a big impact in the Federal Republic of Germany as a dynamic diplomat for Zambia. We were only too ready to accept that our observation was correct because his background was well known to us at home. He was a political activist in the Copperbelt area before independence. He was among the few highly educated UNIP cadres in the Copperbelt. Although a militant by nature, he demonstrated maturity and wisdom at all times. He was admired by his peers and elders alike because he was a hands on politician. His aim was to get things done and never to give excuses. Although he was the ambassador for Zambia when Jasper and I visited the Federal Republic of Germany in the first half of 1972, at home he was officially the member of parliament for Kitwe East. He was free, of course, to sit in the House as an MP during his visits to Lusaka when Parliament was in session. It often happens in life that as we grow up we adopt role models for ourselves – the people we wish to emulate because we admire them so much. I know that a few young men looked to me as their role model in our political party – the United National Independence Party. My visit to Bonn enabled me to know the confidence which Moto Nkhama had in me.

He had given the German officials an impression that I had both the qualifications and experience for a top and more senior position one day in Zambia than the post of minister of finance. Often, at meetings and receptions, his remarks about my character, my patriotism and the record of service I had rendered to our country were exaggerated and embarrassing. Although his remarks at such gatherings were flattering, nevertheless in my responses, where possible, I tried to show in a diplomatic way that there were colleagues in the political arena at home who were more dedicated and experienced than I. Accompanied by an equally capable and experienced colleague, Jasper Soko, the credibility of my remarks was unquestionable. Fortunately, our visit to Bonn was the most successful of all those the delegation made.

It was standard practice for the head of an official delegation to a conference to report to President Kaunda the delegation's activities and achievements at the conference. This practice also applied to a mission like the one I led to some foreign countries. Within a week after our return to Zambia, I secured an appointment to brief President Kaunda at State House about the success of the two man ministerial delegation to North America and Europe. President Kaunda was always friendly and courteous to his ministers. On this particular occasion he was exceptionally jovial and appeared to know much already about the success of our mission. I described our activities in the various countries we visited. However, he showed most interest in our visit to the Federal Republic of Germany. Without any prompting from me at all, President Kaunda told me that he was pleased that we were very well received by the government in the Federal Republic of Germany. And then he

228

dropped a bombshell. He told me that he was particularly pleased that I displayed a sense of humility and patriotism during our delegation's visit to Bonn! It dawned on me then that he had received a report on our mission to the Federal Republic of Germany even before we returned home. It became obvious to me that someone was monitoring our delegation's activities at all times. Actually, this realisation pleased me. I realised that gradually our government was becoming more and more efficient.

In the remaining months of the 1972 financial year, I chose to spend more time in Zambia in order to enforce strictly the rules for avoidance of over-expenditure of funds approved in the budget for 1972. For this and other reasons, I did not attend the Eighth Meeting of the African Development Bank held in Algiers in 1972. At that meeting two important resolutions were adopted. They were of particular interest to Zambia. The first decision concerned the setting up of a fund to be known as the African Development Fund. Its purpose was to give financial assistance to its members on the lines of the International Development Assistance (IDA). We supported this new initiative because we knew the advantages of soft loans to developing countries at a time when the cost of borrowing was increasing. We also supported the Bank's decision in Algiers at the Eighth Annual Meeting to hold the Ninth Meeting of the Board of Governors in Lusaka. In the budget address to the House on 26 January 1973, I informed the House that Zambia had accepted the honour to host the conference later in the year.

In my budget address of 1972, I had also informed the House that the African Development Bank had given Zambia a loan for agriculture. That was a good beginning. However, I informed the House that it was nonetheless necessary to intensify the search for additional fields of cooperation. The aim was to find other suitable areas for the Bank's further assistance to Zambia. It was in this context that I personally attached importance to the prospect of hosting a successful meeting of the Board of Governors of the African Development Bank in

Lusaka from 2 to 7 July 1973.

By virtue of holding the office of minister of finance I was *ipso facto* the governor for Zambia on the Board of Governors of the African Development Bank. I was due to take over the chairmanship of the Board of Governors at its Ninth Annual Meeting in Lusaka. As the host country, we had a large delegation at the conference. Our delegation included Jasper Soko, as temporary alternate governor. He was the minister of trade and industry. Ephraim Chibwe and James Mapoma were also included in our delegation as alternate governor and adviser respectively. The former was permanent secretary in the Ministry of Finance; the latter was permanent secretary in the Ministry of Trade and Industry. The governor of the Bank of Zambia, Bitwell Kuwani, was among five additional advisers in the Zambian delegation. As the delegation's leader, I was satisfied that I had able men to provide the necessary advice in the course of the Bank's deliberations in Lusaka. I was privileged to lead a strong delegation.

Before the arrival of the delegates, the president of the African Development Bank, A Labidi, organised a meeting in Lusaka to brief me on the various items on the agenda of the Ninth Annual Meeting of the Board of Governors which I was expected to chair. In the course of our discussions, he disclosed that two items were particularly sensitive. He was worried that the discussions on those items might be acrimonious. The first related to the desire of the Arab nations to seek the recognition of Arabic as the third official language for use in all activities organised by the Bank. Yet the Bank's statutes were specific on this issue. Under the statutes there were only two official languages – English and French. The second item which was likely to be contentious was a proposal to open up the capital stock of the Bank to non-African countries for participation. He briefed me fully on the advantages and disadvantages of adopting each of these proposals. Our government's position was predetermined on the issues which in the opinion of the Bank's president were likely to be contentious. In an organisation run on democratic principles, like the African Development Bank, we expected that on each item on the agenda the will of the majority would prevail. The plenary sessions of the Annual Meeting were held from 2 July to 7 July 1973 inclusive.

The opening speech by President Kaunda was delivered to the delegates in the morning at the Mulungushi International Conference Centre Hall on Monday 2 July. President Kaunda gave a clear and concise account of the progress the Bank had made during the nine years of its existence. The financial operations of the Bank had increased tremendously during that period and it had continued to grow. It was a source of pride and inspiration to President Kaunda that the Bank had built up "an unquestionable solid reputation as a source of technical assistance and advice to member countries". He was particularly pleased that the Bank was already effective as a promoter of multinational and regional projects and that it had become a useful "channel for the flow of development resources from abroad to the African continent".

Not surprisingly, as a prominent leader among frontline states, President Kaunda used the occasion to remind the delegates that the meeting was held in Lusaka at a time of grave threats. That was a demonstration of "a clear manifestation of the unity of the entire African people against the enemies of Africa". He believed that with such unity the attempts by adversaries and mercenaries to frustrate the efforts of frontline countries such as Zambia would meet with "the wrath of the entire African people". President Kaunda concluded his speech wishing that "the decisions made in... Mulungushi Hall would be for the benefit of Africa as a whole". He believed that the delegates had the wisdom and experience to resolve African problems of development and cooperation.

The outgoing chairman of the Board of Governors, Idriss Jazairy, addressed the Ninth Annual Meeting after President Kaunda's opening speech. He gave a comprehensive account of the growth and achievements of the African Development Bank since the adoption of the agreement by thirty three African countries at a meeting in Khartoum. He also reminded delegates about the significance of the Ninth Annual Meeting in that the Bank and non-African states were expected to meet for the first time to set up a joint institution designed to promote the development of the African continent. Idriss Jazairy did not conceal the fact that he regarded the need to reach the target of UA 130 million quickly as a priority. He, of course, accepted that the target was achievable earlier rather than later if an appropriate resolution was adopted inviting non-African members to contribute to the capital stock of the Bank without seriously diminishing its purely African character.

Idriss Jazairy also clearly stated in his address that he supported the proposal to introduce Arabic as an additional working language side by side with English and French. He cited the OAU as one organisation in Africa which recognised the Arabic language for official use. He surmised that by the end of the ninth meeting of the Bank its membership would be equal to the total membership of African countries in the OAU. On this particularly sensitive issue, he believed that it was appropriate to contemplate the introduction of the same working languages within our institution, namely, French, English and Arabic. Furthermore, acceptance of the proposal to introduce Arabic as another working language was necessary so that we did not any longer remain behind the United Nations specialised agencies which had taken a similar decision.

The outgoing chairman also raised several other important issues for debate. However, it was the general view that they were not as sensitive as the two I have dealt with in some detail. As Idriss Jazairy delivered his address, he was undoubtedly conscious that he was at the same time stirring up a hornet's nest. I think that is why he concluded his remarks thus:

> It is with this appeal for African solidarity that I should like to conclude my remarks, while asking you to pardon me for having taken a stand on some of the burning issues you will have to consider at the present session. Perhaps in my defence, I might

recall that on the occasion of my election in Algiers last year, I warned you that I would not possibly be able to perform my duties in the spirit of neutrality, for it is impossible not to feel a commitment in all matters concerning the future of our continent. I made it clear, however, that I would discharge my duties in an objective manner guided by the higher interest of Africa, of which the Bank is an emanation.

The address by the outgoing chairman of the Board of Governors was received with mixed feelings by the delegates. It was a precursor of the acrimonious debate on these two subjects later in the meeting. However, on the first day of the meeting the items on the provisional agenda were not controversial. They related to routine subjects which were easily settled without arousing heated discussions. They included adoption of two separate resolutions for an increase in the capital stock of the Bank to allow the Kingdom of Lesotho and Mauritius accession to the African Development Bank Agreement. Item eight on the agenda of the meeting allowed delegates to elect the chairman and vice chairman of the Board of Governors. That was the time when I assumed responsibility for the meeting as chairman. I was then privileged to address the delegates to the Ninth Annual Meeting of the Board of Governors of the African Development Bank. At the beginning of my address, I hastily recorded my own gratitude to the Board of Governors for their affection and regard for Zambia and President Kaunda. It was appropriate at that stage also to thank the outgoing chairman, Idriss Jazairy, for his enlightened leadership of the Bank during his term of office. To A Labidi, president of the Bank, and the able team of executive directors, I conveyed the gratitude of all the people of Zambia for their dedication to the promotion of the interests of the African Development Bank.

In anticipation of the controversial nature of some items on the agenda of the meeting, I appealed for the cooperation of all members to ensure successful deliberations. I also made a strong plea to the members to make brief contributions because the agenda of the two meetings was long. But I was not shy of my determination to show firmness if that was necessary during discussions. I concluded my address as incoming chairman of the Board of Governors with these words:

> Mr President and distinguished governors, I shall be obliged on some occasions to exercise a firm hand, but I must assure you all that in so doing I shall be guided by considerations of equity and justice, the interests of the African Development Bank, our own institution in which we place so much hope for promoting the economic independence of our continent. I am sure I can count on all of you to cooperate with me and give me the guidance necessary to ensure the success of the Ninth Annual Meeting of the Board of Governors of the African Development Bank.

On Wednesday 4 July I encountered the first difficulty in controlling the discussion on what I had thought earlier to be a non-controversial subject. On that day, the president of the Bank tabled the report of the Board of Directors on the recovery of arrears in subscriptions to the Bank's capital stock. I drew the governors' attention to the document and requested them to consider the recommendation in the report. At the Eighth Annual Meeting of the Bank, it was established that six countries were still in arrears in spite of the efforts by the management to get them to honour their pledges. At the end of the Eighth Annual Meeting the Board decided to set up an *ad hoc* committee to make proposals concerning recovery of arrears in subscription to the Bank's capital stock. It was an *ad hoc* committee of ministers from seven countries which elected the governor for Nigeria as its chairman. Its report recommended that the question of arrears was properly the responsibility of the Board of Governors for consideration.

It was this simple recommendation which sparked a heated but otherwise lively and interesting debate. The governor for Sudan, for example, thought it was necessary to give the management more time to intensify its efforts to persuade countries in arrears to honour their pledges and settle the arrears. Other countries believed that leniency towards countries in arrears would ruin the Bank's good image. In particular, the temporary governor for Liberia was not in a mood for compromise on the failure by some countries to pay their arrears to the Bank. She dismissed the argument by one country that it had failed to pay its arrears because it was in a state of war. Miss Ellen Johnson Sirleaf was adamant that countries which were in arrears were unfair and irresponsible. Without pulling punches, she recorded her contribution as a hard-liner was recorded in the minutes thus:

> While also appreciating management's efforts, since only six countries were still in arrears (the governor for Liberia) felt it inadmissible that those countries which had made pledges to the Bank in Khartoum had not honoured them. The argument by one member country with over Unit of Account 14 million in arrears (namely that it was in a state of war), was untenable for many were African countries which, though victims of wars – if not external at least internal – had nonetheless fulfilled their obligations. She commended the goodwill displayed by another state which had been in a similar difficult situation.
>
> She was prepared to join other governors wishing to have coercive measures taken against defaulting members.

However, the governor for Cameroon was even more uncompromising than the governor for Liberia on the problem of arrears. He stated that his country deplored the fact that some member countries refused to honour their commitments to the Bank, although they willingly fulfilled their commitments to bodies such as the International Monetary Fund and the International Bank for Reconstruction and Development. He then warned the governors that "any country could offer a high initial subscription, acquire proportionally high voting power and then proceed to build up an alliance and try to bend the Bank to its will."

I was unhappy with the acrimonious sentiments of some governors in their contributions to the debate. Twice I interrupted debates and "appealed to the Board to discuss the admittedly sensitive problem in a frank yet dispassionate atmosphere." Fortunately, my appeal was heeded by the governors. After the participation of the governor for Ethiopia and the governor for Mauritania, the governor for Nigeria proposed the adoption of the proposal by the steering committee to appoint an *ad hoc* committee to find a satisfactory solution to the problem. The governors for Mauritania and Swaziland supported the proposal and it was accepted unanimously. Later in the evening at home, I realised that it was fortunate I had allowed governors with strong feelings "to let off steam" before I intervened.

The following day, Thursday 5 July, the Board of Governors convened at 10.20 hours. The governors quickly disposed of the business of setting up an *ad hoc* committee on the implementation of the recovery of arrears in subscriptions to the Bank's capital stock. Seven member countries were elected members of the *ad hoc* committee including Nigeria. I then suggested the election of the governor for Nigeria as chairman of the *ad hoc* committee. The governor for Cameroon supported the suggestion. It was accepted unanimously.

After setting up the *ad hoc* committee, I tabled the report concerning the mobilisation of additional financial resources for the Bank for discussion by the governors. The report was prepared by a steering committee which was mandated specifically to report "on ways and means of mobilizing additional financial resources by opening up the Bank's capital stock to non-African countries or other appropriate means." Because the steering committee recognised the importance of the report, the members had proposed the formation of an *ad hoc* committee to study the report and make its own recommendations on it. Therefore, as a first step, I asked the Board to discuss the proposed formation of an *ad hoc* committee. In the discussion, the governor for Kenya stated that since two meetings had previously discussed the subject, it was unnecessary to waste time by setting up an *ad hoc* committee to suggest other possible ways of mobilizing additional resources for the Bank. He requested the Board to take a decision on the recommendations contained in the relevant documents. He further requested the Board to consider referring only the formulation of a draft resolution to an *ad hoc* committee. His suggestions were accepted. I was also quite comfortable with the suggestions made by Mwai Kibaki, the governor for Kenya.

In guiding the Board, I emphasised the need for a decision at the end of the discussion. I did not hesitate to stress that mere rhetoric was unlikely to be helpful to the African Development Bank. However, while emphasising the need for a decision, I reminded the governors "to propose other solutions if they were not satisfied with the recommendations in the report." The debate on the proposal to open the Bank's capital stock to non-African countries aroused considerable interest and revealed divergent views. Some were of the opinion that non-African participation in the capital stock was "inevitable" because the task of the Bank was beyond purely African resources. They appealed to the governors to adopt a pragmatic approach. The governors who maintained this position pointed out that after all "...only borrowers were to be found among the Bank's members". This viewpoint was strongly canvassed by the governors for Ethiopia, Kenya and Liberia, among many other governors. I was particularly impressed, like some other governors, with the frankness of the governor for Liberia, Miss Ellen Johnson Sirleaf, and the logic of her argument. She reminded us that the African Development Bank had been set up, unlike other political institutions, primarily to mobilise financial resources for the continent's development efforts. She warned that unless the Board "faced up to the reality and seriousness of the matter confronting it, the cries for African needs and African fraternity would sound hollower and hollower until the Bank sank into oblivion." She emphasised that Liberia wanted to preserve the African character of the Bank, "but it was a fact that there was already cooperation with non-African countries within national development banks.... there was no need to pretend therefore otherwise."

On the other hand, the governor for Mauritania voiced his country's firm opposition to the proposal to open up the capital stock of the Bank to non-African countries. He pleaded with the governors to opt for the preservation of the African character of the Bank which was in its long-term interest. His country believed that political independence must be reinforced by economic independence. The governor for Algeria also opposed the proposal. His country believed that such a course of action would change the African nature of the institution. It was not the way to make the Bank a truly authentic institution for African development. The governor for Tanzania also opposed the proposal because it would make a fundamental change in the Bank's original charter. He believed that even if non-African countries participated to the extent of forty per cent in the capital stock there would still be insufficient resources for the development needed. Therefore, Tanzania held the view that the Bank's priority was to mobilise fully the potential of the African economies themselves before opening up the equity to non-African countries. Some governors also expressed similar sentiments.

The discussion clearly showed that the governors were deeply divided on this issue. The governor for Ethiopia intervened in the discussion to bring to my attention the fact that there were two camps at the Ninth Annual Meeting of the Board – one for governors who opposed the proposal to open up the Bank's capital stock to non-African countries and another of governors who supported the proposal. He suggested deferment of a decision on non-African participation in the Bank's capital stock "to a more auspicious moment." I agreed to allow the governor for Ethiopia's proposal to be discussed although I observed: "It would be regrettable to give the impression that the African countries were incapable of taking decisions .... besides, the president of the Bank needed guidance in his quest for resources." After a short, lively debate on the suggestion by the governor for Ethiopia, the governor for Cameroon formally proposed the rejection of the suggestion to open up the capital stock of the Bank to non-African countries. He was supported by the governors for Algeria and Zaire. However, the governor for Senegal disagreed with the proposal to reject the recommendation contained in the report of the steering committee. Consequently, the governor for Algeria requested me to put the proposal to the vote. I agreed. The proposal was adopted by 61.41 per cent in favour and 29.96 per cent against, with 3.10 per cent abstentions. The figure of votes not cast was negligible. Accordingly, the proposal to open the Bank's capital stock to the participation of non-African countries was rejected at the Ninth Annual Meeting of the African Development Bank held in Lusaka in Zambia.

The items on the agenda which were discussed subsequently were less contentious. Among various resolutions adopted by the Board of Governors, two were particularly important. One was the adoption of a resolution concerning the problem of unpredictable disasters in Africa. The governors decided to set up a Special Relief Fund at the African Development Bank and to make the first appropriation for the Special Relief Fund from the General Reserve. They also invited the African Development Fund to give priority consideration to the financing of projects for combating disasters in affected member states. The second resolution concerned the increase in the capital stock of the African Development Bank. The Board of Governors decided to increase the authorised capital of the Bank from 259,400,000 Units of Account to 320,000,000 Units of Account and accordingly the number of shares from 25,940 to 32,000 of a par value of 10,000 Units of Account each share. Furthermore, payment of the amounts voluntarily subscribed to the increased capital stock of the Bank by a member state was to be made in two years.

With the adoption of these two important resolutions, on the last day of the meeting I expected a happy conclusion of the deliberations, devoid of acrimonious remarks. That was wishful thinking. A heated short discussion erupted when I invited the governors to consider the last draft resolution concerning the adoption of Arabic as a working language at the African Development Bank. At previous annual meetings the suggestion for the management's study of the possibility of adopting Arabic as a working language was mooted by the governor for Algeria. At the Ninth Annual Meeting in Lusaka, the governor for Libya strongly supported the draft resolution concerning the adoption of Arabic. Quite clearly the Arabic-speaking member countries supported the draft resolution which was strongly opposed by other member states. The discussion on the draft resolution was later recorded as follows:

> The governor for Senegal pointed out that, according to Article 41 (1) of the ADB Agreement, "the working languages of the Bank shall be, if possible, African languages, English and French." Despite their knowledge of foreign languages, Africans should not lose sight of the "African authenticity" or forget their mother tongues. Even if no resolution had been adopted, the Board could ask management to study the possibility of using an African language.

> The governor for Libya concurred with the governor for Senegal. After Arabic, management could study the possibility of adopting Swahili as another working language.

> The chairman, noting the general approval of the Algerian governor's decision to withdraw his draft resolution, ruled that there was no need to vote on the Ivory Coast governor's proposal since no formal decision had been taken in Algiers inviting management to carry out the study mentioned by the president of the Bank. He then gave the floor to the governor for Libya who was attending the Board's meeting for the first time since his country's accession to the ADB Agreement.

> The governor for Libya wished to deliver his speech in Arabic but assured the Board that simultaneous interpretation would be provided in English and French.

The governor for Ivory Coast, speaking on a point of order argued that since Arabic was not an official working language of the Bank, the governor for Libya should either make his speech in one of the working languages – English or French – or not make it at all.

The Chairman upheld that point of order.

The governor for Libya, after expressing regret at the chairman's decision, praised the president, the government and people of Zambia for the warm welcome which had been extended to his delegation.

It was surprising, although interesting too, that the governor for Libya spoke in English after his failure to persuade other governors to allow him to deliver his maiden speech in Arabic. He certainly did not like me for ruling in favour of the governor for the Ivory Coast. The governor for Libya left the conference hall after his short maiden speech. He left the conference hall for the Lusaka International Airport an hour before I delivered my closing speech. It appeared to me and many others that the timing of his departure was a deliberate act of protest against the decision of the Board of Governors at the Ninth Annual Meeting not to allow him to deliver his maiden speech in Arabic. His behaviour did not worry me at all. His theatrical behaviour made the deliberations interesting and enriching in terms of experience for all of us.

In my closing speech on Saturday 7 July, I summarised the achievements of the Board of Governors at the Ninth Annual Meeting of the Bank. Those achievements were due to the commitment of the delegates, their spirit of cooperation and hard work. I was conscious that on many occasions I was compelled to be firm in guiding deliberations. Yet none of my fellow governors raised a finger in protest against the chair's authoritarianism. It was necessary at the end of the meeting to record my grateful thanks to all the delegations and, indeed, to the president and management, for their spirit of accommodation and cooperation. I said:

> It was a great honour, distinguished governors, which you bestowed on me by electing me to this high office. It is even a greater honour for me now to thank you all for the most courteous and affectionate considerations you showed to the chair throughout the conference. But for your splendid spirit of accommodation and cooperation I would not have been able to discharge my onerous duties.

> I must also thank most profusely my two colleagues, distinguished governor for Nigeria and distinguished governor for Mauritania for sharing the burden of this high office with great ease and competence. I am sure they would wish to join me in thanking our indefatigable, ever resourceful and most able president, Mr Labidi, and vice president, Mr Alamoody, who constantly guided the chair on the highly technical and complex points of substance and procedure.

> It is inevitable, distinguished governors, during the frank and free exchange of views which we purposely have every year, that the chairman has sometimes to do the unpleasant, unwelcome and indeed the thankless job of exercising a heavy hand in order to assure what he considers to be in the best interest of the conference and for the maintenance of due decorum and respect for procedures. This is a must in the conduct of any civilised business. If, therefore, any harsh word escaped from my lips and if I have thus injured the sentiments of any of my very close friends and colleagues around this table, I must sincerely apologise. I can reiterate that this was done entirely in the best interest of the organisation we all cherish so much – the African Development Bank.

The closing ceremony is an occasion I shall always remember, an occasion when I played a part, albeit a small one, in demonstrating that Zambia was not a nation in retreat. It was a vibrant nation. To many governors who attended the Ninth Annual Meeting of the Bank, I became a source of inspiration and encouragement and we all rejoiced at the success of our meeting in Lusaka.

As our winter of 1973 moved into summer, the political climate began slowly, but unmistakably, to hot up. I had been under pressure for a long time to accept an invitation to stand as a parliamentary candidate for UNIP in a constituency in my home district at the end of the year. I accepted the invitation. From time to time in the second half of the year, I was obliged to visit my home area to familiarise myself with the needs and aspirations of the people. Without much effort during the election campaign, I was elected as the member of parliament for Mpulungu Constituency with an overwhelming majority at the end of the year. Quite clearly, my decision to stand as the UNIP candidate for Mpulungu Constituency was not in vain.

C H A P T E R

10

Commission of Inquiry into Salaries

My term of office at the Ministry of Finance ended in the middle of December 1973, just a week or two before the next presidential and general elections. I had been invited by the UNIP party officials to stand as a candidate in my own home area. With the approval of the party's Central Committee, I agreed to contest the seat in Mpulungu Constituency in Mbala district, nearly six hundred miles north of Lusaka. I was elected subsequently with a very comfortable majority as member of parliament for Mpulungu Constituency for a period of five years.

During two previous five year terms as an MP, I had been privileged to serve in President Kaunda's administration as minister of education, minister of lands and mines, minister of finance and at the Cabinet Office as the secretary general to the government. Over a period of ten years, I had been sufficiently exposed to the rigours of ministerial responsibilities and the trials and tribulations of politics generally to have reached the stage of trying to identify a fresh career path. My inclination was obvious. I decided to explore the possibility of a career as a lawyer – indeed a life-time career in which I expected to find peace and tranquillity. It was not necessary to canvass my wife's support. She embraced my idea of permanent retirement from politics enthusiastically. My decision in any event was consistent with her belief that politics was a thankless job. But she, too, agreed that law practice and sitting in Parliament as a backbencher could be complementary functions beneficial at times to clients and to my constituents in Mpulungu. It was difficult to persuade President Kaunda to leave me out of his new cabinet. However, eventually he relented and accepted my decision.

I had two options at the beginning of 1974 – the establishment of my own law firm or joining an existing law firm. I preferred the latter option which I considered as convenient and advantageous. I had identified a suitable law firm to join, Jaques and Partners, and mutually acceptable conditions were negotiated. It was one of the largest law firms in our country at that time with offices in Kitwe and Ndola on the Copperbelt and, of course, in Lusaka, the capital city. There were at least six partners with an equal number of assistant lawyers, among them two or three expatriates. With my background and credentials, the partners expressed their willingness to accept me as a partner in their law firm. I readily complied with the requirements the senior partner, Paul Cave, had stipulated in writing. Within a week, I was well settled in the firm. It was quite clear that I had embarked on a lifelong career which I was not likely to abandon for another career in future. For my share in the capital of the partnership, I obtained a bank loan which the law firm guaranteed. It was repayable from my drawings and profits. The arrangement was convenient to all stakeholders.

Early in July 1974, I was requested one morning to meet President Kaunda at State House. It was not an invitation I could decline. After all, I was still a member of parliament although not a cabinet minister. In any event, my relations with him remained cordial after declining reappointment to the cabinet in 1974. During our discussion in State House, after his usual courtesies of asking about my family, President Kaunda told me that he required my assistance. The government had decided to appoint a commission to inquire into the salaries, salary structures and conditions of service for the public services and the parastatal sector. Furthermore, the government had decided to appoint me a member and chairman of the Commission of

Inquiry. He asked me to accept the challenge of an important national assignment. Two other members of the Commission of Inquiry were Jones Nyirongo and Kenan Nkwabilo, the permanent secretary in the Ministry of Labour and Social Services and deputy governor of the Bank of Zambia. President Kaunda was convinced that together we were a formidable team capable of reviewing salaries and salary structures properly and fairly to the satisfaction of all concerned. He quite rightly emphasized that adequate and fair remuneration of public servants was critical to the achievement of stability, efficiency and continuity in the public services.

Often, when faced with a difficult situation, I have counted on my wife for advice and comfort. On this particular occasion, there was also a need to consult my partners in the law firm. That is why I had insisted on President Kaunda's confirmation that we were required to work for the commission at our own pace and on a part-time basis. My wife surprisingly urged me to accept the appointment. She felt very strongly indeed that I was likely to be misunderstood if I declined it. When I chose to remain an ordinary backbencher, some of my political colleagues indulged in childish gossip that I intended to make a comeback and to take over a top position in the government. Equally surprisingly, my partners in the law firm encouraged me to accept chairmanship of the Commission of Inquiry into Salaries, Salary Structures and Conditions of Service. They thought that the appointment would boost the law firm's image in the eyes of the public. However, they were confronted with one hurdle – the likelihood of a distortion of income and expenditure projections over the period of my supposed irregular contributions to income through expected earnings of fees.

These were not really serious problems. It was my intention to work in my office daily attending to clients' instructions, except when I was obliged to attend meetings of the Commission of Inquiry at its secretariat. I was not expected to work in the office at our law firm when the commission left Lusaka to visit provincial centres in order to receive evidence from members of the public. Members of the commission were entitled to receive sitting allowances paid monthly. I gave instructions to the commission's secretary to make direct payment of my sitting allowances to Jaques and Partners. It was a pleasing revelation that, quite apart from such remittances to the law firm, my own monthly earnings from legal work exceeded the monthly target of income. At one of the regular meetings of the partners, Stephen Malama, a partner resident in Kitwe, made favourable observations on this trend. On the basis of my scheme of performing work for the law firm and for the Commission of Inquiry, no one was disappointed with the result when we submitted the report to the government on 10 July 1975.

I had one other compelling reason for accepting the appointment. The government had selected two eminent public figures to serve as members of the Commission of Inquiry. Jones Nyirongo had served for many years in the Ministry of Labour and Social Services since independence, rising through the ranks to the top post of permanent secretary. He was an authority on and highly respected in labour relations matters. On the other hand, Kenan Nkwabilo was an economist who held the post of deputy governor in the Bank of Zambia at the time of his appointment as a member of the Commission of Inquiry. Even more importantly, however, I had known both men when they were schooling at Munali Secondary School. There was not the slightest doubt in my mind that their cooperation was assured in carrying out the onerous and arduous duties of the commissioners. Fortunately, the government appointed two able men from the Cabinet Office to service the commission's secretariat, namely Alan Simmance and Evaristo Kasunga, as secretary and assistant secretary respectively.

The terms of reference for the commission were published in a Statutory Instrument dated 2 August 1974. For the first time since independence in October 1964, the government appointed a commission of inquiry with the widest possible terms of reference to review salaries, salary structures and conditions of service of public services. The "public services" included the Zambia Public and Teaching Services, the Zambia Police Force and Prisons Service, the Defence Forces and the staffs of local authorities, including casual and daily-paid employees. Such a review also necessitated, *inter alia*, consideration of the rise in the cost of living since the last review of salaries in 1967. It also necessitated consideration of the need to provide adequate incentives to particular categories of staff and to attract persons to service in rural areas. The second term of reference required the commissioners for the first time after careful investigation "to report on the salaries, salary structures and conditions of service of personnel employed by statutory boards and corporations and by companies in which the state has a majority interest and to make whatever changes were necessary". In this term of reference, the commissioners were required to pay particular regard to the need to establish a closer relationship between salaries, salary structures and conditions of service in the public services and those applicable to the staffs of parastatal organizations. The government's confidence in the commission was clearly demonstrated in the third term of reference. The commissioners were authorized to consider any other matter and report on it with appropriate recommendations if, in the opinion of the commission, it was in the public interest to inquire into the matter.

The terms of reference were very wide indeed. The task before the commissioners was truly daunting. The government was under pressure from its employees in various departments, members of the Defence Forces, the Police Force and the Teaching Service to revise wages and salaries upward relative to the rise in the cost of living. The economy was not sufficiently strong to enable the government to increase salaries to meet the demands of its employees for positive action immediately. The government killed two birds with one stone when it appointed the Commission of Inquiry at the beginning of August in 1974. To cries from its employees for immediate salary increases, the government's reply was simple and straightforward: "Wait for the Commission of Inquiry to submit its report to the government with the appropriate recommendations". The government bought time following the commission's appointment; its employees turned to the commission and urged the commissioners to complete the assignment expeditiously. They did not appreciate the enormity and complexity of the assignment. In these circumstances, it was understandable that the Commission of Inquiry became the "whipping boy" of the Government by the end of 1974.

Before arranging meetings of the commission, it was necessary for members of the Commission of Inquiry to be sworn-in by the chief justice. They and senior officials were sworn-in by the chief justice on 21 August 1974 at the High Court of Zambia. Our first meeting was held at the commission's secretariat immediately after the swearing-in ceremony. Regular meetings were held at the secretariat subsequently to plan the work of the Commission of Inquiry systematically. In the early days of the commission's work, we made two important decisions. Firstly, we took immediate steps to invite written evidence from interested organizations and individuals in Zambia and abroad. We issued Salaries Commission Circular No. 1 of 22 August 1974 for this purpose. It was widely distributed to government ministries and departments, local authorities and parastatal bodies. Secondly, we also invited the general public to submit written or oral testimony for the consideration of the Commission of Inquiry. These separate invitations were given wide publicity through the available mass media of radio, television and the national and regional press. This first phase was successful.

Our next strategy was to deliberate on the method of conducting public hearings to ensure that witnesses were not inhibited in any way from presenting their views and recommendations. Our task at public hearings was to receive the evidence of witnesses before us even if their evidence was weird or unreasonable. However, we accepted that in the course of receiving oral evidence the commissioners were entitled to question witnesses for the purpose of clarification of their statements. Accordingly, wherever public hearings were held, proceedings were informal and witnesses were not required to give their evidence on oath. Due to the time factor and to financial constraints, the commission decided to hold public hearings at provincial capitals only. Witnesses from the districts were free to appear before the commission at the nearest provincial capital. The commissioners resolved to begin their hearings in the rural areas. This approach surprised many observers for in previous years urban areas received priority from similar commissions of inquiry seeking the views and needs of the people. On the other hand, we preferred to base our impressions on a rural rather than on an urban perspective of Zambian life. Our commission's first public hearings were in Mongu on 17 September 1974. The programme of public hearings was tight and tiresome but we worked as a dedicated team and endured the ordeal. In the event, we heard a total of 601 witnesses in the provinces and a further 206 in Lusaka at public sessions, making a total of 807 in all. We received about 1,500 written submissions. Each commissioner received a copy of every written submission sent to the secretariat of the Commission of Inquiry.

The number of witnesses who appeared before us during the public hearings and the large number of written submissions sent to the commission was ample evidence of our commission's popularity and how strongly people felt about the issue. It was a demonstration of the people's confidence in the members of the Commission of Inquiry and its staff. Two previous salaries commissions received fewer witnesses and oral submissions. The Hadow Commission heard oral evidence from 282 people and received 189 written representations. A subsequent commission, the Whelan Commission, heard 531 witnesses and received evidence in writing from 431. I have always felt that a commission of inquiry is appointed mainly to enable the appointing authority firstly to solicit the views of a cross-section of interested parties; and, secondly, to assess the views, comment on them and make, if necessary, the necessary recommendations. These objectives cannot be truly achieved if the number of people who come forward to assist a commission of inquiry is negligible. A record number of men and women volunteered vital information on our commission's terms of reference. For me, however, the cheerfulness and cooperation of nearly all witnesses we heard at public sessions was a source of joy and encouragement. I was personally satisfied that whatever conclusions we reached would reflect the will of stakeholders. In our report in paragraph 1.9 on page 6, this observation is recorded thus:

> Although the O'Riordan Commission left no record of the number of witnesses heard or of written evidence received, it seems highly probably that we have elicited a broader response than any previous salaries commission and we are certainly convinced that no important point of view has failed to reach us or has been subsequently overlooked. The end result, and one which we believe to be in keeping with the principles of participatory democracy, is that we have been able to relate our recommendations at every point to the evidence presented to us.

The submissions we received from witnesses revealed a wide range of claims from one extreme to the other. On wages and salaries, some witnesses requested the commission to increase them by one hundred per cent. They claimed that even doubling wages and salaries would not relieve government employees from hardship. Others recommended an increase of at least fifty per cent across the board for the wages of government employees. However, many witnesses were moderate in their submissions. They were careful to relate proposed increases in salaries and wages to the rise in the cost of living since the last revisions were effected. Curiously, one witness appeared before the commission and testified that he was personally happy with his salary. He claimed that employees in government were fortunate to live relatively comfortable lives in one of the poorest countries in the world! On the whole, the commission's most difficult problem was to find a formula for determining award of salary increases if any were to be recommended. We found that since independence a poverty datum line had not been determined in Zambia.

During 1969 – 1970, when I served as secretary general to the government, we invited Professor Turner of Cambridge University to visit Zambia and report on wages, incomes and prices policy. He was sponsored by the International Labour Organisation. After completing his studies, Profession Turner's findings were published jointly by the government and the ILO. His recommendations led eventually to the establishment of the Industrial Relations Court, but the issue of determining the poverty datum line remained unsettled. A wages and incomes policy to guide the commission was nonexistent at that time. We were content in performing our task to consider vague concepts such as "the threshold" level below which "the basic necessities of life" or "a minimum standard of health and decency" cannot be maintained. However, to a very large extent the Central Statistical Office rescued the commission by providing comprehensive figures illustrating cost of living changes from May 1967 – the implementation date of the last salaries review – up to April 1975. We safely relied on the figures. The director of the Central Statistical Office confirmed to us that the figures we were given were based on firm price index data up to February 1975. They were also based on returns received and projections thereafter. In these circumstances, we were confident that the figures represented the most reasonably accurate estimate of cost of living changes that could be provided to us for this exercise.

It was indeed helpful to commissioners to use the cost of living index for assessing the amount by which to increase wages and salaries for various categories of government employees. However, agreement was necessary among the commissioners on two other key issues. We considered if it was fair to apply the same percentage increase to highly paid government

1. The author.

2. The author's mother & father-in-law, Jacob & Lizzie Chimpampata, with their children in January 1939.

3. (l. to r.) Tengo Jabavu, Herbert Chitepo & the author.
Form V class, Adams College, 1948.

4. Victor Mcunu (standing), the author's best friend in Durban - a farewell picture "to my dear John from Victor 09/12/48".

5. (l. to r.) Lewis Changufu, the author & Mathew Kang'ombe in Kabwata when the author received his degree examination results from the University of South Africa in January, 1951.

6. Margaret Chipampata in January 1952.

7. The author as housemaster of the winning team (Maybin House) in Inter-House
Athletics Competition, Munali Secondary School.

8. The author with his wife at Kasama Secondary School, 1957.

9. (l. to r.) Margaret Mwanakatwe with June Kashita & Mphumie Mwemba at her home in Thornton Heath, London in 1962.

10. The author, his wife & a Maltese guide at the independence celebrations of Malta in September, 1964. We represented Northern Rhodesia at the celebrations.

11. President Kaunda, second from left, & the first Zambian cabinet with Sir Evelyn Hone (in the centre front row) & Martin Wray who retired as governor of Northern Rhodesia and chief secretary respectively on the eve of Independence Day on 24 October 1964.

12. (l. to r.) Yvonne Goma, Betty Kaunda & Margaret Mwanakatwe inspecting a kindergarten for a local community organized by ministers' wives.

13. Kansenji Secondary School, Ndola, becomes multi-racial, 1964.

14. The author's wife & children, Mupanga (left) & Chitalu (right).

15. Reuben Kamanga, vice-president & James Skinner, minister of legal affairs with the author in 1966.

16. (l. to r.) Margaret Mwanakatwe, her cousin Mercy Shikopa & the author's elder sister, Emily Nakazwe.

17. Deputy minister Andrew Mutemba, second from left, with the author on mine inspection in Zambia.

18. The author, Fines Bulawayo and Henry Thornicroft visit Northern Technical College, Mufulira, May 1967.

19. The author & the secretary of state in the Federal Foreign Office in Germany, Sigismund Von Braun, signing the ratification documents in Bonn for an investment promotion agreement, July, 1972. Moto Nkhama & Jasper Soko standing behind the author.

20. The author as chancellor of the University of Zambia.

21. The author's eldest brother, Joseph.

22. The author, his wife and eldest son, Mupanga, on Budget Day in January, 1973.

23. The author's mother seated in the front row in the middle with grandchildren in Lusaka, 1975, with Margaret Mwanakatwe standing.

24. The author with his wife and Jimmie Vangelatos on holiday on the island of Odyssey in Kelafonia, Greece, in 2001.

25. The author with Grey Zulu at the Oasis Forum in Lusaka in 2001.

26. The author as guest of honour with his wife at the wedding of Hrishi, son of Mohan & Raji Unni, of the State of Kerala in India, December, 2002.

27. SOS Children's Village, Zambia (SOS Kindergarten Graduation, December 2002).

28. Fiftieth wedding anniversary celebration in December, 2002. The author, Lewis Changufu, Elijah Mudenda & Mrs Zine Mudenda.

employees and lowly paid employees when wages and salaries were revised. We opted for adoption of the principle of narrowing the difference between recipients of high salaries and others who were paid low salaries. There was also the question of attracting civil servants, especially professional men and women like medical doctors, agricultural officers, engineers and veterinary doctors, to work in the rural areas. Such highly qualified staff were required to serve in rural areas to accelerate development. Practical considerations made it difficult to devise special salary scales for such personnel willing to work in rural areas. In our view, payment of a "hardship allowance" to professional employees of the government would be an appropriate incentive. In urban areas, some medical doctors were tempted to establish their own private clinics where they practiced medicine in order to supplement their income from working in government-controlled hospitals. To encourage medical doctors in urban areas to concentrate on practicing in government medical institutions only we recommended payment of a non-private practice allowance for doctors. Our greatest difficulty was to agree on a proper method of determining pay for the civil service salaries. We had endless discussions on this difficult subject. No one found an acceptable formula. Ultimately, we agreed to adopt a quotation from the Second Report (Review Body on Higher Remuneration in the Public Sector: Stationery Office, Dublin, 1972) that "There is no scientific method of determining pay". On this point on which we agonized so much, we stated in paragraph 11.2 at page 375 of our report the reason for adopting the quotation as follows:

> The quotation ... aptly summarises our view that there is no known scientific formula for determining absolute rates of pay. There are, of course, developed techniques of staff inspection and job evaluation which can measure the relatives between jobs in a reasonably accurate and objective manner .... That can only be done by weighing of many factors and by attempting a balance which takes account of both the needs of the individual and the interests of the community at large.

We attached significance in our deliberations to the words "which takes account of both the needs of the individual and the interests of the community at large" from the "Red" Devlin Report. Kenan Nkwabilo, the economist in our midst, suggested that these words begged the question "Can the government afford to pay?" assuming that the commission recommended wages and salary increases. This question was relevant. At the beginning of our deliberations we made an analysis of our country's economic situation. Based on the analysis, we established that the government faced a very serious budget deficit. Its financial situation was getting worse. Therefore, any salary award was likely to aggravate balance of payments problems with adverse effects on inflationary trends. Although we accepted that the Zambian economy was susceptible to short-term fluctuations, nevertheless we felt quite strongly that based on the economic analysis no salary increases were justified.

But we found it prudent also to ask ourselves not only the economic question "Can the government afford to pay?" but to consider the wider social consequences of an affirmative reply. It was common knowledge that the civil service was the key instrument for the implementation of development programmes. Prospects for economic growth largely depended on development. We reached the conclusion that a negative attitude to remuneration of civil servants would negatively affect their morale and performance. We decided ultimately that there was justification for the review of salaries upwards. Apart from the justification of an upward review of salaries, we felt that the government had an important responsibility to be a model employer. In the Zambian industrial environment at that time, the government had an obligation to set a good example for other employers to emulate.

Since the appointment of the Commission of Inquiry into Salaries, Salary Structures and Conditions of Service for the Public Services and Parastatal Sector, I was from time to time in the limelight. The anxiety of civil servants was understandable. The Cabinet Office prodded by the commission, issued a circular to all ministries and departments and parastatal bodies freezing revision of salaries before our work was completed. There were high expectations. There was optimism among employees that the commission would award them high salary increases. Information leaked to me revealed the government's expectation of very small, almost insignificant awards of salary increases in view of a serious budget deficit and balance of payments difficulties at that time. I made every possible effort to avoid public statements before the commission completed its work. Neither of my colleagues nor senior members of the commission's secretariat disappointed me by leaking information to the media or members of the public.

We recommended generally an upwards salary review for practically all civil servants and other categories of government employees. The thorny issue of the quantum of the award was resolved in favour of the lowest paid civil servants. In determining the award, we began with an analysis of the remuneration ladder. Therefore, we decided to raise the top of the normal civil service range from K9,000 to K9,500 per annum. This represented a salary increase of 5.56 per cent. At the other end of the ladder, the lowest civil service salary was K396 per annum. We decided to raise the lowest civil service salary from K396 to K540 per annum, an increase of 36.36 per cent. The effect of these awards was to reduce the ratio between the highest and the lowest civil service salaries from 1:25 to 1:20. That achieved an appreciable narrowing of the incomes gap. We, therefore, recommended to the government in our report the sum of K540 per annum for the lowest civil service salary and K9,500 per annum at the top of the remuneration ladder.

In our report, as a guide to the government, we stated that the cost of living, the economic situation, the need to narrow the gap between lower and higher incomes and generally to improve conditions of service were the most important factors which influenced us. Our estimated annual cost of increases in salaries and wages was K37,527,599 for the civil service, the teaching service and local authorities. We also recommended backdating the introduction of new salaries and wages to 1 April 1975. In response to the recommendations in our report, the government issued a white paper in June 1975. Most of the major recommendations in our report were accepted by the government. Even more importantly, the salary increases which we recommended and the improvements in conditions of service were well received by the civil servants and other categories of government employees.

The favourable reaction of civil servants to the recommendations in our report was a source of great satisfaction to me and my colleagues. The world in which we live is so unpredictable! Overnight, the members of the commission became popular figures in our country. I recall receiving messages of congratulations for the work our commission had done from many people – most of them completely unknown to me. The other members of the commission, erstwhile ordinary humble citizens who had served our country honourably as public servants, came into the limelight overnight. However, apparently some politicians found the consequences of our appointment as commissioners to inquire into salaries, salary structures and conditions of service of public servants embarrassing.

When we completed our work on the Commission of Inquiry, I resumed my law practice in Jaques and Partners on a full time basis. One day I met purely accidentally an old intimate friend, the vivacious and humorous Sikota Wina, once my student at Munali Secondary School. He told me that our commission's recommendations had caused some confusion among political big wigs in President Kaunda's government. As minister of finance, I had always emphasized the importance of maintaining strict control of recurrent expenditure as one way of stabilizing the value of the Kwacha and the economy generally. Therefore, some leading politicians did not expect the commission to recommend any salary increases at all in the light of the country's economic situation. He then remarked wittily that ambitious politicians do not like to see potential rivals gaining popularity. There was some truth in his remark although they knew that I had no political ambitions. But, of course, fear of the unknown is a disease among some politicians. The best reward I received for our toil and sweat on the Commission of Inquiry was the appreciation and gratitude of the beneficiaries of our work. Twenty five years later, I continued to receive compliments from many erstwhile civil servants with remarks such as "you know I bought my first wardrobe with the back-pay I received under the recommendations of the Mwanakatwe Salaries Commission!"

Undoubtedly, I was personally satisfied and proud of the work of the Commission of Inquiry and the positive response of civil servants to the recommendations in our report. Nonetheless, I was happy to resume the more interesting and remunerative work of law practice in Jaques and Partners. I settled down again quite satisfactorily in the law firm. In any case, I had continued to attend to the interests of my clients as far as it was possible to do so during my involvement with the work of the Commission of Inquiry. I was back in the law office for only a few months when I was approached by a well known businessman in Lusaka to join his accountancy firm. Oliver Irwin was the senior partner of Coopers & Lybrand in Zambia, a member of Coopers & Lybrand (International). It was one of the largest accountancy firms in the country. On 1 July 1975, the firm of Coopers & Lybrand in Zambia had 151 professional staff, forty five administrative staff, with three partners, a total of 199 personnel. Oliver Irwin's vision for the firm was to increase its client base, particularly from parastatals. However, he was unhappy that the full complement of 151 professional employees of his accountancy firm were expatriates. His efforts in previous years to employ indigenous personnel as professional staff had proved futile. Very few were available locally. Therefore, he decided on a programme of identifying capable and intelligent young Zambians with suitable academic qualifications and encouraging them to train in the United Kingdom as fully qualified accountants. He expected that in this way and over the years a large proportion of professional staff in the local accountancy firm would be Zambians. He attached importance and urgency to his programme of Zambianisation of the professional staff of Coopers and Lybrand.

However, Oliver Irwin also believed that his programme of Zambianisation of the firm's professional staff was not likely to succeed without the guidance and support of a suitable Zambian citizen. He was advised to invite me to join his firm and work with him to achieve his objectives. It is likely that someone told him that I had a soft spot for training young men and women. I had done legal work for Coopers & Lybrand from time to time. I met Oliver Irwin when I was privileged to sit on the Board of Directors of ZIMCO Limited, a holding company of several state-owned enterprises. President Kaunda chaired board meetings on which I sat by virtue of holding the position of minister of finance. When Oliver requested me to join his accountancy firm, he emphasized that the London office had approved my appointment as a partner in view of the senior position I had held previously in the government. In Jaques & Partners, too, I was a partner of the firm. Consequently, I was eligible to purchase shares in Coopers & Lybrand, thereby reducing the percentage of shares held by Coopers & Lybrand in London. The terms I was offered for partnership in Coopers & Lybrand in Zambia were attractive; my partners in Jaques & Partners encouraged me to accept the offer; and the remunerations and conditions of service were attractive too. Above all, I was assured of a steady flow of legal work within the accountancy firm itself for my performance "in-house" or for reference to Jaques & Partners. My wife had no objection.

I have always thought that she would have objected to my decision to accept the challenge of promoting Zambianisation in Coopers & Lybrand if it meant more involvement in politics. Even over a relatively short period, we were happy in the Jaques & Partners family. Fortunately, when

I moved eventually to Coopers & Lybrand, we integrated ourselves easily into an equally friendly association of professional men and women and their families. I was not loaded with as much work as I was obliged to carry out on behalf of clients in Jaques & Partners although I had a competent legal assistant, Ranjit Fernando, a Sri-Lankan, to work with me exclusively. Otherwise, in Coopers & Lybrand the work was mainly of a routine nature relating to interviewing potential students for sponsorship to train as accountants, providing legal opinions on a wide range of issues and coordinating operations in the firm's offices in Kitwe, Ndola and Livingstone.

It was a joy to work with Oliver Irwin our senior partner in Zambia. An experienced accountant, he had wide connections with influential businessmen and politicians. Many people admired him because he was a practical man of few words who often achieved the desired results. Over the years of practising accountancy in Zambia, he had gained the reputation of helping many men in the world and he and I had one common characteristic – by nature we were both *trouble-shooters*. He considered no problem insurmountable. Therefore, in practically every difficult situation, he tried to find an acceptable solution by adopting a proactive attitude. Above all, I enjoyed working with him because he trusted me as much as I trusted him. On every important issue we consulted each other.

Early in September, Oliver Irwin invited me to travel with him to London to attend a meeting of the international firm of Coopers & Lybrand in October. Such meetings were held in selected member countries once every two years. The partners attending the meetings were allowed to invite their wives to accompany them. After consulting my wife, I accepted the invitation to represent the firm of Coopers & Lybrand in Zambia with Oliver Irwin at the 19th Meeting of the General Partners to be held in London on 3 October 1975. Partners, principals and representatives of member and associated firms were invited to attend.

We had an unusual journey to London. Ordinarily we

should have travelled from Lusaka to London on either a Zambian Airways or British Airways flight. However, we travelled to London in a small twin-engine jet aircraft. Oliver was the pilot and his wife, Joan, was the co-pilot. Because Lusaka to London was a long journey, they sometimes exchanged their roles with Joan taking over as pilot and Oliver performing the functions of a co-pilot. At first, Margaret and I were visibly uneasy, in fact frightened, at the prospect of flying in a small aircraft from Lusaka to London. Oliver had expected me to put on a brave face. I did not – I was as frightened as a rabbit! With only one stop for refuelling, somewhere in Zaire, now called the Democratic Republic of Congo, after some hours we were flying over the Sahara desert. After another stop in North Africa we flew over the English Channel and landed safely at an airport in the Midlands. Apart from the joy of meeting other members of the Coopers & Lybrand family from various parts of the world, the real benefit I derived from attending the Meeting of General Partners was exposure to a wide range of publications – books, periodicals and journals. I made a list of books and journals of interest to me and bought some books before returning to Zambia. On my wife's part, the evening entertainment we were given on two occasions was the climax of our visit to London. The senior partner from Tanzania at the meeting was Reginald Mengi, accompanied by his wife Mercy. Margaret and Mercy had a common background from two neighbouring countries and by the end of the meeting, they had developed a friendship which has endured the passage of time.

One particular item on the agenda was of special interest to me. Apart from supporting Oliver Irwin's programme for the Zambianisation of the professional staff of the firm in Zambia, I had also a special interest in efforts to promote and strengthen some degree of independence of local firms, such as Coopers & Lybrand in Zambia, from their parent firms in London. At the meeting the chairman undertook to circulate a new draft policy statement on "independence" of member and associated firms. The thrust of the draft policy statement was to lay down the "minimum standards (that) should be observed by member and associated firms in this respect" and member and associated firms were urged to "study carefully the exposure draft setting out these minimum standards and comment on it as they thought appropriate".

Although there was undoubtedly a critical shortage of indigenous professional accountants in Zambia, a very small number was nonetheless available. The few who were available were trained overseas under various types of sponsorship. Some students were sponsored by accounting firms or by their employers or the government. I was anxious to try and fish in a pond which appeared dry of any fish for the sake of slowly progressing the employment of Zambian professional staff in Coopers & Lybrand. In 1975, we identified one young man who was fully qualified as a chartered accountant. He was intelligent, energetic and had remarkable qualities of leadership. George Sokota was the first Zambian qualified accountant. Oliver Irwin and I tried to attract him to join our firm in Lusaka. Our effort failed. In fact our attempt to attract him to join the ranks of our firm's professional staff backfired. He was employed by the local branch of public accountants, Deloitte & Touche, which had sponsored his training in England. His employers objected to our overtures to attract George Sokota to join Coopers & Lybrand. As the Senior Partner in Coopers & Lybrand, Oliver Irwin was queried by Coopers & Lybrand in London about the propriety of our action. I requested Oliver Irwin to inform our office in London that if our action was in any way improper, I was primarily responsible. I was prepared to accept the blame. Today, twenty five years down the road, George Sokota is the doyen of the accountancy profession, respected in Zambia and abroad as a well qualified and experienced accountant. At least history has not questioned our value judgement at the time George Sokota was invited to join Coopers & Lybrand as an accountant in a senior position in the firm's office in Lusaka.

Our failure to attract George Sokota to work in Coopers & Lybrand underscored the urgency of formulating our programme of training accountants and implementing it. I worked enthusiastically on a policy document on "ways and means of improving and accelerating the training of accountants in Zambia" which was intended to interest both the partners in Coopers & Lybrand and in other local accountancy firms. The paper was also intended to interest the government in a subject of national interest.

At the end of March 1976, I completed the preparation of my paper after extensive consultations. On 29 March, the Lusaka office of our accountancy firm released my paper to the partners in Zambia and to the professional and administrative staff. Copies of the paper were sent to relevant government departments and various stakeholders. The recommendations contained in the paper were well received. I sometimes look back with a sense of satisfaction to my small contribution to the sensitisation of various agencies in the government and private sector to the need to improve and accelerate the training of accountants in Zambia.

CHAPTER

11

Back to Finance

In 1976, during the last week of the month of April, I visited the Copperbelt Province in connection with our programme for training Zambian accountants locally and abroad. At first I visited Kitwe for a day and then returned to Ndola, where I intended to spend the weekend before returning to Lusaka. My wife's sister and her husband lived in Ndola. It was convenient to meet them while on duty in Ndola although I had chosen to stay at the Savoy Hotel.

That weekend early in the morning on Sunday, a senior officer of the Zambia Police Service came to the hotel to see me. The receptionist on the ground floor of the hotel informed me that the police officer brought a message for me from State House. That was a real surprise, for I was not expecting that the president of Zambia would send me a message with such urgency. I was requested to travel to Lusaka at the earliest opportunity to meet him at the University Teaching Hospital where he was admitted for a routine medical check-up. Not knowing why President Kaunda was anxious to meet urgently, I confirmed my willingness to travel as soon as possible. Fortunately a seat was available on a Zambia Airways flight to Lusaka late in the afternoon. The rest of the arrangements to meet him in the hospital ward were straightforward. My wife met me at the airport and we drove directly to the hospital.

At about eight o'clock in the evening I found myself again discussing national affairs of grave concern with President Kaunda. He described to me his grief when he decided to relieve our senior executives from their offices in the Bank of Zambia and Zambia National Commercial Bank Limited for their misdeeds. He was anxious to replace them with people capable of restoring the good name of Zambia "in important financial circles throughout the world." He had decided, therefore, to appoint me minister of finance again. He appealed to me to accept the appointment. For a while I was dumbfounded. I remained silent in order to recover from my shock. All sorts of concerns came to my mind immediately – the political, social and financial implications of accepting public office alarmed me considerably. Instead of giving President Kaunda a negative response, which my instinct dictated at that time, I asked him to give me some time to chew over what I considered a difficult problem. However, he insisted that the matter was urgent and that the nation was waiting to know his response to the crisis. In these circumstances we reached a fair compromise. I undertook to consult with my wife and close friends and relatives the same night. I also undertook to communicate my final decision to him the following day.

Very late that same night a few close friends and family members came together in my house for consultations. After listening to my ordeal that day, they all sympathized and appreciated my dilemma. One of my closest relatives fortified his preference for my acceptance of the offer by suggesting that the consequences of rejection were too ghastly to contemplate. Fortunately, I was supported by nearly everyone in my belief that only one criterion required proper consideration – to put the national interests above my own or vice-versa. At that consultative gathering, I opted for acceptance of reappointment to the portfolio of finance in the national interest. My wife, perhaps reluctantly, also supported my decision.

Early the following morning, I also consulted my colleagues at Coopers and Lybrand. All of them advised that it was an honour for the president to reappoint me minister of finance. Although they would regret the loss of my services in the firm, nonetheless they were inclined to encourage me to

264

accept the appointment. Oliver Irwin, our senior partner in the firm, was particularly enthusiastic that I should accept the appointment. He was prepared to persuade partners in the London office to agree payment of my full salary in lieu of the government's salary and allowances which were less than my total remuneration as a partner in our firm. However, I rejected the offer. If I decided to accept reappointment to the office of minister of finance, I believed that on purely moral grounds I would be obliged to forfeit all benefits from the firm in the form of salary and allowances. For I regarded an arrangement of receiving pay from a private business organization while in the government's service as likely to compromise my position in a particularly sensitive ministry. For, indeed, the person who pays the piper also quite often calls the tune. On the other hand, I was quite happy to continue to hold shares in the firm so that if I so wished at the end of my term of office as a minister I could return to the firm or dispose of them.

Later that Monday morning, I again conferred with President Kaunda in an effort to conclude our discussion of the previous day. He was pleased with my positive response to his call on me to serve the nation again as minister of finance. I briefed him fully on my discussion with Oliver Irwin and other partners in Coopers and Lybrand. In the afternoon, President Kaunda sent me a letter of appointment as follows:-

Following up our discussions last night and early this morning, I am very glad to appoint you once again Minister of Finance. You will take over this post at a time when the whole nation is disgraced by the activities of two of our brothers, namely Mr Kuwani and Mr Nkwabilo, former Governor and former Deputy Governor of the Central Bank of Zambia.

Their activities which led to their being arrested have disastrous implications on Zambia which are impossible to imagine. Adding to this, the steps which we have had to take against Mr Nyambe, former Managing Director of the National Commercial Bank of Zambia and his Deputy Mr Kazunga,

TEACHER, POLITICIAN, LAWYER

presents before you a complete picture of how low the name
Zambia must be in important financial circles throughout the
world. However, against what I have said above, one is glad to
pitch your name and that of the new Governor of the Central
Bank, Comrade LJ Mwananshiku. You are going to form a
formidable team which, I am sure, is going to bring joy to all
our friends and gloom to all our foes. Needless for me to say,
Mupanga, that I have full confidence in you.

May I now end by saying that I hope and pray that the good
Lord will ever be your source of love for your fellow men,
dedication, commitment to the cause of the people of Zambia,
kindness to them and, indeed the spirit of hard work throughout
your life.

I was naturally overwhelmed by President Kaunda's
expression of confidence in my ability to stand shoulder to
shoulder with other ministers in the cabinet to restore the
government's ability to manage the economy in a prudent and
effective manner. I had worked with the new governor of the
Bank of Zambia, Mr Luke Mwananshiku, during my first term
of office at the Ministry of Finance. In that period, he held the
post of senior under secretary responsible for the budget office
and subsequently, he was appointed permanent secretary. I
assessed him as one of the most dedicated and efficient civil
servants. He was a technocrat through and through. With his
economic background and wide experience in administration, I
was satisfied that he was well prepared to perform the functions
of governor of the Bank of Zambia. The rest of the senior staff
at the headquarters of the Ministry of Finance were old familiar
faces with whom I had worked happily and satisfactorily.
Therefore, I expected no rebellion following my reappointment
to the finance portfolio, but rather loyalty and cooperation. One
fact was obvious and unchangeable about the finance portfolio
– that it is in Zambia as in most countries in the world one of
the busiest offices in government. A minister of finance often
has to curtail expenditure and that is why some refer to the

Treasury as 'the graveyard of politics'. Yet for me the Treasury at the political level also offers opportunities to influence the pattern or pace of development. That was again my experience when I went back to the Ministry of Finance at the beginning of May 1976. It is a ministry which offers room for innovation and making bold decisions depending on the style and temperament of the holder of the office.

By way of prologue, let me first reflect upon public reaction to my reappointment in May 1976. It received overwhelming support from men and women in all walks of life in Zambia. In 1958 when I was appointed education officer by the Northern Rhodesian government, I received many congratulatory messages. That was understandable. It was the first time an indigenous civil servant made the grade for appointment to a post previously reserved for expatriates. My appointment to the post of education officer was in that context an historical event. In this case, however, there was nothing particularly significant in the exercise of the president's prerogative to effect a minor reshuffle of the cabinet at the beginning of May 1976. Yet the number of congratulatory messages I received was truly overwhelming. I received messages from ordinary men and women in Zambia, in South Africa and West Africa, and from representatives of business and international organizations both in the United States of America and the United Kingdom. In the letter of appointment which I received from President Kaunda on 3 May 1976, he stated that "...activities which led to their (the men in charge of the Bank of Zambia and Zambia National Commercial Bank) being arrested have disastrous implications on Zambia which are impossible to imagine." The congratulatory messages I received were an expression of hope by many that the new team would restore people's confidence in the proper management of two key financial institutions, the Bank of Zambia and Zambia National Commercial Bank Limited.

My records show that I received more than one hundred and twenty written letters of congratulation messages on my reappointment to the Ministry of Finance. One category of such messages came from some members of UNIP's Central Committee and cabinet ministers. This was to a large extent comforting. At least from the beginning I had the feeling that the cooperation of my political colleagues was assured in performing my unenviable duties and responsibilities. For I have always believed that a minister of finance who looks for popularity can never succeed. The nature of his work is such that he is sometimes obliged to take rather unpopular decisions. Often he will find himself stepping on other people's toes. That he should take in his stride if it is in the national interest to do so. Paul Lusaka, minister of rural development, wrote: "I wish to assure you of my support and cooperation in your assignment. Wishing you all the best of luck in all you do during your term of office." From the political party cadres, a young female member of parliament, Miss Zeniah Ndhlovu, also conveyed her congratulations to me on my reappointment as follows:

> I sincerely congratulate you for accepting the portfolio belatedly. I am also aware that it was your genuine wish to decline such and stay in the background but as an elected popular representative of the people, it is only fair that the same should be reflected at cabinet level.

> I am sure it is the feeling of most backbenchers that we have lost strong representation but we are grateful that the nation has made one more stride forwards as actual participation by the people in the running of their own affairs through you.

> May God bless you always.

Apart from representatives of the ruling party, my reappointment as minister of finance was welcomed by a broad spectrum of members of the business community who also welcomed my return to the helm of the Ministry of Finance. At that time Chisambwe Kapihya was the general manager of the National Breweries Limited. He wrote a letter to me and stated that: "It gave me great pleasure to hear of your appointment on the radio and I could not resist the temptation to put my feelings of joy on paper and communicate them to you." From the Coopers and Lybrand office in Dublin, Ireland, the senior partner, Donald Flynn, wrote a congratulatory letter to me which touched me considerably. He wrote, "I have read with considerable interest your reappointment as minister for finance.... congratulations and good wishes for this onerous responsibility which you have reassumed .... The financial management of any nation is a difficult undertaking which I am sure you will perform with resolution and skill." While serving as a partner in the Lusaka office of Coopers and Lybrand, I accepted an invitation from Andrew Sardanis to act as "business advisor" to the Board of Wilfrid Watson Ltd which was a subsidiary company of Sardanis Associates Services Ltd. Andrew Sardanis was its chairman. The day after I was appointed minister of finance by President Kaunda I wrote a letter to Andrew Sardanis resigning as business advisor. He responded:

Naturally it was with great regret that I received your letter of the 4 May 1976 resigning as business advisor to the Board of Wilfrid Watson Ltd. However, when I did hear of your call to another term of office in the service of the nation I was, of course, expecting it.

Let me congratulate you on your decision to go back to the Ministry of Finance. It must have been an agonizing one coming so soon after the beginning of a very promising career in the private sector, but nevertheless the correct one. The state of the economy and our reputation in international financial circles are at an all time low but I am absolutely confident that a team led by you as minister of finance with Luke at the Bank of Zambia will go a long way towards restoring economic order and our reputation.

From abroad, I received many letters and telex messages of congratulations. They included messages from Charles

Billmyer, vice president, London Regional Office for Africa, Bank of America; Messrs Robert Hoen, David Davis and Thomas Shattan on behalf of the Chase Manhattan Bank NA; Timothy Tahane, alternate executive director, African Development Bank; and Bob Liebenthal, formerly an economist with the Ministry of Agriculture in Lusaka but then with the World Bank. However, although I valued all the messages I received from well-wishers, the message of congratulations which I received from the president of the World Bank, Mr Robert S McNamara, was the most significant of them all. He wrote a letter on 17 May welcoming me again to the Board of Governors of the World Bank. He wrote:

> I am happy to learn that you have again become the Governor for Zambia on the Board of Governors of the World Bank.
>
> The Executive Directors, Officers and Staff join me in welcoming your return to our Board. We look forward with pleasure to a renewal of our contacts with you in the activities of the Bank.

There was one aspect of some of the messages which gave me comfort and satisfaction. Many well wishers apparently knew that taking up the reins and the responsibilities of government again involved considerable personal sacrifices. In congratulating me on my reappointment as minister of finance, the chief justice, hon. Annel M Silungwe, observed in his letter that "... no doubt this must have entailed a great deal of personal sacrifice on your part, and I consider it to be very commendable indeed because it was done purely in the national interest." I felt equally encouraged by the accolade I received from one of the younger generation of politicians, Boniface Zulu, chairman of the Water Development Board of Zambia. He wrote thus: "I have been one of your greatest admirers in Zambian politics; I like your honesty and dedication to the cause of the common man and I hope that you will continue with your principles for the benefit of the young people who are now joining the party and government." One of my closest friends in the political arena was the veteran politician, Reuben Chitandika Kamanga. He was especially happy, indeed excited, about my decision to accept service as a cabinet minister again in President Kaunda's government. He was a senior member of the ruling party's Central Committee.

Before my appointment as minister of finance, a rumour was taking the rounds in Lusaka that some of my personal friends who remained in the government after the 1973 presidential and general elections were uncomfortable with my role as a backbencher in Parliament. Others believed that the Commission of Inquiry into Salaries for the Public Service should not have awarded generous salary increases in their report. They thought that in spite of the country's ailing economy, salary increases were recommended in order to make the government unpopular if the recommendations were not accepted. An old friend, Sikota Wina, once hinted to me about this feeling among die-hard party activists. Sikota Wina was merely alerting me jokingly about the concerns of political die-hards. Of course, I did not take his remark seriously. However, from some of the congratulatory letters I received, it became obvious to me that there can be no smoke without fire. My active role in Parliament as a backbencher was underscored by Miss Zeniah Ndhlovu in her congratulatory message. Reuben Kamanga, who was my closest friend among politicians, summed up his feelings about my acceptance of appointment as minister of finance in a particularly hilarious style. Unwittingly, he spilled the beans! He undoubtedly gave substance to some rumours I had heard since the submission of the Report of the Commission of Inquiry into Salaries for the Public Service. In his letter, he wrote:

> Just to confirm what I said to you by telephone on that great evening of my comrade's re-re-re-re-re-re-appointment as Minister of Finance.

> I said then and I say it now that His Excellency the President could not have made a better choice at this very critical time.

271

The economy of our country needs expert hands and brilliant brains. Above all it requires people who can inspire confidence into the nation.

Comrade, I am aware of the inconveniences this re-appointment has made to you personally and indeed to immediate members of your family. All your plans which you made and were still making in your previous employment have been frustrated. Speaking as one of your close friends, the re-appointment has cost you far more in terms of personal benefits. This is not to say you had stopped making your contribution towards the building of our country. No, this is not. But in your present position you will give away even the little you had attempted to begin doing. To you Comrade, therefore, it is the nation first and then Mupanga second.

As I said that evening we are once again in the same boat. You and me must now implement the findings of the Mwanakatwe Salaries Commission. How do you like that?

I was undaunted by Reuben Kamanga's rhetorical question in the ultimate paragraph of his letter. The team of senior officials at the headquarters of my new ministry were competent, experienced and loyal to me. The letter I received on 7 May 1976 from the general manager of the Bank of Zambia, FL Bvulani, was a general expression of the feelings of many of his colleagues both at the central bank and in the Ministry of Finance. In a short letter, firstly he conveyed to me his heartiest congratulations on my appointment as minister of finance by the president of Zambia. He then concluded his letter courteously: "May I take this opportunity to assure you, Sir, that I will give you full support and cooperation in your undertakings." With the assurance of support and encouragement from technocrats and key administrative staff in both the Ministry of Finance and the Bank of Zambia, I assumed my responsibilities with confidence that I would live up to the expectations of my fellow countrymen and women. So, within five days of my appointment, I was back in the

272

Ministry of Finance and another permanent secretary received me in the same office which I had previously occupied from October 1970 to December 1973.

My team of workmates at the Ministry of Finance, both technocrats and administrative staff, was excellent. They were capable of surviving the rigours of my style of work. However, I also required the advisory services of an independent expert who was not an ordinary civil servant. I had such an adviser in the Ministry of Education, although I did not find him particularly useful. Professor John Mars, the prolific writer, was my adviser in the Ministry of Lands and Mines. During my first term in the Treasury, I had Dr Raj Sharma as my adviser on economic and fiscal policies. He was still available, albeit for a limited period only, when I returned to the Ministry of Finance at the beginning of May 1976.

When I held the portfolio of finance for the first time from 1970 to 1973, Dr Sharma's performance was outstanding. Because of his special abilities and experience, I often relied on him for advice which he always rendered with exceptional competence and humility. That was the reason for his rapid promotion through the ranks in the civil service in Zambia to the post of senior economist and subsequently the post of assistant secretary with special responsibility for providing advisory services to the minister of finance.

Therefore, in the first week of my return to the Treasury when I requested the permanent secretary to instruct a team of senior officials to prepare a comprehensive brief on "Zambia's economic problems and prospects" I asked him to involve Dr Sharma in the preparation of the brief. It was my intention to be updated on the current state of the economy, with an assessment of the successes and failures of economic policies adopted by my successors at the Treasury. It was an urgent assignment and I was given a comprehensive brief with a summary in a short time. Among many important issues, it contained an account of the collapse of copper prices and its disastrous effects on Zambia's economy. Consequently, the balance of payments position had deteriorated from a current account surplus to an increased deficit. In fact, it had deteriorated from a current account surplus of US$112 million in 1973, my last year at the helm of the Treasury, to a massive deficit of US$471 million in 1975, a year which saw a deficit on the balance of trade for the first time since independence. Therefore, the deficit had to be financed by utilization of foreign reserves and by the accumulation of arrears on external payments. Another notable consequence of the decline of copper prices was that the mining companies experienced a period of non-profitability unprecedented in their history. In 1975, the mining companies were obliged to sell copper at prices which on average were less than the cost of production. The brief indicated that the trend was likely to continue. Thirdly, due to these factors, the government budget was seriously affected. For example, in 1974 revenue from mineral taxation yielded K339 million, representing over 50 per cent of total revenue. After 1974, there was a sharp decline in revenue from mineral taxation.

These external influences had another negative impact on Zambia's economy. Between 1974 and 1976, the decline in per capita national income declined by nearly 12 per cent. When adjusted for the terms of trade, real per capita gross domestic product fell by a staggering 37.4 per cent.

From the brief my officials prepared, it would have been unreasonable to expect any comfort during my second term of office at the Treasury. It was certainly my conviction that in the medium term the prospects for the price of copper were bleak. I realized that I returned to the Treasury when Zambia was passing through what was undoubtedly a serious and prolonged economic crisis caused mainly by our country's dependence on a single commodity, copper, and a series of external factors completely beyond our control. Copper prices were determined outside Zambia on the London Metal Exchange. Furthermore, in January 1973, the illegal regime in Rhodesia after sustained provocation of our country had sealed the border with Zambia. It remained closed when I returned to the Ministry of Finance.

Despite a massive re-routing exercise in 1973, the cost to Zambia of the closure of a major trading route was heavy. It was heavy both in financial terms and in the relative slowness of moving goods through the overburdened port of Dar es Salaam in Tanzania.

From this scenario, it was obvious to me that our country's economic survival would largely depend on the preparedness of all the people in Zambia to make the necessary sacrifices. I viewed at that time the expenditure in the government budget as my number one target. In this regard, I anticipated an immediate stoppage of over-expenditure on the allocations in the 1976 budget. Secondly, I anticipated reductions in capital expenditure. This was to lead inevitably to abandonment of some capital projects or deceleration on their progress with consequential savings on capital expenditure. In all my anticipated efforts to resuscitate the economy, attraction of external assistance was a key component. Above all considerations for stabilisation of the economy in the long term, improvement of the performance of the agricultural sector was paramount.

As I was studying briefs on the economy of our country and discussing the feasibility of proposals for improving it the Central Committee of the ruling United National Independence Party was preparing feverishly to hold its regular General Conference at Mulungushi. It was due to be held at the end of May or early in June. Apart from delegates from every district throughout the country, Central Committee members were expected to attend the party's General Conference. It was also mandatory for cabinet ministers to attend as accredited members. The attendance at the General Conference usually exceeded two thousand.

One day towards the end of the one week long General Conference, I was informed that the national chairman had decided to include my name on the list of speakers. Each specially invited speaker's intervention was limited to not more than ten minutes. In my case, the national chairman, as presiding officer, advised me to speak on the economy of Zambia. Later as I reflected on his invitation to participate in that day's proceedings, I wondered what I was expected to say to the delegates on the economy of Zambia in a period of not more than ten minutes. I decided to speak extempore – in other words off-the-cuff according to my instinct. Not unexpectedly, I was not called to address the conference before the break for lunch. I was invited by the national chairman to address the General Conference half-way down the list of afternoon speakers. There was a warm and heartening applause when my name was called for the purpose of making a short intervention. However, the applause was not as thunderous as it had been for others who spoke before me, especially representatives of foreign governments who read messages of goodwill to the people of Zambia from their governments.

In my short speech to the delegates and visitors at the General Conference, I expressed my gratitude to President Kaunda for appointing me again as minister of finance. I assured the delegates of my determination to work hard to improve the economy which had deteriorated considerably due largely to external factors. I emphasized that the Zambian economy was a classic example of a "dual economy". It was an economy in which a small but wealthy highly industrialized urban sector existed side-by-side with a large, poor rural subsistence sector. It was characterized by large disparity between urban and rural incomes. I further explained that growth rates in the two sectors were due to the government's policies which in general favoured the urban sector. I then told the delegates at the General Conference that a careful study of economic indicators showed that between 1974, when I left the Ministry of Finance, and 1976 when I was reassigned the portfolio of finance, real per capita national income fell by nearly ten per cent. When adjusted for the terms of trade real per capita gross domestic product had fallen by twenty five per cent in the same period. In a nutshell, I summed up, the people had become poorer over the same period. After these words, I walked down from the platform. The delegates were unexpectedly moved by my short intervention. They applauded, whistled and cheered as I walked back to my seat.

However, later in the evening it transpired that my address was not appreciated by some members of the Central Committee, the all-powerful political bureau of the ruling United National Independence Party. In particular, they took offence at my assertion that according to economic indicators people had gradually become poorer over the period between 1974 and 1976. They believed that my remarks were likely to be misunderstood by ordinary delegates to imply that the government's economic policies had failed. To the hawks among members of the ruling party's Central Committee, my remarks were calculated to make UNIP unpopular. One of the more erudite and outspoken political activists, Alexander Chikwanda, took exception to the murmurs of unhappiness among the conservative-minded party leaders with my short speech. He reminded me that enlightened men and women knew that certain economic indicators were necessary to determine poverty levels in society. Therefore, any significant decline in per capita income indicates an increase in poverty levels, more especially in the less developed countries. He gave me the encouragement I required now that I was back in a political game – a game in which many are tempted to gain cheap popularity by appeasement of their followers. This incident reminded me of my experience as minister of education. It was my nature at all times to tell the truth even when the truth was unpleasant to some people. That is how I apparently earned among teachers this nickname: 'Mr speak straight'.

In June 1976, I received a letter from President Kaunda instructing me as minister of finance in turn to instruct the governor of the Bank of Zambia to freeze Lonrho's bank accounts in Zambia. The background to this request was that early in 1976, a well known British businessman faced a rebellion of his co-directors of his company at its head office in London. It was Tiny Rowland, the major shareholder in Lonrho, a multinational company with extensive business interests in Eastern and Southern African countries, including Kenya, Malawi, Zambia and Rhodesia. His companies were involved in agriculture, motor vehicle trade, engineering and construction. Lonrho was an important company for promoting development. In particular, it also provided employment opportunities in these countries because of its extensive investments.

Without doubt, Lonrho's outstanding business success in these countries was due to Tiny Rowland's close connections with heads of state, especially Jomo Kenyatta, Hastings Banda and Kenneth Kaunda for Kenya, Malawi and Zambia respectively. In particular, he espoused the cause of African majority rule for countries which were still under white minority rule in Southern Africa. He was also a close ally of Joshua Nkhomo who led the Zimbabwe African People's Union (ZAPU) in the liberation war against Ian Smith's white minority rule in Rhodesia. These relationships with leading African statesmen in Southern Africa placed him in a particularly influential position. Therefore, faced with a boardroom crisis of his London-based company, he turned to some African leaders for support against his rivals who had conspired to remove him from his position as chairman of Lonrho. He expected to maintain his position if his African friends took appropriate measures in their own countries to disadvantage Lonrho companies if he was removed from office. President Kaunda was among the leaders approached by Tiny Rowland for support and he responded by instructing me to have Lonrho's bank accounts frozen.

He gave in the letter some background information about Lonrho's boardroom crisis. It threatened the position of Tiny Rowland who was known to be a friend of Zambia. President Kaunda feared that the removal of Tiny Rowland as chairman of Lonrho was likely to affect the development of our country. His successor in office might be a reactionary with retrogressive policies. Under the existing law at that time, it was not possible for President Kaunda to issue such instructions directly to the governor of the Bank of Zambia. Only the minister of finance was authorized to give such instructions in writing to the governor of the Bank of Zambia.

The letter I received from President Kaunda was a real test of my determination and strength to resist pressure to act at any time, as minister of finance, on instructions to promote a cause which was politically expedient but totally unacceptable on purely economic grounds. I agonized alone about the wisdom of refusing to carry out President Kaunda's instruction. I concluded that there was no justification for freezing Lonrho's bank accounts in Zambia in order to support Tiny Rowland in his desperate attempt to maintain leadership of the board of directors of a foreign company. More importantly, I agonized about the social consequences of freezing Lonrho's bank accounts in Zambia. It was obvious that payment of month-end wages and salaries would be impossible if the bank accounts of the company and its subsidiaries were frozen. The logical, not merely instinctive, reaction to President Kaunda's instruction was to avoid its implementation.

However, I decided to consult senior civil servants for their own views on the best way of implementing President Kaunda's instruction. Fortunately, I had a very good team of advisors, Francis Walusiku, Lloyd Sichilongo and Dr Raj Sharma. They, too, expressed concern about implementing President Kaunda's instruction. They reminded me that in the event of a Parliamentary question on the issue being raised subsequently the government would find itself in an extremely difficult situation. Zambian people generally were not concerned with the boardroom affairs of Lonrho in London. It was at this stage that I consulted Luke Mwananshiku, governor of the Bank of Zambia, for advice. His views were not different from my own and the views of senior officials in the Ministry of Finance. The governor of the Bank of Zambia and the senior civil servants preferred to take over the responsibility of preparing a suitable draft reply to send to the president through official channels after my approval. The suggestion was unacceptable. The

279

president's letter was addressed to me in the first instance. Secondly, it was essentially a political issue which required my personal attention. One of the officials revealed their concern that President Kaunda might dismiss me as minister of finance if I expressed unwillingness to carry out his instructions. To the surprise of the governor and the civil servants, I reminded them that President Kaunda enjoyed the prerogative of relieving any minister of his portfolio at any time. My own wish prevailed. I wrote a letter respectfully to President Kaunda setting out the reasons for my own reluctance to instruct the governor of the Bank of Zambia to freeze Lonrho's bank accounts throughout Zambia. There was no further correspondence between President Kaunda's office and my office on the Lonrho affair. That was President Kaunda's open expression of confidence in me after my re-appointment as minister of finance.

The economic situation in Zambia continued to worsen in 1977. Kaunda summoned Parliament and addressed an emergency session on 11 October 1977. It was the first emergency meeting of Parliament since the independence of Zambia in October 1964. In his address, President Kaunda challenged the members of parliament to consider ways and means of revamping the country's ailing economy. The House took up the challenge. A special select committee of Parliament was appointed under my chairmanship as minister of finance to study President Kaunda's address and recommend measures for stimulating the economy. The composition of the committee included prominent backbenchers like Arthur Wina and Valentine Kayope and an influential member of the Central Committee, Daniel Lisulo, was appointed. The composition of the special Parliamentary Select Committee was as follows:-

Hon JM Mwanakatwe, MP (Chairman)
Hon MJ Lumina, MP (Member)
Hon DM Lisulo, MCC, MP, SC (Member)
Hon AB Chikwanda, MP (Member)
Hon Professor LKH Goma, MP (Member)

Hon R Chisupa, MP (Member)
Hon ANL Wina, MP (Member)
Hon VWC Kayope, MP (Member)
Hon L Lubamba, MP (Member)

The committee was required to examine the desirability of maintaining the existing institutional and organizational structures of the government, parastatal bodies and the party with a view to devising ways and means of strengthening the economy.

Members of the Select Committee attached significance to the third term of reference which was of general application by which they were required to "recommend any necessary actions" which should be taken by the executive to give effect to any conclusion reached by the Select Committee.

We met seventeen times during the period 21 October to 24 November 1977 to hear oral evidence and to consider written submissions from witnesses. The Select Committee received overwhelming support from a cross-section of MPs, civil servants, trade union leaders, farmers, business men, industrialists and representatives of Non-Governmental Organisations. In particular, we appreciated the good response of chiefs of parastatal bodies who voluntarily offered to give oral evidence or submit written memoranda. The list of 107 persons who gave oral evidence or submitted written memoranda was attached to the Select Committee's Report as Appendix III.

The Select Committee presented its report to the National Assembly on 30 November 1977. It contained many radical recommendations, including abolition of the post of provincial member of the Central Committee; abolition of the post of provincial political secretary; designation of a number of members of the Central Committee for service on a part-time basis; phasing out mealie meal subsidies gradually; introducing a more acceptable method of electing members of the Central Committee in accordance with the basic principles of participatory democracy; and reduction of public expenditure in order to reduce the government's budget deficit.

Basic to the recommendations was the fact that the people were saddled with a top-heavy administrative superstructure, that in effect the people were over-governed and the dual administrative structures of party and government were a heavy drain on the economy. The top-heavy provincial superstructures were severally criticized because they were also a serious constraint on the administration as a whole. Parliament debated the report and unanimously accepted the recommendations of the Special Parliamentary Select Committee.

President Kaunda naturally saw red. Perhaps he would have made an objective consideration of the recommendations for revamping the economy if the issue of reforming the Central Committee had not featured as one of the recommendations in the report. He was incensed by the committee's audacity in questioning the desirability of appointing provincial members of the Central Committee and the method of election of members to that body. He had reorganized the political superstructures to maintain a balance of sectional interests, thereby achieving peace and stability. In their report, members of the Special Parliamentary Select Committee stated, "There is presently considerable duplication of effort. It would appear that there is no clear demarcation between the functions and responsibilities of members of the Central Committee on the one hand and members of the cabinet on the other, leading to confusion and overlapping of functions." That was a critical observation on the necessity of the Central Committee in the Zambian political process. The Central Committee was President Kaunda's sacred cow.

Before the end of the year, President Kaunda summoned a meeting of the National Council consisting of an overwhelming majority of UNIP officials who were dependent on his patronage for their livelihood. At the National Council meeting on 12 December 1977, he denounced the recommendations contained in the Select Committee's report. President Kaunda's main concern was that the recommendation to reorganise UNIP's

Central Committee was an intolerable challenge to the supremacy of UNIP. The effect of his attitude to the report was to negate even the more straightforward recommendations which were intended more directly to promote structural reform of the country's ailing economy.

However, there was also another important ramification to President Kaunda's response to the recommendations contained in the Special Parliamentary Select Committee's report. His reaction showed clearly the dangers of the one-party system which inevitably concentrated power in the hands of a few individuals. It was widely known that many members of the Central Committee had been alarmed by some of the recommendations which threatened their positions and livelihood. The report had been adopted unanimously in Parliament, yet an outside body without any legal standing was able to obstruct its business. In subsequent years, similar conflicts between the executive on one hand and Parliament on the other arose under the one-party state. Parliament survived such conflict and maintained independence because of the courage, patience and experience of the first speaker of the House under the one-party system. He always gave the necessary protection to the "minority opposition" when it was justified to do so. Although he was subjected to unwarranted abuse and intimidation, Mr Robinson Nabulyato continued to hold the torch of democracy and freedom in Zambia under the one-party state.

Apparently, the officials in both the IMF and World Bank in Washington read the Special Parliamentary Select Committee's report. Perhaps it was the World Bank's country representative who made available our committee's report to the officials for study. Both the World Bank and IMF officials passed favourable judgment on the efficacy of our committee. They apparently supported practically all the recommendations for revamping the economy both in the short-term and the long-term. At least their positive reaction to our report gave us some comfort. We began to appreciate that our efforts were not entirely in vain – that the administration in our own country might one day consider objectively the recommendations in our report. After all, Parliament had debated the report and unanimously accepted its recommendations.

My first three years in the House as minister of finance from October 1970 to December 1973 taught me some basic housekeeping lessons. I learnt during these years one very important lesson – that a minister responsible for the portfolio of finance at first enjoys immense popularity from political colleagues, especially other ministers. Often, however, much of their love for him is not genuine. It is shown to the minister of finance merely to promote their own interests. Such ministers expect their ministries to receive favours when funds are requested for expenditure above allocations approved by Parliament. When such favours are not forthcoming their friendship does not last for a long time. I learnt in my first three years at the helm of the Treasury that one measure of success of a minister responsible for finance in any government is the extent of his or her unpopularity among ministerial colleagues. This may be a crude way of emphasizing the fact that a minister responsible for finance cannot please all his colleagues at all times. Ministers rarely admit (often for very good reasons) that funds allocated by the Treasury for recurrent or capital expenditure in the annual budget are adequate. Therefore, when they are under attack for poor performance of their ministries, the minister of finance is the scapegoat. Of course, when their ministries perform well they take all the credit. From very early days in my career at the Treasury, I learnt that politics is made of unexpected twists and turns of fortune. Therefore, in making decisions, especially major decisions, a minister of finance should endeavour at all times to take decisions bearing in mind the national interests only.

Because in those years I came to trust only a few of my colleagues who were prepared to come to my defence in Parliament, I resolved not to take any major decision over the heads of senior officers in the Ministry of Finance. A corollary was my resolve to obtain well prepared briefs on my functions and responsibilities. After reading the main brief I received when I returned to the Ministry of Finance, I selected four subjects on which I required detailed briefs. The effectiveness of a minister in the House largely depends on his ability to participate in debates in the House on short notice or even extempore. It is an advantage for a minister to marshal facts for use in a debate without relying on assistance from officers present in the House. I asked for briefs on four particularly important subjects.

When I returned to the Ministry of Finance, private sector participation in the economy appeared stable from my observations. Some state-owned enterprises had continued to expand their operations although their overall performance was poor. Many state-owned enterprises were loss-making entities which relied on subsidies to sustain their operations. I always believed that even in the aftermath of nationalization of privately owned enterprises, encouragement of private initiative was necessary to stimulate economic growth. Private initiative was also necessary to attract foreign investment. In order to speak authoritatively to businessmen within and outside Zambia, a carefully prepared brief for me was necessary on the government's position with respect to the role of the private sector in the development process. Secondly, I requested a detailed brief on subsidies which were increasing year by year with adverse effects on recurrent expenditure levels. It was necessary to know if cutbacks in subsidies were possible and to know the areas in which subsidies would be maintained. Thirdly, a brief was necessary on the perennial problem of budgetary discipline. It was also necessary to know if the figures for supplementary budgets each year were justified or not. Fourthly, I called for a brief on diversification of the economy through the development of agriculture.

Well prepared briefs for a minister are useful not only for facilitating the process of formulating policies and for parliamentary debates but also for carrying out the important public relations role. Businessmen, industrialists and representatives of the donor community require ministerial assurances on important issues they discuss with officials. After reading the detailed briefs the economic scenario was sufficiently clear to me for the performance of my duties and responsibilities. I returned to the Ministry of Finance three months after my predecessor had presented the 1976 budget to Parliament. My duty was to enforce strict adherence to the monetary and fiscal policies contained in the budget address which were adopted by the House. The briefs I was given clearly showed that the country faced serious economic ills at the beginning of 1976. They originated from persistently low copper prices, the escalation of oil prices and the rather slow growth of the agriculture sector. In the previous financial year, Luke Mwananshiku had introduced austerity measures in the budget. I decided to allow continuation of the austerity measures and to enforce them strictly. Those of my fellow ministers who expected me to be lenient were sadly mistaken. Instead, I used every available opportunity to preach the unpopular message to ministers and senior civil servants that I expected all our people to continue to tighten their belts in order to sustain the economic takeoff. This message meant that I was determined to enforce strict control of government spending and curb all ministerial and departmental extravagance.

My demand for strict control of government spending nearly put me in trouble with my own boss, President Kaunda. The Ministry of Defence made requests on one occasion for funds for the purchase of military ware at a price in excess of the funds available in the estimates of expenditure. Officials in the Ministry of Finance refused to allow the overexpenditure in accordance with our policy of strict control of government spending. The permanent secretary for the Ministry of Defence reported his problem to President Kaunda who was responsible for the Ministry of Defence at the political level. He duly summoned me to State House for a discussion of the problem of a clash of interests between officials in the Ministry of Defence and officials in the Ministry of Finance. At the meeting

President Kaunda reminded me that Zambia was literally under siege by Ian Smith's Rhodesian soldiers on our borders. It was in these circumstances imperative to fully equip our army to enable them defend our country's territorial integrity. I wholeheartedly accepted the absolute importance of fully equipping our army to strengthen the defence capability of Zambia. I strongly argued that it was equally important to recognize that a strong economy for Zambia was an effective bulwark against her enemies. It was necessary to encourage government departments to set a good example of adhering to budgetary controls. We adopted in the Ministry of Finance the strategy of a gradual reduction of the government budget deficit in order to strengthen the country's economy.

President Kaunda accepted my concerns. He invited me to attend another meeting at State House to which he also intended to invite the permanent secretary for the Ministry of Defence and senior officers from the army. His idea was to give me the opportunity of interacting with senior army officers. The senior army officers would also have the opportunity of raising their own concerns about the inadequacy of the equipment available for defending our country effectively. The meeting was cordial from the beginning. It was agreed at the meeting in State House to defer purchase of army equipment above funds available in the budget for 1977. The senior army officers shook my hand one by one as they walked out of the conference room without signs of bitterness. I was happy with the conciliatory outcome of the meeting. It was successful due to President Kaunda's wisdom and diplomacy. As president of the Republic of Zambia, he had the prerogative of reshuffling the cabinet and assigning another portfolio to me, or none at all, in order to support the noble cause of our men and women in the armed forces, indeed a national cause in its own right. But he clearly realized that I, too, espoused a cause which was also in the national interest. If, as we believed in the Ministry of Finance, the economy of our country would be ruined by financial indiscipline the widespread poverty and suffering of our people would be disastrous. My ambition during my second term at the Ministry of Finance was to command a growing economy. That was necessary if I was to meet all representatives of donor countries and institutions on equal terms as full partners in the development of Zambia.

There was considerable relief in the Ministry of Finance among senior officials at the outcome of the discussions at State House on the request for additional budgetary expenditure for the Ministry of Finance. Their earlier concern was understandable. In previous years, we had always experienced problems with the budget with regard to the level of expenditure in relation to the resources available. In the past we had allowed rather large deficits in the government budgets. The 1977 budget had been well received by the IMF because we made a bold decision to reduce the deficit to reasonable proportions. I had successfully persuaded my colleagues in cabinet that the austerity measures I had introduced in the budget for 1977 would have to continue for some time. It was necessary, therefore, to tighten our belts in order to sustain the economic takeoff. To achieve that objective, I was obliged to enforce strict control of government spending.

The disastrous economic consequences of the fall in the price of copper meant that the government's revenue was drastically reduced and thus expenditure was confined to absolute essentials in order to reduce deficits in government budgets. Unfortunately, the drastic and prolonged fall in the price of copper, also caused serious financial problems in the mining sector. In 1974, the price of copper averaged K1,307 per tonne. In 1975, it fell to K722 per tonne although the price increased marginally in 1976 to K1,036 per tonne. In my budget statement in 1978, I explained that the fall in copper prices coupled with inflation had reduced our revenues from the mining industry. The revenue from this sector fell from K339 million in 1974 to zero in 1977. Simultaneously, the fall in copper prices had also greatly affected the mining industry. Their receipts went down drastically while their costs went up. Lack of spare parts and other essential inputs jeopardized production on the mines. In the face of these difficulties, I had no alternative but to allow the banking system to lend extensively to the mining sector. At the end of December 1977 total lending to the mining industry reached K163 million. At the end of February 1978, the figure had increased to K176 million. Projections made at that time showed that the two main companies in the mining industry, namely Nchanga Consolidated Copper Mines and Roan Consolidated Mines, were likely to make a combined loss of K61 million in the calendar year 1978.

Quite clearly, the financial situation of the two giant mining companies was critical. The government studied the situation very carefully. A committee of officials was appointed to study the problem and make recommendations to the government. The team was led by the governor of the Bank of Zambia, Luke Mwananshiku, and also comprised Francis Walusiku, permanent secretary and the senior under secretary in charge of the Budget Office, Lloyd Sichilongo. They were authorized to negotiate with the IMF officials an acceptable package of measures for the economic recovery of the country. The negotiations were conducted over a period of three weeks. Because we were facing a serious crisis, I was available to our officials for consultations and guidance.

The negotiating team suggested in their report two ways of eliminating the loss of K61 million by the mining companies. The first was to ask the two companies to eliminate this loss on their own. The sum of K17.5 million was the loss for elimination by Roan Consolidated Mines. The balance was for elimination by Nchanga Consolidated Copper Mines. For Roan Consolidated Mines to eliminate K17.5 million in about one year would have meant laying off immediately about 2,000 workers. Information available to me indicated that, if 2,000 workers were laid off, about 11,000 people were likely to be deprived of their means of livelihood immediately. The numbers of workers and families to be affected was estimated to be much higher for Nchanga Consolidated Mines. This option was unacceptable to the government. The policy of the government was to stimulate economic growth and create more jobs. It was not the government's wish to encourage employers to lay off workers. The government was obliged to see that workers already in employment were retained.

The second option for removing the loss of K61 million was through depreciation of the Zambian currency by twenty per cent. The government took its final decision on the basis of a compromise between the two options. The government approved a programme which incorporated three basic measures. First, the mines were asked to take measures to reduce their losses from K61 million to K33 million only, in order to avoid massive redundancies of workers on the mines. Secondly, the monetary authorities agreed to a ten per cent depreciation of the currency in order to allow an increase in revenue to the mining industry amounting to about K31 million. Thirdly, the two mining companies were allowed to borrow up to K120 million from the banking system. I had personally intervened to disapprove the figure of twenty per cent for depreciation of our currency which the IMF had suggested. Such a large margin of depreciation would have worsened the price situation in our country. I accepted that ten per cent depreciation would nonetheless lead to some movement in prices but I did not anticipate such movement to be more than five per cent for most imports because the value added in Zambia would remain unchanged. Furthermore, when the government adjusted the value of the Kwacha in 1976, the increased cost was borne by the individual purchaser of foreign exchange. That policy was also applied to existing payments arrears. However, on this particular occasion, the government instructed the Bank of Zambia to bear the loss relating to imports and freight and clearing in order to avoid price increases and to assist importers. Therefore, the policies adopted by the government did not justify any price increases by importers.

The new measures were intended partly to solve the financial problems of the mining industry – the goose responsible for laying golden eggs so to speak! Therefore, it was necessary at an appropriate stage to inform members of parliament about measures taken by the government to stabilize the economy. On 20 March 1978, the speaker of the National Assembly gave me the opportunity to make a ministerial statement. I rose and after summarising the economic problems facing the country stated with pride and confidence:

> As I mentioned last week during the debate on the Bretton Woods Agreements (Amendment) Bill, discussions have been going on in Lusaka for about three weeks between a team from the International Monetary Fund and ourselves. Mr Speaker, Sir, I am pleased to inform the House that these discussions have now been concluded and agreement in principle has been reached. The party and government have accepted the agreement and all that is now remaining is for the Board of the International Monetary Fund to consider it and take a decision.

I went on to assure the House that I had confidence that the measures we had taken would put the mines on the road to recovery, provided the price of copper remained as we had estimated. I then proceeded to conclude my speech with a passionate appeal to all people in our country to work hard. I said:

> Mr Speaker, Sir, it is not simply a formal duty on my part that I would pay tribute to our officials for the success of the negotiations. Knowing what is at stake for our nation and cognizant of the many long hours of hard work they committed to the negotiations, words can hardly record our debt to them all. Perhaps students of history will one day record the great contributions of our officials at a time of grave economic crisis. The great potential of our country for development is universally acknowledged. For example, there are tremendous resources for the development of agriculture and exploitation of minerals apart from copper. We have the means and capability Mr Speaker, Sir, to transform Zambia into a paradise on earth. All the essential requirements for such a

transformation are already within our grasp. Under the wise, humane and dedicated leadership of Dr Kenneth D Kaunda, president of the Republic of Zambia, we enjoy unparalleled political stability and national unity.

Let us now resolve to put our hands to the plough. We do not need any more political slogans today. Our commitment should be to develop Zambia by hard work and the sweat of our brows. Nothing short of such commitment to real hard work and discipline by everybody can bring to an end our dependency on other nations for financial support and assistance because that is the challenge facing all the Zambian people today whatever their occupations in life and wherever they may be. Hon. members of parliament, as elected representatives of the people, have a grave responsibility to explain the intentions of our party and government faithfully, to arouse our people to this new commitment of hard work and discipline, casting aside all trivialities which cause dissension in our midst. We should all strive to promote unity of purpose and love for one another.

Mr Speaker, Sir, no greater service to this nation can be given than urging people in every walk of life to work hard on the land, in factories, on the mines, in production units, in offices, schools and hospitals, practically everywhere. Our poverty as a nation must be brought to an end by the turn of this century or even earlier. The party and government have provided a package for the transformation of our poverty status to affluence and happiness for all. The package will restore confidence in the strength of our economy to weather again the vicissitudes of a depressed copper market.

Mr Speaker, Sir, if my statement has been long, it is only because I have tried to give the House all the information relating to our discussions with the IMF and the programme of action we propose to follow in order to put our economy right in the face of the crisis we face. As I have already stated, the programme will involve some sacrifice but I believe that, over all, the course we have chosen to follow is the correct one. In the case of depreciation, I believe that we all have to make a small sacrifice in order to save the jobs of our workers on the mines who have done so much for the general welfare of our entire nation. It would be wrong to let them down in the present moment of adversity.

Mr Speaker, Sir, Hon Members, I thank you.

Zambia's economic problems included a critical shortfall of funds for investment to promote growth. Donor funding for approved capital projects was limited, in fact almost non-existent, when I returned to the Ministry of Finance. Such funding was necessary for vital projects such as the construction of schools, clinics and feeder roads in rural areas. At the beginning of 1978, Dominic Mulaisho wrote a letter to Mr Michael Wiehen of the World Bank in which he indicated that Zambia was seeking a programme loan. He was President Kaunda's special assistant for economic affairs in State House. President Kaunda had authorized him to apply for a programme loan of a very substantial amount. Programme loans from the World Bank for development purposes had one advantage. They were low interest-bearing. Later, in February 1978, Dominic Mulaisho's request was followed up by Professor WG Phillips in his discussions with the IMF and World Bank officials in Washington. He was President Kaunda's special adviser on economic affairs based in Canada. Both the World Bank and IMF officials informed Professor Phillips that Zambia had previously disappointed both the IMF and the World Bank by failing to live up to the conditionality attached to a standby agreement with the Fund. In a letter to President Kaunda on 9 February 1978, Professor Phillips reported that: "... the World Bank was embarrassed by this and this would not be forgotten" However, he stated quite clearly in the letter that if the Zambian authorities re-engaged in meaningful negotiations an agreement with the World Bank for another programme loan for Zambia would be approved. But he emphasized that "... in any future programme loan the World Bank would need to be assured that Zambia not only had an agreement with the Fund, but in addition, the conditionality was in fact being met." In the discussions with the World Bank and IMF in Washington, Professor Phillips was informed that if senior officials of the Zambian government expedited preparation of documents for consideration at a meeting of a Consultative Group, that was likely to facilitate consideration and approval of a programme loan for Zambia. Professor Phillips reported to President Kaunda that:

> Mr Wiehen indicated that, given the extreme urgency of Zambia's present situation, it would be possible to have a Consultative Group meeting as early as May of this year. It would not be necessary for Zambia to produce a complete five year plan or even a three year plan for such a meeting. Possibly even a comprehensive statement of principles on which planning would be based would be enough.

On 13 February 1978, I received a copy of the report prepared by Professor Phillips for President Kaunda on the discussions he had held with officials of the World Bank and the International Monetary Fund at the beginning of the month. President Kaunda's private secretary advised me to study the letter carefully in preparation for a discussion with President Kaunda later. The president had written comments and marginal notes on the fourteen page letter he received from Professor Phillips. These were helpful indicators of his own views and matters to which he attached urgency. The most important issue was the need to prepare for a meeting of the Consultative Group, sometimes called the Consultative Committee. Our negotiating team of senior officials made good progress in their discussions in Lusaka with representatives of the International Monetary Fund. Zambia negotiated with the International Monetary Fund a programme which involved a total financial package worth Special Drawing Rights (SDR) 315 million. The amount was to be drawn over a two year period. The amount also included a standby arrangement of SDR 250 million, a compensatory financial drawing of SDR 49 million and a trust fund loan of SDR 16 million. We were satisfied that the programme negotiated with the International Monetary Fund was adequate to ease our external payments position and to restore a more normal trade position. With these corrective measures to our country's external position and the wide range of fiscal and monetary measures which were announced in the House on 20 March 1978, I was confident that the country would recover the momentum of its economic growth.

Encouraged by the successful negotiation of a programme with the International Monetary Fund, I urged senior officials in my ministry to work hard on the preparation of the necessary background documents for the Consultative Group meeting to be held in Paris at the end of June 1978. The government had already announced its intention to launch the third five year National Development Plan in January 1979. A meeting of the Consultative Group at the end of June provided an opportunity for mobilization of the resources necessary for capital expenditure under the Development Plan. Although the details of the Development Plan had not been finalized, Professor Phillips had advised that "… even a comprehensive statement of principles on which planning would be based would be enough" for the purpose of holding a meeting of the Consultative Group.

In performing various functions and responsibilities, senior officials were required to give priority to the preparation of the necessary papers and background documents. It was sufficient in my estimation to have a comprehensive brief for members of the delegation and two short papers for the opening statement and another, but a much shorter one, for my closing statement. For the opening statement, as a general guide I intended to give members of the Consultative Group a clear picture of the strengths and weaknesses of the Zambian economy in the past and recently. In this context, it was also necessary to describe the government's policies to stabilize the economy and provide a sound financial base for economic growth. The focus on the development of agriculture to effect the policy of diversification of the economy was another important point for coverage in the opening statement. Finally, it was necessary to inform members of the Consultative Group that Zambia required a very large volume of resources from abroad for development under the Third National Development Plan. When the Second National Development Plan was prepared net foreign assets were high. In 1970, they stood at about US$450 million. However, the Third National Development Plan was being prepared against a situation in which the net foreign assets were in deficit by approximately US$208 million. In these circumstances, our country required a very large volume of resources from abroad, both in the form of official development assistance – loans, grants and technical assistance – and direct investment in the economy.

The World Bank was responsible for organizing the meeting of the Consultative Group at the end of June 1978. It was expected to invite governments and international institutions willing to assist our country in its time of economic difficulty, especially those that had already extended large amounts of assistance in the years after independence. We expected countries such as the United States of America, the United Kingdom, Canada, West Germany, Japan and a number of Scandinavian countries to send representatives to the Consultative Group meeting.

I was privileged as minister of finance to be designated by President Kaunda as leader of the delegation to the first meeting of the Consultative Group for Zambia. On 23 June 1978, I officiated at a ceremony for the official opening of a new office block, Findeco House, by the president. I seized the opportunity of the special occasion to assure the Zambian people that we intended to attend the Consultative Group meeting in Paris at the end of June without in any way compromising our own policies and principles. It was necessary to deliberate at the meeting in a spirit of mutual understanding and mutual respect between representatives of the Zambian government and representatives of various governments and international institutions. I informed the gathering that:

I shall lead a delegation to Paris this weekend to attend the first meeting of the Consultative Group for Zambia against the background of an economy which shows signs of improvement, but one beset by a serious transport constraint. Let me assure the nation that we are not going to Paris as beggars. Zambia is a proud nation. We are proud because of our unassailable record of independence in all that we think or do. No one should be under any illusion that we can compromise our principles simply for the sake of overcoming temporary economic setbacks.

However, our party and government have accepted that our friends in the developed world should be helped to know our needs and priorities, our past achievements and failures and our plans for the development of our country. We shall meet all representatives of donor countries and institutions on equal terms as full partners in the development of Zambia.

The consultations of the first Consultative Group meeting for Zambia were successful. Many representatives of governments and international institutions made pledges to continue supporting Zambia's economic recovery programme. I thanked all who participated in the meeting for making it successful. In particular, special thanks were given to the staff of the World Bank for their dedication. As we concluded the first Consultative Group meeting for Zambia, a letter was delivered to my suite at the hotel in which I was staying in Paris. It was dated 29 June and addressed to me from the vice president of the European Investment Bank in Luxembourg. It read in part:

We are pleased to receive the invitation of the World Bank to attend the inaugural meeting of the Consultative Group on Zambia.

Since the Lomé Convention came into effect in 1976 we have met with your authorities on many occasions and have been able to exchange views on Zambia's development needs and the possibilities for providing financial assistance for priority projects ....

We have paid close attention to the discussions of the Consultative Group meeting and hope that the action being taken to overcome the present difficult situation will permit us to play a full part in the future development of Zambia.

As I reflected further on the contents of the letter from the vice president of the European Development Bank to me, the words 'We have paid close attention to the discussions at the Consultative Group meeting' in the last paragraph kept ringing in my ears. I reached the inescapable conclusion that the public relations exercise we had undertaken in Paris with the World Bank's encouragement and support had been positive and worthwhile.

It is not an exaggeration to say that the busiest times of my political career were the years I spent in the Ministry of Finance from May 1976 to December 1978. My orientation as minister of finance was from October 1970 to December 1973, and in that period I developed a personal interest in the kind of issues entailed by this particularly heavily loaded ministerial job. By nature I have always felt comfortable with the prodigious workload which the Treasury imposes on its ministers. Therefore, I was neither lost nor completely disappointed when President Kaunda assigned the finance portfolio to me for the second time in May 1976. However, I had some misgivings about my ability to continue assisting people in various parts of my parliamentary constituency to complete projects they started with my encouragement and support. As a backbencher, even though a private legal practitioner, I was able to visit my parliamentary constituency frequently to interact with my constituents on national affairs and development issues. With the heavy workload of the ministerial job in the Treasury, the possibility of maintaining regular consultations with the men and women who elected me to parliament became a pipedream.

Fortunately, UNIP was a well organized political party. In fact, at that time, it was among the best organized political parties in independent Africa; perhaps only the Tanganyika African National Union (TANU) was more efficiently organized at the grassroots level. Most of the projects I encouraged or sponsored were well supported by the beneficiaries themselves. They were involved in determining priorities in the projects for implementation in their areas or villages. Even more importantly, the UNIP officials both at the village and district levels were active participants in the process of initiating and executing the projects for the development of various areas in the parliamentary constituency. In any event, the district governor for Mbala had overall responsibility for the supervision of development projects in the district. Thus successful implementation of development projects was possible under the district governor's supervision. At least once in six months, I intended to visit schools, clinics and projects in my constituency, apart from addressing meetings in order to inform people about the policies and programmes of the government.

There were four areas in Mpulungu Constituency in which people desperately needed encouragement and support to undertake projects which were vital for the well being of the communities in those areas. One such area was Isoko village and its environs. The headquarters of Senior Chief Tafuna of the Lungu people was located in Isoko village. It was a heavily populated area in a fertile valley about ten kilometres from Mpulungu port on the shores of Lake Tanganyika. The chief's palace, known as *Musumba*, was only twenty kilometres from Mbala, the administrative centre of the district. There was a clinic in the village and an upper primary school. The villagers occupied themselves by growing maize, millet, bananas, sugar beans and sugar cane. The more hard-working peasant farmers lived comfortably from their farming activities. On the whole, hunger was unknown in Isoko and surrounding areas.

During campaign meetings in and around Isoko before the presidential and parliamentary elections in December 1973, people in this area complained to me about the poor state of the road linking the *Musumba* to Mbala. Secondly, the lack of a telephone link between the *Musumba* and the district headquarters caused great inconvenience to the medical assistant in charge of the clinic when he decided to refer very sick patients to Mbala District Hospital for further treatment. In such a situation, he was obliged to relay a message through a cyclist to the medical superintendent of Mbala District Hospital requesting him to send an ambulance to transport the sick patient to the hospital in Mbala.

During the election campaign in 1973, I agreed with the voters in the Isoko area that their priorities were correct in terms of social needs and development objectives. They deserved encouragement and support to obtain financial assistance for upgrading the road to Mbala to facilitate transportation of farm produce to markets in Mbala and elsewhere in Zambia. I also made an undertaking, once elected as their MP, to lobby the agency responsible for telecommunications to extend the telephone line from Mbala town to Isoko village.

There were also good project proposals from residents of Mpulungu and villagers in the Iyendwe area in Mpulungu Constituency. Quite understandably, residents in Mpulungu, at the port itself and surrounding areas, were dissatisfied with the insufficiency of funds released by the government each year for disbursement as loans to fishermen. Fishermen required loans for the purchase of fishing nets and the engines for their boats. In the light of the high demand for fish by consumers in towns, the request for release of more funds for loans to fishermen was in line with my own thoughts about the necessity of assisting rural dwellers to help themselves. In Mpulungu township itself, there was a critical shortage of water at the time of our election campaign. I was reminded at every turn that the insufficiency or sometimes total lack of piped water risked the lives of the residents due to the threat of cholera breaking out especially during the rainy season. In Iyendwe, where villagers engaged successfully in productive farming, the bad state of the road from Mbala township to Iyendwe was the major constraint on development in the area.

After my election at the end of December 1973, I advised Senior Chief Tafuna to make direct representation to the permanent secretary for the Northern Province for the installation of a telephone to Isoko. The permanent secretary's response was negative. He informed Senior Chief Tafuna that his office had no funds for this project. However, at the same time he advised the director general of the Posts and Telecommunications Corporation in Ndola that "if the senior chief and his people are able to meet the cost of installing the telephone and are able to raise annual rental, I would have no objection to the installation".

At that stage, I took over the responsibility of exploring ways and means of raising the necessary funds, with the participation of the subjects of Senior Chief Tafuna. The director general subsequently sent me a quotation of K2,381.00 for the annual rental and installation fee. When this information was available, I requested the senior chief to obtain a contribution from his subjects. If a reasonable amount of money was raised by the villagers, I did not anticipate any difficulty in raising the balance through appeals to men and women of goodwill for a just cause. The villagers hastily raised K500.00 as their contribution to the cost of the project. On that basis, I appealed to sympathizers in the business community for contributions to cover the shortfall of K1,881.00. By 4 May 1976, the sum of K1,881.00 was raised from Mr B Sharma of Star Jewellers in Lusaka (K680.00), Mr R Patel of City Sales and Wholesalers in Lusaka (K201.00) and Mr HJ Oosthuizen of Central African Engineering Corporation in Kitwe (K1,000.00). Subsequently, I received a letter from the director general of the Posts and Telecommunications Corporation acknowledging receipt of the payment of K1,881.00 and informing me that arrangements were being made for the installation work to commence soon.

This important project for the community in the Isoko area in Mbala District would not have been accomplished without support from three public-spirited members of the business community. Their positive response to my appeal for contribution of funds was spontaneous, based on mutual trust and confidence. This spirit of mutual trust and existence of genuine friendship between me and some businessmen in our country was exemplified in Mr Oosthuizen's letter to me on 6 April 1976 confirming his corporation's willingness to support the project. He wrote thus:

> In response to your letter JMM/jm of 15 March and subsequent telephone calls, we have much pleasure in enclosing our cheque for K1,000.00 (No. ZB 104498) to assist in the payment of the telephone installation to Isoko Musumba.
>
> We would like to congratulate the people of Isoko village on their very fine effort to raise the initial K500.00 for this project and feel they should be encouraged to raise more funds for other services essential in their area, providing we can get the support of other firms and service clubs to make their contribution, as the needs of people in the rural areas are sometimes overlooked for no apparent reason.
>
> The writer has approached a few of the service clubs for their support for additional funds, but unfortunately they are fully committed to various projects for this year.

On economic grounds, officers in the Office of the Cabinet Minister for the Northern Province readily accepted the urgent need to improve the poor access road from the Mbala/Mpulungu road into Isoko. It was about thirty kilometres only to Isoko village off the main Mbala/Mpulungu road. Shortly after my representations for the upgrading of this road, Dominic Mulaisho made a similar plea to the authorities in Kasama. He was the general manager of the National Agricultural Marketing Board. He was anxious to increase his organisation's purchases of good quality bananas from Isoko area. He informed the permanent secretary in a letter dated 9 March 1976 "... that given improved facilities the Board could be purchasing at the rate of up to 20 tonnes of bananas per week from this region". To the good fortune of the Isoko people, on 21 April 1976, the permanent secretary for the Northern Province wrote to me and the general manager of National Agricultural Marketing Board that:

> ...the Roads Department are now working on drainages, culverts and removal of big rocks. This is expected to be completed latest by the end of the month. I am sending a copy of this letter to your representative in the province with a request that they should start purchasing bananas in Isoko as the road is now passable even to big trucks.

Undoubtedly, at that point in time, my rating in Mpulungu constituency was quite high. I would have received at least an A grade! However, our third project for Isoko village was initially unsuccessful. It related to the provision of piped water to Isoko village from a nearby perennial river. At first, lack of progress on this project was due to non-provision of funds. However, later when the government provided funds, the Department of Water Affairs was incapable of implementing the project. In a letter to me dated 31 March 1976, the permanent secretary for the Northern Province apologized for the department's failure to complete the project on schedule due to "lack of experienced manpower". He requested me "to appeal to the people of Isoko village to exercise some patience". He pleaded with me to assure them "that everything possible is being done to have the scheme completed".

The fishermen living in and around Mpulungu township were fortunate. I did not encounter any problems in soliciting assistance for them from the appropriate authorities in government. By the middle of 1975, I had obtained assurance that funds for loans to fishermen were available on application to the Zambia Fisheries and Fish Marketing Corporation (ZFFC). They were as anxious as I was that "...the funds voted for loans will be utilized and thus avoid the frustration of the past two to three years". I was particularly happy with the assurance I was given by James Mapoma, minister of lands, natural resources and tourism, in a letter to me on 9 October 1975 that "I have already written to the Ministry of Planning and Finance asking them to release all funds voted for loans to fishermen – to the ZFFC directly now that agreement has been reached on the administrative machinery". Early in February 1978, the Office of the Cabinet Minister for Northern Province gave a grant of K22,500 to assist Mbala Rural Council to improve feeder roads to productive agricultural areas, especially the Mbala-Chitimbwa-Iyendwe road.

The Mpulungu township problem was settled in the second half of 1978, under the Norwegian Aid Scheme. Initially the sum of K35,000 was allocated for improvement of water supplies in general to be followed later by the Mpulungu Water Supply Upgrading scheme under the Norwegian Aid Scheme.

When I look back at my political career, I inescapably recall some successes and of course, failures – failure to do things I ought to have done or merely partially achieving my objectives. Both in government service as a minister and as a mere backbencher I derived some happiness with achievements in my efforts to promote the development of our country. At the end of my political career in December 1978, I was quite naturally pleased with many kind messages I received from friends and well wishers. Their messages thanking me for the services I had rendered to our country in the early years of its development were acknowledged gratefully. However, in my responses, I was quick to remind them all how grateful I was to President Kaunda and the people of Zambia for the opportunity they gave me to serve my country in key positions after independence. I was deeply thankful to President Kaunda for his understanding and sympathy in those difficult and testing times when I chose to disagree with him on major policy issues. The loyalty of my staff, senior and junior staff alike, at the Treasury had given me encouragement and strength during trying moments. The love and affection we had for each other was conspicuous at the farewell function the staff organized for me and my wife a week before my retirement in December 1978. To date, I still treasure the gifts they presented to us, especially the miniature scale made in copper.

Then on 12 December 1978, the last day in my office at the Treasury, I received a letter from President Kaunda. He had also decided to thank me for the services I had rendered to the nation at the political level for a period of sixteen years from 1962 to 1978. President Kaunda was overgenerous in describing my contribution to the development of our country. I was quite advanced in age when I received his letter; in fact, I had reached fifty two years of age the previous month – on 1 November 1978. Yet tears rolled down my cheeks as I read President Kaunda's letter. He was so sincere and so compassionate that it was impossible for me to control my emotions. Fortunately, I was alone in the office. Every word and every sentence in the letter portrayed his sincerity and magnanimity.

In the fourth paragraph of President Kaunda's letter, he observed quite rightly that I was not hypocritical by nature; that in a nutshell I preferred to call a spade a spade and nothing else. One thing I learnt quite early in my political career is that many politicians thrive on cheap popularity gained by sheer appeasement of other politicians all the time. Such politicians can never be useful in any society. Apparently, President Kaunda did not simply tolerate my frankness in the way I advised him or other political leaders. He considered my "forthrightness" a virtue. Sharp differences between us arose following the adoption of recommendations in the Report of the Special Parliamentary Select Committee on ways and means of strengthening the economy of Zambia. Although some of our committee's recommendations were distasteful and unacceptable to President Kaunda and members of the Central Committee of the United National Independence Party, nevertheless we remained friends. He accepted that all my actions were done in good faith. He observed in the fourth paragraph of his letter that "you are always forthright in your handling of public affairs" and stated that "...I personally will miss you a great deal".

Each time I have reread the letter again over the years, I have come to realize the depth of President Kaunda's wisdom. I have always thought that I might, God willing, share with other fellow men and women the wisdom of the first president of our country and founding father of our nation. This is what he wrote in the letter:

> I thank you for your personal and confidential letter MF/P/2 dated 11 December, 1978. Although I have known all along that you would not like to extend your serving this nation as minister due to poor health, nonetheless your letter bringing your message confirming this state of affairs is very sad indeed.
>
> As we grow older both in our jobs as well as biologically, one begins to learn to understand one's fellow man a little better. One of the things that has become an experience is that no one man can run a country without identifying men of calibre, integrity, dignity and honour with whom to work. I want to say I thank God for having made it possible for me to see one of such men in you.
>
> As you know, in Humanism we believe that we all are instruments in God's hands in His service which we do by working for and with our fellow men. You have developed your brain to the point where you are not only an educationalist but also a lawyer with an abundant knowledge in the management of finance. In spite of all these acquisitions, each time I have called upon you to serve God and his people, you have done so.
>
> I want to record my sincere and heartfelt appreciation to you, Mrs Mwanakatwe and your family. As you leave do know that you leave a gap difficult to fill and I personally will miss you a great deal. You are always forthright in your handling of public affairs. You have earned yourself a good name through these many qualities that I have referred to already.
>
> I pray to God Almighty that as you join private life, the

blessings that God has bestowed on you, He will continue to maintain in you. The honourable name such as you have built is worth more than millions of Kwacha. I pray to God that he will guard and protect you from any developments within you towards the animal in man. You have defeated so much of this already. It is because I know this to be the case that I did not think it was necessary for me to ask for a medical certificate. You have been, you are and I pray that you will always be a man of honour. One therefore grows to trust men and women he has classified in his own mind as honourable.

If I do not take a firm decision to stop writing I would bore you with a terribly long letter but I am sure you will understand how it feels to begin to miss the services of one's dedicated and committed colleagues to a common cause.

Please accept from me and Mrs Kaunda this copper tray to you as a small token of appreciation for all you have done. In this I must include Mrs Mwanakatwe who has stood so much and so well by your side when you have had to face many difficult budget sessions burning the midnight oil. May God bless her too.

God's blessings.

More than twenty years down the lane I do not regret the decision I took in 1978 to retire completely from politics. I occasionally suffer from hypertension but today this illness is no longer a cause of anxiety to me, my medical doctors or members of my family. In that year, I led a delegation to the first meeting of the Consultative Group for Zambia in Paris with representatives of governments and international institutions which were willing to assist our country to overcome its economic difficulties. In my opening statement, I emphasized that we had not gone to Paris as beggars. We had gone to the meeting to meet all representatives of donor countries and institutions on equal terms as full partners in the development of Zambia. In the year 2000, for the first time a meeting of the

Consultative Group for Zambia met in Lusaka. A representative of the cooperating partners in his address at the opening of the meeting on 17 July 2000 emphasised the equality of participants in the deliberations. He concluded his remarks by emphasizing that "... the Consultative Group exercise is first and foremost one of partnership, based on frank and open communication". He went on to say: "The views... presented are those of the cooperating partners as a whole.... We offer them in a spirit of partnership and the shared goal of a successful and prosperous Zambia". The seed we sowed in Paris at the first meeting of the Consultative Group for Zambia was certainly not in vain.

CHAPTER

12

1980 Coup Attempt

My second term of office as minister of finance ended in mid December 1978. That year marked the end of my political career. Undoubtedly it had its own fascination which my wife hardly shared with me. It was not my intention, of course, to retire from politics into oblivion. At the age of fifty two, I was still energetic. During my term of office at the Treasury, my health was sometimes failing me because of pressure of work and anxiety generally about our country's economic difficulties. In any case, I was obliged at that stage to continue working in order to earn a living. Even more importantly, all my children, except my eldest daughter, were learning in schools or universities. They required financial support to complete their studies. Although I had many offers of employment from reputable organisations within Zambia, my preferred option was to be engaged again in practising law. Instinctively, after sixteen years of "politicking" I was only too anxious to opt for a professional career and to join the league of private legal practitioners.

In 1977, when I became certain about my retirement from politics at the end of the following year, I made enquiries about the possibility of establishing a large firm of legal private practitioners comparable to Ellis and Company, Lloyd Jones and Collins, Jaques and Partners and one or two others. I had had the feeling for some time that there were too few large enough law firms in the country capable of providing a wide range of legal services in a timely and expert manner for the benefit of their clients. That was the achievement and attraction of Jaques and Partners. For example, in the 1970s it had a team of eight partners and several assistant lawyers in Lusaka, Ndola and Kitwe. Of course, the 'one man' or 'one woman' law firms also have an important role to perform in any society. However, ideally such law firms should be supported by a fair proportion of large law firms in order to serve the needs of clients adequately and satisfactorily in our country.

In an effort to contribute to the achievement of this objective, Wila Mung'omba, his wife Linda Mung'omba and Bevin Willombe agreed to team up with me as partners in a new law firm to be established at the beginning of 1979. Wila Mung'omba expected to complete his term of office on the Board of the International Monetary Fund in Washington at the end of 1978. Bevin Willombe had already planned to resign his post of commissioner of lands in the civil service at the end of 1977. He offered to register the law firm of Willombe and Company in 1978 as a forerunner to the law firm of MMW and Company. MMW is the acronym of Mwanakatwe, Mung'omba and Willombe. Bevin Willombe acquired suitable offices in Electra House in Cairo Road. He used the offices initially for Willombe and Company in which he was the sole legal practitioner until the end of December 1978. From January 1979 the law firm of MMW and Company was in full operation. It enjoyed considerable goodwill from the public both in Lusaka and other towns. The law firm was established to provide a wide range of legal services. Partners did not specialise. Each partner was available to render legal services required by any client at anytime. However, partners consulted each other from time to time. In fact, reference of clients by one partner to another was encouraged if that was in the client's interests.

Back in private law practice in the firm of MMW and Company, I felt more relaxed than I had been when I was in politics, with all the power and influence which go with it. There is a distinct difference between the practice of politics and the practice of law. Lord Bolingbroke once observed that the practice

310

of law is by its nature the noblest and most beneficial to mankind; in its abuse an abasement of the most sordid kind. Cynics of lawyers sometimes say that "lawyers aren't made, they are born – out of wedlock"! Like many lawyers, I do not believe that lawyering is simply in the genes. I agree with the writer JR Elkins who states in his book *The Legal Persona: An Essay on the Professional Mark* that instead "a complex of dispositional factors, social background, education, training and work experience go to make up the *legal persona*." I have always believed that lawyers owe allegiance generally to the cause of truth, justice and public interest in the administration of justice. As officers of the court, lawyers owe a duty to their clients and to the courts primarily to be truthful and candid at all times. They are expected to represent their clients by fair and proper means. Whatever tactics lawyers may choose in representing the interests of their clients, the hallmark of proper conduct is determined by their honesty and fairness.

I was sometimes confronted with situations when these principles which I cherished so much were tested. In 1980, the government uncovered a coup plot which the officials considered serious. At first, the government alleged that altogether eighty men were suspected to have been involved in the plot. However, eventually only thirteen men were arrested and charged with the offence of treason. The charges were that they had conspired to overthrow the government by unlawful means, that they had plotted to kidnap Kenneth Kaunda, the president of Zambia, and fly him to an isolated place or foreign country for safe custody while the conspirators executed a bloodless coup d'etat. The conspirators relied on Katangese mercenaries to support their attempt to overthrow the government with perhaps some assistance from South African troops. It was alleged also that the thirteen men arrested in October 1980 hired a mercenary army which they stationed privately on a farm near Lusaka, and that they arranged to procure or purchase arms for the execution of the coup plot. The charges also included an allegation that they had attempted

311

to corrupt members of the armed forces to support their bid to overthrow the government by unlawful means. The Katangese mercenaries had fled from Zaire to Zambia because they did not like the government of President Mobutu Sese Seko. The conspirators were alleged to have promised them assistance in ousting President Mobutu from power once Kaunda's government was overthrown.

Three prominent businessmen were among the thirteen arrested in October 1980 and charged with treason, namely Valentine Musakanya, Edward Shamwana and Yoram Mumba. Musakanya was a well known intellectual who had retired from government service after a distinguished career as a civil servant and a holder of high political office in Kaunda's administration. After his retirement, Kaunda appointed him governor of the Bank of Zambia. Later, he fell into disfavour and Kaunda fired him. Shamwana was also a well known intellectual who had pioneered the admission of Africans into the legal profession in Zambia. Kaunda had recognised Shamwana's abilities and experience as a lawyer by appointing him a High Court Commissioner, a part-time job, which he held at the time of his arrest in October 1980. Mumba was a younger man. He was a former manager of the Industrial Finance Company and Zambia National Building Society. Godfrey Miyanda, a quiet, firm and principled brigadier general and General Christopher Kabwe were the most senior military men arrested and charged with treason. Others were Air Force Major Anderson Mporokoso and Major Macpherson Mbulo. Only one European was allegedly involved in the attempted coup plot, namely Pierce Annfield, who had fled the country. General Christopher Kabwe was later given an indemnity. He then turned a state's witness. Eight persons were originally arraigned together with five others. Later, one of them was struck off the information on account of illness. Four others were acquitted after the close of the prosecution's case and submissions of no case to answer. Eventually, the treason trial before the High Court involved Edward Shamwana, Valentine Musakanya, Goodwin Mumba,

Anderson Mporokoso, Thomas Mulewa, Albert Chimbalile, Laurent Kabwita and Deogratias Symba. They were put on their defence as charged except Anderson Mporokoso, who had a case to answer for misprision of treason after acquittal on the treason charge. By 3 December 1981, the judge had considered various preliminary issues raised by the defence. Ruling had been made by the judge on one particularly important preliminary issue related to the objection by the defence to the prosecution's proposal to amend the information. The judge allowed the information to be amended but only after he had ordered two counts to be struck off from the information because they were embarrassing to the accused persons. After the ruling on the amended information, pleas were then taken.

The coup attempt uncovered early in 1980 was not the first such attempt in Zambia. After independence in 1964, a few instances of unsuccessful coup attempts were reported. They were all of them fairly insignificant and passed almost unnoticed. However, the coup plot which the government uncovered in 1980 was more dangerous than previous coup attempts. An attempt to overthrow the lawfully established government by unlawful means may constitute the offence of treason. Upon conviction on a charge of treason, the accused person is liable to be sentenced to death. In fact, the death penalty is mandatory in Zambia. Furthermore, treason is an offence for which bail is not available.

Among the accused persons, I had a special family relationship with Valentine Musakanya. His wife, Flavia Musakanya, was a niece of my own wife. Flavia Musakanya's mother was my wife's first cousin. Therefore, Valentine Musakanya was not merely a close friend to me but also a son-in-law of my wife. In these circumstances, I was among the first people in Lusaka to know about Valentine Musakanya's arrest by the police and his detention subsequently at Lilayi Police Station. A few days after his arrest and detention, Valentine Musakanya wrote a note in which he requested me to go to the prison to discuss arrangements for his legal representation. When I visited him in prison, we also discussed the possibility of negotiating his release or applying for the writ of *habeas corpus ad subjiciendum*. If such an application were successful, his release would be secured. That occasion marked the beginning of my involvement in the defence of Valentine Musakanya in one of the most celebrated criminal trials in the history of Zambia. When eventually a full bench of Supreme Court judges heard the appeals of the eight appellants four years later, Chief Justice Annel Silungwe observed in the judgment that:

> This was a long and complex trial the record of which runs into some 5,500 pages. The case commenced in the High Court on November 2, 1981 and lasted, on and off, until January 20, 1983, when judgment was delivered and the appellants were convicted and sentenced. The complexity of the case was compounded by the fact that there were 122 prosecution witnesses (who will hereinafter be referred to as PW1, PW2 and so on), in the main trial; 158 exhibits; and an abundance of applications, objections and the trial court's rulings thereon. The period between January 20, 1983, and August 8, 1984 (when the hearing of the appeals started) was used for the preparation of the case record on appeal, the formulation of grounds and additional grounds of appeal by the appellants and also of heads of argument by the appellants and the State and replies thereto by the appellants. Altogether, 85 substantive grounds of appeal (let alone the numerous subsidiary ones) were argued. The hearing of the appeals took twenty eight days.

After my discussions with Valentine Musakanya, I engaged in consultations with Bevin Willombe to determine the best arrangement for the protection of the legal interests of Valentine Musakanya. He was at that time the second partner available in our law firm. Wila Mung'omba and his wife Linda were temporarily resident in Abidjan in the Ivory Coast where Wila was in the service of the African Development Bank as its president. The views of Mrs Flavia Musakanya and her relatives were required about the best ways and means of protecting her husband's legal interests. In the consultations it became quite clear to us that Valentine Musakanya preferred to instruct our law firm to represent him in all legal matters. He expected me to lead the team of lawyers representing his interests. In this regard, he had the tacit support of his brother-in-law, Henry Shikopa. I personally favoured another proposal, that of engaging a good lawyer in Lusaka who was likely to be totally detached from Valentine Musakanya himself and his relatives. Lawyers should be as objective as humanly possible in advising their clients, especially in very serious criminal matters such as the offence of treason. Sometimes lack of objectivity by a lawyer can prejudice his client's interests. We put our viewpoint to Valentine Musakanya quite firmly.

After completing consultations with interested parties, we advised Valentine Musakanya to instruct George Chaane of Chaane and Company, a Lusaka-based lawyer with a good reputation in the legal profession. Originally from South Africa, I knew him in the early 1950s when he was a teacher at Chalimbana Teacher Training College and I was teaching at Munali. We undertook to represent Valentine Musakanya in the pre-trial court proceedings and more particularly in the preparation of the application of the writ of *habeas corpus* in the High Court. We also undertook to research for George Chaane and to advise him from time to time. Both Valentine Musakanya and George Chaane were assured that we were prepared to attend court sittings regularly during the trial. Valentine Musakanya accepted the arrangement grudgingly. His brother-in-law, Henry Shikopa, was also not wholly pleased with this arrangement. He had pleaded with me not to appoint George Chaane as the lead counsel for Valentine Musakanya's defence. Otherwise, many relatives and friends of Valentine Musakanya were satisfied with our arrangements for his defence.

Apart from the expected trial of the accused persons in the High Court, we had a more immediate legal problem to consider. It was an accepted fact that the prosecution might take several months to prepare their case against the accused persons.

In the meantime, they would continue to languish in police custody pending their trial. Bevin Willombe and I had failed to negotiate with the police to release our client from police custody in the same manner they had released Elias Chipimo, Patrick Chisanga and others. In our opinion Valentine Musakanya was also innocent. One other way open to us for securing his release and total freedom was to apply to the High Court for the writ of *habeas corpus ad subjiciendum*. The right to the writ is a right which exists at common law independently of any statute. Its jurisdiction in Zambia is vested in the High Court of Zambia. It is a writ primarily used "for securing the liberty of the subject." Furthermore, the remedy by *habeas corpus* is equally available in civil and criminal proceedings provided that there is a deprivation of personal liberty without legal justification. In Zambia, applications to the High Court for writs of *habeas corpus* have been concerned primarily with the committal or detention of prisoners.

For an application for the writ of *habeas corpus* to succeed and thereby secure the liberty of the applicant it is necessary to prove to the court that the applicant was deprived of personal liberty "without legal justification". These three words "without legal justification" are crucial to the success or failure of the application. Nonetheless, it is a writ of the highest constitutional importance because it is available against the executive. It is a remedy which is available to the lowliest person in society against the most powerful. Therefore, in Zambia the writ is used to test the legality of detention under the Preservation of Public Security Act and the Regulations made under this Act.

Valentine Musakanya was initially detained on 24 October 1980 by the police under the provisions of Regulation 33(6) of the Preservation of Public Security Regulations. His detention under Regulation 33(b) was revoked subsequently on 31 October 1980. On that same day, the Presidential Detention Order under Regulation 33(1) of the Preservation of Public Security was served on Valentine Musakanya. Therefore, from 31 October 1980, he was detained under Regulation 33(1) of the

Preservation of Public Security Regulations. The first attempt to secure the release of our client from police custody was made by a lawyer based in Ndola before Mr Justice Bweupe in the High Court. On 26 November 1980, Mr Justice Bweupe declared Valentine Musakanya's detention unlawful following consideration of his application for the writ of *habeas corpus ad subjiciendum*. With remarkable speed, a police officer later charged him again with the offence of treason at the Ndola Police Station contrary to Section 43 (1) (a) of the Penal Code under Chapter 146 of the Laws of Zambia. The attorney-general, who was dissatisfied with the judgment of Mr Justice Bweupe, notified his intention to appeal to the Supreme Court against the judgment. On 1 December 1980, an assistant superintendent in the Zambia Police served on Valentine Musakanya another Presidential Detention Order.

The Constitution of Zambia contained provisions for the protection of a person's freedom of movement. Where a person's freedom of movement was restricted or he was detained under the authority of any law, Article 27 (D) of the constitution contained provisions for the protection of his liberty. One such provision imposed an obligation on the detaining authority to furnish the detainee or restrictee with the grounds upon which he was detained or restricted. Article 27 (1) (a) of the constitution further provided that such grounds were to be furnished to the detainee "as soon as is reasonably practicable" but "not more than fourteen days after the commencement of his detention or restriction". The detaining authority was obliged to furnish the detainee or restrictee with "a statement in writing specifying in detail the grounds upon which he is restricted or detained."

The grounds of detention for Valentine Musakanya's second detention were served on him on 13 December 1980 as follows:

"WHEREAS ON THE 1st day of December, 1980 you were detained by the Order of the President made on the same day namely 1st December, 1980 under Regulation 33 (1) of the

Preservation of Public Security Regulations Cap. 106 of the Laws of Zambia;

AND WHEREAS it is provided by Article 27 (1) (a) of the constitution that every person detained shall, not more than fourteen days after the commencement of his detention be furnished with a statement in writing specifying in detail the grounds upon which he is detained;

NOW THEREFORE, you are hereby informed that the grounds upon which you are detained are:-

1.   That on a date unknown but in or about the early part of April, 1980 you together with Messrs Jack Edward Shamwana and Goodwin Yoram Mumba attended an unlawful meeting at the residence of Mr Pierce Annfield situated in Kabulonga Area, Lusaka where Mr Pierce Annfield disclosed a plan to overthrow the lawfully constituted government of the Republic of Zambia by force.

2.   That subsequent to the aforesaid meeting and on a date unknown but between the 1st day of April and 31st day of May, 1980 you together with Messrs Goodwin Yoram Mumba, Edward Jack Shamwana, Anderson Mporokoso, Deogratias Symba and other persons whose names are unknown attended an unlawful meeting chaired by Mr Pierce Annfield at the residence of Mr Edward Jack Shamwana situated in Kabulonga Area, Lusaka where yourself and other persons mentioned herein agreed to overthrow the lawfully constituted government of the Republic of Zambia by force.

3.   That you failed to report the above meeting to the police or other lawful authorities.

Your aforesaid activities are prejudicial to the public security and there is a genuine apprehension that if left at large, you will continue to persist in the said unlawful activities, and therefore, for the preservation of public security, it has been found necessary to detain you.

After careful consideration of the grounds for the second detention of our client, we were instructed to file a writ of *habeas corpus ad subjiciendum* in another effort to secure his release from detention. We had noted particularly that earlier our client had applied for leave to issue a writ of *habeas corpus ad subjiciendum*. The application to the High Court at its Ndola Registry was successful. Judge Bweupe found the grounds for our client's detention "insufficient, vague and roving" and declared Valentine Musakanya's detention unlawful. However, subsequently our client was rearrested and served with a Presidential Detention Order issued on 1 December 1980 in pursuance of the Preservation of Public Security Regulations. We observed that the grounds of our client's second detention were substantially the same as the grounds furnished to him earlier in a statement in writing on 13 November 1980. However, in the new grounds upon which he was detained again it was alleged that on a date unknown but in or about the early part of April 1980 Valentine Musakanya attended an unlawful meeting with Edward Shamwana and Goodwin Mumba at the home of Pierce Annfield in Kabulonga, Lusaka. The new grounds of his second detention included another allegation that he attended a second unlawful meeting at the residence of Edward Shamwana with Goodwin Mumba, Edward Shamwana, Anderson Mporokoso, Deogratias Syimba and other unknown persons.

With this background information, we did not hesitate to confirm to our client our willingness to challenge the state on his continued detention under provisions of the Preservation of Public Security Regulations. We prepared a detailed affidavit in which Valentine Musakanya deposed to the relevant facts in support of his application for the writ of *habeas corpus ad subjiciendum*. The last paragraph of the affidavit summed up the gist of his application for leave to issue the writ. It was couched in these words:

I humbly submit to this honourable court that I am the said VALENTINE SHULA MUSAKANYA detained at Lusaka Central Prison, Lusaka, that I believe my detention to be unlawful, malicious and motivated by *malafides* and I pray that this honourable court will grant me leave to issue a writ of *habeas corpus ad subjiciendum* directing the attorney-general as principal legal adviser to the government of the Republic of Zambia and the inspector general of police to show cause why I should not be released immediately.

Later, the respondent also filed an affidavit in opposition sworn by Mubuka Sinyinda, a senior assistant commissioner of police in the Criminal Investigation Department. He did not admit most of the allegations in the applicant's affidavit. In particular, he denied that the grounds set out in the statement of 12 December 1980 to justify the second detention of the applicant were "inadequate or improper to found lawfully the applicant's detention". I had also sworn an affidavit in support of Valentine Musakanya's application for the writ of *habeas corpus ad subjiciendum*. In my affidavit, I averred as Valentine Musakanya's legal adviser that the grounds of his second detention demonstrated *malafides* on the part of the police in arresting him again on a charge of treason. I also averred in my affidavit that the grounds of the applicant's detention contained in the statement of 12 December 1980 were "as vague or as insufficient or as exploratory as those contained in the statement dated 12 November 1980 which were declared illegal by the Honourable Mr. Justice Bweupe". In his affidavit in opposition, Mubuka Sinyinda denied that the applicant's detention was punitive or unlawful as alleged.

When the application was heard on 6 January 1981 before Judge Chaila in the High Court in Lusaka, the attorney-general, as the respondent, was represented by AG Kinariwala, assistant senior state advocate in the attorney-general's chambers. I was the sole legal representative of the applicant in court. Most of the issues raised in the applicant's affidavit and the affidavit of the respondent were not in dispute. To fortify the applicant's position it was necessary to rely on case law. The counsel for the respondent adopted the same approach. I was particularly anxious in my arguments to persuade the court that Judge Bweupe's decision in the High Court in Ndola had merit although Judge Chaila was not bound by his decision. In my arguments, I emphasised facts which supported the applicant's contention that his detention after his release by Judge Bweupe in the High Court in Ndola was malicious or motivated by *malafides* and, therefore, unlawful. In addition, I argued on behalf of the applicant, that the detaining authority had failed to supply to the applicant a statement in writing specifying *in detail* the grounds upon which the applicant was detained as required by law. The assistant senior state advocate's main submission on behalf of the respondent was that the applicant's activities were prejudicial to the public security and there was a genuine apprehension "that if left at large would continue to persist in the said unlawful activities ... therefore ... it was found necessary to detain him".

On 20 January 1981, Judge Chaila delivered his judgment. It was a long judgment of twenty eight pages. The judge decided that the applicant was being held for the purpose of preserving public security. He concluded in the judgment thus: "All contentions which have been put forward in this application have failed. The application is therefore dismissed with costs".

Our client, Valentine Musakanya, was quite naturally disappointed with Judge Chaila's decision. He had expected a repetition of his success with the application for the writ of *habeas corpus ad subjiciendum* which was heard earlier in the High Court in Ndola before Judge Bweupe. However, the dismissal of his application by Judge Chaila did not demoralise him completely. He was determined to continue the fight against the authorities on his detention. Subsequently, he instructed our law firm to advise him if there were strong grounds for lodging an appeal to the Supreme Court of Zambia against Judge Chaila's dismissal of his application. After studying the judgment and examining the relevant case law, initially we advised against lodgement of an appeal to the Supreme Court. We considered the chances of success to be quite remote. After further discussions with our client and consultations with his close relatives, we agreed to file the necessary documents for setting the appeal procedures in motion. Matters relating to the freedom or liberty of a subject are given priority when cause lists for the High Court are prepared. Bevin Willombe and I relegated less important legal issues to our partners or legal assistants. It was important to allow ourselves all the time necessary for the preparation of the grounds of appeal and heads of argument with a list of authorities on which we relied in the appeal.

The respondent in the appeal was the attorney-general. In the High Court, during the hearing of our client's application before Judge Chaila, AG Kinariwala, assistant state advocate, appeared for the attorney-general as the respondent. It was quite clear from the time Judge Chaila delivered his judgment that Kinariwala was determined to defend the decision all the way. He employed every conceivable trick in the book to delay our client's appeal process. However, eventually Valentine Musakanya's appeal was heard in the Supreme Court of Zambia on 10 July 1981 before Chief Justice Annel Silungwe, Deputy Chief Justice Brian Gardner and Supreme Court Justice James Cullinan. In my submissions, I argued four grounds of appeal. I emphasised that the appellant was detained under regulation 33 (1) of the Preservation of Public Security Regulations. His application for a writ of *habeas corpus ad subjiciendum* was unsuccessful in the High Court. Therefore, he appealed to the Supreme Court arguing, *inter alia*, that (i) the trial judge erred in law in holding that the provisions of Article 15 (3) (b) of the constitution do not apply to persons detained under Regulation 33 (1) of the Preservation of Public Security Regulations; (ii) the trial judge erred in law in holding that the appellant's grounds for detention were not vague; (iii) the trial judge also erred in law in refusing to accept the appellant's plea of *alibi*; and (iv) the unreasonableness of the trial judge's order on costs made against the appellant in the court below. The senior state advocate opposed my arguments vehemently. In particular, he argued strongly that the provisions of Article 15 (3) of the Constitution of Zambia did not apply to the applicant because he was detained for the purposes of preserving public security.

On 8 October 1981, the chief justice delivered the unanimous judgment of the Supreme Court. The appeal was dismissed. In a nutshell, the Supreme Court judgement drew a distinction between detention governed by Article 27 (1) (a) of the Constitution of Zambia and detention under Article 15 (3). It was held that a detention which is made for the purpose of preserving public security is a constitutional derogation from the provisions of Article 15. Therefore, such a detention cannot be challenged on grounds that it is in contravention of that article. However, although the appeal was dismissed, the appellant was not condemned in costs. The Supreme Court acknowledged that the appellant had raised "a constitutional point of public importance concerning the interpretation of Article 15 (3) (b) of the constitution which has not been decided before". Therefore, the court ordered each party to bear its own costs. For our client the dismissal of the appeal was a great disappointment. However, the court's order for each party to bear its own costs was a welcome although small consolation.

The trial of the thirteen men accused of treason opened in the High Court on 19 November 1981. Apparently, Valentine Musakanya was all along unhappy with the engagement of George Chaane as his defence counsel. Totally unknown to me and Bevin Willombe, he had made up his mind to inform the court that he did not want George Chaane to continue representing him during the trial. In the morning on that day or earlier, he had informed George Chaane that he intended to appoint another lawyer to represent his interests in the trial. Of course, Valentine Musakanya had a constitutional right to be represented in the trial by a lawyer of his own choice, but decency or mere courtesy obliged him to inform George Chaane about the decision he had made. George Chaane, too, was obliged by rules of professional conduct to accept his client's wish to replace him with another lawyer of his choice. Just as hearing started in Lusaka High Court before Judge Dennis Chirwa, defence counsel for Valentine Musakanya stood up and told the judge that he had been instructed by his client to step down.

Valentine Musakanya's decision to replace his lawyer came as a shock to the other accused persons and to the prosecuting team comprising of the attorney-general, Gibson Chigaga; the director of public prosecutions, Joshua Simuziya; senior state advocate, Gulam Sheikh; and assistant senior state advocate, Raja Balachandran. To me it was clear that the die was cast. I knew that Valentine Musakanya wanted his will to prevail – to confirm the law firm of MMW and Company as his legal representatives, but it took some time for me to recover from his bombshell. The following day, the *Times of Zambia* carried the story of Valentine Musakanya's decision to dismiss George Chaane as his lawyer with a more sensational caption than the language George Chaane himself had used in court. The newspaper's caption was "Musakanya drops lawyer". The article described the court's proceedings after the dramatic event and showed how easily counsel for the prosecution and the defence crossed swords in an effort to gain an advantage for their own cause. Its text was as follows:

> Submissions in the case of thirteen men charged with treason were yesterday adjourned to November 25 in Lusaka High Court to enable new defence counsel for former Bank of Zambia governor Valentine Musakanya to obtain full instructions after his lawyer stepped down.

> Legal affairs minister and attorney-general Mr Gibson Chigaga, who is leading the prosecution's case, was supposed to reply to a preliminary issue raised by one of the thirteen, lawyer and former High Court Commissioner Edward Shamwana and agreed to by others urging the court to quash the first count in the indictment as it was bad.

As the hearing started defence counsel Mr George Chaane told Mr Justice Dennis Chirwa he had been instructed by Musakanya to step down.

"He has his own reasons and he is entitled to do so". Mr Chaane said.

Mr Bevin Willombe said he and former finance minister Mr John Mwanakatwe will represent Musakanya.

He applied for an adjournment so he could obtain instructions from Musakanya on the preliminary issue raised by Shamwana.

.... No plea has been taken as the thirteen men have raised preliminary issues,

Mr Chigaga – who will be helped in prosecuting by director of public prosecutions Mr Joshua Simuziya, senior state advocate Mr Gulam Hussein Sheikh and assistant senior state advocate Mr Raja Balachandran – said the defence was given time for any preliminary issued from November 18 to 20.

Mr Chigaga said Mr Willombe was in court as one of the defence counsel helping Mr Musakanya's lawyer.

He said on Wednesday Mr Chaane was given an opportunity to submit on the objection and he agreed with Shamwana's submissions.

There must be an effort by the state and defence not to delay the trial unduly.

Mr Willombe, apparently annoyed, said he took exception to Mr Chigaga's submission.

He said it took the state more than a year to bring the case to court and it was not his or Musakanya's intention to delay the proceedings.

He needed time to argue his points to help the court arrive at a reasonable conclusion.

The judge's ruling in our client's favour on Bevin Willombe's application was fair. Following the withdrawal of George Chaane from Valentine Musakanya's defence team, it was necessary to again confer with him. He might give us new instructions for conducting his defence in the trial. However, our first duty during the adjournment was to arrange immediately settlement of costs for George Chaane's professional services at the beginning of the treason trial. A deposit was held in the clients' account at MMW and Company for this purpose. Therefore, when we received a fee note from G Chaane and Company, it was paid immediately with Henry Shikopa's guidance and assistance. He had undertaken to coordinate Mrs Flavia Musakanya's efforts to raise funds for legal costs on behalf of her husband. After settlement of the fee note, George Chaane surrendered Valentine Musakanya's case file to us together with relevant notes and documents which were in his possession. That is how George Chaane's involvement in the treason trial came to an amicable end.

Our next responsibility was to review our brief on this matter and discuss it again with our client during the adjournment. Because I attached great importance to this particular responsibility, it would have been unfair to ask Bevin Willombe to undertake its performance. I chose to grapple with this responsibility myself. That, in fact, was a convenient arrangement for us. For Bevin Willombe required sufficient time during the adjournment to prepare his submission in support of the preliminary issue Edward Shamwana raised urging the court to quash the first count in the indictment because it was bad in law. After reviewing the brief and in the light of the information we obtained during the proceedings in court on preliminary issues, I realised that the time had come to adopt a specific strategy for Valentine Musakanya's defence in the treason trial.

On the eve of Independence Day in October 1980, a

combined team of paramilitary men, police and security officers raided the home of Valentine Musakanya off Leopards Hill Road, east of Lusaka. The police suspected his involvement in a clandestine plan to overthrow the government by unlawful means. They had planned to search his house before whisking him away to a police station for interrogation and his subsequent arrest. To carry out their mission effectively, the police and security men produced a search warrant. At that stage, Valentine Musakanya could have exercised his right not to allow them to search his house in the absence of his lawyer. Nonetheless, he allowed the officers to search his house and the premises. During the search, the armed paramilitary men were guarding the premises. None of the members of Valentine Musakanya's family was allowed to make any telephone call or to leave. The search was thorough. It started after midnight and continued long after dawn. The police and security men were interested especially in a careful examination of documents which might contain information related to the alleged plan to topple the government. However, their search did not apparently yield the desired result.

At the end of the search, Valentine Musakanya was asked to accompany the police and security men to a police station for questioning. He was taken to Lilayi Police Station where he was later arrested and detained on 24 October 1980 under the provisions of Regulation 33 (6) of the Preservation of Public Security Regulations. The Police Detention Order was revoked on 31 October 1980 and he was on the same day served with a Presidential Detention Order under Regulation 33 (1) of the Preservation of Public Security Regulations. For several days the place where Valentine Musakanya was held in custody remained a secret. It was in the early days of his detention at Lilayi that he was subjected to prolonged interrogation. Eventually, the police managed to get him "to tell it all" to their satisfaction. The so-called "Interrogation Notes" were later perceived by the police as a convenient confession by Valentine Musakanya during the treason trial. Yet the police officers responsible for his interrogation did not follow the usual Judges' Rules when obtaining a statement from a suspect which might be used against him in criminal proceedings. Actually, it occurred to us later in the treason trial that the police intended originally to use the copious notes they wrote during the informal dialogue at Lilayi Police Station as a basis for the formulation of questions for Valentine Musakanya's statement after the usual "warn and caution".

Indeed, a week or two after the police had completed interrogating Valentine Musakanya at Lilayi Police Station, he was advised to inform a lawyer to be present at the headquarters of the Zambia Police in Lusaka where he was required to give his statement to the police on the alleged coup plot. He had already engaged MMW and Company to represent his interests. I refused to accompany our client to the Zambia Police headquarters on the date the police had set because it was not convenient for me. More importantly, I informed them that it was again necessary to obtain instructions from our client. In reality, I wanted to know as much as possible from our own client about the police interrogations at Lilayi Police Station.

That was a useful tactic. Within a few days Valentine Musakanya had felt at ease with the officers at Lilayi. They were friendly and courteous. He told them all that they wanted to know. However, he emphasised that he was not at any time warned or cautioned by any of the interrogators. In addition, he did not sign any statement or document at the conclusion of the interrogations. I advised him that, in these circumstances, he was free to choose to remain silent or to give a warn and caution statement at the Zambia Police headquarters but avoiding as far as possible contradicting what he told his interrogators earlier. I informed him that he had a constitutional right to remain silent during trial for a criminal offence. It was enshrined in the Constitution of Zambia that every person charged with a criminal offence shall be presumed innocent until he or she is proved or has pleaded guilty.

Subsequently, our session with the police officers at the

328

Zambia Police headquarters did not complicate the strategy I conceived for our client's trial in the High Court. Our client had reflected carefully on my advice before attending the Zambia Police headquarters for recording his statement. During preliminary discussions, the defence team for the accused persons was divided on whether or not the accused should testify. Some asserted that it would harm our clients if they chose to testify. Quite clearly, eventually each lawyer was responsible for advising his client on the best strategy for the defence of his own client. Quite early in the proceedings, I was convinced that it was not in Valentine Musakanya's interest to testify when he had no witness of his own to give evidence in support of his testimony. In any event, in a criminal trial the burden is at all times, with a few exceptions only, upon the prosecution to prove their case beyond reasonable doubt. Valentine Musakanya chose to remain silent when the police recorded a statement from him after he was warned and cautioned. His decision to remain silent in my presence undoubtedly disappointed the police officers. I have always thought that with the interrogation notes they wrote at Lilayi Police Station the police officers hoped to obtain a statement from Valentine Musakanya which was free and voluntary and in line with the interrogation notes which were already in their possession. Therefore, what would have truly been a field day for the police officers at the headquarters in Lusaka turned out to be a lost opportunity.

I always discussed with Bevin Willombe each development in our strategy for the defence of our client. However, he was uncertain about the wisdom of advising our client to remain silent throughout the trial. He agreed that our client had been wise to remain silent when the police officers requested him to make a formal statement at the Zambia Police headquarters. We knew that we were engaged in a long and complex trial. We knew that the prosecution intended to call more than one hundred witnesses in the main trial and to produce more than one hundred and fifty exhibits. We also knew that before the commencement of the main trial the court had a duty to consider and give rulings on numerous applications and objections by the accused or by their counsel. Although Bevin Willombe and I were obliged to attend every sitting of the court to represent our client, I undertook additionally to plan and conduct further research on various aspects of our client's defence. There was need to consult legal experts available in Zambia and abroad. While I researched to improve our brief for the defence of Valentine Musakanya, Bevin Willombe was occupied with routine work – the administration of our law firm. We had also a joint responsibility of attending to legal work of other clients.

Indeed, due to numerous preliminary matters and objections raised mainly by counsel, the treason trial in the early stages proceeded very slowly. However, those preliminary matters, objections and rulings on them were of concern not only to the accused and their lawyers but also to members of the public generally. The accused persons, their counsel and families were interested in a fair trial in a properly constituted court of law. The concern of the accused was understandable. They were charged with treason, a very serious criminal offence which carried a mandatory death sentence. Publishers of newspapers knew, of course, that the trial of the accused was of great interest to the public, anxious to know why the government accused them of conspiring to overthrow it.

The accused were concerned that adverse pre-trial publicity in the press might prejudice their fair trial in court. Therefore, the danger of pre-trial publicity was among complaints which were brought to the judge's attention because it was considered prejudicial to a fair trial. Edward Shamwana quite early in the trial complained that once in Lusaka and once in Maputo, Mozambique, President Kaunda held press conferences at which he claimed that the state had a watertight case. President Kaunda's statements were given wide publicity in the newspapers. However, in the judge's ruling on the complaint raised by Edward Shamwana on behalf of all accused persons, a distinction was drawn between publicity which takes place well before criminal proceedings and publicity at the pre-trial stage. The complaint against President Kaunda's pre-trial publicity was invalid. The publicity was not prejudicial to the fair trial of the accused persons.

A similar complaint was raised by Edward Shamwana against a pronouncement by Grey Zulu, secretary for defence and security, which all lawyers supported on behalf of their clients. Grey Zulu was the third ranking political leader in the government. He addressed a meeting in Serenje at which he told UNIP officials that Pierce Annfield, one of the suspects in the treason case, had gone into hiding because he knew he had committed a serious offence. On 17 November 1981, the *Times of Zambia* newspaper published an article headlined "Why Annfield is still hiding" which reported Grey Zulu's comments. The complaint was that Mr Grey Zulu and the newspaper's editor-in-chief, Naphy Nyalugwe, were in contempt of court. Accordingly, the thirteen accused persons urged the court to decide whether or not Mr Grey Zulu and Mr Nyalugwe, were not in contempt of court. The court later summoned them for contempt of court for the article referring to Pierce Annfield who was a suspect in the treason case. Before Judge Chirwa, both Mr Grey Zulu and Mr Nyalugwe were represented by two leading lawyers, Sebastian Zulu and John Jearey respectively, at a hearing on 9 December 1981 for alleged contempt of court. Mr Grey Zulu was the first to give evidence. He denied that he had told a meeting in Serenje that lawyer Pierce Annfield was in hiding because he was guilty of an offence. Mr Nyalugwe also gave evidence and relied on the fact that he had not been aware of the contempt of court. His counsel in a submission emphasised that journalists in Zambia considered it their obligation to report statements of national importance made by political leaders. John Jearey, counsel for Naphy Nyalugwe, told the court that Mr Grey Zulu had been "occupying high positions in society and what he says is always news".

On 15 December 1981, Judge Chirwa delivered his mini-judgment in Lusaka High Court. He issued an injunction restraining Mr Grey Zulu and Mr Nyalugwe from issuing statements outside court which might prejudice the fair trial of the thirteen men charged with treason. In addition, Judge Chirwa fined Mr Grey Zulu and Mr Nyalugwe K15 each or in default seven days simple imprisonment for contempt of court. He delivered a clear, well reasoned judgment which was widely reported both in Zambia and in the foreign press. It was a landmark decision which demonstrated beyond doubt that the judiciary was truly independent in Zambia. On 16 December 1981, the *Times of Zambia* carried an article on the historic judgment captioned in large glaring letters: 'Zulu, Times guilty'.

At the beginning of the treason trial, the prosecutors were visibly overconfident about the strength of the prosecution's case. That was the reason for President Kaunda's observations at two press conferences that the state had a "watertight case". The leader of the prosecution team was Gibson Chigaga, the minister of legal affairs and attorney-general. It was rare for the attorney-general to assume prosecution of criminal offences except in especially selected cases of fundamental significance to the country's security and integrity. He was assisted by a formidable team of senior advocates, among them the director of public prosecutions, including Joshua Simuziya, GM Sheik and RR Balachandran, director of legal services corporation and principal state advocate respectively. The treason trial was understandably a high profile case. Security at the High Court in Lusaka was particularly tight. The environment as a whole was intimidating to the accused persons and their lawyers.

The atmosphere surrounding the High Court in Lusaka was tense on 2 November 1981, when thirteen men charged with treason and misprision of treason appeared before Judge Chirwa for plea. However, Gibson Chigaga applied for an adjournment to enable defence lawyers to obtain instructions from their clients. He conceded that statements of offence had not been served on the accused fourteen days before the trial as required by law. Leading the prosecution team, the attorney-general told the court that to give defence lawyers sufficient time to obtain full instructions from their clients an adjournment was necessary. The following day in an article on High Court proceedings, the reporter for the *Times of Zambia* described the atmosphere at the High Court graphically as follows:

> The High Court was a hive of activity as about one hundred heavily armed security, paramilitary and police officers who had put up two camps, searched everybody entering the courts.
>
> The High Court building was sealed off as early as 07.30 hours when roadblocks were put up on four roads leading to the court building.
>
> Motorists parked their vehicles at nearby office buildings and walked to security tents erected for identification before entering the courts.
>
> There were two tents for men and women in which security officers used metal detectors to screen people and search for concealed weapons that might be carried into the court.
>
> Paramilitary officers were armed with rocket and grenade launchers, machine guns and pistols.
>
> A crowd watched curiously from the nearby Cathedral of the Holy Cross.
>
> The accused men were immediately whisked away to Lusaka Central prison after the hearing. Traffic which was halted for almost five hours was back to normal at 12.00 hours.
>
> Two prominent lawyers, a former Bank of Zambia governor, and four senior army officers and others were only asked their names and in which language they would like the proceedings to be interpreted....
>
> The accused complained to the court that prison authorities constantly refused them to meet their lawyers and prepare their defence.

The court was told that the accused men were "tossed around" in so many detention centres in the country that some of them had found it impossible to secure any lawyers to defend them.

They appealed to the court to intervene to uphold their constitutional rights....

Adjourning the case Mr Justice Chirwa said he hoped the trial would go on with no further delay.

He said Mr Chigaga should not only issue instructions to the Prisons Department allowing lawyers to see their clients as promised but should ensure his orders were followed.

Mr Justice Chirwa said Mr Chigaga must protect the interests of the citizens and he hoped something would be worked out for the case to go on.

He would have a different view if on November 18 he was told lawyers were prevented from seeing their clients.

I will make no orders. I leave it in the good hands of the attorney-general to see that the accused men prepare their cases, Mr Justice Chirwa said.

Earlier, I have described the powerful and no-nonsense ruling by Judge Chirwa, which I called a mini-judgment, on the contempt allegation; it was of considerable significance. It was an embarrassment to the government and a boost to our morale. For the first time, we believed that a fair trial under Judge Chirwa was possible. Before the treason trial, the judge was neither famous nor infamous. He rose to fame during the treason trial. It was a complex case which lasted over a year. I do not remember a single day when the judge was late for trial of the case. He sat calmly in court in his flowing red robes. He was always friendly and courteous to counsel but quite firm, if necessary. He was a pokerfaced judge who had no patience with fools.

However, within a short time it was our turn as counsel for the accused persons to suffer defeat on an important application. The application concerned admissibility of the evidence of General Christopher Kabwe on behalf of the prosecution. Who was General Christopher Kabwe? Why was his evidence critical to the defence of the accused, including Valentine Musakanya? On the basis of the strategy we adopted for the defence of Valentine Musakanya, it was important to persuade Judge Chirwa that the evidence of General Christopher Kabwe was inadmissible. If his evidence was admissible, Valentine Musakanya's direct implication in the coup plot would be established by the prosecution.

General Christopher Kabwe was the principal witness for the prosecution. He was, at the material time, head of the Zambia Air Force in his capacity as chief of staff. He had jointly been arraigned with the other accused persons but was later granted immunity against prosecution: a *nolle prosequi* was entered in his favour and he became a state witness. He was, of course, presented by the prosecution as an accomplice witness. Therefore, by law, support for his evidence was necessary.

The case for the prosecution was that, sometime between the months of April and May 1980, General Kabwe had been approached at the Lusaka Flying Club by Goodwin Mumba, a former schoolmate who informed him of a plan – which had reached a very advanced stage – to carry out a coup d'etat in Zambia. General Kabwe was to be one of the participants in the coup d'etat. It was to be financed by powerful people within and outside the country.

At a subsequent meeting held at Edward Shamwana's house in Kabulonga, Lusaka, attended by a number of the accused, namely Shamwana, Musakanya, Mumba, and Pierce Annfield the plan for the overthrow of the Zambian government was outlined to General Kabwe. He was told to find suitable Zambia Air Force pilots whose assignment was to be the diversion to a pre-selected place of an aircraft carrying the president of the Republic where he was to be forced, at gunpoint, to renounce his office and to hand over power to someone else. Announcements to that effect were then to be made on Television Zambia, Radio Zambia and other forms of the news media. Following a successful execution of the plot, other national leaders, such as the secretary general of the ruling party, the prime minister, the secretary of state for defence and security, the commander of the Zambia National Defence Forces, and all the service chiefs, including General Kabwe, were to be arrested in order to forestall a possible counter-coup. However, General Kabwe was later to be released. It was stressed that there was to be no loss of blood unless this became an absolute necessity.

With this background, General Kabwe was the key witness for the state. Overt act one alleged a conspiracy in which our client, Valentine Musakanya, was involved. For this overt act, the state intended to call one witness, General Kabwe. In fact, the newspapers referred to him as the state's "star witness". Therefore, Bevin Willombe and I vigorously supported the application for inadmissibility of General Kabwe's evidence as a preliminary issue. We had strong grounds in support of the application. It was a fact that he was an accomplice witness whom the state had indemnified against prosecution for his complicity in the alleged coup plot. Furthermore, the prosecution did not dispute that the witness had been picked up, detained and interrogated for many hours. Subsequently, he was arrested and committed to the High Court for trial. Later, he turned state witness and was issued with an indemnity. We argued that the indemnity had undoubtedly influenced the statement he gave to the police. Therefore, we argued that it was wrong in law to admit in evidence General Kabwe's confession obtained by threats or inducement or in breach of Judges' Rules.

In his ruling, Judge Chirwa found General Kabwe as an honest witness. He ruled that his statement was admissible in evidence. Later in his judgment, he observed that:

Having found General Kabwe a truthful witness, as he is an accomplice, I will look for corroboration, i.e. evidence that will confirm the material points relevant to the case, evidence that should rule out the possibility of false fabrication of the story.

Before I look for such corroborative evidence, I should put it on record that this witness was threatened and interrogated for a prolonged period before he gave his statement in October 1980. When the offer of his turning state witness was made to him he got legal advice from his counsel on it and he accepted the offer on it ....

I do not think that he stuck to his story because of the promised indemnity, I say so because he was told when the offer to turn state witness was made to him that evidence against him was negligible, which in English means that such evidence could not stand against him.

When Judge Chirwa ruled at the beginning of the trial that General Kabwe's confession statement was admissible in evidence, Bevin Willombe and I became concerned about Valentine Musakanya's defence in the treason trial. It was more obvious to us that Valentine Musakanya acted wisely when, upon my advice, he refused to make a voluntary statement to the police interrogators in my presence at the Zambia Police headquarters. It is quite possible that he would have incriminated himself. Such a statement would have been considered relevant for the purpose of "corroborating" the evidence of General Kabwe. After ruling in favour of admission of General Kabwe's confession statement in evidence, Judge Chirwa required further "... independent corroborative evidence to support the material aspects of General Kabwe's evidence". In the absence of Valentine Musakanya's own statement to corroborate General Kabwe's evidence, the prosecution were obliged to find other evidence for this purpose.

During the main trial, confession statements of accused persons were produced by the prosecution to support the case for the state. Such statements were admissible if they were voluntary. All accused persons whose confession statements were produced in court chose to challenge such statements. Consequently, the court was obliged to hold a trial-within-a-trial to establish the *voluntariness* of the confession statements of such accused persons. In Valentine Musakanya's case, the prosecution did not produce a confession statement. None was available. However, the prosecution had decided to produce Valentine Musakanya's "interrogation notes" as exhibit 100. The prosecution did not dispute that a senior police officer, Superintendent Kaulung'ombe, interrogated Valentine Musakanya on 1 and 2 November 1980 at Lilayi Police Station. While interrogating him, other police personnel secretly endeavoured to maintain a handwritten record of the interrogation. No warn and caution was administered to Valentine Musakanya. The notes were not read to him for approval with or without corrections. They were neither shown to him nor signed by him. Apparently, the notes were originally obtained for the purpose of accumulating as much information as possible on the coup attempt and for Superintendent Kaulung'ombe's use as an *aide-memoire*.

In preparing the strategy for the defence of our client during the trial, we considered the possibility that the prosecution might introduce the interrogation notes for admission in evidence and use by the trial court. If the prosecution introduced the interrogation notes as a substitute for a confession, then our client would be expected to take the stand and testify in a trial-within-a-trial that the purported confession was not voluntary. He had no other person to testify on his behalf. Yet it was likely that the prosecution would call witnesses to give evidence in a trial-within-a-trial. At the end of the trial-within-a-trial, the Judge was at liberty upon the evidence led in court to exercise his discretion to exclude or admit the interrogation notes in evidence. I was personally inclined to advise our client to avoid giving evidence in the witness box in a trial-within-a-trial. There was a real danger that the prosecution might easily line up as many as three or more witnesses to testify in the trial-within-a-trial. The outcome of a trial-within-a-trial is always a gamble. At first, I found Bevin Willombe reluctant to support my proposal.

Lawyers, like medical practitioners, prefer to obtain an opinion from another legal practitioner in difficult cases. Expecting the eventuality of the prosecution introducing the hand-written notes of Valentine Musakanya's interrogation at Lilayi Police Station for admission in evidence, I consulted Geoffrey Care for an opinion. He was an experienced lawyer who had practised law for many years in Zambia. He was qualified as a solicitor in England in 1953. In 1957 he came to Zambia to practise law. For a number of years he was privileged to serve in the judiciary in Zambia as a part-time High Court commissioner capable of exercising powers of a High Court judge. I picked his brains about the advantages of advising Valentine Musakanya to avoid giving testimony on Superintendent Kaulung'ombe's interrogation notes in a trial-within-a-trial. He unhesitatingly supported the idea of advising our client to remain silent. It was advisable for him to rely only on counsel's objection to the production of the interrogation notes as his confession statement. Geoffrey Care emphasised that my proposal had its own risks. However, he firmly believed that asking our client to testify in a trial-within-a-trial had more risks which were likely to prejudice his interests. We were in a situation where we agreed to reverse the truism that "a statement from the dock does not carry the same weight as evidence under oath".

Geoffrey Care had considerable experience of criminal trials in which a trial-within-a-trial was held for the purpose of determining whether or not a confession statement of the accused was voluntary and, therefore, admissible or not. The trial judge was often inclined towards the story of police witnesses in a trial-within-a-trial if two or more police witnesses told the same story against the evidence of the accused. There are exceptions. For example, an accused may testify that he was coerced and tortured by the police investigators in order to extract a confession from him. In such a circumstance, production of a medical certificate to that effect in a trial-within-a-trial might be conclusive evidence for the exclusion of the confession statement. No such circumstance existed in relation to the interrogation notes.

When Superintendent Kaulung'ombe was called to give evidence for the prosecution, he produced Valentine Musakanya's handwritten interrogation notes. He testified that the record of his interrogation was accurate and reflected the true story of his involvement in the coup attempt. However, in cross-examination Superintendent Kaulung'ombe admitted that the interrogation notes did not constitute a warn and caution statement of the accused. He also admitted that the accused did not sign the interrogation notes which, in fact, were never read to him at any stage during the interrogation. In our submission, we emphasised that it was wrong to admit the interrogation notes in evidence even if they were taken as a confession statement. On the other hand, Balachandran, on behalf of the state, submitted that the interrogation notes were a "contemporaneous record" of the information given by our client to Superintendent Kaulung'ombe who testified as a prosecution witness in the trial. At that stage I received two written messages from defence lawyers enquiring if we intended to apply to the court for a trial-within-a-trial to be held to afford the accused an opportunity of discrediting the interrogation notes as a confession statement. It was too late for us to abandon a tactic for our client's defence which we had adopted after careful reflection and consultation with Geoffrey Care. Personally I was not keen to encourage our client to testify in a trial-within-a-trial because I considered the interrogation notes of very little evidential value.

On 20 January 1983, Judge Chirwa delivered the marathon judgment in the treason trial. The written judgment took five hours to read to a packed court room. It was crowded with relatives and friends of the accused, with local news reporters and others from various parts of the world. Many curious onlookers stood outside the High Court building in the midst of tight security maintained by security men in plain clothes and regular police and paramilitary men.

Judge Chirwa found that "on the totality of the evidence" Edward Shamwana, Valentine Musakanya, Goodwin Mumba, Anderson Mporokoso, Thomas Mulewa, Deogratias Syimba, Albert Chimbalile and Laurent Kabwita did conspire to overthrow the government of the Republic of Zambia by unlawful means and did endeavour to persuade General Kabwe to arrange for the diversion of the presidential plane to a previously selected place where the president was to be forced to renounce his office at gunpoint and to hand over his office to another person. Accused Anderson Mporokoso was found guilty of the offence of misprison of treason, the offence of failing to report a treason contrary to Section 44 (b) of the Penal Code, Chapter 146 of the Laws of Zambia. The rest of the accused were found guilty of the more serious offence of treason which carries a mandatory death penalty. In his judgment, Judge Chirwa stated that:

> I am, therefore, satisfied beyond all reasonable doubt that the prosecution has proved the case of treason, contrary to Section 43 (1) (a) of the Penal Code, Chapter 146 of the Laws of Zambia, against the accused and I convict each and every one of them as charged.

In the judgment, Judge Chirwa stated that from the evidence a conspiracy had been proved. Therefore, he concluded that any act or omission by any conspirator in pursuance of the conspiracy was deemed to be an act or omission of conspirators. Judge Chirwa relied heavily on the evidence of General Kabwe on the meeting he had with Goodwin Mumba together with Pierce Annfield at Edward Shamwana's house. He went on to say that "the meeting was clearly in furtherance of the conspiracy". Judge Chirwa also stated quite clearly that he relied on the warn and caution statement of Goodwin Mumba and the "interrogation notes in respect of the second accused, Valentine

Musakanya" for the necessary corroboration of General Kabwe's evidence. The conviction of our client on the treason charge was dependent on the admission of the interrogation notes in evidence. They were used by the trial court as if they were a properly admitted confession.

At the end of the judgment and as Judge Chirwa walked out of the courtroom, lawyers were completely stunned. Suddenly, we all had melancholy faces. The judgment sent shock waves through the crowd outside the High Court. Men and women, both young and old, showed their total disbelief at the realisation that seven men were found guilty on a charge of treason which carried a mandatory death sentence. I recall turning to Bevin Willombe in disbelief. I asked him: "What next?", after Judge Chirwa's departure from the courtroom. I do not remember his response.

The next day on 21 November 1983, the *Zambia Daily Mail* carried a front page story captioned "Mporokoso Jailed For Ten Years" and below it another caption in big letters "Treason Seven to Hang". Another story by a *Zambia Daily Mail* reporter summarised the judgment. He wrote in the article that "all eight men indicated soon after the verdict was pronounced that they would appeal to the Supreme Court against conviction in the case of those who were charged with treason". Anderson Mporokoso also indicated his desire to appeal to the Supreme Court against conviction and sentence on a charge of misprison of treason. Kingston Ndawa's article also had a photograph showing some relatives of the seven men who were sentenced to death weeping outside the High Court after judgment. Another *Zambia Daily Mail* reporter described the sombre mood of the people who stood outside the High Court building throughout Judge Chirwa's five hour long judgment:

> Relatives broke down and wept yesterday when Mr Justice Dennis Chirwa pronounced death sentences on seven men whom he convicted of treason.

As the judge pronounced the sentences, saying: "I sentence each one of you to death and direct that you shall be hanged by the neck until you are dead," there were murmurs of bewilderment in the packed public gallery.

And then there was brief silence during which one could see relatives weeping in the gallery.

Meanwhile, in the dock, former High Court commissioner, Edward Shamwana, former Bank of Zambia governor, Valentine Musakanya, Zairean politician, Deogratias Syimba, Thomas Mulewa Mpunga and Roger Kabwita remained quiet as the capital sentences were being handed down to them.

But former Industrial Finance Company general manager Goodwin Yoram Mumba and Albert Chimbalile reacted to the verdict with smiles. They looked completely unmoved by the verdict.

After the judge had retired to his chambers, a weeping female relative waved at Mumba, who waved back at her, a smile still written on his face. Other condemned accused persons also waved at their relatives, some of whom were also weeping.

Tight security was slapped around the entire High Court building. Armed paramilitary police officers were stationed both outside and inside the building to check for any trouble. Members of the public had to be screened first before entering the court premises.

Because of the importance of the case and the wide publicity given to it, the courtroom where the treason judgment was to take place was packed to capacity by 0700 hours so that many people who wished to attend the judgment had to be turned away.

And for the first time since the treason trial started, the eight accused persons (including Major Anderson Mporokoso, who got 10 years for misprision of treason) were guarded by a group of about 15 prison warders who formed a human wall between the public gallery and the dock.

At about 1200 hours, as Mr Justice Chirwa was delivering his judgment, two military jet planes flew over the High Court building, their piercing noise forcing some of the people in the courtroom to close their ears.

The same or similar planes flew over the court building again in the afternoon at about 1600 hours, just after the sentences were pronounced.

The weeks following Judge Chirwa's judgment and conviction of all the accused in the treason trial were difficult for both clients and their counsel. The convicted men had decided to appeal to the Supreme Court. However, they were mainly concerned about the length of time they would remain in prison before the Supreme Court would hear the appeals. Convicted persons were known to languish in prison for several months or years before prosecuting their appeals in the Supreme Court. The delays were partly due to the backlog of pending appeals and to the length of time taken to prepare transcripts and case records. For counsel, prosecution of appeals to the Supreme Court is always a laborious exercise. In complicated criminal cases, the amount of time spent in preparing appeal documents is often disproportionate to the financial reward at the end of the day.

Valentine Musakanya did not delay in conveying to me his decision to appeal to the Supreme Court against Judge Chirwa's judgment. Both Bevin Willombe and I agreed that an appeal to the higher court was necessary. With the written instructions he gave us, we agreed to proceed with the formalities for lodgement of the notice of appeal to the Supreme Court. Furthermore, there were important issues to settle while waiting to receive copies of transcripts of the treason trial from the High Court Registry. As Valentine Musakanya's counsel, both Bevin Willombe and I were dissatisfied with Judge Chirwa for convicting our client on the treason charge. We strongly believed that Judge Chirwa erred when he held in his judgment that, "As to accused Valentine Musakanya the corroborative evidence is contained in the interrogation notes written by witness Mr Kaulung'ombe". Apart from other errors in the judgment, our considered opinion was that the admission of the interrogation notes in evidence was a serious error which scandalously perverted the course of justice.

Our client's family consulted us about the possibility of instructing a senior counsel from England to lead our team at the stage of hearing of the appeal in the Supreme Court. We thought that their suggestion was excellent. We did not anticipate any difficulty with collaborating with a senior lawyer from England. However, such an arrangement was only workable if procedural requirements were ironed out in advance of the arrival of such a senior counsel in Zambia to argue the appeal of our client in the Supreme Court. In Zambia, no person has the right of audience in the law courts unless he is in possession of a certificate issued by the Law Association of Zambia authorising him to perform the functions of a legal practitioner. Such a practising certificate should be valid at the time of its production in court. However, even more importantly, the Council of the Law Association of Zambia cannot issue a practising certificate to an applicant whose name does not appear on the official roll of legal practitioners in Zambia maintained by the Registrar of the High Court pursuant to provisions of the Legal Practitioners Act of 1973. For a person to be enrolled as a practitioner entitled to practise as an advocate, it is necessary to pass the qualifying examinations conducted by the Institute for Advanced Legal Studies. Lastly, payment of legal fees to a lawyer based outside Zambia required exchange control permission. This was the easiest procedural matter to resolve on application to the Bank of Zambia.

After making the necessary searches at the High Court, we found two eminent lawyers both with Queen's Counsel (QC) status whose names appeared on the roll of legal practitioners in Zambia. The two men were Mr Robert Gatehouse, QC and Mr Arthur Suzman, QC, of London and Johannesburg respectively. I discussed with Valentine Musakanya the credentials of the lawyers. They were both good lawyers with rich experience. Both men qualified as barristers in England. Mr Arthur Suzman's experience was richer, with over fifty years of law practice to his credit. However, we agreed that the more practical approach was to choose Mr Robert Gatehouse who was engaged in the practice of law in England which has similarities with Zambia. In the Republic of South Africa on the other hand Roman Dutch law was the basis of the judicial system.

Through useful contacts abroad, the credentials of our law firm were acceptable to Mr Robert Gatehouse who readily accepted our instructions to argue our client's appeal in the Supreme Court. A senior member of the Bar in England, a person who has "taken silk", does not appear alone in court. Ordinarily a QC has a junior barrister who researches and prepares an appropriate brief under the guidance of the senior counsel. He proposed Anthony Wood, who was ready at short notice to come to Zambia for consultations, as his junior. These arrangements were satisfactory to us. Consequently, exchange control permission was obtained for remission of funds for lawyers' fees and a practising certificate was issued to Mr Robert Gatehouse by the Law Association of Zambia. Valentine Musakanya and members of his family were especially pleased with the choice of Mr Robert Gatehouse as the senior counsel at the hearing of our client's appeal in the Supreme Court. They were even more encouraged when Anthony Wood arrived in Zambia to discuss all legal issues of the treason case and the trial in the High Court. The objective of his first mission to Lusaka was to meet our client, discuss with us suggested grounds of appeal and draft heads of argument. After working with Anthony Wood for a few days, we discovered that he was a competent lawyer, energetic, lively, with a flair for thoroughness. In a short time, he became one of us. We simply called him

Tony as a sign of our fondness for him.

Bevin and I continued to be responsible for the preparation of all the necessary documents for our client's appeal, including the brief for the senior counsel. That burden of responsibility was ours as instructing counsel. In any event, Mr Robert Gatehouse expected to rely on us because we were especially knowledgeable on law and practice in Zambia. Therefore, in the months between August 1983 and March 1984, Bevin and I spent many long hours preparing the appeal documents and attending conferences in Lusaka and London. Anthony Wood commuted more frequently between London and Lusaka for this purpose. Eventually, on 17 May 1984 we filed successfully in the Supreme Court the "Additional and Amended Grounds of Appeal in substitution for the Grounds of Appeal dated 20 January 1983". Simultaneously, copies of the "Heads of Argument in the Appeal of Valentine Shula Musakanya" were also filed. With the filing of these documents in May 1984, the die was cast. We looked forward thereafter to the day when the appeals would be heard, including that of our own client.

The authorities in the Supreme Court undoubtedly favoured the treason trial appellants by setting an early date for hearing the appeals. We received notices that the appeals were due to be heard in the Supreme Court of Zambia from 8 to 10 August 1984, approximately fourteen months from the date the "Additional and Amended Grounds of Appeal" and the "Heads of Argument in the Appeal" were filed in the Supreme Court on behalf of our client. The appeals were scheduled to be heard before five judges of the Supreme Court, namely Chief Justice Silungwe, Deputy Chief Justice Ngulube, Supreme Court Judge Muwo and Acting Supreme Court Judges Bweupe and Sakala. The panel of judges selected to hear the appeals in the Supreme Court reflected the complexity of the trial in the High Court. The appointment of a bench of five Supreme Court judges also underlines the political significance of the treason case. Usually, three Supreme Court judges were considered adequate to dispose of appeals from courts below. The appointment of five judges of the Supreme Court to hear the appeals was wholly justified. It was an acknowledgement of the complexity of the legal issues raised in the appeals.

Mr Robert Gatehouse and Mr Anthony Wood arrived in Zambia one week before the judges were expected to begin hearing appeals in the Supreme Court. We considered a period of one week to be adequate for a review of our brief and the details of the various heads of argument. In our consultations, Mr Robert Gatehouse felt that our client's appeal was weakened by my failure to ask the trial judge in the High Court to allow a trial-within-a-trial which would have given Valentine Musakanya an opportunity to challenge the admissibility of interrogation notes in evidence. However, I emphasised in our discussion that there was also another side of the coin. I firmly believed that a trial-within-a-trial might provide the judge an opportunity to exercise his discretion to believe the story of police officers (two, three or more) called by counsel for the people to testify during the trial-within-a-trial. In that event, the defence of our client might be completely ruined. Mr Robert Gatehouse accepted my viewpoint. In our discussions, we also considered other legal issues and reviewed carefully our client's grounds of appeal and heads of argument.

The thrust of our argument in the Supreme Court in support of our client's appeal was that Judge Chirwa erred in law when he decided to admit Superintendent Kaulung'ombe's interrogation notes in evidence. In the lower court, the state's submission was that the interrogation notes had been made as an *aide-memoire* and not for the purpose of production in court. The state's submission was that the interrogation notes were nonetheless admissible in evidence "as a contemporaneous record of information supplied by the accused Valentine Musakanya to Superintendent Kaulung'ombe". Yet in law such notes were ordinarily intended to be used by a witness merely for refreshing his memory. In any event, we argued that even if the interrogation notes were intended to be produced as a confession they would have been inadmissible in evidence without first of all holding a trial-within-a-trial.

When Mr Robert Gatehouse reached that stage of his argument, he regretted that I had by lapse of memory failed to remind Judge Chirwa that it was necessary to hold a trial-within-a-trial to determine the admissibility of the interrogation notes in evidence. Immediately, the deputy chief justice, Mr Matthew Ngulube, interrupted the proceedings. He interjected clearly and loudly that no regret or apology was necessary for my failure to plead with the court below to hold a trial-within-a-trial. The deputy chief justice stated emphatically that it was the trial court's duty to hold a trial-within-a-trial with or without persuasion from accused Valentine Musakanya's counsel to determine the admissibility of the interrogation notes in evidence. The chief justice and other judges of the Supreme Court on the bench did not make any comment on deputy chief justice Matthew Ngulube's interjection. Mr Robert Gatehouse continued with his arguments in support of our client's appeal.

However, to Mr Robert Gatehouse and other experienced lawyers in court it was obvious that the Supreme Court judges had considered carefully our submissions on the impropriety of the admission of interrogation notes in evidence. The notes on this issue were copious in the "Heads of Argument in the appeal of Valentine Musakanya", a document which we had filed in the Supreme Court on 17 May 1984. After the court's adjournment, it was unnatural to avoid speculation about the fate of Valentine Musakanya's appeal to the Supreme Court against his conviction for treason and the consequential mandatory death sentence. However, although I was not keen to offer a bet to anyone, I had a strong feeling nonetheless that the tactic I had conceived for Valentine Musakanya's appeal with Geoffrey Care's encouragement, might succeed. The Supreme Court sat for eighteen days in August and for eleven days in September 1984 to hear appeals against convictions by eight appellants.

Unfortunately, we had to wait for six months before the judgment was ready for delivery on 2 April 1985. Indeed, a very long time. That day eventually came. It was a very exciting day indeed as the lawyers, appellants, news reporters and members of the public crowded the courtroom. The atmosphere in the courtroom was tense. No one among the appellants knew what was in store for them – liberty, dismissal of appeal and a sentence of imprisonment or dismissal of appeal followed by the mandatory death sentence. Valentine Musakanya's appeal against conviction was allowed at the end of the Supreme Court's marathon judgment on 2 April 1985. Therefore, sentence was set aside. The appeals of two other appellants were also successful. In respect of these three appellants, namely Valentine Musakanya, Anderson Mporokoso and Laurent Kanyimbu, the Supreme Court judges observed that "there is no evidence on which their convictions can be sustained" that "the appeals by these three appellants against convictions are allowed".

The Supreme Court in its judgment held that Valentine Musakanya's interrogation notes should never have been brought before the trial court. They were in fact admitted in evidence which was wrongful. A number of passages in the judgment illustrate the Supreme Court's abhorrence of the state's effort to use the interrogation notes "as a substitute for a confession":

Clearly, the interrogation notes were, to all intents and purposes, admitted in evidence and used by the trial court as if they were a substitute for a properly admitted confession. This was a misdirection.

The significance and purpose of interrogations is to aid police investigations, not to later turn into evidence. It would be undesirable to promote the status of interrogation notes to the status or quasi status of a confession since, for obvious reasons, the police would usually be tempted to prefer the former.

In this case Appellant Valentine Musakanya made a statement to the police subsequent to the interrogations, but because it was apparently of no interest to them, they preferred to fall back on the interrogation notes which had been made as an *aide-memoire*, and not for the purpose of production in course.

There was joy and happiness among relatives and friends of the men whose appeals to the Supreme Court were successful. I was among the first well-wishers to congratulate Valentine Musakanya and hug him in the courtroom. At that stage, I was still mesmerized by the success of his appeal against conviction for treason in the High Court. Unfortunately, the appeals of five other appellants were dismissed. The unsuccessful appeals included Edward Shamwana's appeal. He was an intimate friend of Valentine Musakanya, a fact which dampened his spirit to rejoice following the declaration of his innocence by the Supreme Court.

While Valentine Musakanya's relatives and friends were rejoicing and hugging each other outside the High Court building, I was preoccupied in negotiations with the prison warders to get him released from Lusaka Central Prison forthwith. However, I was fighting against the odds. By the time the chief justice delivered the Supreme Court's long judgment, the prison gates were already closed at Lusaka Central Prison. Nevertheless, I was determined to persuade the prison authorities to allow completion of the formalities for his release, albeit after the official hours. One senior prison warder was kind and understanding. He allowed us to complete the formalities. It was a great relief to me when Valentine Musakanya was released from prison.

I drove him in my car to his house at Nkunkulusha farm. It was less than six kilometres to the east of Lusaka along Leopards Hill Road. When we arrived at his house a large crowd of well-wishers surged forward to welcome him. It was an emotional occasion for many men and women who had not seen him for a long time. It was an emotional moment for me too. After many trials, tribulations, risks and temptations, our mission was accomplished. Valentine Musakanya was a free person again in his own land. The success of his appeal to the Supreme Court vindicated his confidence in my suitability to represent his interests satisfactorily during the treason trial.

Apparently, after the judgment, many well-wishers, relatives and friends took wine and champagne bottles to his house to celebrate his release from prison. I refused to participate in the spontaneous celebration. I felt emotional when I accompanied Valentine Musakanya out of the prison gates. My mission was accomplished the moment he came out of my car to go into his house at Nkunkulusha farm. I returned home immediately and went straight to our bedroom. After lying on my bed for some time, I slept soundly for a long time. Fortunately, some good Samaritan had taken my wife to Nkunkulusha farm for the celebrations when I was at Lusaka Central Prison negotiating with prison warders the release of Valentine Musakanya. At least I was well represented at the informal function.

C H A P T E R

13

Lawyer for Multinationals

During the four years when I was preoccupied with Valentine Musakanya's defence both in the High Court and the Supreme Court, I was busy also with the affairs of other clients. From the time I began to practise law at the beginning of 1974, my preference was commercial work although another important and unavoidable aspect of an advocate's practice of law is giving advice and representing clients in court. Both are important. But if a lawyer's work meant spending all my time performing in front of a judge its attraction for me would have been minimal. While a criminal lawyer may expect to be in court every other day, a lawyer who specializes in property, or tax work, or commercial transactions may find that weeks go by without going to court. It is in this context that over the years I have preferred to do more commercial work than to deal with other aspects of law practice. Moreover, in developing countries, a successful commercial lawyer is more likely to gain influence at both the national and international levels. It is true that in high profile civil or criminal cases court appearances can give a good lawyer welcome but unsolicited publicity and fame. However, such high profile civil and criminal cases are rare.

A lawyer in Zambia has a variety of options for earning a living after admission to the Bar. He may opt to set up a private law firm and practise independently. On the other hand, he may join a law firm and practise law as a partner with other lawyers. Some lawyers in Zambia prefer to practise law as employees in established law firms. Nonetheless, even in fairly large law firms with four, five or more partners and employees, practitioners rarely specialize in the kind of legal work they do. But lawyers who are constantly instructed to act for large corporations or multinational companies may specialize in one type of legal work, such as property or tax work, commercial law or industrial relations work. In financial terms, lawyers who receive instructions regularly from large corporations or multinational companies to do specialized work are rewarded handsomely.

In the final analysis, however, a lawyer should possess the necessary skills in order to succeed in his profession. Three of these are particularly important. The first is that a good lawyer should possess good communication skills. In negotiating with other advocates in conferences or arguing a case in court, an advocate is expected to convey his message effectively. In drafting legal documents or giving a legal opinion, it is important that what an advocate writes is clear and easy to understand. The second important skill for an advocate to possess is careful planning and preparation of the work which he is required to perform. An advocate's care and concentration in planning his work easily gains for him a good reputation and more work from his clients. Finally, ability to work under pressure and yet perform well is an important attribute for an ambitious lawyer. Clients admire a lawyer who remains calm in the face of pressure. Every advocate will experience occasions when a great deal of work has to be done in a short time. Ability to cope with the pressure of last minute preparations will always create a favourable impression of an advocate's suitability to perform well in complex matters.

Throughout my legal career, I found commercial law more interesting to practise than any other branch of the law. I always enjoyed drafting opinions and legal documents. The occasional court appearances were also interesting and stimulating, especially in high profile civil or criminal matters. As early as 1964, when I was called to the Bar at Lincoln's Inn in London, it was obvious to me that lawyers who specialize in their work rise quickly to prominence in the profession and in the community generally. From the time of my call to the Bar, Margaret Thatcher, now the Rt. Hon. The Baroness Thatcher, was my role model. After obtaining a degree in Natural Science (Chemistry) at Oxford University, she worked for four years as a research chemist for an industrial firm in Great Britain. In her spare time, she read for the Bar examinations in preparation for fulfilment of her political ambitions. She was called to the Bar at Lincoln's Inn in 1954 and subsequently she practised as a barrister, specializing in tax law. Five years later, she was elected to the House of Commons as MP for Finchley. Lady Thatcher's first ministerial appointment came in 1961 when she became a parliamentary secretary to the then Ministry of Pensions and National Insurance. Later, she became the first woman to hold the office of prime minister of Great Britain from 1979 to 1990.

I have always been proud of the fact that Great Britain's first woman prime minister is a product of Lincoln's Inn which was established in England more than five hundred years ago. I was also called to the Bar at Lincoln's Inn by Lord Denning on 24 November 1964. On that occasion Lord Denning, as the treasurer of Lincoln's Inn, presided over the ceremony. In fact, Lord Denning, too, was a product of Lincoln's Inn. He was one of the most renowned judges of the Supreme Court of Judicature in Great Britain in the twentieth century. In my efforts as a practising lawyer, the successes of Lord Denning and Lady Thatcher were always a great inspiration to me.

On 19 August 1982, I received a telex message from Equator Bank's general counsel, Laurence Friedman. He informed me that Equator Bank Limited had successfully concluded negotiations with the Bank of Zambia for a loan to the Bank of Zambia of US$10,000,000 to facilitate financing "purchases of essential imports of capital goods, equipment and spare parts". Therefore, he wished to retain my services again as the Zambian counsel for Equator Bank. He wrote that the format of the agreement with the Bank of Zambia followed the "format of two previous transactions between other lenders and the Bank of Zambia done earlier this year. I believe you represented lenders in both cases". On a previous occasion, I had also acted for Equator Bank when a loan of US$34,840,000 was extended to Nchanga Consolidated Copper Mines Limited in August 1981. Equator Bank Limited acted as the manager of the syndicated loan which was co-managed by Commerzbank AG, Chicago Branch and SIFDA Investment Company. Altogether, there were seven participating banks in this syndicated loan. However, I did not find the credit structure for the latest loan to the Bank of Zambia complicated. The most difficult legal document for a commercial transaction structured with my involvement was in London early in 1981 for the Bank of America International Limited. It was the successful drafting of the credit documents for the Zambian oil import facility which publicized the usefulness of my legal services in commercial transactions.

Owing to chronic foreign exchange shortages, at the beginning of 1981 the governor of the Bank of Zambia successfully negotiated an oil import facility of US$150,000,000. The credit was desperately required for the purchase of oil when the nation was not able to source its oil imports for spot-cash. Under the law, the Bank of Zambia was authorized to borrow money with the approval of the minister of finance "in accordance with such conditions and on such terms as the minister shall, in respect of such loan, direct". The amount required by the Bank of Zambia for the oil facility was a large sum which necessitated the participation of several banks in a syndication. That, of course, complicated the process of structuring the credit document. I was invited to travel to London to join two lawyers instructed to finalise the oil facility agreement between the Bank of America International Limited and the Bank of Zambia. For three days we worked very hard indeed. We always worked until very late in the night before retiring to bed at a hotel near our working place. I did not know how far away my workmates lived from our place of work. During those days, for our lunch we survived only on tea and sandwiches. At the end of the mammoth task I derived little comfort in the following weeks from the small fee which the Bank of Zambia paid to our law firm – MMW and Company – on behalf of Bank of America Limited for my professional services. However, I derived satisfaction from the letter of appreciation which I received from Jaques Favillier and Enrique Bacalao, associate director and manager respectively on behalf of the Bank of America International Limited in London. I received the letter with the "encapsulated tombstone announcement of the Zambian oil facility". Both the letter and the encapsulated tombstone are valuable possessions which have, indeed, reminded me "over time" of my "personal involvement in ironing out the complexities of this financial milestone". In their letter of 11 May 1981, Jaques Favillier and Enrique Bacalao expressed sincere appreciation of my contribution to the efforts to devise a letter of credit "issued by a syndicate of banks on a several basis". The language in which the letter was couched expressed their genuine feelings thus:

Dear Mr Mwanakatwe,

Enclosed please find an encapsulated tombstone announcement of the Zambian oil import facility we arranged recently. We thought you might enjoy receiving a tangible memento of this transaction, which was structured with your help and cooperation. To the best of our knowledge a letter of credit has never before been issued by a syndicate of banks on a several basis, primarily due to the legal and operational complexities involved. We trust this tombstone will remind you over time of your personal involvement in ironing out the complexities of this financial milestone.

Please accept our best personal regards.

Sincerely yours,

Jacques Favillier   Enrique Bacalao
Associate Director   Manager

With this experience behind me I had no reservations in accepting appointment as Zambian counsel for Equator Bank Limited to prepare all the necessary legal documents for securing the loan to the Bank of Zambia in the sum of US$10,000,000. Subsequently, on 30 September 1982, at the request of the Bank of Zambia, I forwarded the draft Credit Facility Agreement to Charles Kachapulula who was the legal advisor for the Bank of Zambia. I advised him in the letter accompanying the credit document that "our client bank has attached urgency to the completion of this transaction". Therefore, I implored him to study my document and advise expeditiously the extent to which it was unacceptable. In the meantime, early in October 1982, Eddie Alexander arrived in Lusaka from Equator Bank in Nassau, Bahamas to review with me several key documents for approval as a condition precedent of the eventual disbursement of funds under provisions of the Credit Agreement. The key documents we reviewed included drafts of the promissory note, the power of attorney to sign the agreement, certificate of signatures of officials of the Bank of Zambia and letters to the Zambia National Commercial Bank, London and the permanent representative to the United Nations in New York appointing both as agents of the Bank of Zambia for service of process in respect of the Credit Agreement.

Apart from preparing the draft Credit Agreement and various supporting documents, as the Zambian counsel for the Lender, Equator Bank Limited, I was especially responsible for preparing a draft "Opinion" to be rendered by our law firm confirming the fulfilment of all the requirements and obligations of the Borrower under the Credit Agreement. In addition to confirmation of the fulfilment of certain obligations by the Borrower, our law firm's opinion on specified issues relating to the status of the Borrower was required. Out of fifteen such issues, three were the most important. On the basis of our confirmations and having regard to the laws of Zambia, we advised in our opinion that:

(a) The Borrower, the Central Bank of Zambia, is a body corporate duly established, validly existing and in good standing as a separate legal entity under the laws of Zambia and is fully qualified and empowered to own its assets and carry on its business and activities in each jurisdiction in which it owns assets or carried on business or activities and has and will have full power, authority and legal right to execute and deliver the Credit Agreement and the Note, to borrow the maximum principal amount of the commitment and to perform and observe the terms of the Credit Agreement and the Note.

(b) The execution and delivery of, and the performance and observance of the terms of, the Credit Agreement and the Note by the Borrower and the borrowing of the maximum amount of the Commitment have been validly authorized by all appropriate corporate and other action, and the Credit Agreement and the Note constitute, legal, valid and binding obligations of the Borrower enforceable in accordance with their respective terms and are and will be direct, unconditional and general obligations of the Borrower.

(c) The Borrower is and will be subject to civil and commercial law with respect to its obligations under the Credit Agreement and the Note and with respect to the transactions contemplated thereby; the execution, delivery, performance and observance of the Credit Agreement and the Note by the Borrower constitute and will constitute private and commercial acts rather than governmental or public acts, and neither the Borrower nor any of its assets enjoys or will enjoy, under the laws of Zambia, any right of immunity from service of process, jurisdiction, judgment, setoff, counterclaim, enforcement of or execution on a judgment, attachment (whether before judgment or in aid of execution) or other legal process in respect of any of the obligations of the Borrower under the Credit Agreement or the Note or with

359

respect to the transactions contemplated thereby. To the extent that in any jurisdiction in which proceedings arising out of or in connection with the Credit Agreement may at any time be taken there may be attributed to the Borrower or any of its assets any such immunity (whether or not claimed) the waiver contained in Section 7.8 of the Credit Agreement is irrevocably binding on the Borrower.

In an opinion of this nature, the responsibility undertaken by a law firm is enormous. Therefore, the law firm inevitably assumes grave risks in the event of default by the Borrower. I recall arguing at length with London-based lawyers for Equator Bank Limited about the desirability of qualifying our opinion. Ultimately, Laurence Friedman, Equator Bank's general counsel accepted my proposal.

Later in the 1980s, the number of clients instructing me to prepare similar legal documents increased by leaps and bounds. They included local banks like Zambia National Commercial Bank Limited and Meridien International Bank of Zambia Limited. In August 1982, I received interesting instructions from Zambia National Commercial Bank, a government-controlled commercial bank. The Bank's legal counsel instructed our law firm to draft a Loan Agreement between Central Province Cooperative Marketing Union Limited as the Borrower, Zambia National Commercial Bank Limited as the Agent for the Lenders and the Republic of Zambia acting by and through its minister of finance as the Guarantor. The Central Province Cooperative Marketing Union was granted a loan of twenty two million Kwacha syndicated by Zambia National Commercial Bank Limited as the Agent for seven other participating financial institutions, including Barclays Bank, Bank of Credit and Commerce, Standard Bank Zambia Limited and Zambia State Insurance Corporation Limited. The loan was granted to the Borrower for purposes of purchases of crops from farmers in the Central Province and the purchase of fertilizers from National Agricultural Marketing Board (Namboard). The

Lenders were required under the Loan Agreement to advance their respective proportions of the loan by payment of the amount to the Agent before the specified date.

The legal documents for the syndicated loan transaction were expeditiously prepared and subsequently approved after meetings on two separate occasions to correct the drafts and effect amendments as desired by parties to the Loan Agreement. On 17 September 1982, I received a letter from the managing director of Zambia National Commercial Bank Limited inviting me to attend the ceremony for signing the loan facility agreement at 11.00 hours at Hotel Intercontinental in Lusaka on 21 September 1982 followed by a luncheon at the same hotel. The business transaction was completed in about four weeks only – in record time. My contribution to the successful structuring of the loan facility was appreciated by the management of Zambia National Commercial Bank Limited. The Bank's legal counsel, Clement Mabutwe, wrote a letter to me on 27 September, 1982 as follows:

Further to discussions herein, we write to confirm that the Loan Facility Agreement was approved as slightly amended and finally executed by all the parties concerned on 21st September, 1982.

Noting your busy schedule and since we had the "meat", so to say, we proceeded with the preparation of the final document. We did not get back in time because of the urgency of the matter.

We would once again take this opportunity to thank you most sincerely for the commendable job done and advice given in this matter and please find enclosed herewith a copy of the Loan Facility Agreement for your records.

We await a note on your fees.

I always derived joy from letters in which my clients

expressed gratitude for services I had provided on their instructions. It was gratifying when a client on his or her own volition reminded me to submit my fee note for payment in due course of time. In all the years of practising law, I do not remember taking legal action against a client for failing or refusing to pay fees for the work I had done. One exception, however, was in 2001 when the government of the Republic of Zambia failed to pay my fees under a World Bank funded project for the revision of the Roads and Road Traffic Act and related legislation. Subsequently, on 21 March 2002, I obtained an order from the High Court for reference of the dispute to Arbitration with the Honourable Justice F. Chomba, state counsel, as the sole arbitrator of the Arbitration proceedings. I have always accepted that lawyers owe overriding duties to the courts and the administration of justice; and, secondly, that they are obliged at all times to be truthful and candid and to represent their clients by fair and proper means. Otherwise, like their fellow men and women in various walks of life, lawyers, too, are entitled to fair remuneration for the work they do for their clients.

Sometimes commercial transactions are involved and difficult to complete to the satisfaction of the parties concerned. Often, commercial transactions which involve multinational corporations are subject to a vast body of governmental controls designed to protect the citizen or the country in general to ensure fair treatment. I was involved in such a commercial transaction as Zambian counsel for Meridien International Bank Limited at the beginning of 1982. The Bank of Zambia and Meridien International Bank Limited intended to enter into a US$30,000,000 Medium Term Credit Facility Agreement. Under the proposed Agreement, Meridien International Bank Limited was to act as the agent for other banks participating in the syndicated Medium Term Credit Facility. My clients retained me as Zambian counsel to assist with structuring the Agreement and writing an opinion on the borrower's fulfilment of its obligations under the Agreement. The instructions were conveyed to me clearly but succinctly that my services were required "for the purposes of the review of loan documentation, drafting of any additional documents required, and provision of ... legal opinion to the Lenders in accordance with the specimen opinion".

The completion of this particular transaction took a very long time – just over one year! It took too long to complete because my advice to the Lender's lawyer in New York from time to time was ignored. The bank officials and their lawyer in New York were in a hurry to complete the commercial transaction. However, quite often their efforts to shorten the usual procedures led to other difficulties. Sometimes in law practice it is advantageous to hasten slowly – to follow the dictum of the ancient Romans, *festina lente*. Consequently, many documents were sent to the Bank of Zambia without incorporating my recommendations. Later, they were returned to the bank's lawyer in New York for redrafting.

I recall one particular difficulty which arose when the loan transaction was about to be completed. The Bank of Zambia and Meridien Bank had agreed to enter into a medium term loan in the maximum principal amount of US$ 30,000,000 to the Bank of Zambia as Borrower. The Bank of Zambia fulfilled all its obligations and obtained the necessary authorizations stipulated in the loan agreement. One such authorization was a letter which the minister of finance wrote to the governor of the Bank of Zambia authorizing it to borrow the maximum principal amount of US$30,000,000 on the terms and conditions contained in the loan agreement. However, subsequently at the request of the Bank of Zambia, Thomas Ryan, vice president of Meridien International Bank Limited, wrote a letter to the Bank of Zambia advising arrangement of a further loan in the amount of US$4,254,302 under the Credit Facility. The government required additional funds "to finance the purchase of new Capital Tractor Company equipment" and Meridien International Bank Limited was prepared to loan the additional sum.

I strongly objected to the proposal by Meridien International Bank Limited to offer to the Bank of Zambia an additional loan in the sum of US$4,254,302 on the terms of the Credit Facility Agreement which the minister of finance had already approved. I was morally bound as the Zambian counsel for the Lender to advise that this was improper and unacceptable because the minister of finance had already authorized the Bank of Zambia to raise a loan in the maximum principal amount of only US$30,000,000. The legal instruments for various authorizations had already been issued in favour of the Bank of Zambia by the minister of finance. The legal instruments provided, inter-alia, for exemption of Meridien International Bank Limited from tax and stamp duty payments on the understanding that the loan was for the maximum principal amount of US$30,000,000. In these circumstances, I advised the governor of the Bank of Zambia to obtain further authorization from the minister of finance to borrow the additional amount of US$4,254,302. However, among businessmen time is always an expensive commodity. My advice to the Lender and the Borrower was ignored. On behalf of the Bank of Zambia, on 22 July 1982, the deputy general manager sent a letter to Meridien International Bank Limited confirming acceptance of "the proposal for the making of a loan by yourselves to Bank of Zambia for the purposes of and on the terms and conditions as specified in the Notice of Commitment and Credit Facility Agreement on condition that the existing US$30,000,000 Credit Facility is increased to US$34,254,302 and the cost of the additional US$4,254,302 will not be met by the Bank of Zambia ... the position will be ratified by exchange of letters between the Bank of Zambia and Meridien International Bank Limited".

However, the governor of the Bank of Zambia, Bitwell Kuwani, was the first person to realize that the approach of incorporating the additional loan in the original Credit Facility Agreement was unworkable. The legal advisor for the Bank of Zambia, Charles Kachapulula, also agreed with the governor of the Bank of Zambia. Both men realized that the approval of the minister of finance was necessary to increase the original

Credit Facility of US$30,000,000 by the sum of US$4,254,302. Subsequently, the lawyer for the Lenders also capitulated. He, too, went down on his knees and requested again for my guidance and assistance. Some paragraphs in his letter to me on 17 August 1982 were as follows:-

> In connection with the most recent loan proposed under the Facility, in the amount of US$4,254,302, the governor of the Bank of Zambia requested that the maximum amount of the Facility be increased by that amount. This proposal was made in the Bank of Zambia's Notice of Drawing accepting the proposed loan as outlined in a Notice of Commitment. Copies of the Notice of Commitment and Notice of Drawing are enclosed for your information.

> Because the Notice of Drawing had the somewhat mystifying words "and the cost of the additional $4,254,302 will not be met by the Bank of Zambia", our client, Meridien, felt that the situation should be clarified, and therefore sent a letter indicating that the increase would be agreeable, but on the basis of the terms and conditions of the credit facility as set forth in the Credit Facility Agreement. A copy of this letter is also enclosed.

> I am told by Tom Ryan of Meridien, with whom the question of the increase was raised by Mr Kuwani, that both Mr Kuwani and Mr Kachapulula feel that it will be necessary to obtain the approval of the minister of finance before such an increase can be placed in effect. That requirement does not stand out from the bare language of section 23 (m) of the Bank of Zambia Act, which seems to require that the minister approve only the "manner", "rate of interest", and "terms and conditions" of foreign currency borrowings by Bank of Zambia, all of which he presumably did when he originally approved the Credit Facility Agreement (pursuant to which the increased amount will be borrowed).

> Nonetheless, these are matters of Zambian law, and of the interpretation by the Bank of Zambia of its relationship with

the minister of finance, and therefore must rest on your expertise and judgment. We understand that Mr Kachapulula has set in motion the steps necessary to obtain the necessary approvals, and Meridien expects that they will be forthcoming in due course.

I wanted to write to keep you informed of the status of the matter and to advise you of these recent developments. In view of these events, it may be necessary for Mr Ryan to call upon you for advice when he is next in Zambia if questions arise requiring your attention.

The lawyer for the Lenders in New York, John Stotsenburg, was undoubtedly anxious to complete the commercial transaction satisfactorily at the earliest opportunity. Therefore, I did not hesitate to assume the responsibility of preparing additional legal documents for consideration and approval by the minister of finance. On 11 November 1982, I received a letter from the Ministry of Finance with the advice that "the two statutory orders; that is the Exemption from Stamp Duty (No. 3) Notice, 1982 (Statutory Instrument No. 152 and the Income Tax (Foreign Organisations) (Exemption Approval) (No. 8) Order, 1982 (Statutory Instrument No. 153) were gazetted on 22 October 1982". That letter from the Ministry of Finance marked a happy ending to the commercial transaction to which both the Lenders and the Bank of Zambia attached great importance. In John Stotsenburg's letter to me early in December his gratitude for my services were succinctly expressed thus: "I appreciate the skill and effort you expended to obtain these certificates subsequent to the signing of the facility, and I am writing on behalf of our client, Meridien International Bank Limited, and myself to thank you for this achievement". Although I was retained to provide legal services to Meridien International Bank Limited, I also received a complimentary letter from the legal advisor to the Bank of Zambia after completion of the commercial transaction. The words of his complimentary message were carefully chosen. I was touched. He wrote thus: "On behalf of the governor Mr BR Kuwani, may I express his personal as well as our sincere thanks to your firm for the wonderful assistance and cooperation we have received from you. We hope to receive more of it in future transactions".

Although I was retained as a lawyer for various multinational companies from time to time in the mid 1980s, nonetheless I spent more time doing other types of legal work in my chambers. Commercial transactions formed a small proportion of my work in our law firm. It was the kind of work which I never found exciting although the measure of responsibility I assumed on each such transaction was immeasurable. The importance of such work was brought to my attention by Charles Kachapulula in a letter he wrote to me fifteen years later. His father died on 2nd January 1999. He implied in his letter that he had decided to adopt me unofficially as his "father". Apparently, from the time we collaborated in the preparation and completion of commercial transactions, he took a keen interest in my background and my humble contribution to the development of our country. His account of my contribution to the nation-building effort was exaggerated. However, the significance of his letter was the sincerity of his feelings and that it was totally unsolicited. It came to me "like a bolt from the blue". Much of what he wrote in the letter was about the efficient manner in which I performed my duties and responsibilities in assisting my clients who were negotiating terms for oil facilities with the Bank of Zambia. Often, I pick up Charles Kachapulula's letter to read it in the hope that I would derive encouragement from it to continue to render services to our country even in my old age. To show his affection for me, the salutation "Dear John" was chosen. Yet he is about my daughter's age.

It has been such an important and inspiring letter to me that I prefer to reproduce it without exercising the author's privilege to edit it. He wrote the letter to me on 2 May 2000 as follows:

Dear John

Peace be with you.

I looked around for you at the last Annual General Meeting of the Law Association of Zambia hoping to see you. I hope you are well.

I have been thinking of writing this letter to you for a long time. The urge for me to do so even became greater when I read Jonathan Chileshe: *Abe Galaun*. At page 152 of this book, Mainza Chona, SC quoting Rev Nevers Mumba, it reads: "learn to thank and recognize heroes while they are alive and for their ears."

I write this letter to you as my dear father, learned friend and colleague to thank you for what you have done.

My father was born in 1924. He died on 2nd January last year. So you see why I mean to call you Abba. Not only that. You are one of the fathers of Zambia. Your personal contribution to the struggle for the independence of mother Zambia is in such volumes and abundantly rich. Your patriotism, for what you have done and continue to do for mother Zambia, selflessly and with such great humility, is a ball of fire, so bright for every one to see and warm to all. I love you dear John.

I love you for that independent mind and your frankness. I recall one day during the Second Republic. You were reported as having opposed the economic policies of the day. Those whose corns you stepped on did not hesitate to scream. I remember somebody retorted, "Those who left us on their own must leave us alone."

In the mid 1980s I had the privilege to work with you as a learned friend over loan syndications. The nation could not source its oil imports spot cash. Year after year a syndicate of banks from America and Europe would put up a finance arrangement for Zambia. The syndicate of banks found so much trust and confidence in the person of JMM of MMW & Company. Without the legal opinion of dear John to those banks, no L/c would be opened, no crude oil would be loaded for shipment to Zambia. Here again you rose to the occasion in terms of patriotism. Yet without compromising your professional integrity as counsel. So much work was involved, with such responsibility, no one has ever realized, yet for so little pay to you. But "you dunnit year after year." "Who dunnit?" It was you of course. Late (By Zambian standards at 19.00 hours), I remember on one occasion, anxieties were high already whether documentation would be in place, you walked into my office at Bank of Zambia and handed over your legal opinion to me for onward, of course immediate, delivery to London. It was on a Friday. That evening there was a Zambia Airways flight direct to London Heathrow.

The English in their literature (William Shakespeare: *Julius Caesar*) would want to convince us that the good that man does is often buried with him but the evil lives after him. I am sure that all the good things dear John has done for mother Zambia in his social and political endeavours, in his professional career as a lawyer, will live after him.

I thank you Lord our God that you gave this society dear John and pray to you that you will reward him abundantly with your mercy. Amen.

You are my hero.

Yours sincerely

In May 1995, I received a letter from Richard Duffy, the director of operations for Zamanglo Industrial Corporation Limited (Zamanglo) in the company's head office in Lusaka. He requested me to give an opinion to his company's management on the merits of the company's intention to exercise its pre-emptive rights in Chilanga Cement plc. Zamanglo was a shareholder in Chilanga Cement Limited which became

369

Chilanga Cement plc. when it was privatised by the government under the privatisation programme. During the 1970s when the government vigorously pursued the policy of nationalisation of selected industrial and business enterprises, Zamanglo and the Commonwealth Development Corporation (CDC) were compelled to sell some of their shares to the government. Consequently, the government acquired a controlling interest in the Chilanga Cement Limited through Indeco Limited which was wholly owned by the government. A Shareholders Agreement was signed to this effect between CDC, Zamanglo and Indeco Limited in 1973. In terms of the Shareholders Agreement CDC and Zamanglo were granted pre-emptive rights. Therefore, under the 1973 Shareholders Agreement, CDC and Zamanglo were entitled to equal treatment and similar terms and conditions for purchasing shares on offer subsequently. This provision remained in the 1973 Shareholders Agreement when the privatisation programme started in July 1992.

Following the launch of the privatisation programme, CDC and Zamanglo were each offered additional shares in Chilanga Cement in exercise of their pre-emptive rights. CDC were allowed by the minister of finance to acquire their additional shares in Chilanga Cement on favourable terms by utilising pipeline funds. However, Zamanglo was refused similar treatment.

Yet the management of the Zambia Privatisation Agency (ZPA) consistently maintained that Zamanglo was entitled to purchase its additional shares in Chilanga Cement Limited on the same terms and conditions as CDC. However, the minister of finance consistently refused to authorise Zamanglo to purchase additional shares in Chilanga Cement Limited by using pipeline funds or at a discount. The minister of finance maintained the right to exercise his discretion not to allow Zamanglo to purchase the additional shares at a discounted price. He also claimed that the International Monetary Fund (IMF) had signed an agreement which discontinued the utilisation of available pipeline funds.

After careful study of the law and more especially the principles established in decided English cases in which the facts were similar to Zamanglo's problem, I advised that "the refusal by the minister of finance to give Zamanglo permission to buy shares in Chilanga Cement plc. while allowing CDC to use their pipeline funds for the same purpose was a blatant act of discrimination which was totally against the letter and spirit of the 1973 Shareholders Agreement". I further advised that Zamanglo was entitled to purchase its additional shares in Chilanga Cement on the same terms and conditions as CDC. My opinion was accepted by the company's management. I was instructed to make representations on behalf of Zamanglo to the attorney-general as the principal legal advisor to the government. It was hoped that if he accepted that Zamanglo was entitled to purchase its additional shares on similar terms and conditions as CDC, the attorney-general would prevail on the minister of finance to revoke his previous prohibition. The attorney-general's response to my representations was negative. I was obliged to advise Zamanglo's management to institute civil action against the attorney-general to compel the ZPA to sell Zamanglo's additional shares in Chilanga Cement on terms and conditions similar to those extended to CDC. The further advice I gave to Zamanglo was also accepted by the management.

At that stage, I was confronted with a difficult problem. Like in many countries in Africa and elsewhere in the world, our judicial system functions too slowly to the detriment of the interests of innocent litigants. It was in the interest of Zamanglo to obtain a court order early to facilitate the purchase of the additional shares which formed a part of shares for Chilanga Cement already floated on the Lusaka Stock Exchange for sale to the public. Law officers in the attorney-general's chambers have been known often to handle their briefs casually. Their lackadaisical manner of dealing with briefs may be aggravated when the case they are obliged to defend is weak. After some soul-searching, I decided to adopt a not so common procedure for prosecuting a client's claim in court. I chose to proceed by way of an application for a court order for a "trial without pleadings" under Order 29 Rule 2 of the Rules of the Supreme Court in England. Initially, a writ of summons was filed in the High Court in which Zamanglo's claim was stated against the Zambia Privatisation Agency and the attorney-general as the first defendant and second defendant respectively. Zamanglo, of course, was the plaintiff in the action. For the trial without pleadings, the last three paragraphs in the "Summary of the Plaintiff's submissions" were as follows:

> We submit that on the facts before the court in the available documents and in affidavits, there is no doubt whatsoever that the minister of finance has not given equal treatment to CDC and the plaintiff in the matter of purchasing their additional shares in Chilanga Cement plc. The refusal by the minister of finance to allow the plaintiff to purchase shares in Chilanga Cement plc. on the similar terms and conditions as CDC is an act of discrimination contrary to the provisions contained in the 1973 Shareholders Agreement.

> The court is prayed to order that the plaintiff be allowed to purchase additional shares in Chilanga Cement plc. on terms and conditions similar to those extended to Commonwealth Development Corporation by paying the offer price of US$0.1050 per share as described in the preceding paragraph 6. Therefore, at 11 cents to the US$ per share, the price to be paid by the plaintiff (Zamanglo) for its additional shares in Chilanga Cement plc. is US$150,092.60.

> The court is prayed to allow the plaintiff's claim in the writ of summons and grant such further or other relief and costs as the court may deem fit.

The trial before Judge Kabazo Chanda was brisk and conducted in a fair and businesslike manner. The attorney-general was represented by a senior counsel from his chambers. A few days later, the judgment was delivered in favour of the plaintiff. The order as prayed was granted by the court. The favourable judgment I obtained brought great relief and joy to the management of Zamanglo. Curiously, officials of the Zambia Privatisation Agency did not show any disappointment with Judge Kabazo Chanda's judgment. It seemed to the management of Zamanglo and equally to the ZPA's management that it was a matter of "all is well that ends well". I was happy, too, that I had played an important role in ensuring fair and equal treatment of parties involved in a commercial transaction.

A commercial lawyer's work is quite often varied. In the early 1980s, I was more frequently involved in commercial transactions in which the government of the Republic of Zambia, through the Bank of Zambia, borrowed funds to pay for necessary imports such as oil or to purchase vital equipment required for development purposes. In the late 1980s, there was a noticeable shift in the nature of commercial transactions for which my legal services were required. I became more involved in commercial transactions which related to the process of the sale and resale of goods by terms of credit and the process of payment. There were also commercial transactions which involved very large investments in land development. I have always encouraged investors to undertake large-scale farming in our country with its abundant natural resources. Of course, large-scale farming is initially a very costly undertaking but quite profitable in the long term to investors and the country.

The opportunity to assist such investors came to me early in 1985. In late 1984, Lummus Agricultural Services Company Limited (LASCO) proposed to undertake a farming project in Zambia. LASCO were international agricultural project specialists. The company was incorporated in the United Kingdom. Early in 1985, the proposal was approved by the government. The promoters chose a suitable piece of land in the Sinazongwe area in Gwembe District for the implementation of an ambitious project to develop underutilised agricultural land in the Southern Province of Zambia. LASCO was an experienced company in putting up total agricultural project packages whose areas of expertise included initial identification of a project and determination of its commercial viability, negotiation with central and local government authorities, coordination of international finance partners, site selection, operational management and marketing of the end product.

I first met Thomas Koshy, the Managing Director of LASCO, in the Lusaka office of Coopers and Lybrand. After obtaining the government's recognition of the relevance of the project to the development of the Sinazongwe area, Thomas Koshy requested me to serve as LASCO's legal adviser in Zambia. It was a responsibility I willingly accepted, not least because I was convinced that the project marked a new era in the development of rural parts of our country.

Early in 1985 the Gwembe Valley Development Company Limited (GVDC) was formed and registered in Zambia. Its formation was promoted by Thomas Koshy specifically for the implementation of the Sinazongwe project. The project area was 2,500 hectares approximately south-west of the Kariba Dam, bounded by the lake to the east and the Sikalimba River in the north. The promoters of the project intended to grow cotton on the farm during the rainy season (November to April). It was regarded as an important export crop. During the dry season, they intended to grow wheat under irrigation. Other crops such as ginger, soyabeans and maize were also to be grown according to world market needs and local requirements. It was a pioneering large-scale private sector agricultural project in the country. It opened up a traditionally drought-ridden and undeveloped part of the country for large-scale agricultural production.

Two investors, Lummus Industries Inc. (Lummus) and Hoechst Zambia participated in GVDC's equity. As legal advisor of both LASCO and GVDC, the success of the Sinazongwe project was dear to my heart. Legal pundits quite often remind us that lawyers are entitled, without moral disquiet, "to pursue clients' ends zealously no matter how immoral or unjust they or the means necessary to their achievement may be". However,

I have always maintained that lawyers are not merely "mouthpieces of clients" but also "vehicles for societal development and progress". A few years after the official launch of the Sinazongwe project, GVDC had created job opportunities for 400 permanent staff. In addition, the company also employed several thousand labourers during the cotton weeding and harvesting seasons. In the early years of the company's operations, the sum of US$1,400,000 was spent in setting up a ginnery at the farm. That investment led to the introduction of a large-scale scheme for out-growers of cotton in the Gwembe Valley. The scheme was of great benefit to the many families who joined it.

Without capital for investment in the project, it would have remained a grandiose scheme only on paper. GVDC was a registered company under the Companies Act with a share capital of only One Million Kwacha. Therefore, it was necessary to mobilise additional funds for the company's working capital. Fortunately, LASCO's large-scale private sector agricultural project was well presented to potential investors by Thomas Koshy. The response from potential investors was overwhelming. It was estimated that the total investment required for the development of the Sinazongwe project was in excess of US$15,000,000. Three major shareholders in GVDC gave loans to the company in order to increase its working capital. GVDC created a mortgage over Farm number 4906 situated in the Tonga Choma Reserve number XXI in the Southern Province of Zambia. The property was mortgaged in favour of International Finance Corporation (IFC), DE-Deutsche Finanzierungsgesellschaft fur Beteiligungen in Entwicklungslandern GmbH (DEG) and Lummus Agricultural Services Company Limited to secure their loans to GVDC. The mortgage was registered on 5 January 1988.

In the months of November and December in 1987 and in January in 1988, my main preoccupation was with the preparation of a variety of legal instruments for financing the development and operation of the large-scale mechanized farm.

They included the Project Funds and Share Retention Agreement, Investment Agreement, Foreign Exchange Account Agreement and the Security Sharing Agreement. Whilst I represented the GVDC's interests in the preparation of these legal instruments, David Ffinlo Quirk of Ellis and Company represented the interests of DEG and IFC. He was one of the oldest and most experienced legal practitioners in Zambia. He qualified to practise in England as a solicitor in 1935. About twenty years later, he came to Zambia, then Northern Rhodesia. He was admitted to the Bar as an advocate of the High Court of Zambia on 22 January 1954. I enjoyed cordial relations with the doyen of the legal profession in Zambia at that time. In fact, working with him on a major commercial transaction was a great pleasure and unforgettable experience.

The Sinazongwe agricultural project was initially quite successful. It was the first large-scale private sector agricultural project in Zambia. The anticipated total investment in the project was in excess of US$15 million. GVDC was quite successful with its wheat operation. Unfortunately, the company's operation with its cotton production was unsatisfactory because it was more dependent on the weather. The heating curve in the Sinazongwe area was long and difficult. Consequently, GVDC incurred heavy financial losses in the first few years of its operations. Due to these losses LASCO, as the majority shareholder in GVDC, made efforts to raise new capital to revitalise the company's operations. LASCO's efforts were unsuccessful. Consequently, in June 1993, Zambia National Commercial Bank (ZNBC) appointed receivers to enforce recovery of the whole or part of its credit to GVDC. A few months later, DEG which was the largest secured creditor also appointed its own receiver.

Whilst LASCO always adopted a long term outlook towards its investment and was willing to invest new capital because of its confidence in the eventual success of the project, DEG was more conservative in its approach. Its concern was that it should not risk losing even one Deutche Mark of its investment. LASCO's confidence in the project was amply demonstrated by the amount of money it injected into the project without seeking any security from the company, whereas DEG had taken the precaution of obtaining security for all its loans. DEG had every right to protect its investment by appointing receivers. It was, however, hypocritical for it to pretend that it was concerned more about the adverse effects that the failure of GVDC had on the economy of the country in general and in the development of the Gwembe Valley area in particular than in the recovery of its investment. DEG's real intention was to prevent LASCO from continuing to manage GVDC. I always thought that LASCO's interest was in promoting the revival of activities of a company which had earlier proved the potential of the neglected Gwembe Valley in the economic development of our country. There were serious differences between DEG and LASCO when DEG appointed a receiver without following the laid down consultation procedure. LASCO made several appeals to DEG with a view to saving the project but DEG did not respond positively. In fact, DEG, due to its antipathy to LASCO, preferred to offer the farm to new managers using the receivers it had appointed.

Early in April 1994, LASCO received information that in January 1994 the receivers appointed by DEG had advertised the sale of the farm and its assets. LASCO was not given an opportunity to bid for the farm's purchase. In April 1994, LASCO was informed that the receivers had concluded the sale of the farm and its assets. In the event, the sale of the farm by the receivers to new managers precipitated a fierce legal battle between LASCO and DEG both in Zambian and English courts. DEG engaged a local law firm to represent its interests in Zambia. I was instructed to represent both LASCO and LASCO (Zambia) in the Zambian courts. LASCO (Zambia), a subsidiary of LASCO, an English company, sought an injunction to prevent the receivers using property and facilities which it owned exclusively adjacent to the GVDC's farm. The new buyers of the Sinazongwe farm, Northern Grain Growers Limited (NGG), were placed in a difficult position. They were prevented from using water from the pumping station on a piece of land owned by LASCO (Zambia).

Late in November 1994, President Chiluba's administration appointed a commission of inquiry to review the Constitution of Zambia. I was appointed a member of the Commission of Inquiry and its chairman. Consequently, I reduced the legal services regularly provided to my clients in order to concentrate on the work of the Commission of Inquiry.

Therefore, my regular clients, both LASCO and LASCO (Zambia), were obliged to retain other lawyers. Disputes continued in the High Court of Zambia between LASCO and LASCO (Zambia) on the one hand and DEG on the other hand. Roger Chongwe for LASCO and LASCO (Zambia) filed an Originating Notice of Motion in the High Court for a declaration that the appointment of the receivers was null and void because the instrument of appointment did not comply with the requirements of the Authentication of Documents Act, Chapter 85 of the Laws of Zambia. The court avoided making a ruling on the application. It was referred for hearing *de novo* before another judge.

In the meantime, the management of LASCO discovered an unusual entry in the records at the Registry of Lands and Deeds in Lusaka. During its investigations, LASCO discovered that a partner in a law firm in London had visited Zambia and conspired with the receivers on 16 and 17 March 1995 in Lusaka for the purpose of effecting the transfer of the farm to DEG with the connivance of the receivers. LASCO believed that the receivers and the lawyer from London had acted in bad faith in order to facilitate the sale of the Sinazongwe farm to NGG. When DEG and the receivers advised LASCO on 27 March 1995 that the transfer of the farm from GVDC to NGG had been effected on 16 March 1995, LASCO's management challenged the validity of the transfer. They took this position for two reasons. Firstly, they claimed that the receivers who had possession of the title deeds on behalf of all secured creditors knew about LASCO's refusal to release its security. Secondly, LASCO had previously placed a caveat against the transfer of the property. The transfer had been effected by DEG, as mortgagee under powers contained in the mortgage.

Although I was preoccupied at that time with the work of the Constitutional Review Commission at the River Motel in Kafue, Thomas Koshy instructed me to intervene on behalf of LASCO. Consequently, I wrote a strongly worded letter to the registrar of lands and deeds and protested against the improper manner in which DEG had acquired legal ownership of the Sinazongwe farm. I stated in the letter that DEG, the receivers and their lawyer from London, had acted in bad faith by arranging the transfer of the property on which LASCO had previously placed a caveat against its transfer. My representations were successful. On 18 April 1995, the registrar of lands and deeds reversed the transfer of the farm because it had been procured in an improper manner. He accepted my submission that DEG had acted in bad faith when they arranged to have the farm property transferred without LASCO's consent. The decision to reverse the transfer of the farm to DEG was a devastating blow to its strategy.

Having failed in its bid to arrange the farm property transfer without LASCO's consent, DEG then started a new initiative to achieve the much desired objective of acquiring legal ownership of the farm property. Consequently, with the assistance of officials in the German Embassy in Lusaka, a meeting was arranged at State House with the special assistant to the president to discuss the conflict which had arisen between DEG and LASCO over the transfer of the farm. The meeting was held either late in December 1995 or early in January 1996. It was attended by officials from the German Embassy in Lusaka and the Ministry of Lands, including representatives from DEG and Zambia National Commercial Bank Limited. Neither LASCO nor LASCO (Zambia) were requested to send representatives to the meeting which was chaired by the special assistant to the president for economic affairs. At the meeting, the permanent secretary for the Ministry of Lands was requested to review the reversal of the transfer of the farm property. The official from Zambia National Commercial Bank Limited was queried as to why it was not pressing its claim against LASCO for its indebtedness to the bank.

Immediately this information was known to LASCO, I was instructed to write a letter to the special assistant protesting about the meeting. Our client's position was that matters discussed at the meeting were *subjudice*. Secondly, our client company, LASCO, as the majority shareholder in GVDC, was not invited to the meeting. Its officials should have been invited to attend the meeting and afforded an opportunity to explain LASCO's position in the dispute. One important principle of natural justice is that no one shall be condemned unheard, often expressed by lawyers in the Latin maxim *audi alteram partem*. I wrote a letter to the president's special assistant for economic affairs and lodged a formal complaint on behalf of LASCO about the impropriety of the meeting he had arranged at State House through the offices of the German ambassador to enable DEG to make representations to the government. Subsequently, I received a favourable reply from the special assistant. He requested LASCO to give its own views on GVDC's problems. LASCO's position was described in a long letter I wrote to him on 23 February 1996. The punch line in my letter was on page three in the concluding paragraph as follows:

> Again, I thank you for giving me the opportunity of stating another side of this rather sad story. My clients have believed that DEG's approach to you in State House through the German ambassador on a matter under litigation in court was with sinister motives.

The meeting at State House certainly did not bring about the results desired by DEG and the receivers. Our clients observed that after my letter of representation to the special assistant to the president for economic affairs inaction characterized the attitude of officials in both the Ministry of

380

Lands and Zambia National Commercial Bank Limited.

During the first quarter of 1996, members of the Commission of Inquiry appointed to review the constitution were camped at River Motel in Kafue. The arduous task of visiting districts in various provinces to solicit views from the public on the revision of the constitution had ended. Therefore, I was readily available to provide legal services again on a regular basis. In May 1996, I filed for the second time the Originating Notice of Motion challenging the validity of the appointment of receivers by DEG without first consulting LASCO. In any event, I had advised my clients that their claim was strong because the instrument of appointment of the receivers was not valid for use in Zambia. It did not comply with the provisions of the Authentication Act. The court in its ruling agreed that the instrument of appointment of the receivers was invalid under provisions contained in the Authentication of Documents Act. However, the High Court Judge also ruled that because the instrument of appointment was later rectified in accordance with the provisions of the Authentication of Documents Act in March 1966, there was no merit in the application to review the Order dated 11 October 1994, restraining LASCO from appointing its own receiver.

In this circumstance, I advised LASCO that an appeal to the Supreme Court against the ruling in the High Court would not be considered frivolous and vexatious. It was my considered opinion that it was unjust and improper to allow the rectified instrument of the appointment of the receiver to be effective retrospectively. My opinion was that the receivers were empowered to act as such only from a date in March 1996 when a new instrument of their appointment was executed in compliance with provisions of the Authentication Act.

My clients decided to appeal against the High Court's finding that the subsequent rectification of the notice of appointment of joint receivers and managers of the respondent dated 28 September 1993 had a retrospective effect and that the notice was valid for use in Zambia in terms of Section 3 of the

Authentication of Documents Act, Chapter 75 of the Laws of Zambia. In the appeal to the Supreme Court, LASCO and LASCO (Zambia) were the 1st and 2nd appellant respectively. I, of course, represented the appellants assisted by Robert Simeza, an advocate in the law firm of Simeza Sangwa and Associates. Gwembe Valley Development Company Limited, the respondent, was represented by Musa Dudhia and Company another law firm in Lusaka. After filing the Notice of Appeal on behalf of our clients, the respondent cross appealed against a finding that the notice of appointment was a document within the definition of that word in Section 2 of the Authentication of Documents Act and that if not authenticated it was not available for use in Zambia.

The appeals were heard in the Supreme Court on 10 December 1998 and 5 February 1999. The appeal of our clients was allowed. On the other hand, the cross appeal of the respondent was dismissed and their lordships declared that "costs of both appeals shall abide by the event and to be taxed in default of agreement".

I remember very well that the Supreme Court gave its decision in the morning on Friday 5 February 1999. The favourable result of the appeal was particularly pleasing because it vindicated the just cause of my clients in the dispute with DEG. Thomas Koshy, on behalf of LASCO, subsequently sent a transcript of the judgment to his company's solicitors and counsel in England. Later, I was informed that Thomas Koshy's counsel was of the opinion that the judgment was well reasoned and instructive on a point of law which was argued before the Supreme Court of Zambia for the first time. I had retired from active law practice when I reached the age of seventy. However, I was obliged to continue in law practice and appear in court in order to dispose of matters which were not completed by the end of 1996. Nonetheless, when I rose on my feet in the Supreme Court on 5 February 1996 to say "thank you" to their lordships for their judgment allowing the appeal of my clients, I was conscious that it was my last appearance in action in the Supreme

Court of Zambia. I bowed three times to Supreme Court Judges Ernest Sakala, David Lewanika and Weston Muzyamba as if to say to them "goodbye" on that occasion.

As a lawyer for multinational companies, I was from time to time blessed with a fair amount of good luck in our law firm, MMW and Company. In the early 1980s, Zambia was occasionally a beneficiary of sizeable loans from the African Development Bank (ADB) in Abidjan for development purposes. On one occasion I was retained by the ADB to prepare and register security documents for a loan to a local authority in Zambia for improvement of water supply for the benefit of residents. However, it was the Eastern and Southern African Trade and Development Bank (PTA Bank) which engaged my legal services regularly in the 1980s for the purposes of perfecting its securities for loans given to corporate bodies for development projects in Zambia. The PTA Bank was a body corporate established by charter pursuant to Chapter Nine of the Treaty for the Establishment of the Preferential Trade Area for Eastern and Southern African States. At first, its head office was in Bujumbura in Burundi. Later, owing to political instability in war-torn Burundi, the PTA Bank's head office was moved to Nairobi in Kenya. The PTA Bank's record of contribution to the development of Zambia in the 1980s and 1990s is probably unsurpassed by any other financial institution in the African continent.

My career has spanned a period of more than twenty five years of active law practice. I was called to the Bar in England in November 1964 and to the Bar in Zambia in January 1966. I was unable to practise law from 1966 to the end of 1973 because I was a full time politician and a cabinet minister in President Kaunda's administration. My legal career was again interrupted when President Kaunda requested me to return to the Ministry of Finance as a cabinet minister from May 1976 to December 1978. In all these years of active law practice, I have learnt one lesson – that hard work and dedication to the interests of clients is the real secret of a lawyer's success. Often before appointing a lawyer, a lawyer's prospective client asks himself or herself these questions – "is the lawyer effective?" or "can the lawyer deliver?" However, even if positive answers to these questions are given, some prospective clients often want to know if a lawyer, however capable, is also "trustworthy". In other words, a lawyer's "integrity" should always be above board and unquestionable. Surprisingly, some clients who look for proven qualities of integrity in lawyers they wish to employ fall short of minimum standards of civilized behaviour and decency which lawyers in turn expect from their clients. For example, I remember acting as a lawyer for a black American businessman whose company's offices were in a prestigious suburb of London. He was owed money by Zambia Police Force for goods and services which his company had supplied to the organisation by Indent through the Crown Agents in London.

After successful representation to the office of the attorney-general in Zambia, the government provided the funds required in full settlement of the claim. The Bank of Zambia was authorised to externalise the funds for payment in the claimant's bank account in London. Subsequently, I sent him a fee note for payment for the services we had successfully provided to his company. Our fees have never been paid. Subsequently, we received a letter from our client's solicitors in London advising us that the company was bankrupt. I experienced a similar misfortune in the 1980s with a foreign client whom I served faithfully as lawyer for several months without taking a deposit from them. However, I was never tempted by such bitter experiences to compromise professional legal ethics.

During those years, our law firm's popularity with clients needing work involving commercial transactions increased from strength to strength. It was a source of pride and satisfaction when I was unexpectedly invited to undertake responsibility for the legal component of a World Bank funded consultancy service on how to improve the management and financing of roads in Zambia. The project had been won by an American-based company, Louis Berger International of New Jersey, on the basis of competitive tender. Under the government's contract with Louis Berger International, the consulting firm was obliged to include in the team of consultants a legal expert to draft legislation for the establishment of the Road Fund and the National Roads Authority. Other experts were recruited locally by William Saunders to provide consulting services in financial management and civil engineering. He is the person who requested me to accept the assignment to advise Louis Berger International on legal issues involved in the study to improve management and financing of roads in Zambia. It was a great challenge to me. However, the responsibility of preparing draft legislation for the establishment of the Road Fund and the National Roads Authority was indeed an even greater challenge. Eventually, I submitted my final report to Louis Berger International on the legal issues involved in the study. I emphasised in the report that legal reform was fundamental to any effort to improve the management and financing of roads in the country. In particular, the need to revise the Roads and Road Traffic Act, Chapter 464 of the Laws of Zambia, was absolutely necessary to achieve the government's intention of improving the administration of road infrastructure, road transport and road safety. The final report I sent to Louis Berger International included draft legislation for the establishment of the Road Fund and the National Roads Authority.

It pleased me and I felt that I was amply rewarded for my efforts when both Louis Berger International and the World Bank expressed satisfaction with the draft legislation I had prepared for the proposed Road Fund and the National Roads Authority. While the cabinet was deliberating on policy issues for the roads and transport sectors in Zambia, the World Bank officials freely used the model legislation I had prepared to guide policy makers in other African countries where governments were eager to introduce legal reforms in the roads and road transport sectors as one way of mobilising resources to meet recurrent and capital expenditure requirements in the transport sector. Two years later, the government of Malawi established a National Roads Authority under provisions of an act modelled on the legislation I had prepared for the World Bank and the Zambian Government. Apparently, the work I had done for multinational companies, financial development institutions like the ADB and the PTA Bank, the World Bank and many others had given me unexpected exposure in legal circles internationally. In January 1998, I received an interesting letter from New York in the United States of America. At the beginning of 1998, the Association of the Bar of the City of New York decided to undertake a study of the capital markets in Africa. The objective was ultimately "to compile and publish in a single volume studies of capital markets in each African country where there is an active stock exchange". Members of the Association of the Bar of the City of New York believed that the study would be "invaluable to lawyers, investors and bankers in the United States and elsewhere with an interest in the emerging markets of Africa".

The importance the members of the Association of the Bar of the City of New York attached to the study was prompted by the interest of President Bill Clinton's administration in political and economic developments in Africa during his last term in office. To promote the objective, the Bar Association mandated its Committee on African Affairs to undertake a study of the capital markets in Africa. The Committee's chairman, Michael E Thoyer, earnestly requested me to contribute to the study. In his letter dated 20 January 1998, Michael Thoyer pleaded thus: "We very much hope that you will seriously consider participating in this study". What I found rather intriguing was to know how I was selected as a suitable person to participate in the proposed study on a highly technical subject to lawyers. The opening sentence in the third paragraph of Michael Thoyer's letter gave a clue to some extent. He wrote, "We understand that you or your firm have the *expertise* required to participate in this project". However, the person who recommended my name was not revealed in the letter I received from Michael Thoyer. Perhaps, I shall never know!

I confirmed my willingness to participate in the proposed project. Because the organizers invited about five other participants in this study from various African countries, they were anxious to maintain a standard of uniformity for each country study. Therefore, they prepared a suggested table of contents. The table of contents was given to participants "more as a proposed guideline than an absolute standard for the study". Acceptance of the invitation meant additional work for me when I was winding up activities in my law firm in readiness for retirement. The work, of course, was not remunerative. All that Michael Thoyer promised the participants was that:

> There are many benefits to such participation including the opportunity to work with members on the Bar Association and for you to have your name identified in the final volume which we hope will have a wide circulation.

However, the challenge of the study for me lay in its novelty and the necessity to research extensively before writing about the capital market in Zambia. The task was consistent with my hobby since boyhood – researching and writing. Of course, being human, I was also motivated by the prospect of having my name "identified in the final volume" if my country study was completely satisfactory.

Participants were given a deadline for submission of first drafts to New York by June, 1998. On 20 June 1998, I forwarded my paper to Michael Thoyer with an apology for a short delay in delivering it to him due to circumstances beyond my control. Later, he advised that my paper was the first to be received. He expressed the gratitude of his committee for the work I had done. It was evident that members of the committee had studied the forty one page document carefully. Part four of the document was the conclusion. In it I summarised my perception of developments of the capital markets in Zambia as follows:-

> We conclude this article on a note of optimism. There is

387

undoubtedly a bright future for emerging African capital markets. From our earlier account of the Zambian economy it is reasonable to link the growth of African capital markets to the improvement of the economies of countries in Sub-Saharan Africa.

It will be necessary, indeed desirable, in the years ahead to constantly review the efficacy of the existing regulatory framework for the securities markets. This is absolutely necessary to ensure that the securities laws and regulations are not outpaced by economic and social changes happening in Zambia. We foresee that future laws and regulations and amendments thereto might incorporate views and recommendations of professionals who have participated in the local securities market since its inception. For the long-term objective should be the achievement of what the chairman of the Securities and Exchange Commission once described as "a careful balance between over-regulation and under-regulation of the industry to ensure that the players on the capital market as well as the investors feel equally secure in their activities".

Finally, relatively few indigenous people have participated so far in the activities of the local stock market. The authorities ought to invest more in their dissemination efforts. Such investment will yield dividends by increasing the number of local participants in the securities markets in future.

I really derived joy from Michael Thoyer's letter confirming acceptability of my paper on the study of African capital markets with particular reference to the Zambian experience. The paper was accepted without revision. However, this achievement was not comparable to my great joy ten years earlier when on 10 August 1988, the president of the Republic of Zambia elevated me to the status and dignity of state counsel in Zambia. In the president's Letters Patent, President Kaunda declared, "I being well satisfied of the loyalty, integrity and ability of *John Mupanga Mwanakatwe,* Advocate of the High

Court of Zambia, have thought fit to constitute and appoint him, the said *John Mupanga Mwanakatwe* to be of State Counsel". The elevation to the status and dignity of state counsel enables the appointee to enjoy the privileges described in the Letters Patent such as "the right to take precedence and to have pre-audience within the Bar as by law established and ordained in all Courts of Justice".

The much sought-after status of state counsel among advocates is not acquired merely by successful practice at the Bar. Applicants for this respected position among advocates of the High Court are subjected to microscopic examination of their suitability by established institutions more especially the judiciary through the chief justice; the government through the minister of legal affairs; and the Bar itself through members of the Law Association of Zambia. Of course, ultimately the final decision whether to appoint an applicant as a state counsel or not is made by the president who is entitled to exercise his prerogative as he deems fit. It is probably true to say that the president considers carefully the integrity of the applicant on the basis of comments from the chief justice, the minister of legal affairs and the recommendations of advocates who already hold the rank and dignity of state counsel.

When I retired from politics completely at the end of 1978, I was too preoccupied with my law practice and the interests of my clients to consider applying for the rank and dignity of state counsel. However, early in 1988 two senior members of the Bar, Mainza Chona and Daniel Lisulo, persuaded me to submit an application to the minister of legal affairs for appointment as a state counsel. Both men held the rank and dignity of state counsel. Both men had at different times held the office of prime minister in the First Republic and the Second Republic.

The unwritten rules which govern procedure for applications for this appointment are followed strictly. An applicant should obtain two favourable references from practising lawyers of the rank of State Counsel. He or she should also obtain at least one reference from an ordinary advocate who was called to the Bar before the applicant was admitted as if to say "no objection" to the application by his "junior" at the Bar. When I decided to apply for the rank and dignity of state counsel, Mainza Chona and Daniel Lisulo readily provided the references in support of the application. I then approached Harry Smallwood, who was called to the Bar in England in July 1957 and was an advocate of the High Court of Zambia in March 1962. Therefore, Harry Smallwood was considered my senior at the Bar in Zambia. I requested a reference from him which he readily agreed to give me in support of my application. He knew that if my application was successful I would supersede him in the order of seniority at the Bar in Zambia. Yet Harry Smallwood gave me a glowing testimonial.

In 1987 and 1988, Ali Hamir was the chairman of the Executive Council of the Law Association of Zambia. I had not approached him for a reference in support of my application for appointment to the status and dignity of State Counsel. The references I was given by Mainza Chona, Daniel Lisulo and Harry Smallwood were sufficient. Nevertheless, without my knowledge he sent a good reference to the Ministry of Legal Affairs in support of my application. He knew that his reference was unnecessary but I learnt later from sources in the Ministry of Legal Affairs that he merely wanted to be on record, as chairman of the Law Association of Zambia, that he had fully endorsed my application which he supported unreservedly. After President Kaunda bestowed on me the rank and dignity of state counsel Ali Hamir telephoned and congratulated me heartily. However, he complained I had not arranged a sherry party at my house to celebrate my new appointment. He had expected to receive an invitation to a party at my house on the evening on 10 August 1988. Unfortunately, merry-making with sherry and wine flowing in my home late at night has never been my favourite pastime.

Anyway, when I look back on the goodwill of all my professional colleagues when I applied for the state counsel status, I thank God Almighty with all my heart. As for Ali

Hamir's unsolicited support for my application, what an unforgettable demonstration of one man's genuine desire for another man's success in life!

C H A P T E R

14

Community Service

My wife, Margaret, has often told our children that "the old man, having retired, can't stand having nothing to do". Recently, three grandchildren – Kambole, Chitalu and Mwiza – sent me a card on Father's Day (which presumably included grandfathers too). The card carried a funny message but it echoed their grandmother's fear that I shall never completely retire from work of one sort or another. Our grandchildren's message on the card was "Happy Father's Day to a Grandad who's always on the move".

At seventy five and a half years of age, I keep myself busy in one way or the other, often to my wife's disappointment. She wishes to see me spend most of my time at home resting or merely chatting with her about this and that. Unfortunately, that kind of life would be against my nature. Instead, for me retirement from political and professional responsibilities is a welcome opportunity to devote more time to a variety of other activities in which I have become involved over the years. On retirement, I certainly did not need a new hobby to keep myself occupied. Yes, Margaret's observation was correct that "the old man, having retired can't stand having nothing to do". I believe that professional men and women can and should serve the community by volunteering their services in professional-related areas. Indeed, quite often their services are required in business-related areas too. Communities do not lack ideas for improvement of the living standards of their members. Often, it is leadership, encouragement and support they require to translate ideas into reality, thereby promoting the welfare of their members.

My interest in community service dates back to the early 1950s when I was teaching at Munali Secondary School. In 1953, I offered to teach students enrolled in evening classes for adults studying for Form 1 and Form 2 secondary school examinations at Kabwata Primary School. In the early 1950s, recognizing the important role of adult education in the development of our country, some teachers began to agitate for improvement of the facilities offered by the Ministry of African Education for adult education. Before independence, the ministry's adult education effort was hampered by a serious shortage of staff and funds. In 1964, only 4,498 students were enrolled in the evening classes organized by the Ministry of African Education under the supervision of provincial education officers. Adult education, which is defined as the further academic education of adults in courses leading to recognized educational standards, was confined in pre-independence days mainly to centres along the line of rail, although a few classes were organized also in more densely populated rural centres. Yet there has always been a great demand for adult education in all parts of the country as the following passage from the Triennial Survey of the Ministry of African Education (1961 to 1963 inclusive) shows:

A very great unsatisfied demand for adult education exists, particularly in the more densely populated rural areas. Elderly men travel by bicycle as much as twelve miles along rough tracks which entails wading rivers to attend classes three times a week, and back home again, late at night. In one class a father and son sat side by side studying for the Standard VI examination; the father hoped to be spared the embarrassment of failing while his son passed; he was. In one prison, warders and prisoners attended evening classes together; it was perhaps as well for discipline that the warders achieved better results in the final examinations than their charges.

After independence, the government embarked upon a

vast expansion of adult education, deeply aware that to be truly independent a country must be able to supply its own skilled manpower at all levels from within its own borders. The government realized that several major projects for the expansion of educational facilities were long-term in character and the benefits to the nation could not be expected for many years. It was recognized, therefore, that improved and extended facilities for adult education were a means of alleviating the manpower difficulties of the nation. For many capable workers who possess experience in their specialized jobs, additional knowledge of arithmetic and English is a prerequisite for advancement to positions of responsibility. Many well-paid jobs in industry require workers who know how to read charts or meters fixed to machines and are able to write reports at the end of the day.

The Lockwood Commission on the establishment of a university in Zambia recognized the need in a developing country to provide facilities for the education and training of adults and notes that: "Intelligence and ability are not the prerogatives of any generation. Many men and women now in lowly positions possess the potential for more responsible positions". Since independence, the government has undertaken to increase facilities for adult education so that those with intelligence and ability, from whatever generation they may come, shall be given the opportunity to develop their talents to the full. While in the past government efforts merely supplemented the more extensive effort of voluntary agencies – Rotary Clubs, Municipal Councils, mining companies, YMCA, YWCA, welfare clubs and others – after independence it was desirable that the main burden of the cost of adult education should rest on government shoulders. Only government's full participation in adult education work could ensure the even spread of facilities in the country and a reasonable measure of efficiency.

I was actively involved with other progressive men and women teachers in Northern Rhodesia in efforts towards the formation of an adult education association. Before independence our efforts did not bear fruit. However, after independence many educators began to appreciate the important role of adult education in development, especially in the new nation states in various parts of the world. On the occasion of International Literacy Day in August 1968, President Kaunda referred in his speech to Article 26 of the Universal Declaration of Human Rights of the United Nations. In his speech, the president emphasized the value of providing education for all, both young and old. President Kaunda's speech on that occasion gave the necessary impetus to the idea of forming an adult education association in Zambia. In fact the environment was appropriate for the promotion of such an idea with the establishment of the University of Zambia in March 1966. The men and women who proposed the formation of an adult education association received encouragement from personalities like Lalage Brown, who was the director of the Department of Extramural Studies in the University of Zambia, and William Capstick from Evelyn Hone College in Lusaka.

The Adult Education Association of Zambia was formed in October 1968 and registered in that year under the Registration of Societies Act. The association's main objective is to promote adult education in all its forms through conferences, study courses, seminars, research and publications. It also aims at being the forum for all adult educators for the exchange of ideas and experience in adult education. Other important objectives and functions of the association include the promotion of gender sensitivity in society, acting as a clearing house for information on all forms of adult education in Zambia, cooperating with any society, association or body whether private or public, in matters conducive to the attainment of the association's goals and undertaking objective study of and research into the problems of adult education in Zambia. Membership of the association is open to "those individuals who apply for membership through the branch and pay an annual subscription fee to be determined from time to time". Such ordinary members are all entitled to vote. Other categories of members include associate members, life members and affiliate members.

I have been associated with the Adult Education Association of Zambia since its formation and registration in 1968 as an ordinary member, a trustee or patron. For a very long time, I have served the association as its patron – an honorary position which I still hold today. The constitution of the association provides in Section III (7) for the position of a patron as the association's figurehead. The role of a patron is to provide guidance to the national executive committee of the association when it is required. Secondly, a patron should be a friend of the association who is ready at all times to support and encourage the efforts of members of the national executive committee.

In August 1969, the national executive committee of the association organized the first national seminar on "Adult Education and Development". It was held at the Ridgeway Campus of the University of Zambia in Lusaka. The national executive committee invited Wesley Nyirenda, the minister of education to deliver the opening address. I was also requested by the national executive committee to deliver a key note address on the theme "Adult Education and Political and Social Change". The subject for discussion at the seminar was of great significance in a country striving to promote rapid development. In my address, among other things, I stated that:

It is important that societies in all parts of the world should accept that the youth are concerned about better prospects of life for themselves in the future, the future which only the old men and women who form the establishment today can shape either to the advantage or disadvantage of the youth. This latent conflict of interests of the youth and the old people of our times can be reduced by comprehensive programmes of adult education. We need to offer more opportunities in evening adult education classes to the young boys and girls who require further education and vocational training to minimize their frustration. It is recognized widely that adult education constitutes an important element in promoting better understanding between generations. Providing more education facilities in any country helps to increase the educational influence which parents are able to exercise on their children.

In the present supersonic age, an age when man's technological advances have brought about his greatest achievement since the beginning of history, adult education can be useful in providing adults with the opportunity to fill the gaps in their knowledge. This is most important to enable adults "to prepare themselves for the many new tasks which are continually arising, to become actively aware of contemporary life, and to adapt themselves with flexibility and inventiveness to the new values, ideals and ways of living which are associated with a constantly changing society".

In the sense that continuing education of adults provides useful practical skills and knowledge, it is useful and important to the individual and to the state in terms of material considerations. Yet, the most important role of adult education is in the civic, cultural and moral development of the individual. In this sense, the continuing education of adults is a potential force for development and for promoting political and social change. Kuan-Tzu, a famous Chinese poet, once said: "If you give a man a fish, he will have a single meal. If you teach him how to fish, he will eat all his life".

My address was well received and was discussed constructively by the participants. In 1970, the address was published in *Convergence* (Vol III, No 1 1970), the journal of the International Council for Adult Education (ICAE) in Toronto, Ontario, Canada. That publication had unexpected spin-offs later. Apparently, many readers of *Convergence* were interested in some of my comments and observations in the article. The article gave me unsolicited publicity as an enthusiastic advocate of the value of adult education in a society. From its inception, the Adult Education Association of Zambia was affiliated to the African Association for Literacy and Adult Education

(AALAE) which was based in Nairobi. Other national adult education associations in Africa, like the National Council for Adult Education in Zimbabwe, were also affiliated to AALAE. The African Association for Literacy and Adult Education, in consultation with national associations affiliated to it, sponsored my candidature for the vacant post of vice president for Africa on the International Council for Adult Education in 1986.

Following AALAE's successful campaign, I was elected as vice president for Africa on the International Council for Adult Education. My election to this office was for a term of four years. It was in this capacity that I attended the ICAE'S Executive Committee meeting at the Conference of the ICAE in Sri Lanka from 19 to 27 October 1986. The Executive Committee of ICAE is an important and influential body. In one of the reports for ICAE's Conference in Sri Lanka, Budd Hall, the secretary general, described the Executive Committee as "... composed of active and concerned individuals with a depth of experience and influence. The combination of the continuity of older members with a strong new presence gives us the broadest base for action which we have had to-date. Twenty nine countries and all regions of the world are now represented". Unfortunately, although Budd Hall invited me to attend the ICAE Executive Committee meeting in Harare in January 1989, I failed to go to Harare for the meeting. Zambia was at that time experiencing foreign exchange difficulties. It was not easy to obtain approval for an application for a business allowance for such a purpose.

After my retirement from active politics, I did not restrict my community services to the realm of development of human resources. Wherever possible, I offered to assist service providers such as Lions Clubs, Rotary Clubs and many others. Such assistance was sometimes by way of advice, guidance or merely encouragement through speeches in response to invitations. In recognition of such services to the community, in 1989 I was honoured by the Rotary Club of Nkwazi, Lusaka. In June 1989, I received an award from the club president, Rajiv

K Dewan titled "Community Service Award for distinguished and selfless service to the community without financial gain". That is an award which I value and cherish. It is an award more valuable to me today than all my possessions. It was given to me by men who have themselves dedicated their lives to the improvement of the living standards of their fellow human beings. I believe that our lives are increasingly complex and that lifelong learning is called for today. There are many situations in which an individual cannot cope with the new challenges through the acquisition of knowledge and skills alone. Today what is frequently required is to organize the learning process in groups and communities in organizations or companies.

In July 1996, I joined the Board of Trustees of SOS Children's Village of Zambia Trust. It is a trust which was registered subsequently under the Land (Perpetual Succession) Act, Chapter 288 of the Laws of Zambia. In June 1996, I received a letter from Rainer Kruger, regional director for Southern Africa I in Harare, Zimbabwe, requesting me to assist him in the organization of an SOS Children's Village in Lusaka. His letter of 24 June came to me like a bolt from the blue. I did not know the writer, neither did I know anything about SOS-Kinderdorf International, the organization which had reached an agreement with the government of Zambia to construct an SOS Children's Village in Zambia. He tried hard in his letter to throw some light on the kind of assistance he was requesting me to provide, presumably on the basis of my legal qualifications and experience.

It was Demetre Vangelatos who informed Rainer Kruger about the change of government in Zambia in 1991. He invited Rainer Kruger to come to Zambia and resume negotiations. Demetre Vangelatos was a prominent businessman who was well known to me. On many occasions I had acted as his lawyer in business transactions. However, more importantly Demetre Vangelatos was a personal friend. When I received Rainer Kruger's letter, he was available to tell me about the objectives of SOS Kinderdorf International and about SOS Children's Village worldwide. Basically, SOS Kinderdorf International was established to provide a permanent family environment for children who have lost their parents or whose parents are unable to care properly for them. SOS Kinderdorf International is based in Innsbruck, Austria. The organization was founded in 1949 by Hermann Gmeiner. He remained the founder of SOS Children's Villages until his death in 1986. Herman Gmeiner was born in 1919 in Tannen, near Alberschwende, Voralberg in Austria. He was one of many children of a farming family. After the Second World War, he studied medicine at Innsbruck University. Later in life, he was confronted with the problem of orphans. He saw how inadequately society cared for them. Hermann Gmeiner resolved to find ways and means of providing family-oriented care and education for orphans. Each SOS family lives in a house of its own. Usually, ten to twelve children consisting of boys and girls grow up together like brothers and sisters. The head of each SOS family is the SOS mother. She provides the children entrusted to her care with the affection and sense of security they need to ensure their sound development.

Children are accepted to SOS Children's Villages irrespective of race, nationality or creed. They are accepted from infancy to the age of ten years entirely on the basis of their need for care. In most SOS Children's Villages, children stay until they are able to begin their own lives as adults. SOS Children's Villages have been established in various countries in all five continents of the world. There are more than 1,350 in over 125 countries. SOS Children's Village Association is the largest private child care organization in the world.

The information brochures on SOS Children's Villages which were attached to Rainer Kruger's letter to me were helpful. After reading the brochures, I was assured that the organization was established solely for the promotion of a noble cause – to provide a permanent family environment for children who have lost their parents or whose parents were unable to care properly for them. The prospect of participating in a project for the construction of an SOS Children's Village in Lusaka was exciting. After a period of reflection, I sent a letter to Rainer Kruger confirming my willingness to cooperate and assist him. He replied on 4 July 1996 informing me that he hoped by the end of the month the agreement with government would be signed. He wrote:

> I shall be travelling to Lusaka during the period 15-18 July in the hope that we can finalise the agreement, sign it and begin further negotiations for land etc. I would be very pleased to be able to meet with you during that time so that we can further discuss the plans.
>
> Perhaps your office could be of assistance with the registration and implementation of the Trust itself?
>
> Thank you for giving me Reinhold Bonkat's name and for advising me that he would be a good trustee, and I will be sure to contact him during my visit.
>
> I look forward to meeting you shortly.

As Regional Director for Southern Africa I, Rainer Kruger was responsible for the supervision of SOS Children's Villages in Zimbabwe, Malawi, Mauritius and Swaziland. He had knowledge and experience of the registration and implementation of a trust in each of those countries. However, law and practice in a matter of this kind was likely to differ from one country to the other. Therefore, I agreed to assist him with the registration of the trust. I had drawn up trust documents on many occasions as a legal practitioner for my clients for registration in the Deeds Registry. Unfortunately on this occasion it was preferable to engage an independent lawyer in Lusaka to act for SOS-Kinderdorf International. Because I had already agreed to serve on the Board of Trustees, it was desirable to instruct another legal practitioner to effect the registration and implementation of the trust. My professional opinion was acceptable to Rainer Kruger and he relied on me to suggest a suitable legal practitioner. We settled for Solly Patel of Solly Patel Hamir & Lawrence, a firm of Advocates in Lusaka. I had known him for many years as a senior colleague at the Bar in the High Court in Lusaka. On 16 July 1996, an agreement was signed between the government of the Republic of Zambia and SOS-Kinderdorf International for "the construction, equipment and operation of an SOS Children's Village in the Republic of Zambia". Subsequently, the trust deed for "SOS Children's Village of Zambia Trust" was signed on 24 July 1996 by "John Mupanga Mwanakatwe of Lusaka in the Republic of Zambia and Rainer Kruger (a representative of SOS-Kinderdorf International) of Harare, Zimbabwe (hereinafter called 'the Trustees')". Both the agreement and the trust deed were filed and registered in the Lands and Deeds Registry by Solly Patel of Solly Patel Hamir & Lawrence.

Before 1996 Rainer Kruger had tried unsuccessfully to negotiate with the government an agreement for the construction of the SOS Children's Village in Lusaka. Although he had credentials showing the readiness of SOS-Kinderdorf International to provide funds, officials did not embrace the project enthusiastically. During the Second Republic especially in the seventies and eighties, foreign voluntary organizations were usually suspected of being agents of the American CIA. Rainer Kruger was often told by civil servants and politicians alike that the problem of orphans and abandoned children was not serious in Zambia. They claimed that the government had both the capacity and competence to ameliorate their plight.

The financial resources earmarked by SOS-Kinderdorf International for the construction of an SOS Children's Village in Lusaka were diverted for use elsewhere in countries where governments welcomed their participation. In Zimbabwe, where the activities of SOS-Kinderdorf International started in the early eighties, there are today three SOS Children's Villages with one or two additional facilities for orphaned and abandoned children over the age of eighteen years. Nelson Mandela attended the opening of the SOS Children's Village in Cape Town in 1996. He was so impressed with its design and construction that he requested the SOS-Kinderdorf International organization to construct an SOS Children's Village in his home district of Eastern Cape Province. The SOS Journal No. 3/2001, the magazine for staff and friends of the SOS Children's Village, reported the official opening of the SOS Children's Village in Umtata in Eastern Cape Province as follows:

> Eighty children now have a new home at SOS Children's Village Umtata, which was officially opened in January 2001. The village comprises fifteen family houses, an SOS Hermann Gmeiner School, an SOS Kindergarten and a small clinic. The SOS Hermann Gmeiner School in Umtata has admitted the maximum number of two hundred and fifty pupils and is the first school of its kind in South Africa. The location of these new facilities is in keeping with the personal wishes of Nelson Mandela who was at the opening of the SOS Children's Village in Cape Town in 1996. At the opening, he requested that an SOS Children's Village be built in Southern Africa's new Eastern Cape Province, formerly Transkei.

In my discussions with Rainer Kruger and Demetre Vangelatos about the proposal to construct an SOS Children's Village in Zambia, I was told about Nelson Mandela's approval of the noble ideals of SOS Children's Villages. The ideals incorporate what orphans and abandoned children need most – love and care from adults. This ideal is achieved because fifteen houses are grouped together as SOS Children's Village which forms a community. Therefore, it provides a community for all the children. The SOS Children's Village is supervised by a village father who supports the mothers and, together with other male employees, represent father figures. The children grow up in conditions very similar to those in a normal family. They attend schools and are encouraged to integrate with the surrounding community. Nelson Mandela, who has exceptional love for young children, appreciated the advantages of SOS Children's Villages in any community. I have always admired the Madiba. He has been my role model for many years. Therefore, when Rainer Kruger told me the story of Nelson Mandela's interest in SOS Children's Villages, he was literally pushing an open door when he asked me to become one of the trustees of the new trust. I agreed to be one of two original trustees as provided in clause 4.2 of the trust deed. Other members were appointed later in accordance with the provisions of the constitution.

Under clause 4 of the trust deed the composition of the Board of Trustees was prescribed to "comprise of six persons appointed by SOS-Kinderdorf International from time to time, provided that these trustees shall be Zambian residents". The trust deed also prescribed that "one Trustee shall be appointed from an appropriate government ministry in Zambia with its approval". Finally, the Board of Trustees will always include two representatives of SOS-Kinderdorf International. The trust deed prohibits remuneration of the trustees for their services. The composition of the first Board of Trustees included the permanent secretary in the Ministry of Sport, Youth and Child Development, Bernard Simpokolwe, and Rainer Kruger, the Regional Director for Southern Africa I. Others were Demetre Vangelatos, Christine Ng'ambi, Reinhold Bonkat and Mrs Hamir. At the first meeting of the Board of Trustees, I was elected chairperson. Reinhold Bonkat was elected honorary treasurer.

In June 1998, the Board of Trustees authorized me to attend the Ordinary General Assembly at SOS Children's Village, Imst where I received the Certificate of Registration of the SOS Children's Village of Zambia Trust as a member of SOS-Kinderdorf International. I gave a short speech to the General Assembly thanking the fraternity for the admission of our organization which was well received.*

I returned from the meeting of the 16th Ordinary General Assembly in Austria conscious that the SOS-Kinderdorf

---

* See Appendix II

International encourages SOS Children's Village national associations to raise funds to build and run Children's Villages in their own countries. There are also associations of Friends of SOS Children's Villages who support the building and running of SOS Children's Villages in developing countries. All these associations are members of SOS-Kinderdorf International which coordinates the work of SOS Children's Villages, and helps and advises its member associations. It also trains and sends out experts to help with the construction of new SOS Children's Villages in developing countries. The immediate task for the Board of Trustees is to expedite the construction of the SOS Children's Village in Kitwe. The trustees will spare no effort to achieve this objective within two years. When the SOS Children's Village in Kitwe is fully operational, efforts will be made to establish a national association for SOS Children's Villages in Zambia. Meanwhile, proposals will be submitted to the Board of Trustees for raising funds to supplement grants and donations for SOS Children's Village in Lusaka.

The accreditation of our organization following the issue of the certificate gave encouragement to the Board of Trustees. The trustees became more determined to complete the construction of the SOS Children's Village in Lusaka expeditiously. It is situated on the outskirts of Lusaka. By the end of 2000 considerable progress was made in the construction of the SOS Children's Village with the accompanying facilities such as the kindergarten and the SOS Hermann Gmeiner School. The SOS Children's Village in the capital was officially opened on 3 November 2000 by the president of the Republic of Zambia, Mr FJT Chiluba, in the presence of Richard Pichler, the secretary general of SOS-Kinderdorf International. By the end of May 2002, the village had fifteen family houses, one hundred and eighty children whose ages ranged from one year to fifteen years. Thirty mothers were employed to take care of the children on a twenty four hours basis. Each family house with at least ten but not more than twelve children had two mothers to look after the children. In June 2002, the Hermann Gmeiner Medical Social

Centre was officially opened by Levison Mumba the minister responsible for Sport, Youth and Child Development. The objective of the facility is to complement the existing medical facilities in the area surrounding the Children's Village. The centre provides clinical and laboratory services as well as conducting HIV/AIDS awareness and care programmes. It also offers child immunizations and under-five clinics. Even more importantly, an outreach programme was launched in 2002 to assist alleviate the negative impact of poverty. The outreach programme will help to mitigate conditions that lead to the situation of street children and orphans.

SOS-Kinderdorf International at the headquarters in Vienna have approved in principle the construction of a second SOS Children's Village to be situated in Kitwe in the Copperbelt Province. The decision by SOS-Kinderdorf International to provide funds for the construction of another SOS Children's Village is a demonstration of their confidence in the dedication of the Board of Trustees and the efficiency of the national director who is responsible for coordinating the day-to-day activities of the SOS Children's Village of Zambia Trust. SOS-Kinderdorf International provided the necessary funds for the construction of the SOS Children's Village in Lusaka. The Board of Trustees ensured that the funds for the construction and upkeep of the SOS Children's Village in Lusaka were properly accounted for. Every year an audit of our organisation's accounts was carried out by a firm of public accountants approved by SOS-Kinderdorf International. All trustees have known my personal interest to ensure proper accountability of our organisation's financial resources. Indeed, SOS-Kinderdorf International's obligation in this regard was equally onerous. I have always been mindful of the fact that the funds made available by SOS-Kinderdorf International for the construction and upkeep of SOS Children's Villages in various parts of the world are derived primarily from donations and contributions received from members and supporters of the organization. The organization's motto is "Doing good is easy when many help".

There are now more than five million people in over a hundred countries of the world whose regular donations make the work of SOS Children's Villages possible. In addition, sponsorships are taken out by generous donors, companies and associations for an SOS Children's Village family or for a whole SOS Children's Village. For these reasons, I was pleased when the Board of Trustees approved the annual audit for the year 2001 at a Board meeting on 27 February 2002. Later, to the credit of our Board of Trustees, we received a report that "SOS Zambia was the first country to finalise the audit, long before the deadline of 30 June given by the Regional Office".

I have been involved directly and indirectly in community work for many years. About fifteen years ago I was requested by the Executive Committee of the UNZA Law Association to accept the position of patron of the association in the Law School. Interacting with law students in their activities was interesting although a demanding responsibility. I was regarded by members of the association as their guide, philosopher and friend. Consequently, members of the executive of the association were inclined to raise issues on which I was not competent to advise as their patron. But I was always willing to help the association or its members individually. Some members required assistance to find a suitable law firm for attachment after completing the law degree in the University of Zambia. Others requested for advice on employment opportunities after passing their final examinations. Sometimes I felt that my goodwill to the association was unfairly exploited by its members. However, such feelings were often tempered by the realization that I was helping an association whose members were destined to play an important role in Zambia's cultural and political life. My position as patron of the University of Zambia Law Association had other spin-offs. Over the years I had the opportunity of meeting some distinguished academics in the School of Law. For example, I first met Dr Joshua Kanganja and Dr Ngosa Simbyakula when they were lecturers in the School of Law in the University of Zambia. That was when I developed friendship with two notable academics in our society.

Since my retirement some years ago, I have occasionally accepted an invitation to be a director of a company although I do not find such invitations attractive. Company boards meet often and the amount of homework that is required can be overwhelming. On the other hand, I feel that even at seventy five years of age I can continue to make a meaningful contribution to community service activities for a few more years.

C H A P T E R

15

UPND Appointment

The Common Market for Eastern and Southern Africa (COMESA) is a well known regional organization established to create an economic community. Its forerunner was the Preferential Trade Area for Eastern and Southern African States (PTA) which was established by the treaty signed on 21 December 1981. Its objectives were pursued through trade liberalization measures and through arrangements for cooperation in the fields of agriculture, industry, transport and communications. When the treaty was signed on 21 December 1981, the members and potential members of the organization comprised Angola, Botswana, Burundi, Comoros, Djibouti, Ethiopia, Kenya, Lesotho, Madagascar, Malawi, Mauritius, Mozambique, Rwanda, Seychelles, Somalia, Sudan, Swaziland, Uganda, United Republic of Tanzania, Zaire, Zambia and Zimbabwe.

The establishment of the PTA was predicated on a gradual and systematic programme of the elimination of tariff and non-tariff barriers among participating states. That was the thrust of the programmes and activities undertaken in the field of trade, customs and monetary affairs. In order to achieve the objective of trade liberalization, a clearing house was established in February 1984 to facilitate the use of the national currencies of the PTA member states for intra-PTA transactions. Under the PTA clearing system, settlement in convertible currencies arose only at the end of a transactions period of two months. The most important advantage of the PTA clearing system was that settlement in foreign exchange was limited to the difference between imports and exports of the participating countries. Therefore, the benefits of the clearing house depended largely on its full utilization by the member states. However, although the volume of transactions channelled through the clearing house increased from UAPTA 43 million in 1984/85, to UAPTA 88 million in 1987/88 (1 UAPTA = 1 PTA Unit of Account = 1 SDR), the latter amount represented only twenty per cent of the total intra-PTA trade. Consequently, the percentage of transactions settled in foreign exchange was still high.

In early 1988, the PTA Secretariat in Lusaka carried out a study in order to identify the reasons for the underutilization of the clearing house. The study concluded that the advantages of using the clearing facilities had not been adequately promoted and that this constituted the single most important reason for the low volume of intra-PTA trade transacted through the clearing house. Subsequently the PTA Secretariat requested assistance in the execution of a programme for the promotion of the PTA clearing facilities.

Fortunately, the United Nations Development Programme (UNDP) responded favourably to the request. The UNDP undertook to fund what later became known as Project No. RAF/89/006 for "Intra-PTA trade expansion through promotion of the PTA clearing facilities". Under this project, the post of senior adviser on the promotion of PTA clearing facilities was established. The duration of the project was designated to be for two years commencing March 1989.

Primarily, the adviser's function was to promote the utilization of PTA clearing facilities in order to achieve intra-PTA trade expansion. The overall terms of reference were broad, including a review of the state of implementation of PTA policy organs' decisions regarding the use of the clearing house on a country to country basis; assessment of training needs at the national level taking into account the need for simplification of the overall intra-PTA trading operations; the need to analyse training needs at the national level of PTA businessmen and

410

women in relation to using the PTA clearing house as part of their intra-PTA trading operations; and the need to perform any other related duties required for the attainment of the objectives, as agreed upon by the International Trade Centre (ITC) and the PTA Secretariat.

An expert was successfully recruited for the post of senior adviser before commencement of the project at the end of March 1989. Unfortunately, in May 1989 the expert appointed to implement the project died. The PTA Secretariat was again authorized to identify a suitable candidate for the vacant post. The UNDP representative in Lusaka was expected to receive the new nomination with the curriculum vitae for transmission to the headquarters of the ITC in Geneva for consideration. It was in this context that one day, totally unexpectedly, Mr Bax Nomvete, the PTA's secretary general, invited me to his office at the PTA Secretariat for a cup of tea! I had not the slightest idea of the subject he intended to discuss with me. I knew him to be an exile from South Africa, which was at that time under white minority rule. Before his appointment as secretary general, he had served with distinction in a senior position in the headquarters of the Economic Commission for Africa (ECA) in Addis Ababa, Ethiopia. I did not anticipate any devilish motive for inviting me to his office for a cup of tea. I, therefore, accepted his invitation.

During our discussion, Mr Bax Nomvete revealed that I was his preferred candidate for appointment to fill the vacant post of senior adviser on promotion of PTA clearing facilities. He also revealed that it was Bitwell Kuwani who had first been appointed to this post. He was a qualified professional banker with wide experience in banking. For some years he had served as governor of the Bank of Zambia. He said that Bitwell Kuwani was particularly suitable for the appointment because he had good connections with the central bank governors and ministers of finance who were involved in the formulation and implementation of the policy on the clearing and payments system. He emphasized that the adviser was expected to

411

undertake missions to PTA member countries to hold meetings with the business community in groups and at their business premises as individual businessmen and women. Therefore, in Mr Bax Nomvete's opinion the public relations aspect of the adviser's functions was important to the promotion of the utilization of PTA clearing facilities. He believed that my successful interaction previously with ministers responsible for finance and central bank governors in the PTA member states would be a distinct advantage in the implementation of the project effectively if I accepted the appointment.

Two aspects of the invitation to apply for the vacant post were very attractive to me indeed. Firstly, the successful candidate was expected to complete the assignment within a stipulated period of not more than twenty months. The UNDP was designated as the employer organization responsible for the employee's terms and conditions of service. The ITC in Geneva was designated as the executing agency responsible for supervision of the employee's programmes and activities for the promotion of PTA clearing facilities. The remuneration package was not particularly exciting because the successful applicant would not be entitled to the usual benefits of UNDP employees. The vacant post was primarily interesting for the opportunity it provided to get to know some of the countries in the East, Central and Southern African sub-region which I had not visited before. The responsibility to promote intra-PTA trade expansion through increased utilization of the PTA clearing facilities was a short term assignment which was unlikely to disturb my legal career in the long term if the appointment was accepted.

On further reflection and following consultations with my family I gave the green light to Mr Bax Nomvete to forward my name and credentials to the ITC Headquarters in Geneva. A few weeks later, I received an official invitation to visit Geneva for discussions with the officials responsible for the supervision of the implementation of the project on behalf of the ITC as the executing agency.

During the one week long visit to the headquarters of the ITC in Geneva, I wrote two short papers on the methodology I expected to adopt in order to implement the project's main objective – the promotion of utilization of the PTA clearing facilities for the purpose of achieving intra-PTA trade expansion. Later, I was privileged to discuss the content of my papers with the officials of the ITC in Geneva. It was during these discussions that one official revealed that he had read a paper I wrote in 1989 for the World Bank's publication *The Long-Term Perspective Study of sub-Saharan Africa*. In preparing the *Long-Term Perspective Study* (LTPS), "The Board and the management of the World Bank insisted that inputs be mobilized from the development community in Africa, and that these views be reflected in the LTPS report": (vide paragraph three of the preface on page (v)). I was privileged to be among the men and women from "the development community in Africa" whose views were invited on this subject. I was even more privileged when the World Bank's editorial board for this exercise decided to publish my paper entitled "Reflections and Long-term Perspectives for Sub-Saharan Africa with particular reference to Zambia" in Volume 1: *Country Perspective*. This unsolicited remark by one of the ITC's officials in Geneva during our discussion prompted me to think that I had a good chance of receiving an offer of appointment to fill the post of senior adviser on promotion of PTA clearing facilities.

It was a good premonition. Before my return to Zambia, I received a letter of appointment. A copy of the letter was sent by the ITC to the PTA Secretariat. Another copy was sent to the UNDP's resident representative in Lusaka. To my surprise, on my last day in Geneva all the necessary formalities were completed for the issue of a United Nations passport to me. I felt happy and proud to be a *bona fide* holder of a United Nations passport for the first time in my life. During my short stay in Geneva, I rated the performance of the bureaucracy of the International Trade Centre as *par excellence*.

My term of office as senior adviser on promotion of PTA

413

clearing facilities started on 13 November 1989. My office was located at the PTA Secretariat in Ndeke House in Lusaka. A full time secretary was employed to manage the affairs of my office. This arrangement was convenient. It facilitated consultations on a regular basis with the secretary general and senior staff of the PTA organization. Facilities at the PTA Secretariat, such as the telexes and telephones, were readily available to me for use in performing my functions.

One function required urgent attention after the establishment of my office at the PTA Secretariat. It was necessary to inform relevant authorities in various PTA member states about the establishment of my post at the PTA Secretariat in Lusaka. It was equally important to advise the authorities on the terms of reference attached to this post. In my circular letter to the ministers responsible for finance and ministers responsible for trade and industry in the PTA member states, I emphasized the significance of the finding under a study conducted by the PTA Secretariat on the utilization of PTA clearing facilities. It was emphasized in the report that the reason for the under-utilization of the PTA Clearing House was that "the advantages of using the clearing facilities were not adequately promoted". Consequently, my office was set up at the PTA Secretariat to sensitise both the government officials in the member states and the business communities as to the benefits of using the clearing facilities. I was specifically responsible for the formulation and execution of a programme for the promotion of the PTA clearing facilities. The role of central bank governors in the member states was crucial to the success or failure of the programme. I appealed earnestly to them for encouragement and support to ensure the success of the programme for intra-PTA trade expansion through promotion of the PTA clearing facilities.

Later in my activities, I realized that often I was preaching to the converted. Many key players in the sensitisation programme were ministers and governors of the central banks of member states whom I knew when I served the government of Zambia as minister of finance. For this reason, I was not surprised by the warm reception I received from many political figures and their officials in some PTA member countries. In nearly all the countries in the PTA sub-region, the key ministers and officials assured me of their support.

Following my appointment I devoted six weeks to the preparation of programmes for missions to PTA member countries. Initially, I planned missions to four countries. The programme for each country encompassed meetings with the business community in groups and at their business premises as individual businessmen. It was necessary for the programme suggested for each mission to receive the approval of the appropriate authorities concerned in each country, especially the authorities responsible for trade and industry activities and the operations of the central bank. Some programmes were designed to include sessions at which some businessmen and women would meet separately with me in order to make complaints about certain inadequacies in the operation of intra-PTA trade arrangements. The relevant authorities in government were expected to arrange the details of each programme, such as the venue and time for the meetings or other activities. During every mission to a PTA member country I allowed myself an opportunity to meet government officials to discuss progress made in the implementation of PTA Policy Organs decisions. The ITC expected to receive a written report at the end of every mission to a PTA member country undertaken with the funds provided by the UNDP. I was also expected to submit a terminal report setting out the principal results of the project as well as its most important findings. Obviously, the form, content and usefulness of the terminal report was largely dependent on the content of mission reports submitted to Geneva from time to time. I was determined from the commencement of the project to ensure that during each mission to a PTA member country all activities were focused particularly on the sensitisation of businessmen and women to the benefits of using the PTA clearing facilities. It was equally important to sensitise government officials to appreciate that the clearing house was established in 1984 to facilitate the use of national currencies for intra-PTA transactions.

I undertook my first mission to Harare in Zimbabwe. The choice of Harare was obvious. The PTA clearing house was located in the Reserve Bank of Zimbabwe. I organized the first workshop on utilization of PTA clearing facilities in Harare from 24 to 27 January 1990. It was well attended by many African businessmen and women. Few European businessmen and women attended the workshop. Fortunately, however, a few prominent white businessmen were present at the workshop and participated actively in the discussions. They included P Ellis, chairman of Standard Chartered Bank of Zimbabwe Limited; R King, managing director, PG Industries; D Forbes, managing director, Pinto Group of Companies; and N Norman, managing director, Seed Cooperative Limited. The Ministry of Finance and Economic Planning, the Ministry of Trade and Commerce and the Reserve Bank of Zimbabwe were adequately represented throughout the workshop. The opening of the workshop was graced by Honourable TR Masaya, deputy minister for finance and economic planning.

A similar workshop was organized in Dar es Salaam in the United Republic of Tanzania from 10 to 17 March 1990. Representation of the business community was excellent. In addition the government's strong presence at the workshop was conspicuous. The minister for special duties, Honourable P Bomani, was in attendance from the President's Office. The governor of the Bank of Tanzania, G Rutihinda, led a team of four participants to the workshop. Interest groups represented at the workshop included the high commissioner for Zambia to Tanzania, the International Trade Centre and the UNDP office in Dar es Salaam. Reginald Mengi, senior partner of Coopers and Lybrand, was also in attendance. The discussions during the workshop revealed a genuine desire by participants to contribute positively to the success of the operation of the PTA clearing house in Harare.

From April to September 1990, more workshops were organized in Kenya, Malawi, Lesotho and Zambia. Information had undoubtedly spread to various PTA member countries about the success of workshops organized to promote utilization of PTA clearing facilities. In Lesotho, a record number of seventeen business and industrial institutions were represented at the workshop held from 3 to 14 September 1990. The Honourable Morena M Mokoroane, minister of trade, industry and tourism, led a delegation of three men and three women to the workshop. From the Central Bank of Lesotho, Dr AM Maruping and Mr FM Borotho, the research director, attended the workshop. The workshop was well organized and its conclusions positive. A successful one day workshop was held in Ndola at the Savoy Hotel on 27 September 1990, comprising a large gathering of businessmen, industrialists and bankers. Dr FC Kani, director, represented the Bank of Zambia at the workshop with J Kunda, the deputy director of operations. Altogether, during the period February to December 1990, I undertook missions to ten PTA Member Countries, including visits to Burundi, Mauritius and Swaziland.

Although the project was officially approved in January 1989, I was not appointed until 13 November 1989. The secretary general of the PTA requested that the funds for this project for the period January to June 1991 be used for the study of the Programme for Monetary Harmonization in the PTA sub-region. The UNDP accepted the PTA's request. Therefore, my contract was terminated on 31 January 1991.

Following the expiry of my contract I was obliged to write a report on my activities and findings for the ITC. Guidelines were available for preparing terminal reports. It was a joy for me to write the report although the assignment was for a short period. Nearly all my wishes and expectations from this project had been fulfilled. Therefore, at the end of my contract I was anxious to ensure that my report was written in such a way that it was as clear and concise as possible. Throughout my assignment, I was especially conscious that I was tasked to advocate a good cause – the maximization of utilization of PTA clearing facilities as a first step towards the creation of a common market which would evolve later into an economic community. Therefore, it seemed to me that in preparing the report it was necessary to be not only as clear and concise as possible but also accurate and candid. In the report, I endeavoured to portray the reality on the ground – the complaints by the business community while appreciating the benefits of utilizing the clearing house.

With ten missions undertaken to various PTA member countries preparing a *concise* report was not an easy task. Later, I was informed that my *concise* report was received by officials of the ITC in Geneva with appreciation.

One of the terms of reference of my assignment as senior adviser related to the need to prepare promotional materials for the banking and government staff and the business community. I successfully designed and prepared a brochure on "Promotion of the Utilization of the PTA Clearing House Facility". With the funds provided for this item under the project, I engaged an experienced public relations expert to assist me with the design and format of a pocketsize brochure packed with information on various aspects of the PTA, the objectives of the clearing house and its operations. This attractive pocketsize brochure was printed on both sides of a sheet of paper twenty one centimetres wide and forty nine centimetres long. It had five columns of printed material on one side of each sheet of paper and five on the other side. The information was provided under headings in various columns including "The Preferential Trade Area (PTA)" and "The PTA Clearing House" and "The PTA Trade Information Network". It also included "The PTA Secretariat" and "How to Utilize PTA Clearing Facilities" and other subjects. The brochure was printed by Zambia Printing Company Limited in Lusaka and was published by the PTA Secretariat in association with the ITC as "Promotional Material by PTA-ZEP/ITCUNCTAD/GATT".

The popularity of the brochure was tested in Nairobi where

copies were displayed for sale at the PTA Promotional Exhibition. It was reported at the end of the exhibition that copies of the brochure were sold like hot cakes. The project's supervisor at the ITC headquarters took a personal interest in this particular PTA promotional effort. My appointment's date of expiry was 31 January 1991. Surprisingly, two days before I packed up my bags in order to move out of the PTA Secretariat, I received a letter from Z Demissie, director of trade, customs and monetary division, in the PTA Secretariat in Lusaka. He was the link between my office and the PTA Secretariat. He conveyed good news to me – the interest of the ITC in the brochure I had produced for intra-PTA trade expansion through promotion of the PTA clearing facilities. The full text of his letter dated 29 January 1991 was as follows:

> I acknowledge the receipt of your letter dated 28 January, 1991 reference PTA/JMM/90/11/5/jm the contents of which I have noted with appreciation.

> I would like to take this opportunity to thank you most sincerely for producing the first brochure on the "Promotion of the Utilization of the PTA Clearing House Facility". I sincerely hope that the brochure will assist officials in the central banks, commercial banks as well as economic operators in the sub-region in understanding more thoroughly the benefits and the mechanics of using the PTA Multilateral Clearing and Payments Facility.

> However, as discussed very briefly at Dr Olwa's house, I would be most grateful if we could discuss further the format and the contents of the brochure before it is circulated to the member states. In this regard, Mr Hendrick Roelofsen of the ITC has informed me that we have enough funds to publish additional brochures both in English and French.

Although my appointment as senior adviser on promotion of PTA clearing facilities was not extended beyond 31 January 1991, I was satisfied with my contribution to the consolidation of the activities of the PTA in the Eastern and Southern Africa sub-region. A firm foundation was laid for achieving broader goals of accelerated development of the sub-region through maximum utilization of the PTA clearing facilities. I did not experience any frustrations in performing my duties and responsibilities. I was given maximum support and encouragement by the ITC officials in Geneva who read my mission reports religiously. Their comments and suggestions were constructive. The project funds were controlled by the UNDP's resident representative in Lusaka, Mr Alieu M Sallah. He was a typical international civil servant – quiet, knowledgeable and diplomatic in his actions at all times. Under the project document, the secretary general of the PTA was responsible for provision of "office space, administrative, logistical support and, through member states, conference rooms for training activities". When I encountered difficulties at the PTA Secretariat in Lusaka, due to petty jealousies of some officials, Mr Alieu Sallah always came to my rescue. Although a Gambian national he was often more helpful to me than my fellow Zambians!

I found the UNDP experience extremely interesting. My assignment for a period of fourteen months to promote intra-PTA trade expansion objectives enabled me to gain an insight into the functions of the organization. I gained the impression that, although the United Nations (UN) had its shortcomings, the work of some of its agencies were beneficial to the well-being of mankind.

CHAPTER

16

Movement for Multi-Party Democracy

In November 1989, I accepted a UNDP appointment to serve as senior adviser on promotion of PTA clearing facilities in the PTA headquarters in Lusaka. Under the terms of my appointment, I was not precluded from practising law in MMW and Company when it was convenient to serve the interests of my clients. The UNDP appointment was for a period of not more than eighteen months. In that period, as I later realized, my own country and other African countries were destined to undergo great social and political changes.

Zambia celebrated its twenty fifth independence anniversary on 24 October, 1989. In reality, on that day, there was not much about which to celebrate among the ordinary people in the towns and rural areas. The value of the Kwacha had reached an all time low. There were constant shortages in the shops throughout the country. Even when essential commodities became available, they were unaffordable to the majority of the people. Consequently, the political leadership of UNIP was extremely embarrassed when riots broke out in Ndola early in September 1989 following a rise in the cost of mealie meal. The external debt of Zambia was very high – perhaps at that time the highest per capita in the world. Devaluation at the end of June in 1989 reduced the value of the Kwacha by forty eight per cent. Unemployment levels were exceptionally high. In spite of all the economic difficulties which the people endured, President Kaunda had managed to provide Zambia with twenty five years of peace and stability. Compared to many other countries in Africa, his rule was characterized by relatively few detentions without trial or other dictatorial excesses. Unfortunately, although President Kaunda had provided the country with peace and stability, development and progress, many Zambians were nonetheless tired of him. They felt that he had overstayed in office as president of Zambia.

Therefore, when events in Eastern Europe stirred latent pro-democracy movements in Africa, there were widespread demands for what was later called cultural political pluralism. Overnight, new movements were started by men and women in various countries in Africa who pledged to promote democracy on the basis of political pluralism and respect for fundamental human rights. The movements were a direct challenge to the established order of autocratic rule under single-party politics. Zambia was among the earliest countries on the African continent where people quickly rejected the one-party system and embraced the new pro-democracy spirit. The Movement for Multi-Party Democracy (MMD) was formed by pro-democracy groups committed to the establishment of political pluralism. This chapter describes the forces which led to the formation of the MMD towards the end of 1990 and the difficulties which its leaders faced in their effort to break UNIP's monopoly of political power. From the beginning, leaders of the pro-democracy movement solicited my support and encouragement for their efforts.

For "the party and its government" the emergence of the pro-democracy movement in Zambia was as much a threat to its dominance in political activities as the formation of the UPP under the leadership of Simon Kapwepwe had been. However, UNIP leaders knew that the tactics adopted in the 1970s to suppress and eliminate the UPP were not acceptable in a political environment which was completely different. The one-party system of government had become unpopular. Over the years, the number of discontented people in the country had increased as the prevalence of riots had shown. Mwamba Luchembe's short-lived coup in June 1990 also showed that the people wanted to see a change of the politicians who had shaped their country's destiny for more than a quarter of a century. Kaunda had proved over the years to be astute and skilful at the political game. Although he was undoubtedly irritated by the emergence of the pro-democracy movement, nonetheless he expected to beat the people behind the movement at their own game. Rather than appear to obstruct directly the emergence of the pro-democracy movement, it was more tactful to discredit it by showing after a national referendum that it was devoid of any popular support. Even before the pro-democracy movement gained momentum in Zambia, many industrial countries in Western Europe and North America had begun insisting on democratisation of governments as a condition for development aid. The major powers, after the dramatic political changes in the old Soviet Union and the fall of the Berlin Wall, were no longer interested in placating African dictators. In these circumstances, with a totally broken-down economy largely dependent on donor aid, the Zambian government was in a way impotent to clash head-on with the pro-democracy activists.

The Movement for Multi-Party Democracy owes its origin to many scholars in institutions of learning who canvassed businessmen, professional men and women, farmers and trade union leaders for support. Akashambatwa Mbikusita Lewanika undertook with courage and conviction the difficult responsibility of propagating the pro-democracy movement openly. He was a good scholar who enjoyed respect among his peers for his academic achievements in the United States of America in economics and public administration studies. A soft-spoken and principled advocate of political pluralism, Akashambatwa Mbikusita Lewanika is the son of the late Godwin Mbikusita Lewanika, who was a founder member of the African National Congress and its first president. He was following his father's footsteps when he undertook to publicise the cause of multi-party politics at the beginning of 1990. Mbita Chitala at the University of Zambia later joined forces with Akashambatwa Mbikusita Lewanika in mobilizing funds for the organization of an inaugural national convention for supporters of the movement for multi-party democracy. Mbita Chitala's late father had been a politician too. He had served two terms as a UNIP member of parliament. Therefore, Mbita Chitala also was following in the footsteps of his father when he abandoned teaching in a university in order to further his political ambitions. The birth of the MMD and its rapid growth in 1990 was due largely to the efforts and dedication of these men.

On various occasions I was approached by prominent Zambian citizens and requested to openly support the new pro-democracy movement in Zambia. Many of them knew about my tacit support for the reintroduction of multi-party politics. It was well known that I, too, had lost faith in the capacity of the one-party system of government to build a democratic society. My support for the pro-democracy movement was unequivocal. Unfortunately, my position as an international civil servant with the UNDP put me in an invidious position. I was not allowed as an international civil servant to participate actively in partisan politics in any member country. I had quietly consulted the UNDP country representative, Mr AM Sallah, and sought his advice. His advice was firm. As an employee of the UNDP, I was not allowed to mix politics with my duties of promoting intra-PTA trade expansion by encouraging utilization of PTA clearing facilities. His word was final and I accepted it.

Meanwhile, the pro-democracy movement continued to grow by leaps and bounds. Akashambatwa Mbikusita Lewanika and Mbita Chitala had succeeded by the end of the first half of 1990 in recruiting the support of influential political figures. They included academics and other scholars from universities and colleges, lawyers, businessmen and trade union leaders, retired civil servants, journalists and former politicians. Consequently, together with their supporters they successfully organized the first important meeting of representatives of interest groups at Garden Motel in Lusaka West on 20 July 1990. It was an historic meeting attended by men and women from all walks of life who were anxious to strengthen the campaign for the reintroduction of multi-party politics in Zambia.

The organizers of the inaugural national convention had invited Dr Robinson Nabulyato to deliver a keynote speech on the occasion of the official opening of the inaugural national convention of the MMD. Dr Robinson Nabulyato was chosen to perform a key role at the conference because he was universally accepted as a distinguished Zambian citizen. After serving as speaker of the National Assembly for many years, he had retired to his home in Namwala in the Southern Province. However, although he supported and encouraged the pro-democracy movement, nonetheless he was unable to guarantee his availability on 20 July 1990. Therefore, Akashambatwa Mbikusita Lewanika and his colleague, Mbita Chitala, approached me to stand in for Dr Nabulyato as the guest of honour in the event that he failed to attend the national convention. I readily accepted their invitation provided the UNDP country representative approved the arrangement. When Mr AM Sallah received my request for permission to attend the inaugural national convention, he referred it to the headquarters of the International Trade Centre in Geneva for consideration. The reply was negative. I was disappointed. The organizers of the inaugural national convention were more disappointed than I was. However, I remained a passive member of the MMD until the expiry of my contract of employment with the UNDP.

The government had followed and observed the proceedings at the inaugural national convention in July 1990. By that time the pro-democracy movement had gained momentum and it was obvious to many keen observers of the Zambian political scene that for the first time since the banning of the United Progressive Party, UNIP was faced with formidable opposition. However, at first the top officials in UNIP derived comfort from the fact that pro-democracy activists had merely formed a movement, not a political party. They were unlikely to succeed in mobilizing people to support the formation of another political party. In the opinion of many leaders in UNIP, once the time came for registering political parties differences among the new political leaders would emerge and there was every possibility of disintegration of the movement. Certainly the people who combined to start the movement came from all walks of life but they all had only one thing in common - the desire to eliminate the single-party rule in Zambia and re-introduce multi-party democracy. Probably there were divergences in political ideology. However, such divergences were suppressed. In the UNIP ranks, the belief was strong that the Multi-Party Movement for Democracy was destined to disintegrate once multi-party politics were restored.

In 1990, the PTA's Secretariat undertook a review of its priorities in the sub-region. Consequently, the project for promotion of clearing facilities for the purpose of increasing intra-PTA trade was downgraded and the ITC in Geneva approved the transfer of funds at the beginning of 1991 to projects of greater priority to the organization. After consultations with the headquarters of the ITC, I confirmed my ability to complete the remaining tour reports and prepare the terminal report on my activities and findings within one month. Therefore, 31 January 1991 was agreed as the convenient date for the termination of my employment with the UNDP. Thereafter, I was free to participate actively in the politics of our country.

In March 1991, I decided to make my stand publicly known on what was undoubtedly an important national issue – the popular demand for reintroduction of multi-party politics in Zambia. In fact, for a long time many friends and foes alike were anxious to know if the pro-democracy movement had my blessing. After the termination of my appointment with the UNDP it was against my conscience to remain silent on the issue.

At the inaugural national convention at Garden Motel in July 1990, a strong team was elected to the national interim committee of the MMD. Arthur Wina was elected chairman. Frederick Chiluba was elected vice chairman for operations and organization. The office of vice-chairman for public relations was scooped by Vernon Mwaanga. He was a professional journalist with wide experience in newspaper publication. More importantly, Vernon Mwaanga was also an astute politician who had at one time served our country as permanent representative to the United Nations in New York. During the early 1980s, I developed a close relationship with Vernon Mwaanga as his legal adviser in the firm of MMW and Company. That is why I chose him to organize and manage the press conference at which I intended to announce my decision to join MMD. On 14 March 1991 my press conference was held in his office at Curray Limited.

The press conference was well attended although it was organized at short notice. I distributed a short press statement which avoided controversial announcements. At that stage I was neither an official in the MMD's national interim committee nor an expert on its policies and programmes. That strategy was acceptable to Vernon Mwaanga, popularly known as 'VJ', who managed the press conference satisfactorily. On 15 March 1991, the *Times of Zambia* carried a short story of the press conference captioned "Mwanakatwe joins MMD as Mututwa quits". The *Times* reporter's account was published as follows:

PROMINENT Lusaka lawyer and former cabinet minister Mr John Mwanakatwe has joined the Movement for Multi-Party Democracy (MMD) as a member.

He said time had come for the old guard to pave the way for young people to shape Zambia's political destiny.

Mr Mwanakatwe, formerly minister of education and finance, dispelled speculation at a press briefing held at Curray Limited in Lusaka that he planned to re-enter active politics.

He had delayed to join the party because he was still serving as senior adviser to the Preferential Trade Area (PTA) clearing house. As an international civil servant he could not participate in politics. His tenure of office for the post ended last January and from 1 February he ceased to be an international civil servant.

On Zambia's political rebirth, Mr Mwanakatwe said: "I take this opportunity to pay tribute to the people everywhere in our country who worked tirelessly to pressurize the government to legislate for the re-introduction of multi-partyism in Zambia."

Meanwhile, district chairman of the MMD in Senanga, Maxwell Mututwa, has resigned from the movement and rejoined UNIP, reports Zana.

Surprisingly, this news item in the *Times of Zambia* aroused great interest. It provoked endless discussion, with some political analysts convinced that I intended to re-enter active politics sooner or later. It was merely a question of time. Others had been persuaded that I sincerely believed that the time had come for young people to assume the responsibility of guiding the political and economic destiny of our country. However, it was in UNIP political circles where my decision to join the MMD was discussed emotionally and often with conspicuous bitterness. They were free, of course, to express their views and vent their feelings. Some extremists among the rank and file of UNIP members believed that I chose to abandon UNIP in 1991 in order to fulfil personal political ambitions. Yet since 1978, when I announced my retirement from active politics, I have never changed my mind. Some MMD leaders indeed used to tempt me at various times after 1991 to return to active politics but I always spurned their overtures instinctively. I have never wavered from my strong belief that a time comes in a nation when the older men and women in politics should facilitate the transfer of political responsibility to the younger men and women in their midst.

One of my closest friends among top UNIP leaders, Reuben Kamanga, wrote a letter to me to express his disappointment that I had joined the Movement for Multi-Party

Democracy. His letter was full of courtesies and niceties. It also had hard punches and vitriolic accusations which saddened me. I had always appreciated Reuben Kamanga's respect for me because he held senior political positions both in UNIP and Dr Kenneth Kaunda's government since independence. In pre-independence days he was greatly admired for his courage and determination in the fight against British colonialism. His contemporaries in the 1950s remember how he challenged a British colonial officer in his own office to arrest him for holding an unauthorized political meeting with UNIP followers. The district officer decided not to arrest him. That was the measure of the courage of Reuben Kamanga.

Because Reuben Kamanga was a traditionalist, he always gave me respect commensurate with my age advantage over him. In the protest letter he wrote to me, he added the word "senior" in the salutation to make it respectful. His salutation was couched thus: "My dear senior Brother". In the same spirit, throughout the letter, he chose to refer to me as "Ba Shikulu Chileshe" where another intimate friend would have simply called me "John". In IciBemba the prefix "Ba" before a person's name denotes respect for that person. Hence, "Ba Shikulu Chileshe" means the "Respected Grandfather of Chileshe".

He was my closest friend in and outside politics. Reuben Kamanga raised three main issues in his letter. Firstly, he bitterly complained that he was not forewarned by me personally that I intended to join MMD after I ceased to be an international civil servant. In the second paragraph of the protest letter, he stated bluntly that "… my only complaint is that you decided to keep me in darkness maybe, of course, for reasons best known to yourself". He went on to justify this particular reason for his complaint that "… I am only saying this because I have all along felt I was one of the closest friends to you". The second serious complaint my friend raised was that I had occasionally used his office to make telephone calls or to ask his personal secretary to type manuscripts for me. Yet he "never complained at all just to show how close we worked together". I understood the complaint to mean that I should not have joined MMD before consulting him. The third complaint was vaguely phrased but more serious than the first two complaints. He implied that I had decided to leave UNIP and join MMD in order to satisfy my political ambitions. He did not elaborate the nature of my political ambitions. However his letter concluded:

> Hatred is no doubt a negative force by whoever harbours it. Hatred must therefore be avoided at all costs by all of us in the leadership of whatever party or organization.

> Finally, as brothers as well as friends nothing is going to change my personal relations with you. I would like to believe that love will continue to take its rightful course between the two of us and indeed between our two families. I am more than convinced that Banakulu Chileshe will continue to exercise her loving instincts as she had done in the past.

It was quite clear from the last two paragraphs of Reuben Kamanga's letter that he wrote in a spirit of reconciliation, not hostility and in a spirit of love but not hatred. Therefore, it would have been unwise and improper to adopt an uncompromising attitude in my reply. However, I was also justified in clarifying various issues Reuben Kamanga had raised in his letter which tended to stigmatise my character.

Reuben Kamanga's letter was three pages long. My reply was longer – four pages in all. Of the eight issues covered in my letter, only four were particularly significant; namely, failure to give my intimate friend notice about my intention to leave UNIP and join MMD; visits to my friend's office; celebration of my sixtieth birthday; and competition for political leadership in the country. I was certain that on these issues my position was clear, plain and obvious. I wrote that I had only informed my wife of my decision to join MMD; that I had visited his office as a friend and that my birthday celebrations, to which he had been invited, were purely social. I reiterated that I was not interested in political leadership.

In spite of my decision to join MMD in 1991, personal relations with Reuben Kamanga remained cordial. In fact, the bonds of friendship between my own and Reuben Kamanga's family became stronger in the 1990s than before. My intimate friend had predicted accurately in the last paragraph of his letter when he stated that "… as brothers as well as friends nothing is going to change my personal relations with you".

President Kaunda unexpectedly invited me to meet him at State House on 5 March 1991. It was about two weeks before Reuben Kamanga sent me a letter protesting against my decision to leave UNIP and join MMD. I was invited to meet Dr Kaunda "to discuss current political developments in our country". I accepted the invitation and attended the meeting in State House, a week before the press briefing in Vernon Mwaanga's office at which I announced my decision to join MMD. At the meeting in State House, the president commented on current political developments. The discussion was interesting. It became clear and obvious to me that he had received intelligence reports that I intended to join MMD in the near future. In Dr Kenneth Kaunda's informal observations on the political situation at that time, he stated that I was free like any other citizen to join any political party of my choice at any time. However, he emphasized that if I made such a decision he personally would be "hurt". He added that if I took such a decision his respect for me would not be affected.

Throughout the discussion, President Kaunda was, as usual, friendly and courteous. However, he had quite clearly, albeit obliquely, sent a message to me that he was not in favour of my intention to leave UNIP and join MMD. His feelings were natural and understandable. But President Kaunda's position was rather contradictory. On the one hand he would not interfere with my freedom to choose membership of any political party although we had been close friends in UNIP for a long time. On the other hand, he also emphasized that he would be "hurt" if I decided to leave UNIP in order to join another political party. I found the two propositions contradictory. I was puzzled. After the meeting in State House, I rushed to my office in MMW and Company to compose a letter to President Kaunda about my reaction to his observations on "current political developments in our country". The first draft of the letter was strongly worded because I thought that President Kaunda was indirectly interfering with my right to join any political party. I expected him to know that I would not wish at any time to take any action which was likely to "hurt" him. I stated in the introductory parts of the letter that he had known me over many years as "... blunt and unhypocritical ...."

On further reflection, I decided that it was unwise to send a letter to President Kaunda which I had written hurriedly after the meeting at State House. It was necessary to sleep over the matter and chew it over beforehand to allow for revision of the letter, if necessary, after my nerves had cooled down. On 12 March 1991, two days before the press briefing in Vernon Mwaanga's office, I sent a revised letter to Dr Kaunda at State House. It was not couched in acrimonious language. I dealt mainly with his concern that if I left UNIP and joined another political party he would feel "hurt". I explained my position to His Excellency the President and added:

> As a Christian who reminds us to show love to one another – even to our enemies – I would hope that you will not be "hurt" when friends exercise their right to belong to a political party other than the one you lead.

> Speaking for myself, I have tried throughout my life to value my friends even when they have treated me unfairly. For example when I was unfairly called a "dissident" in 1980, I harboured no bitterness or hatred, as the attached newspaper article I wrote at that time shows quite clearly.

> God bless you.

On 25 March 1991, I received President Kaunda's reply. In a short letter, the President stated thus: "I have never hated in my life for any reason at all" and he continued "I always pray to the living God that He will continue to place this gift at my disposal". The words he chose to use in these two affirmations were appropriate to allay the concern I had conveyed to him in my letter of 12 March 1991. He was at pains to emphasize that he felt "hurt" and "injured" that I would not be available to continue working with him in national development efforts if I left UNIP and joined another political party. In President Kenneth Kaunda's opinion being "hurt" and being "injured" "does not mean you break friendship". The impact of his argument was conveyed to me in the third paragraph of his letter in beautiful rhetorical language I have never forgotten. He wrote thus:

> Nobody denies you that right, nobody at all. Nobody says do not change your mind and do something else, nobody at all. But do you honestly believe that after we have worked together in public life for so many years, not only as minister of education, not only as minister of finance, as secretary general of the government of the Republic of Zambia, that you would leave the party I have been privileged to lead and that this would not injure my feelings; it would not hurt my feelings? I want you to know my feelings were injured, I was hurt when I heard this especially after our last meeting when I got the impression that you had no other thoughts apart from staying with the United National Independence Party. Please note the fact that I am saying you gave me the impression that you will be staying in UNIP.

After the press briefing in Vernon Mwaanga's office, I was officially known to be a supporter of the MMD wherever I went in Zambia. I joined the new political party purely on the principle that a multi-party system of government was comparatively better than the one-party system we introduced in Zambia in 1972. I had no intention whatsoever of re-entering active politics by joining MMD. My ambition was only to devote my energies to the service of my fellow countrymen and women as a lawyer for the rest of my life.

Since I had gained experience in politics as a member of the United National Independence Party, I was available to give advice to MMD leaders when they requested for it. For I believed then, as I do even today, that the younger generation deserves support and encouragement from the older generation in their efforts to maintain good governance of our country. Because the MMD decided to participate in the 1991 presidential and parliamentary elections, MMD officials began to invite me to join the election campaign teams during weekends. I was introduced as an MMD member at a public rally in Matero for the first time in the presence of Mr Frederick Chiluba, the party president. Later, I attended similar gatherings in Kafue township and Ndola.

Perhaps due to the kind of support I gave to the MMD leaders, it was wrongly assumed that I was keen to contest the election in October 1991 as a parliamentary candidate. At that time, Emmanuel Kasonde was the MMD provincial chairman for the Northern Province. Apparently with the approval of some senior colleagues in the National Executive Committee of the MMD, he formally requested me to contest the Mpulungu Constituency seat in the Northern Province on the MMD ticket. He knew that my home area was in Mpulungu Constituency. In fact, a large number of influential men and women, including UNIP leaders in Mpulungu Constituency, had strongly protested when I decided to retire from politics at the end of December 1978. I believe that Mpulungu Constituency would have been a safe seat for me in the elections on an MMD ticket. However, I declined the offer. Instead, I promised to join the election team to campaign for any person selected to contest the Mpulungu parliamentary seat on the MMD ticket.

Late in September, about four weeks before the elections in October 1991, I joined the team Emmanuel Kasonde had organized to campaign for Dean Mung'omba as the MMD candidate for Mpulungu. Our efforts in the election campaign were amply rewarded. Dean Mung'omba was elected with a comfortable majority. In the presidential election, Mr Frederick Chiluba defeated Dr Kenneth Kaunda, the founding father of the Zambian nation. The Movement for Multi-Party Democracy won a landslide victory in the parliamentary elections. Dr Kenneth Kaunda, the man who had ruled Zambia for twenty seven years after independence, conceded defeat to Mr Frederick Chiluba, the well known trade union leader.

Before the president-elect moved into State House, he lived for some days in the government house designated primarily for use by the vice president. While in transit to State House he started interviewing the men and women he had earmarked for ministerial and other appointments in the MMD administration. One morning I received an invitation by telephone to meet the new president for consultations. The nature of the consultations was not revealed. However, at the meeting President Frederick Chiluba informed me that he intended to appoint me to a senior position in the parastatal sector. He was anxious to know my reaction to his proposal. I informed him that I had no intention of accepting re-employment in the civil service or the parastatal sector. At that time, early in November 1991, I was sixty five years old. I told him bluntly that at that age I was not interested in any position in the public service or private sector which might oblige me to leave home early in order to sit in my office by eight hours in the morning. Then I quipped, "How would you feel, Mr President, to call me at my office at nine hours in the morning only to be advised by my personal secretary that I had not yet arrived for work?".

He was sincerely anxious to find a position for me in the new administration. Then he requested me to consider accepting a diplomatic appointment. Although he did not indicate the country which he considered suitable for my appointment, I told him that his suggestion was unacceptable. At that stage, he was visibly disappointed. To avoid misunderstanding, I reiterated in our discussion that I was not interested in any kind of employment. However, I informed President Chiluba that I was prepared to accept short term assignments which did not mean employment by the state. Otherwise, I made every effort to convince him that I was prepared to assist the new administration in every possible way on condition that my law practice was not adversely affected and I was convinced that my temporary services were required in the overall national interests.

Such an opportunity arose quite unexpectedly in July 1992. In June the Privatisation Act, No. 21 of 1992, was enacted "to provide for the privatisation and commercialisation of state-owned enterprises, to provide for the establishment of the Zambia Privatisation Agency and to define the functions of the Agency". The Privatisation Bill was debated in Parliament during June 1992. It received presidential assent on 3rd July 1992. The inaugural meeting of the Agency was held on 6 August 1992. Before the inaugural meting was held, under the provisions of the Privatisation Act, it was necessary for a select committee of the National Assembly to scrutinize the proposed members of the Agency to determine their suitability and acceptability. The recommendations of the Select Committee were later ratified by the National Assembly. Members of the Agency were appointed by the president of Zambia after ratification by the National Assembly. At the inaugural meeting and in terms of section 5 (2) of the Privatisation Act, the Agency elected "from amongst its members" the chairman and the vice chairman. I was unanimously elected chairman and Ben L Ngenda was elected vice chairman of the Agency.

The establishment of the Zambia Privatisation Agency was an important step in the MMD's fulfilment of its manifesto presented to the electorate in 1991. The manifesto gave priority to the privatisation of state-owned enterprises. The previous UNIP government had nationalized privately-owned enterprises in the 1970s. It was a fact, although an unpalatable one, that most parastatals in Zambia were not profit-making enterprises in the 1980s. The government's restraints upon state-owned enterprises and the country's crippling debts meant that those companies which needed foreign exchange for essential inputs – spare parts and raw materials – were working at reduced capacity. The result was economic stagnation. Yet Zambia had in the 1970s and 1980s a first class infrastructure – good roads, a rail system which connected the entire southern region and an indigenous entrepreneurial class capable of making the economy boom.

A Zambian of Asian origin was indirectly instrumental for my nomination by the Zambia Confederation of Chambers of Commerce and Industry (ZACCI) as a member of the Zambia Privatisation Agency. Dr Beejay Sharma was a prominent businessman in Lusaka and a well known and influential member of ZACCI. I was the major shareholder and chairman of a small company called JJ Express Enterprises Limited, formed early in the 1980s mainly to trade in agricultural inputs imported from South Africa and Zimbabwe. Although after my retirement from active politics at the end of 1978 I concentrated mainly on my law practice, I had an interest in promoting the development of agriculture in our country. My partner in the business was Jimmie Walker – hence the company's name "JJ Express Enterprises Limited" with the initials J and J for John and Jimmie. Later, I invited a close friend, Andrew Mutemba, to join our company as a shareholder and co-director. Our company was a registered member of the Lusaka Chamber of Commerce which was affiliated to ZACCI.

I enthusiastically accepted the challenge of leading the Agency in its early stages. Members of ZPA were drawn from various interest groups, including the Bankers Association of Zambia, the School of Business of the Copperbelt University, a representative of the Zambia Confederation of Chambers of Commerce and Industry and the Zambia Congress of Trade Unions. Other members included the attorney-general and government officials. The high calibre of the members of ZPA was a source of great encouragement to me as the chairman. They included George Sokota, a leading Zambian accountant, who represented the Zambia Institute of Certified Accountants and Ben Ngenda from the Law Association of Zambia. With these qualified and experienced members, I was confident that

ZPA would successfully perform the functions described in section 8 of the Act, "to plan, manage, implement and control the privatisation of state-owned enterprises". To achieve this main objective the Agency was expected also to prepare a long-term divestiture sequence plan for submission to the cabinet for approval.

My greatest concern was to encourage ZPA to formulate policies and programmes which would ensure transparency and accountability in all its operations. For example, the mode of sale ZPA adopted *ab initio* for most of the state-owned enterprises was by competitive bidding. It meant that companies were packaged for sale and bids were invited from prospective investors who competed for the purchase of the companies offered for sale. Whether the sale of a company was by competitive bid or by negotiation, independent consultants or experts, such as lawyers and accountants, were employed to process the bids and later submit reports and recommendations to the Zambia Privatisation Agency. In its function of privatising state-owned enterprises, ZPA acted independently without political interference from the minister of commerce, trade and industry or any other officer in government. It was responsible for the submission of its reports and recommendations only to the cabinet for final approval. That objective – the transparency of the Agency and accountability for its operations – was achieved by the time I relinquished my position as chairman and the representative of ZACCI at the end of December 1993.

In September 1992, President Chiluba invited me to accept appointment as chancellor of the University of Zambia. The University of Zambia was established in 1965 by an Act of Parliament, which designated the chancellor as "the head of the University". The president of Zambia was responsible for the appointment of the chancellor on the advice of the Council of the University. From March 1966 when the University of Zambia opened its doors to students, the Council of the University set the precedent of advising the appointment of the president of Zambia as chancellor. In July 1966, Dr Kenneth Kaunda was installed as the first chancellor of the University of Zambia at a colourful ceremony in Lusaka. Dr Julius Nyerere, president of the United Republic of Tanzania, attended the installation ceremony. The chancellor's term of office was for five years. However, a person appointed chancellor was eligible for re-appointment. Dr Kenneth Kaunda continued to hold the office of chancellor of the University of Zambia until early in 1992 when the new government of Dr Frederick Chiluba changed the law relating to the establishment, regulation, control and functions of public and private universities in Zambia. In terms of the provisions of the University Act of 1992, the president of the Republic of Zambia was empowered to appoint a chancellor of a public university from among eminent Zambian citizens for a period of five years on the recommendation of the minister.

It was a great honour and privilege when I was appointed chancellor of the University of Zambia by the president in September 1992. I had been involved in education in our country for many years, indeed for almost all my life as an adult. At the political level, as minister of education, I collaborated with my colleagues in the post-independence administration of President Kenneth Kaunda to establish the University of Zambia and other institutions of learning. Therefore, it was a great honour to have my educational career crowned by being appointed chancellor of the University of Zambia.

In July 2001, I was interviewed by Father Miha Drevensek for a special feature article he intended to write on my contribution to the "democratic development of Zambia as a nation". He was the editor of the *Challenge Magazine*, a Roman Catholic publication for the promotion of Christian living in Zambia. In the interview, I was asked by Father Miha Drevensek about the challenges I encountered as chancellor of the University of Zambia. He recorded my response in the *Challenge Magazine* as follows:

> .... the minister responsible for higher education was obliged to recommend three persons to the president for consideration

for this appointment. Nominees had to be persons who had distinguished themselves in the manner described in the Act. The president was expected to select one person for appointment as chancellor of a specified public university for a period of five years.

Although my credentials certainly fulfilled the statutory requirement for prospective candidates, I have always believed that the appointment was in recognition of my contribution to the development of education in our country. The office of chancellor of a public university is largely ceremonial for under the Act he is merely "the titular head of the university". It is not a remunerative position at all. Nonetheless, it is a position of honour and respect in the community.

I would say that I did not find the office of chancellor of the University onerous or especially challenging. As the University's father-figure, I avoided involvement in purely administrative problems. I expected the management of the University to settle such problems using, when necessary, organs such as the Senate or the Council of the University. However, I was always available to assist officers who requested for advice. I preferred to act as a philosopher and friend of members of diverse interest groups in the university community, such interest groups as the students' union, the trade unions, lecturers and researchers group *inter-alia*. My aim was to reconcile interest groups where there was conflict and establish mutual trust where there was misunderstanding.

In February 2000, President Frederick Chiluba decided to launch the Frederick JT Chiluba Centre, an institute for democratic and industrial relations studies. The officials arranged two stages for the official launch of the centre. Firstly, invited guests were expected to attend the ground-breaking ceremony on 15 February 2000 in the afternoon. A programme was prepared which included unveiling of the commemorative plaque by the president preceded by introductory remarks by the *raconteur*. Before refreshments, invited guests were expected to plant trees led by the president. Secondly, a fund-raising dinner was arranged for invited guests in the evening on 15 February 2000. Later, the date for the fundraising dinner was postponed to 10 March 2000 which was a more convenient date for the guest of honour, Dr Bakili Muluzi, president of the Republic of Malawi.

On 11 February 2000, I received a letter from Richard Sakala, the special assistant to the president for public relations and press inviting me to attend both the ground-breaking ceremony and the fund-raising dinner at Mulungushi Conference Centre. He requested me to act as the *raconteur* at both functions. President Chiluba knew that I would support his project because I have had throughout my life a soft heart for efforts intended to advance education and training in our country. The first two paragraphs of Richard Sakala's letter portrayed to me a sense of seriousness by President Frederick Chiluba to continue promoting the noble cause of democracy, peace and stability in the region at the end of his term of office as president of Zambia in December 2001. In the first paragraph, Richard Sakala emphasized President Frederick Chiluba's intention to retire from the presidency in 2001. He wrote, "President Frederick Chiluba will be launching the Frederick JT Chiluba Centre ... where he hopes to devote most of his time when he leaves the presidency in 2001". In the second and third paragraphs, he wrote that:

The intention of the programme is to raise funds to commence the construction of the institute which will deal with formal and informal studies in democracy and industrial relations. It is intended that the centre will service the region through regular academic programmes, seminars, workshops and summits on contemporary issues on the two programmes.

As *raconteur* we expect that you will give a speech to introduce the president, the idea of the institute and indeed the guest of honour. Thereafter you may wish to invite for pledges and finally the president will autograph his two books for a fee.

President Frederick Chiluba's idea of establishing a centre for formal and informal studies in democracy and industrial relations was similar to Jimmie Carter's idea of establishing the Carter Centre after completing his term of office as president of the United States of America in 1978. Before accepting Richard Sakala's invitation, I decided to do some homework. My eldest son, Mupanga, who is more computer literate than I, obtained on the internet all the information I wanted to know about the Carter Centre in the USA – its constitution and organization, objectives and functions, and the composition of its board of trustees. From the information I obtained, there was no valid reason to doubt the desirability of the proposed institute for studies in democracy and industrial relations. Consequently, I accepted the invitation to attend both functions and to act as the *raconteur*.

When President Frederick Chiluba was actively canvassing for support from Zambians to raise funds for the construction of the institute for studies in democracy and industrial relations, some people had already started calling for appropriate amendments to the Constitution of Zambia to enable President Frederick Chiluba to make a bid for a third term in the presidential and parliamentary elections in 2001. Such calls were made mostly by MMD cadres in various parts of the country. At first, the party cadres who were calling for President Chiluba's third term in office were not taken seriously. They were simply ignored. However, purely by intuition I suspected the calls by the MMD cadres for a third term had President Frederick Chiluba's tacit approval and perhaps encouragement too.

Because Dr Bakili Muluzi, president of the Republic of Malawi, was the guest of honour at the fundraising dinner at Mulungushi Conference Centre, I decided to write a short speech for the occasion. On such an occasion, an off-the-cuff speech such as the one I made at the ground-breaking ceremony was inappropriate. For my short speech, I chose to reflect on the

442

phrase "real democracy", a phrase which, I conceded, was elusive. However, before theorizing on the phrase "real democracy" it was more important to me to state publicly that the majority of Zambians were proud that President Frederick Chiluba had firmly decided to retire from active politics in spite of pleas from some of his followers to contest the presidency again. I informed the audience, which included the vice president, the speaker of the National Assembly, the chief justice, ministers, ambassadors and high commissioners, that:

Many people in our country have applauded President Chiluba's firm decision to retire from the presidency in 2001. Not that he really has any other choice in the matter. For it is quite clearly stated in the constitution of our country that no person may serve more than two terms of five years each as president of Zambia. On the other hand, we also know countries where similar constitutional provisions have been circumvented by adoption of appropriate constitutional amendments. Thereby, it has been possible for an incumbent president to continue in office, all other things being equal, of course.

I believe that President Chiluba has set a good example for our country by his decision to retire from the presidency in 2001 in spite of calls from some quarters for his continuation in office. A well known British politician, Benjamin Disraeli, observed at one time in the nineteenth century that it is important in life to know when to seize an opportunity. However, he went on to say that it was even more important in life to know when to forego an advantage.

Your Excellencies, distinguished guests, ladies and gentlemen, I believe that in the future historians will write about the successes and failures of Mr Frederick JT Chiluba during his term of office as president of Zambia. Historians will not fail, I think, to credit him with the rare ability of knowing when to forego an advantage. Let us remember that democratisation is, by definition, not revolutionary at all – it is evolutionary. No society can transform the way it governs itself overnight. It will take decades or even generations for new democracies in Africa and elsewhere in the world to make the transition to real democracy. What is important in the process of democratisation is that every step must be taken in the right direction.

My term of office as chancellor of the University of Zambia expired at the end of September 1997. However, I was reappointed for a further period of only three months. Consequently, I was expected to continue in office until 31 December 1997. For a period of four years, from January 1998 to December 2001, the office of chancellor remained vacant. Similarly, during the same period, the Copperbelt University also continued operating without a chancellor in office. New chancellors of these universities were appointed in January 2002 by President Levy Mwanawasa after Dr Frederick Chiluba's term of office as president came to an end.

It was a good omen that President Frederick Chiluba did not reappoint me as chancellor for a further term of five years for I would have found myself in an embarrassing situation during the debate over his bid for a third term in office after amending the Constitution of Zambia. I readily agreed to be a speaker at the famous Oasis Convention, held early in 2001 in Lusaka, at which the civil society undertook to organize a vigorous campaign against calls by the MMD cadres for extension of Dr Frederick Chiluba's tenure of office as president of Zambia.

Father Miha Drevensek requested me to provide background information regarding my participation in the third term debate for his article in *Challenge Magazine*. He wanted to explain what actually motivated me to join hands with other members of the civil society to oppose President Frederick Chiluba's bid for a third term in office. My comments, as published in the *Challenge Magazine*, were as follows:

> The Oasis Convention was organized by the civil society early this year with the participation of representatives of three main

Christian Churches to debate the proposal to amend the Constitution of Zambia. The current constitution restricts the president's tenure of office to two terms only of five years each. In order to enable the incumbent president to participate in this year's elections in an effort to secure a third term of office, the amendment of clause (2) of Article 35 of the constitution is necessary. The Oasis Forum gave citizens an opportunity to discuss whether it was desirable to amend the Constitution of Zambia in order to facilitate the possibility of the incumbent president's bid for a third term of office.

I was invited to participate in what became known as the third term debate by a representative of the Episcopal Conference of Catholic Bishops, the Evangelical Fellowship of Zambia and the Christian Council of Zambia. I accepted the invitation with a sense of gratitude and humility knowing the important role the Church had played in the past to promote peace and stability in times of trouble and uncertainty. I felt that I had an obligation to participate in the third term debate since I had been privileged five years ago to chair the Constitutional Review Commission for transfer of political control of the affairs of our country from the old to the young generation. I felt that it was necessary again to stand up and oppose the proposal to amend the Constitution of Zambia purely on principle.

I considered principles more important than personalities involved in the issue of whether to amend the constitution or not. I regarded then, as I do now, that the Constitution of Zambia is an important and sacred document which citizens are obliged not to change except for truly valid reasons.

The proceedings of the Oasis Convention were widely publicized, especially in the independent print media. That increased the momentum of the anti-third term activities throughout the country. It was evident the intellectuals, businessmen, trade union leaders and student organizations were against the proposal to amend the Constitution of Zambia principally to enable President Frederick Chiluba to bid for a third term in office.

The Evangelical Fellowship of Zambia subsequently organized "A Day of Reflection" at the Cathedral of the Holy Cross in Lusaka on 10 April 2001. It was a day dedicated to "prayer, fasting and reflection on the state of the nation". Men and women from all walks of life were invited to attend the occasion which was non-partisan, non-political and ecumenical in its religious character. The response was overwhelming indeed. Members of parliament from various political parties attended the solemn occasion. Among notable groups in the audience in the Anglican Cathedral there were diplomats representing foreign countries in Zambia, leaders of major political parties, retired politicians and representatives of non-governmental organizations and trade union leaders. The Day of Reflection was supported by all stakeholders who originally organized the Oasis Convention, namely the Episcopal Conference of Catholic Bishops, the Christian Council of Zambia and the Law Association of Zambia. The Anglican Cathedral was packed to its full capacity.

The purpose of organizing a "Day of Reflection" on 10 April 2001 was to galvanize and consolidate public opinion against the proposal to amend the Constitution of Zambia in order to enable President Frederick Chiluba to make a bid for a third term in office. As a retired politician and senior citizen, I received an invitation. In addition the convenor requested me to deliver a keynote speech on a set theme, "The Lord's dealings with Zambia: an oasis of tranquillity". I accepted the invitation to deliver the keynote speech to the august audience with a sense of humility. At that time, a political crisis such as Zambia had not seen before was imminent. After the Oasis Convention, perhaps the gathering at the Anglican Cathedral on 10 April 2001 might be the last opportunity to avert a political crisis in the nation. I had no illusions whatsoever that the organizers of the "Day of Reflection" expected me to rally together the anti-third term forces into a formidable group. Therefore, it was necessary to write a short speech appealing to President

Frederick Chiluba to declare publicly that, in spite of calls from his party followers, he would respect the provisions of the Constitution of Zambia which limited the president's tenure of office to two terms of five years each.

The programme for "A Day of Reflection" included three other participants. They were Bishop Paul Mususu, the executive secretary of the Evangelical Fellowship of Zambia; Pastor Choolwe Mwetwa; and Mark Chona, former special assistant to Dr Kenneth Kaunda. Pastor Choolwe Mwetwa was to preach a sermon on "Responsibilities of leaders to the people they lead". The occasion was a great success. The enthusiasm of the men and women who participated was overwhelming. Indeed, the proceedings on that occasion marked the beginning of the doom of President Frederick Chiluba's tactics to obtain consensus countrywide for amending the Constitution of Zambia to allow him a third term in office.

The Post newspaper carried a front page article on 11 April 2001 on the proceedings in the Anglican Cathedral the previous day. The headline was in bold letters, which readily caught the eye even at a distance, and read as follows: "Kaunda conceded to the Church's calls ...... **EMULATE KK MWANAKATWE URGES CHILUBA**". The newspaper's reporter, Brighton Phiri, summarized my speech as follows:

> President Frederick Chiluba must emulate Dr Kenneth Kaunda's respect for the Church, advised John Mwanakatwe yesterday.
>
> Speaking during the Evangelical Fellowship of Zambia (EFZ) organized "Reflection" prayer meeting at the Cathedral of the Holy Cross, Mwanakatwe who chaired the 1993 Constitution Review Commission said the country's political crisis was caused by President Chiluba's apparent willingness to offer himself to stand as a candidate during this year's presidential elections.
>
> "President Chiluba must emulate what Dr Kaunda did in 1991

447

in June at this same Cathedral where he promised to allow the amendment of the constitution in order to reintroduce multiparty politics", Mwanakatwe said.

According to Mwanakatwe, Dr Kaunda conceded to the Church's calls for change of the constitution and agreed to cut short his term of office.

"That was a historical decision made by Dr Kaunda which is worth emulating", he said.

Mwanakatwe said that it was not too late for President Chiluba to reflect on some of the good things which his government had done and avoid tarnishing them by one mistake.

He explained that a referendum was not the best solution for the current debate because the country could find it difficult to draw a fifty per cent list of potential voters.

Subsequent speeches echoed my message to President Frederick Chiluba that the only solution to the looming political crisis in Zambia was abandonment of the third term debate. The EFZ executive director, Bishop Paul Mususu, disagreed with the pro-Chiluba group which urged the Church to adopt a neutral position on the third term debate. He argued convincingly that the Church's intervention in the past had forestalled serious political crises. In particular, he reminded critics that a political crisis was averted in 1991 because of the Church's intervention. The Bishop then echoed my plea to President Fredrick Chiluba and said, "If Dr Kaunda listened to us, it is our hope and prayer that President Chiluba will listen too". His plea was emphasized when he quipped rhetorically thus: "Why were we not asked to be neutral when we confronted the situation in 1991?" Mark Chona's message to President Frederick Chiluba was simple but quite loud and clear. He, too, informed the audience in the Anglican Cathedral of the Holy Cross that "there was need for President Chiluba to emulate Dr Kaunda's love for the country when he handed over power peacefully". Mark Chona's great concern was that the majority of political leaders in our country "enjoyed love of power instead of power of love". He observed that in public they preached love but privately they practised hatred. He did not pull punches in appealing to President Frederick Chiluba not to seek re-election at the end of his second term of office. In his front page article in the *Post* newspaper of 11 April 2001, Brighton Phiri reported Mark Chona's opening remarks as follows:

> Former special assistant to Dr Kaunda, Mark Chona, said he had advised the former republican president against re-election to avoid a humiliating defeat.
>
> "I am doing the same to President Chiluba; wherever you are please do not seek another term," Chona said. "I hate to see leaders being humiliated and harassed."

Bishop Paul Mususu took a census of the prominent men and women who attended the discussion. In particular, the organizers of the meeting circulated a presidential petition among cabinet ministers and members of parliament. According to Bishop Paul Mususu forty three members of parliament had signed the presidential petition requesting President Chiluba not to seek a third term. It was reported that by press time on 10 April 2001 fifty had signed the presidential petition.

Without a shadow of doubt many people who attended the discussions in the Anglican Cathedral of the Holy Cross on 10 April 2001 felt that President Frederick Chiluba's wish to seek re-election for a third term of office was doomed to failure. He had not one chance out of a million to marshal sufficient support both in Parliament and in a referendum to fulfil the necessary constitutional requirements before amending the Constitution of Zambia. Less than six weeks after the historic "Day of Reflection", President Frederick Chiluba announced to the nation on both radio and television that he had decided not to seek a third term of office. That announcement immediately put an end to the third term debate in Zambia. That outcome made me feel that the support I gave to the Oasis Forum and the civil society in the fight against the third term was not in vain.

C H A P T E R

17

The Constitutional Review Commission

In the second half of 1993, I received and accepted an invitation to attend the graduation ceremony at Kwame Nkhrumah Teacher Training College in Kabwe as guest of honour. It is a well known institution for training successful form five school leavers as teachers in secondary schools. As the guest of honour, I was expected to present prizes to outstanding students in various fields of endeavour – academic excellence, exemplary character, leadership, sportsmanship and so forth. I was invited as the chancellor of the University of Zambia which had a special relationship with the college. The University of Zambia awarded diplomas to successful students at the end of a two year course of training. I was expected as guest of honour to deliver a speech to the staff, students, parents and invited guests.

On graduation day, an odd incident occurred during the ceremony. While reading my address to the audience, someone walked into the hall and gave a note to the principal of the college who read it and immediately walked out. Later, I was informed that he went out of the hall to receive a telephone call from the special assistant for public relations in the President's Office at State House in Lusaka. He was instructed to inform me that President Frederick Chiluba wanted to speak to me urgently after my arrival in Lusaka from Kabwe, a provincial town about eighty five miles north of Lusaka. He knew that late at night on that day I was due to travel with my wife to London. Therefore, after the graduation ceremony, I drove back to Lusaka to report my arrival to the special assistant for public relations at State House with the least possible delay.

In a short discussion, President Frederick Chiluba revealed that the cabinet had decided to appoint a commission under the Inquiries Act to collect views from the general public throughout the country on what type of constitution Zambia should enact. The commission was expected to submit a report containing its recommendations with a draft constitution annexed for the government's consideration. He further stated that the cabinet had decided to appoint me chairman of the Constitutional Review Commission. According to President Chiluba, government regarded the commission's work a priority. Therefore, he was anxious to know what my reaction was since he wanted to announce the commission's appointment without delay.

My initial response was negative. I informed the president that I was unable to accept membership of the commission without knowing its terms of reference. I was unwilling to serve on any commission of inquiry in any capacity if I felt uncomfortable about the adequacy of its terms of reference or their usefulness to the country in the long term. The composition of the Commission of Inquiry was equally of interest to me. I accepted, of course, that it was the government's prerogative to choose the men and women it considered suitable to discharge specified functions and responsibilities. In exercising its prerogative, it was obliged to balance the representation of various interest groups and stakeholders on the commission. On the other hand, I, too, had my interests to protect – not least the desire to be associated at all times with success, not failure and with advancement, not stagnation. Therefore, I wanted to know and assess the calibre of the men and women appointed to serve on the commission.

It pleased me that President Frederick Chiluba received my reservations sympathetically during our short discussion. We reached a reasonable compromise. He agreed to send the necessary documents to me in London so that after studying them carefully I would then be in a position to make an informed decision. Fortunately, at that time – October 1993 – I was privileged to stay with my wife in a flat which belonged to a family friend in St George's Fields near Edgeware Road in central London where a facsimile machine was available for facilitation of communication between Lusaka and London. In less than four days after my arrival in London, I knew the terms of reference and the list of names of members of the Constitutional Review Commission.

The terms of reference were very wide and satisfactory. In particular, I was encouraged by the freedom the commission was given under term of reference number twelve to "examine and recommend any subject matter of a constitutional or political nature which, in the commission's view, has relevance in the strengthening of parliamentary and multi-party democracy". In fact, the succeeding term of reference number thirteen further strengthened the commission's freedom to interpret all other terms of reference widely by instructing it to "examine and recommend on any matter which is connected with or incidental to the foregoing terms of reference". From past experience, I was convinced that the terms of reference were wider than those given to any other previous constitution commission. Later, other members of the commission reached the same conclusion.

The composition of the commission was equally acceptable to me. It consisted largely of intellectuals and respected men and women of high integrity and influence in society. Consequently, having regard to all these observations, I had no reservations whatsoever in accepting appointment as a member of the Constitutional Review Commission. I was also willing to chair the commission's deliberations. In about one week after my arrival in London, I informed President Frederick Chiluba that his government's proposals regarding the terms of reference and composition of the Constitutional Review Commission were acceptable to me.

The government's decision to appoint a commission in 1993 to review the Zambian Constitution was anticipated by many political observers following the MMD's landslide victory in the elections in 1991. The Mvunga Commission successfully produced a constitution for Zambia which was adequate mainly for the restoration of plural politics in Zambia. Its principal task was to produce a constitutional compromise between the ruling party (the United National Independence Party) on the one hand and the opposition parties which emerged in 1990 and 1991 at the height of the campaign for re-introduction of multi-party politics in Zambia. I had never participated in the constitution-making efforts in the post-independence era until my appointment as chairman of the Constitutional Review Commission in 1993.

However, I had gained some experience in the vital field of constitution-making before our country achieved independence. The colonial government at the beginning of 1964 allowed the government of Northern Rhodesia to consult with leaders of the major political parties to prepare a draft independence constitution. The leaders of the major political parties were Dr Kenneth Kaunda, Mr Harry Nkumbula and Mr John Roberts for the United National Independence Party, African National Congress and the United Federal Party respectively. The governor of Northern Rhodesia then set up a committee of colonial civil servants and members of the Legislative Council with the attorney-general as chairman to draft a new constitution for Northern Rhodesia. Each political party nominated two members of the Legislative Council to sit on the committee. Dr Kenneth Kaunda nominated me and James Skinner as UNIP's representatives. He appointed us to serve on what was an *ad-hoc committee* on the basis of our legal qualifications. Although we worked long hours on the committee, I enjoyed participating in the constitution-making exercise. The work was arduous but interesting. James Skinner and I gained some experience by working on the assignment with more experienced legal draftsmen from the attorney-general's chambers in the Ministry of Legal Affairs. Nonetheless, we were pleased that the attorney-general appreciated our efforts and contribution to the preparation of a draft of the 1964 Independence Constitution.

Officially the Constitutional Review Commission was appointed on 22 November 1993 with the publication of Statutory Instrument number 15 in the Government Gazette. The commission's terms of reference were set out in detail in the Statutory Instrument. The terms of reference were very wide indeed – fourteen in all. In fact, they were wider than those of any previous constitution commission in Zambia. The government gave this broad mandate to the commission to enable it to consider provisions for the creation of an open, transparent and democratic society and for a constitution intended "to stand the test of time". As a member of the commission and its chairman, I considered the challenge of the commission's task with awe and trepidation. The work had to be done in any event.

In the afternoon of 9 December 1993, after the commission was sworn-in at State House, we held our first meeting at Mulungushi International Conference Centre. Although we met without a set agenda, a number of important decisions were made at the meeting. The commissioners discussed a draft programme for the primary task of reaching as many people as possible for the purpose of collecting both oral and written submissions. The commissioners decided to visit all the provincial centres in the country. The strategy was initially to undertake an extensive tour of the country and to hold plenary sessions later for the purpose of analysing all the views of the petitioners. That was the best approach – consideration of views of petitioners before determining constitutional principles for incorporation in a new constitution.

The commission's first meeting was particularly important to me. It provided an opportunity to meet some commissioners I only knew on paper. I realised that the government attached great importance to the constitution-making exercise judging by the calibre and eminence of the men and women chosen to be members of the commission. Out of the original list of twenty two commissioners, seven men and women were nominated by the president. The seven nominees included a chief; a chieftainess; a headman of a village in the North-Western Province; a prominent civil rights activist; and the chairman-designate. Political parties were allowed to nominate four commissioners. The political parties selected Professor MP Mvunga, MP; E Mwansa, MP, a lawyer; Dr DK Mwaba, a medical practitioner; and a well known former University of Zambia student activist, Azwell Banda. Two men were selected to represent religious organisations, namely Bishop George Mpundu and Reverend Mwape Chilekwa. Six commissioners were representatives of recognized institutions and professional associations. They included two academics, namely Professor LS Shimba; and Dr EM Beele. Lastly, the non-governmental organisations were represented on the commission by Father I Bantungwa, Mrs H Fyfe and Miss Beatrice Chileshe.

I was satisfied with the calibre and experience of the men and women appointed to sit on the commission entrusted with the responsibility of preparing a draft of a new constitution for Zambia. I personally had no illusions whatsoever about the enormity of our assignment. However, I was confident that working together as a team it would be possible to accomplish the task satisfactorily. It was obvious to me that this would be difficult without a spirit of team work among the commissioners. I resolved from the first meeting of the commissioners that it was my duty to promote team spirit among them in the early days of our work.

Later, I found that the task of building bridges was not easy. In Zambia at that time rivalry between political parties was very strong indeed. Two years after the general elections in 1991 it was understandable that the members of opposing parties distrusted each other. My role as chairman, nonetheless, was to strive at all times to reconcile conflicting positions of commissioners in discussions. When it was impossible to achieve a consensus I preferred then to put proposals to a vote. This seemed to me the only democratic way of resolving contentious issues. I do not remember an occasion when I was obliged to exercise the chairman's casting vote although it was always available if the need arose for its exercise. Indeed, during many years of public service, I learnt this lesson that to succeed in life one must lead others by example. I wanted the commissioners to be objective at all times in the determination of various constitutional issues. My plea would have fallen on deaf ears if I was not objective in the decisions I took every day.

I knew that I had authority as chairman of the Constitutional Review Commission. However, I had also learnt from experience that I was more likely to succeed in my work by soliciting goodwill from my colleagues than by imposing my authority upon them. In that way, I received respect from practically all my colleagues and the supporting administrative staff. That is the way I endeavoured to create *esprit de corps* among the commissioners. I had more friends among commissioners, administrative staff, secretaries, drivers and office orderlies when we completed our task on 16 June 1995.

The second meeting of the commission was held on 10 December 1993 at Mulungushi International Conference Centre. At this meeting, commissioners elected Mrs Lucy Banda Sichone as vice chairperson to the commission. She was a renowned political activist who fearlessly championed the promotion of human rights in Zambia. She fervently supported the movement for promotion of gender equality. Professor Lawrence Shimba was elected vice chairperson in her place subsequently. At first Mr Bilika Simamba was appointed secretary to the commission by the government. Later, on his request, he was relieved of his duties. Consequently, President Frederick Chiluba appointed a constitutional lawyer, Dr Sipula Kabanje, as secretary. Mr Villie Lambanya, a senior civil servant, was the commission's vice secretary. Later, more supporting staff were required to assist the commission in the task of summarising in simple form the major trends from the evidence received from petitioners in various parts of the country. For this task, the commission was fortunate to engage three scholars from the University of Zambia. Dr K Hansungule (now Professor Hansungule) and Dr A Chanda were lecturers in the School of Law and Dr C Namafe was a lecturer in the School of Education.

For the final phase of our work, after the completion of public sittings we planned to meet at the River Motel in Kafue to debate thoroughly the constitutional principles and to develop a consensus on the content of the draft constitution. For this purpose, Pastor Manyema and Mrs Daisy Ng'ambi were in attendance throughout proceedings of the plenary sessions as members of the team of drafting experts. They were appointed on the first day of the commission's plenary session which sat at River Motel in Kafue from 13 February to 2 March, 1995.

Without exception, everywhere during the commission's sittings, the members were warmly welcomed by government officials and leaders of all political parties, by the members of the public generally and representatives of various interest groups. The confidence of the public in general in the Constitutional Review Commission was overwhelming. Often, at public sittings my emotions were aroused by the overwhelming support we received in every district we visited in Zambia. The support was expressed in songs and dance, poems and messages of solidarity. By implication, the universal support we received was a reminder to me that our people did not expect the Constitutional Review Commission to betray them at any stage of the constitution-making process.

In the report we submitted to the government after completion of our task, we recorded public response and support for the Commission thus:

> Everywhere the commission went a variety of petitioners turned up. Among petitioners who appeared and submitted to the commission were children, politicians, traditional rulers, members of the clergy, judges and magistrates. Associations took advantage of the commission's sittings and made representations. Notable among these were the Law Association of Zambia, (LAZ), the Press Association of Zambia, (PAZA), the Zambia Congress of Trade Unions,

(ZCTU) and the Economics Association of Zambia, (EAZ). Political parties also made their submissions. Men and women from all walks of life and different stations in life petitioned the commission. Among them were businessmen, students, farmers, civil servants, diplomats. Able-bodied petitioners as well as the lame and the blind all petitioned. It was a very satisfying and worthwhile experience for commissioners to see the old and the young come, in some cases after covering long distances.

Members of the Constitutional Review Commission travelled extensively throughout Zambia between March 1994 and September 1994. We held in all forty six public sittings in nine provinces. Altogether, the commission received evidence from 996 petitioners. At every public sitting, an interpreter was available to assist the petitioners and the commission. At all public proceedings of the commission, the state of the art equipment made it possible for commissioners to ask questions of clarification of pertinent issues because proceedings were audio recorded. Due regard was, of course, given to written submissions even where a petitioner did not give oral evidence. Anticipating that some petitioners might rely on written or oral evidence only, at its first meeting we advised the secretariat to prepare a questionnaire on constitutional reform. Subsequently, early in January 1994, thousands of neatly folded copies of the questionnaire were distributed throughout Zambia. The brochures were entitled "Guiding Questions on Constitutional Issues". Each brochure had thirteen columns on both sides and carried a total number of twenty four topics, such as "The Constitution and its Objects"; "Citizenship"; "Fundamental Human Rights and Freedoms of Individuals and Groups"; "Political Systems and Political Parties"; "Traditional Rulers"; "The Presidency"; "The Electoral System"; "Judiciary"; "Legislature"; "The Army"; "Leadership Code of Conduct"; and many others. The commission also produced and widely distributed thousands of copies of a small brochure entitled "The Constitutional Review Commission: Terms of Reference: 1994".

Each topic in the questionnaire had a number of sub-topics which were the specific questions a petitioner was required to answer. The total number of sub-topics or questions from twenty four topics was one hundred and ninety seven. Some topics had only two, three or four subtopics. On the other hand, under some topics there might be as many subtopics as ten or fifteen. For example, under "Political Systems and Political Parties" the subtopics were: (a) Should Zambia have traditional rulers at all? (b) If so, what role should they play? and (c) Would it be in the best interest of democracy to revive the political authority of traditional rulers? If so give reasons. If not, give reasons. Under "Leadership code of conduct", the subtopics were as follows:

(a)　　Should Zambians have a Leadership Code and for what reasons?

(b)　　What should be included in such Leadership Code?

(c)　　What categories of leaders should be subjected to such Code?

(d)　　What punishment should accompany breach of the Code of Conduct?

(e)　　What machinery and/or institutions would be effective in enforcing the Leadership Code?

(f)　　How can the contents of the Leadership Code become part of the culture of Zambians?

(g)　　Any other suggestions, besides the Leadership Code, for ensuring that only good leaders get into public office and for punishing those who abuse office?

All written answers to the "Questionnaire on Constitutional Reform" were sent to the secretary at the commission's secretariat in Ndeke House Annex in Lusaka. They were later forwarded to the team of research assistants responsible for summarising the major trends from both oral and written evidence. I was satisfied at the end of the

460

constitution-making assignment that the commission had devised an excellent programme and method of work at its inaugural meeting. The task of collecting views "from the general public both in rural and urban areas ... on what type of constitution Zambia should enact" was satisfactorily accomplished by the commission in accordance with the first term of reference.

However, occasionally I encountered difficulties in guiding members of the commission to ensure that its objective was achieved. The difficulties I encountered were not in any way induced by the more aggressive commissioners during public sittings or in our private discussions but by the tendency among some petitioners to raise totally irrelevant issues in their submissions. In such situations I was obliged to exercise a firm hand and invariably, although politely, refused to allow evidence to be given which had no relevance whatsoever to the commission's terms of reference.

In guiding the proceedings at public sittings, I was conscious of the danger of opening Pandora's box and setting a dangerous precedent if I ever allowed one petitioner to give evidence which was completely outside the commission's terms of reference. For instance, there were men and women in the country who were anxious to petition the commission to recommend the desirability of a federal rather than the existing unitary state in order to promote equity and political stability in Zambia. In the opinion of the commissioners, even the widest interpretation of the terms of reference did not accommodate that viewpoint.

Under the tour programme the commission was expected to hold public hearings in the Western Province from 5 April to 11 April 1994. Public sittings of the commission were arranged in Mongu, the provincial capital, from 6 April to 7 April. Before the commissioners' departure for Western Province, I learnt from the grapevine that advocates of self-rule for "Barotseland" intended to disrupt meetings of the commission in the Western Province to strengthen the demand for the restoration of the

Barotseland Agreement of 1964. Later, I received similar information which was leaked to me deliberately, perhaps through intelligence sources.

It occurred to me at that stage that I was being alerted to take the necessary precautions to ensure that the commission's work was not unduly disrupted in the Western Province. However, after careful reflection I decided to ignore the reports. I thought that they were ill-conceived or exaggerated. I preferred to rely on the reports of the commission's staff responsible for arranging provincial tours under William Muleba, the administrative officer. He was the leader of the advance party which travelled to the Western Province to ensure that all necessary logistics were in place for the arrival of the commission. If the advance party had observed signs of hostility to the commission from the general public or members of the Barotse Royal Establishment, William Muleba would have reported such a situation to the secretary before the commission's departure for the Western Province.

Indeed, there was in reality no evidence of hostility to the commission when we arrived in the Western Province. Our tour of the Western Province was actually the most interesting and successful of all our tours throughout the length and breadth of Zambia. The commission received a warm welcome from the public and from the Litunga, whom I had personally known for many years. We were particularly pleased to receive a message of goodwill from him on behalf of the Lozi people. Furthermore, he had instructed his Ngambela (the prime minister in the administrative structure of the Barotse Royal Establishment) to host a luncheon for the commissioners in Mongu – a rare honour which we were not accorded in any other province.

The Litunga contributed to the deliberations of the commission by instructing trusted representatives of the Barotse Royal Establishment to submit a petition to the commission at a public hearing in Mongu. The petition was intended to emphasise the demand of many Lozi-speaking people for the restoration of the Barotseland Agreement in the new constitution. However, there were some petitioners who rejected this idea. The commission visited five district centres in the Western Province to collect views from the public on what type of constitution Zambia should enact. During public sittings at Kaoma, Mongu, Senanga, Nangweshi and Sesheke from 7 April to 11 April, seventy petitioners made oral submissions. We also received thirty seven written submissions from petitioners and institutions in the Western Province. The contribution by the people of the Western Province to the constitution-making exercise was greatly appreciated.

The enthusiasm of the Zambian people for the work of the Constitutional Review Commission was unabated throughout the country. On my part, it was an honour and indeed a great privilege to chair a commission which enjoyed the confidence of very many people in Zambia. In our final report at the end of the constitution-making exercise, we recorded our gratitude to the people of Zambia for their support as follows:-

> Finally, the commission is greatly indebted to all the Zambian people throughout the country for enthusiastically responding and supporting the review exercise. In many places, the people prayed for members of the commission to succeed in the exercise and travel safely. The contributions made by them, individually, or collectively, greatly helped the commission in addressing a number of critical issues.

Unfortunately, life is not always a bed of roses. Although the commissioners worked as a team over a period of eighteen months, there were times when serious differences of opinion strained relations between some commissioners. In such situations, I endeavoured to reconcile the warring parties. That was my duty as chairman of the Constitutional Review Commission. However, one day at a public sitting in Chipata there was suddenly a war of words between commissioners in the presence of petitioners and other members of the local community. There was a confrontation between two groups on purely tribal lines. They attacked each other on issues which were totally unrelated to the commission's terms of reference. I was embarrassed listening to mudslinging which revealed deep-rooted mistrust or hatred among them. This spectacle also embarrassed the more sober-minded of commissioners present at the public hearing of petitions on 19 September 1994. The efforts I made to restore order were unsuccessful.

Consequently, to the surprise of the commissioners and the audience, I suddenly walked out of the hall without making any statement. It was not my intention to continue chairing the sitting of the commissioners ostensibly for collecting views from the general public when they spent more time quarrelling among themselves. I retired to my room in Luangwa House, the government hostel in Chipata. Later, I was informed that the vice chairman, Professor Lawrence Shimba, refused to take the chair in order to continue the meeting. Therefore, the public meeting on that day ended abruptly.

I agonized considerably in my room over the events of that day. They left me with a feeling that such events might again occur with perhaps more disastrous consequences. The more I reflected on the possibility of a similar occurrence in future, the more I felt that it was necessary at that stage to consider the option of resigning from the Constitutional Review Commission immediately.

Late in the evening on that day, quite unexpectedly, two commissioners came to visit me in my room. The visitors were two respected men of God – Father Ives Bantungwa and Reverend Mwape Chilekwa – who felt concerned about the abrupt manner in which the proceedings of the commission were concluded on that day. Their visit was welcome indeed. It gave me the opportunity of discussing my concerns with them. Even more importantly, I had the opportunity of another opinion on the advantages and disadvantages of resigning from the commission. In the course of our discussion, they convinced me that it was honourable to endure hardship in the service of one's fellow human beings. If I felt that the overall cause of the Constitutional Review Commission was noble, then it was for me to be ready at all times to carry the cross.

I resolved to chair the public sitting of the commission the following day and to carry the cross until the task was accomplished. Then we prayed together. From that day I did not look back on past difficulties and frustration until the commission's task was accomplished in June 1995. Consequently, I have been eternally grateful to Father Ives Bantungwa and Reverend Mwape Chilekwa for their support and encouragement in the evening on that fateful day.

The programme of tours in Zambia started in March 1994. They ended with public hearings for the second time in Lusaka from 28 to 30 September 1994. Public sittings of the commission in the Lusaka Council Chamber gave the public and representatives of various political parties a second and last opportunity to make submissions to the commission. After the last public hearings the commission went into recess. It was necessary to allow sufficient time to its officials to complete the preparation of documents on the views collected from the general public on the type of constitution Zambia was to enact. Later in the new year the commissioners assembled at River Motel in Kafue for the composition of the report and the Draft Constitution of Zambia. The plenary session of the commission sat at the River Motel from 13 February to 2 March 1995 specifically to identify constitutional principles from the evidence received and to debate them fully in order to reach consensus on the basic principles for inclusion in the Draft Constitution. President Frederick Chiluba had directed the commission to submit the report and the Draft Constitution to him "as soon as possible after the commissioners have completed their inquiries and decided upon the recommendations". The government without any doubt attached urgency to the completion of the constitution-making exercise.

Throughout my involvement in this exercise on behalf of the nation, I was not under any illusion about the difficulties ahead after completion of the first phase, that is to say the collecting of views from the general public. In particular, I knew

465

that attempts to reach consensus on the constitutional principles to adopt were likely to be difficult to achieve. I anticipated that that aspect of the commissions work would be the greatest challenge to me and other members of the commission. The task of drafting the constitution after a consensus was achieved was a relatively easy one. By the end of April 1995, the assignment was completed. The efficiency of the drafting teams greatly facilitated completion of the commission's task satisfactorily. However, on certain fundamental issues differences among commissioners were so wide that it was impossible to achieve a consensus. Therefore, in accordance with democratic norms, some commissioners preferred to submit their own minority reports regarding constitutional principles on which they failed to agree with the majority. Professor Patrick Mvunga, MP, Mrs Lucy Sichone and Mr Azwell Banda submitted a ten page minority report which was comprehensive on constitutional issues and proposals on which their reservations were specifically recorded. Other minority reports, two or three pages in length, were submitted by Messrs Richard Mukelebai, Mushota Chakomboka, Humphrey Dyololo and Miss Beatrice Chileshe. The minority reports were reproduced in Part XIII of the main report, a document of about three hundred pages with seven appendices.

Our commission raised a wide range of constitutional issues in its report. Some issues were simple and non-controversial. Others were fundamental constitutional issues which were nonetheless straightforward and non-controversial. For example, we considered the role of English in Zambia and recommended its continued use as an official language. We stated in the report that all petitioners were in favour of the retention of a republican form of government and, therefore, recommended that Zambia remained a sovereign republic. This was a fundamental constitutional issue; yet it was non-controversial even to the government which readily accepted the commission's recommendation.

However, under the terms of reference it was the

commission's obligation to resolve many difficult constitutional principles before incorporating them in the Draft Constitution of Zambia. In this regard, the commissioners' recommendations were mainly based on the views of petitioners in their oral and written submissions. With perhaps only a few exceptions, the commissioners resolved important constitutional issues by adopting the wishes of the majority of petitioners. They accepted that a constitution which reflected the wishes of the people was more likely to stand the test of time. Conversely, they maintained that it was impossible for a constitution to endure even for one generation without popular support. This was a viewpoint I, too, supported for it was compatible with Zambia's multi-party liberal democracy restored in 1991. Indeed, the need to canvass popular support for the Draft Constitution before its adoption in Parliament was really an obsession with me. I firmly believed that in the final analysis the legitimacy of the constitution depended on the popular support it received from the general public in Zambia.

In spite of numerous difficulties which confronted the commissioners, the work was completed in record time. Within three weeks, the plenary session successfully identified constitutional principles from evidence received, thoroughly debated them and developed consensus on principles to be reflected in the Draft Constitution. It was understood that the task of drafting the constitution was more difficult and time-consuming than the process of identifying constitutional principles. Therefore, the commission adjourned on 2 March 1995. The team of drafting experts then took over the responsibility of preparing a Draft Constitution of Zambia. They were in attendance throughout the plenary session.

However, when commissioners left River Motel on 2 March 1995, I remained for consultations with the secretary and the team responsible for drafting the commission's report who required my guidance and assistance from time to time. In order to perform these responsibilities satisfactorily, I needed assistance from one or two commissioners. Therefore, I requested the commission's vice chairman, Professor Lawrence Shimba, to remain with me at the River Motel for the duration of the work of drafting a new Zambian constitution and preparation of the report. Additionally, I requested Dr Ernest Beele to join us. I was satisfied that together we constituted a strong team, a sort of "triumvirate" capable of providing the advice and assistance which the legal draftspersons might require.

When the final plenary session was held at River Motel in mid June 1995, the commissioners had no difficulty in approving the Draft Constitution and the Draft Report after they had re-discussed some of the documents. They also adopted at the final plenary session a resolution to release the Report and Draft Constitution immediately to both the electronic and public media "in order to ensure a high degree of public debate". For this purpose, the secretariat arranged a press briefing at the River Motel at which I issued a statement confirming that the work of the Constitutional Review Commission was completed satisfactorily. The statement also included a summary of the major constitutional principles which the commission had adopted for inclusion in the Draft Constitution. The general public was invited to debate the constitutional proposals in order to advance the democratic process of consultation before the enactment of a constitution intended to stand the test of time.

In order to test the efficacy of the Draft Constitution as a legal document, we had invited Mr Paul Fifoot from the United Kingdom to offer his expert advice. I arranged for this before the commissioners were invited to attend the final plenary session at River Motel to discuss and approve the Draft Constitution. Mr Paul Fifoot was a renowned legal draftsman who had worked for many years in the Commonwealth Office in London before his retirement a year before the appointment of the Constitutional Review Commission. He was not invited to advise the commission on the constitutional principles we had adopted. This was entirely the preserve of commissioners after consideration of the views collected from the general public during sittings of the commission throughout Zambia.

It was a great tribute and a source of pride to our team of drafting experts, Pastor Charles Manyema and Miss Daisy Ng'ambi, when we received Mr Paul Fifoot's complimentary remarks on our Draft Constitution. His satisfaction with our work was expressed in superlative terms. Mr Paul Fifoot was thorough and meticulous where he criticised the Draft Constitution. He made valuable suggestions which greatly improved the document. Therefore, at the end of the constitution-making exercise, I wrote a letter to the British high commissioner in Lusaka to thank the United Kingdom government for sponsoring a renowned legal draftsman to offer his expert advice on the Draft Constitution. Similarly, I conveyed special thanks to the governments of the United States of America, Denmark, and Finland who provided financial and material support to the Constitutional Review Commission in addition to the funding it received from the government of the Republic of Zambia.

In the statement released to the press at River Motel, a number of constitutional principles were accorded special significance. They were constitutional principles which in the opinion of the commission deserved public debate. The commissioners took note of the objective of the term of reference number fourteen which obliged them to "endeavour to ensure a high degree of public debate on constitutional proposals for a democratic Zambia". In December 1991, President Frederick Chiluba declared Zambia a Christian nation. The presidential declaration of Zambia as a Christian nation took many people in Zambia by surprise because it was made less than six weeks after Dr Frederick Chiluba's election as the second republican president. Therefore, it attracted comments from many petitioners during the commission's public hearings in many parts of the country. Some petitioners strongly argued that it was necessary to reaffirm in the constitution that Zambia was a Christian nation. However, other petitioners strongly felt that it was undesirable to include a provision which made Zambia a Christian nation. They maintained that a clear demarcation was necessary between religion and the state. By virtue of the presidential declaration of Zambia as a Christian state Zambia was a *de facto* Christian nation.

The commission noted that the majority of petitioners did not favour the inclusion of a provision in the constitution for making Zambia a Christian nation. It was the commission's conclusion that Christianity or any other religion was secure without any formal declaration in the constitution. We reached this conclusion with the full support of the religious leaders in our midst, namely Father Ives Bantungwa and Reverend Mwape Chilekwa. Therefore, in our report we recommended "that Zambia should not adopt a state religion but should remain a secular state". The recommendation was not accepted by the government. In the white paper (Government Paper No. 1 of 1995), the government stated its position clearly and unambiguously that it was desirable to provide in the preamble to the constitution "that Zambia is a Christian nation which is tolerant of other religions". Presumably, by avoiding inclusion of the provision in the constitution itself but rather inserting it in the preamble, an acceptable compromise was thereby reached.

From term of reference number three, the commissioners noted the government's interest in strengthening the protection of human rights in Zambia. To this end, the government expected the commission to consider inclusion of "appropriate arrangements for the entrenchment and protection of human rights". A majority of petitioners also supported this viewpoint. The commission recommended the establishment of an independent Permanent Human Rights Commission for the enforcement of human rights. The government accepted the recommendation because it was "in fact in line with the government decision made when announcing the Munyama Human Rights Commission but will be established under an Act of Parliament as an investigative commission".

Our commission also recommended for the first time in Zambia the establishment of a Constitutional Court with jurisdiction over a wide range of matters of a constitutional nature including "any violation of a guaranteed fundamental human right". Additionally, the proposed Constitutional Court's jurisdiction included "the determination of any other matters as may be entrusted to it by the constitution or any other law". In its white paper, the government rejected the commission's recommendation for two reasons; that a separate division of the High Court was capable of handling adequately the volume of work proposed for the Constitutional Court, and that existing infrastructure and resources were not adequate to support "a proliferation of courts". Subsequently, experience has shown that the volume of work of a constitutional nature has continued to overwhelm the High Court because a separate division has never been established.

The election of the president was a subject which attracted comments from a large number of petitioners in various parts of the country. Generally, the views of petitioners were divided into two categories. Some petitioners supported the existing provisions in the 1991 Constitution for election of the Zambian president. Others proposed new rules to govern presidential elections. The new rules proposed by some petitioners included citizenship qualifications for a presidential candidate. The evidence received from petitioners on this issue was summarised in the commission's report thus:

> Although it was agreed by petitioners that the presidential candidate ought to be a Zambian citizen, many petitioners felt that in this regard the citizenship ought to be qualified. There were views that the candidate must be a Zambian by birth with both his/her parents being Zambians by birth. The commission observed that the majority of petitioners just fell short of restricting the presidency only to black and indigenous Zambians. These petitioners wished the presidency restricted to those Zambians whose ancestors had villages in Zambia. Yet, other petitioners were attracted to the provisions of the United States Constitution which restricted and qualified the type of citizen who could run for the presidency. Others thought that it was sufficient if the presidential candidate's parents were

born in Zambia.

After careful consideration of various proposals, the commission by a majority agreed that to qualify for the office of president the candidate must be "a Zambian citizen born in Zambia"; with "his or her parents born in Zambia of Zambian citizens"; and must be a person who has been "a resident in Zambia for twenty years". The first two qualifications for a presidential candidate were accepted by the government. However, the first qualification was recast merely to read the presidential candidate "must be a Zambian citizen". The second qualification was also rephrased to read "both his/her parents must be Zambians by birth". The Commission's third qualification was not accepted by the government. The "citizenship clause" in the Zambian Constitution approved by Parliament in May 1996 is contained in Article 34 (3) as follows:

34.(3) A person shall be qualified to be a candidate for election as President if–

(a) he is a Zambian citizen;

(b) both his parents are Zambians by birth or descent;

(c) he has attained the age of thirty five years;

(d) he is a member of, or is sponsored by, a political party;

(e) he is qualified to be elected as a member of the National Assembly; and

(f) has been domiciled in Zambia for a period of at least twenty years.

The "citizenship clause" was undoubtedly a contentious proposal in the Draft Constitution we published with the commission's report in mid June 1995 at River Motel. In subsequent discussions among politicians, the "citizenship clause" was labelled as "discriminatory" and contrary to other provisions in the Draft Constitution on the right to equality before the law under fundamental rights and freedoms. Some political leaders and other people believed that the "citizenship clause" was introduced in the Draft Constitution as a way of eliminating Dr Kenneth Kaunda, the first president of Zambia, from contesting the presidential and parliamentary elections in 1996 against the incumbent president, Dr Frederick Chiluba, and other candidates. They believed that, with Dr Kenneth Kaunda's Malawian parentage, he was unlikely to fulfil the requirements of the citizenship clause proposed in the Draft Constitution. That speculation was, in fact, without foundation. Many petitioners strongly felt that a presidential candidate had to be not only a Zambian citizen but also a Zambian by birth with both his/her parents being Zambian by birth.

The Mvunga Commission of 1991 limited for the first time in the constitutional history of Zambia the tenure of office of president to "two terms of five years each". For avoidance of doubt, it was provided in Article 35 (3) of the 1991 Constitution that "… the period of two terms of five years each shall be computed from the commencement of this Constitution". An overwhelming number of petitioners recommended the retention of the current two five year terms for the office of president. Consequently, in our report the commission recommended that every president should hold the position for a period of five years and should be eligible for re-election to one more five year term. The government accepted the commission's recommendation. In fact, in the government's white paper, the commission's recommendation was recast and phrased in a manner conveying emphatically the concept of only two terms of five years each for the tenure of office of president.

Another non-controversial recommendation in our commission's report related to the institution of chieftainship and its role in society in Zambia. In submissions of petitioners in all parts of Zambia, commissioners were advised that nothing should in any way detract or derogate from the honour and dignity of the institution of chieftaincy. The petitioners also urged the commissioners to include provisions in the Draft Constitution for involvement of chiefs in the governance of the people. The commission made one important recommendation, among others, relating to the institution of chieftaincy. We recommended the restoration of the House of Chiefs as an advisory body to the government on traditional, customary and related matters. The commission's recommendation was accepted by the government.

However, in the opinion of all the commissioners, one of the most important terms of reference for their inquiries concerned the wish of the government to be advised on the "mode of adoption" of the Draft Constitution submitted with the report. In the ninth term of reference, the commission was directed to "recommend on whether the constitution should be adopted by the National Assembly or by a constituent assembly, by a national referendum or by any other method". Essentially, term of reference number nine meant that the government was anxious to be advised on the best method of adoption of the constitution. The approach of the commissioners was to find a method of adoption which satisfied two criteria – the legitimacy and durability of the constitution. Both criteria depended upon the views of the people. The petitioners' views throughout the country favoured adoption of the constitution by a constituent assembly and a national referendum. The commissioners unanimously agreed with the overwhelming views of petitioners. We recorded our finding on this subject as follows:

> In agreeing with the overwhelming views of petitioners and the rationale and reasons advanced, the commission finds it unavoidable and compelling to recommend unanimously adoption by a constituent assembly and a national referendum.

This recommendation was not accepted by the government. In fact, it was at pains to justify the rejection of the commission's recommendation on the mode of adopting the constitution. The reasons given by the government for rejecting the recommendation were trivial and unconvincing. The commission emphasised in its report that its recommendation was based on "the overwhelming views of petitioners and the rationale or reasons advanced ....". Before the commission reached its decision, careful consideration was given to the legal implications of such a decision. Fortunately, there were five lawyers on the commission, including Professor Lawrence Shimba, Professor Patrick Mvunga and Dr Ernest Beele. In spite of the availability of legal expertise on the commission, we sought an independent opinion on this subject from Mr Paul Fifoot. He supported the popular view of adopting the constitution by a constituent assembly and national referendum. He, too, did not anticipate serious legal difficulties in the implementation of such a recommendation.

There was an outcry from many people throughout the country who felt that the government had chosen to deprive them of their democratic right to participate in the all important and final stage of the constitution-making process. Yet it was the same government which had directed the Constitutional Review Commission in terms of referendum number nine to "recommend on whether the constitution should be adopted by the National Assembly or by a constituent assembly, by a national referendum or by any other method". Some sarcastic members of the public stated that the government was quite innocent when the terms of reference were set out for the Constitutional Review Commission. Eighteen months later, when the commissioners submitted their report and Draft Constitution to the president of Zambia, members of the government knew by then that power was sweet! Therefore, at that time adoption of the constitution by the National Assembly made more sense than the adoption of the constitution by a constituent assembly or by a national referendum. In fact, it was a national catastrophe when "it (the government) rejected the people's constitution". Instead, "it dictated amendments to the Draft Constitution".*

Public reaction was hostile to the government's rejection of the mode of adopting the constitution recommended by the

---

* Article on "Constitutional Review" by Green Musonda in Saturday Post newspaper on 30 November 2002.

commission. The Citizens' Convention was organised by the Civil Society Action Committee early in 1996 to intensify the campaign against the government's decision. The convention organized by the Civil Society Action Committee was held at the Mulungushi International Conference Centre from 1 March to 10 March 1996. The convention was a great success. It was attended by 262 people, each participating as a citizen and not representing any organisation. At the end of the convention, the organizers produced the "Citizen's Green Paper".

The chairman of the Steering Committee presented on 11 April 1996 the Citizen's Green Paper on the Constitution of Zambia. On that occasion, he delivered the Civil Society's statement in which he summarised the story of the determination of the Zambian people to participate in the constitution-making process in their country. The presentation stated, in part:

> Unfortunately, government did not keep its word to make the Draft Constitution and Report widely available to the public or to provide fora for the intensive debate of substantive issues therein.

> Instead, the process was begun to enact a constitution that could only be viewed as a government constitution. It was for this reason that a number of church organisations and NGOs came together in October, 1995.

> Their aim was simply to raise awareness and ensure a high degree of public debate on substantive issues in the constitution and agitate for a popular method of adoption.

> When the government insisted on going ahead with the production of a White Paper, Civil Society decided to bring together citizens to debate the Mwanakatwe Draft Constitution and come up with their position. Please note that participants to the Citizen's Convention did not consider any document other than the Mwanakatwe Draft Constitution.

> It is civil society's view that it has carried out the process as it

was envisaged by the government before it was sidetracked. That government had intended for the constitution to be produced by the people of Zambia is evidenced by the terms of reference prepared by the government for the Review Commission. Unfortunately, it would seem that along the way some considerations which have not been revealed to the people of Zambia obliged them to produce a "private constitution".

The green paper is not floated as a final or infallible document. It is a contribution to the ongoing debate which we expect will culminate in a popular mode of adoption of the constitution.

It is a position paper of over 300 citizens who gathered at Mulungushi from the 1st to 10th of March 1996. It is the duty of government to encourage similar process right across the country.

Let me state here that Civil Society is not and has never been against the enactment of the constitution by Parliament. Enactment is Parliament's constitutional duty and right. However, what is enacted should reflect the views of the people of Zambia. In other words, the views of a lot of "green papers" and thus the consensus of the people of Zambia.

The government should ensure that the Constitution Bill tabled before Parliament is a document of the people by the people and for the people of Zambia.

The Civil Society submitted a cast-iron case on the merits of the commission's recommendations in its report on the mode of adopting the constitution. The Civil Society's campaign was supported by Church organisations, in particular the Catholic Commission for Justice and Peace. Yet the government did not relent in its efforts to enact the constitution through Parliament but without a broad consensus of the people of Zambia. That is the manner in which the constitutional issue was settled. On 18 May 1996, Act No. 18 of 1996, the Constitution of Zambia (Amendment) Act, 1996, received the assent of the president and it was to be read as one with the Constitution of Zambia, Act No. 1 of 1991.

Nevertheless, the corridors of power both in State House and the Cabinet Office continue to be haunted by ghosts of men and women no longer living who strenuously advocated the adoption of the constitution by a constituent assembly and a national referendum to ensure the legitimacy and durability of the constitution. Six years later, this issue was raised in an editorial in the *Post* newspaper of 9 September 2002. It is the most popular and influential daily newspaper in Zambia, a newspaper which claims to "dig deeper" and pulls no punches. Fred Mmembe, the *Post* newspaper's managing director, reflected in an editorial on constitutional issues. In some paragraphs of the editorial, Fred Mmembe exposed the insincerity of the political leaders in government when the commission submitted its report and Draft Constitution to the president in 1996. He observed thus:

> The observations on the constitution made by Namwala village headpersons at a Women for Change (WfC) organised human rights, democracy and development workshop deserve serious consideration. Their call for the changing of the constitution because it is at the mercy of the president is well founded.

> In particular, the observation made by Senior Headman Shayawa of Maala village that our country's constitution only serves the interests of the president because he is the one who endorses and rejects the draft copy, has a lot of truth in it.

> And with the way our constitution is made, one cannot disagree with WfC information officer Douglas Chipoya's observation that it is not correct to describe the constitution as the people's constitution when the citizens have never seen it, didn't understand it and didn't take part in formulating it. Governance in Zambia, like in most of Africa, is basically still by trial and error methods; single party hegemony is by no means dead and buried; and the political system continues to be precarious and the constitution transient.

Since the 1960s, when most countries in Africa achieved independence, there has been a remarkable output of national constitutions in almost every state on the continent. The tragedy though is that most of these constitutions tend to be seriously deficient in quality and in meeting legitimate expectations of the people for which they are drafted. More often than not, they correspond to the particular taste of succeeding political regimes. The constitutions which are introduced at fairly short intervals tend to be short-lived.

In 1990, again, a constitutional review commission was appointed to draft a new constitution enshrining principles of political pluralism to guide the proposed Third Republic. One of the MMD's key promises during the election campaign of 1991 was that it would re-write the Republican Constitution to strengthen the protection of civil liberties and to ensure the de-linkage of party and government. The MMD government demonstrated reluctance to deliver on its promise. However, after much pressure both local and international, the MMD relented and in November 1993, a twenty four member review commission was appointed to collect views from the general public and provide proposals for the content of a new constitution. The commission recommended that the constitution be adopted by a constituent assembly. Significantly, President Chiluba rejected the adoption of the revised constitution by a constituent assembly recommended by the commission pursuant to the terms of reference preferring his National Assembly.

It is clear that Zambia has not yet undertaken a popular or people driven comprehensive review of the constitution. It is important to involve the citizens in any constitution-making process. The legitimacy of the constitution is crucial for constitutionalism and democratic consolidation. A constitution should be generally understood by the people and acceptable to them. The people must be made to identify themselves with the constitution. Without this sense of identification, of attachment and involvement, a constitution would always

479

remain a remote artificial object with no more real existence than the paper on which it is written.

Women for Change is a well organised, powerful and influential non-governmental organisation specifically mandated to protect and advance women's interests in Zambia. In promoting the interests of women generally, the relevance of provisions in the Constitution of the Republic of Zambia come under scrutiny at seminars and workshops. The organisation's role supplements in many ways the efforts of other civil society activists in promoting acceptable democratic norms and human rights. The Oasis Forum is another organisation which organized countrywide workshops for the sole purpose of sensitising citizens about the necessity to review the Constitution of Zambia in order to strengthen democracy.

At an Oasis Forum sponsored public debate in Mansa a resolution was adopted on an issue which was controversial in the commission's report – the presidential clause which requires a candidate to be a third generation Zambian to contest elections. *The Daily Mail* newspaper of 5 August 2002 reported on the front page in bold letters "Luapula reaffirms presidential clause". It was reported that at the Oasis Forum at Mansa Hotel the participants "generally and strongly felt that only an indigenous Zambian should be given a chance to lead the country". That resolution illustrated the important fact that a constitution can only endure when it is generally understood by the people and acceptable to them.

In mid June, we came to the end of a truly gruelling and demanding task. I was personally thankful to God that the team responsible for reviewing the Constitution of Zambia remained largely intact at the end of the exercise. It had not disintegrated in spite of the severe difficulties we encountered while collecting views from men and women who came to testify before the commission. It was a great relief to all commissioners when we released the Draft Constitution of Zambia at a press conference at the River Motel in Kafue. The commission's report and Draft

Constitution of Zambia were released to encourage public debate of the Draft Constitution and recommendations in the report in accordance with our terms of reference. I told the press that most commissioners were highly sceptical about the neutrality of the current National Assembly because one party had a majority. The idea of a constituent assembly and national referendum was recommended for the purpose of removing any such suspicions.

Shortly after the release of the Draft Constitution, State House aides were anxious to arrange a ceremony for the presentation of the commission's report and Draft Constitution of Zambia to the president. I confirmed my availability to present the documents at State House on 17 June 1995. Only a few officials from the secretariat of the commission were able to attend the ceremony with only two or three commissioners because the notice was too short. Furthermore, the majority of commissioners returned to their permanent homes after the press conference at River Motel.

Although I am not a suspicious person by nature, nonetheless I was surprised that the president had requested to meet me alone in the conference room in State House before the open-air ceremony his officials had arranged for the presentation of the documents to him. The few commissioners who came to State House to attend the ceremony and officials from our secretariat were excluded from the meeting. Apart from the president, Brigadier General Miyanda, the vice president, attended the meeting. Several cabinet ministers and the secretary to the cabinet, Aldridge Adamson, were in attendance too.

At the meeting the president openly rebuked me for releasing the Draft Constitution of Zambia and the commission's report to the public before the documents were made available to the government. He complained bitterly that no similar commission had in the past acted in the manner in which we had done. He maintained that the government should have been given the first opportunity to examine the documents before their release to the press for public debate.

Although the proceedings in the private meeting took me by surprise, I remained calm and listened attentively. Meanwhile, I was studying with interest the demeanour of the cabinet ministers and officials who were present in the meeting. I observed that Aldridge Adamson was embarrassed to see me being rebuked like a naughty schoolboy by a determined headmaster. I had worked with him for a few years in the Ministry of Education. In fact, I was instrumental in his promotion in 1965 from Ndola as a headmaster of a primary school for coloured children to a senior administrative post at the headquarters in Lusaka. His promotion was on merit and in line with UNIP's post-independence policy of localization of the civil service. He was silent throughout the meeting although his melancholy face betrayed his sympathy for me. We have always enjoyed respect for each other.

When the president concluded his statement, I exercised my right to reply which I did calmly and without equivocation. I was not apologetic at all. The decision to release the contents of the report and Draft Constitution was wholly in accordance with the commission's terms of reference. The terms of reference had been determined by the government. One term of reference directed the commission specifically to encourage public debate of its recommendations following the conclusion of its inquiries. To my surprise, Brigadier-General Godfrey Miyanda, the vice president, intervened in the discussion and strongly supported our commission's position. He reminded the president that a specific term of reference directed the commission to stimulate public debate on its findings and recommendations. Brigadier-General Miyanda's sincerity and courage impressed me considerably. No-one else, apart from Vice-President Godfrey Miyanda, came to my rescue! Not even the dynamic popular political figure – King Cobra!!

The president's agenda on that day was undoubtedly pre-determined. After my short speech prior to the public presentation of the commission's report and Draft Constitution, the president proceeded to castigate the commission for releasing the contents of the report and Draft Constitution to the general public in Zambia before their submission to the government. Pauline Banda of the *Zambia Daily Mail* wrote an article on 20 June on the president's speech published with bold headlines on the front page stating "Chiluba Censures Commissioners". The gist of the president's defence of his government's position was reported as follows:

> Unlike all other commissions which were appointed in the past, this is the first commission which has released reports to the press before the authorities can have a look at them.

> He said that while the government had no intention to doctor the constitution, Zambians should know that it was impossible to include the interests of each one of them in the constitution.

The mandate of the Constitutional Review Commission was to visit various parts of the country for the purpose of obtaining the views of the people on the Constitution of Zambia and their suggestions for improvement of its provisions. That mandate was fulfilled. In terms of reference number fourteen, the commission was directed "in the discharge of its responsibilities" to consult with the public and especially with relevant political and economic groups in order "to ensure a high degree of *public debate on constitutional proposals* on a democratic Zambia". That is precisely what the commission achieved when it released its report and the Draft Constitution of Zambia at a press conference on 16 June 1995 at the River Motel. Furthermore, an overwhelming number of petitioners who appeared before the commission urged the commissioners to publicise their findings and constitutional proposals as a safeguard against the possibility of the government doctoring the recommendations and Draft Constitution. Unfortunately, the reports and constitutional documents submitted by the Chona and Mvunga Commissions were doctored by the government of the day.

Asked by Father Miha Drevensek what was the most

satisfying aspect of my work with the Constitutional Review Commission, I unhesitatingly emphasised the joy I derived from the tremendous confidence of people in the integrity and capability of members of the commission. In his feature article for the *Challenge Magazine*, (3, vol 3 2001) my response was recorded as follows:

> The greatest satisfaction I derived from participating in its work was the tremendous cooperation which we received from men and women throughout the country. The large number of men and women who attended sittings of the commission in towns along the line of rail and in remote rural areas was a clear demonstration of their confidence in the integrity and capability of members of the commission.

We were, of course, aware that not all our recommendations would be acceptable to the government. Unfortunately, the government rejected those recommendations which were vital for according legitimacy and durability to the new Constitution of Zambia. A very large number of commissioners, perhaps all of them, expected the government to consider seriously the proposals intended to give concrete meaning to the idea of the constitution as being derived from the people. That did not come to pass. After presentation of the commission's report and Draft Constitution to the president at State House on 19 June 1995, I resolved not to agonize anymore about their fate. I left it to be determined by the government and historians.

CHAPTER

18

Return to my Second Home

I am often asked by my colleagues which person or institution has influenced my life most. I do not hesitate to inform them that Adams College is the institution to which I owe the greatest debt for what I am in life today. I lived, schooled and trained there from February 1942 to December 1948. It was my *alma mater* from the age of fifteen to the age of twenty two years – the formative years of my life. There I lived with young Zulu men and women and others from various provinces in South Africa. Many foreign students in those days enrolled at Adams College from far away countries in Central and Eastern Africa, such as Kenya and Uganda, Nyasaland and Southern Rhodesia now Malawi and Zimbabwe respectively.

Adams College was an elitist, missionary-run institution. The majority of the teaching staff were white men and women supported by a team of highly qualified African teachers. The tradition of this institution spanned a period of more than one hundred years at the time of my enrolment in form one in the high school department. Adams Mission Station and Adams College were founded by Dr Newton Adams in 1835. For most of the period of my studentship at Adams College, Professor Edgar H Brookes was the principal and his deputy was Dr KR Bruekner.

However, of all the outstanding scholars on the teaching staff of the high school and the teacher training department, Dr Donald GS Mthimkulu was my role model. He was the headmaster of the high school. He had a distinguished academic career in the mid 1920s at Fort Hare University College. It was at that time affiliated to the University of South Africa. He obtained a Bachelor of Arts degree with distinction in English and Ethics. He was also an outstanding athlete. As a sprinter, his record for one hundred yards remained unbeaten for many years. Dr Mthimkulu was also a good tennis player. Later, he obtained a master's degree from the University of South Africa and another master's degree from Yale University in the United States of America. His PhD degree was conferred on him at Yale University.

It was my good fortune that I had an excellent rapport with Dr Mthimkulu, my headmaster and English language teacher from form two through to form five. My interest in English literature, poetry and drama in particular, was stimulated primarily by him and to a lesser extent by Raymond Keet, a Rhodes scholar who was proud to have been an "Oxford Blue" as an outstanding rugby player at Oxford University. These men inspired me to aim for excellence in *all* my undertakings in life. The encouragement I was given by Dr Mthimkulu in my efforts is unforgettable. In the form two end of year examinations in December 1943, I obtained the highest marks in the combined results for three classes of approximately seventy five students. Because I performed badly in mathematics, his remarks in my report were good but qualified with the observation "he lacks the grit to withstand difficulties". Because he was my hero, I was not discouraged by his criticism at a time when I had performed exceptionally in the examinations as a whole. I accepted that Dr Mthimkulu was encouraging me to endeavour to achieve excellence in my academic work. It was at Adams College, quite early in my life, where I learnt that working hard has its rewards. In course of time, the habit of working hard haunted me throughout my life – as a teacher, a politician and a lawyer. Often, I remind my children and grandchildren today that there is some truth in the saying that one can rival a genius (a person with exceptional natural ability) "with ninety nine per cent *perspiration* and one per cent *inspiration*".

Even after my retirement recently from active legal practice, I keep myself occupied with work – sometimes too occupied to the disappointment of my wife and some of my friends. After my retirement, however, I have tried to spend and enjoy my leisure time visiting places of interest in my own country and elsewhere. During the first forty years of our married life, it was not convenient to visit my former institution of learning. Adams College is in Natal, South Africa, a country which was embroiled in the most difficult and complex racial conflicts of the twentieth century until liberated in 1994 by nationalists led by Nelson Mandela. Thereafter, it was my wife's dream that one day she would visit Adams College.

In April 2000, her dream became a reality. Mupanga, our eldest son, had arranged to go to Durban with his wife and children on a short holiday at Easter time. I have always missed the company of our grandchildren because of my personal preoccupations with mundane matters. I was keen to go to Durban during Easter to rest there and enjoy the company of our grandchildren at the same time. My wife was easily persuaded to come along with me for these reasons. However, for her the primary motive for supporting my proposal to holiday in Durban was to use that opportunity to visit Adams College. Thirty eight years after leaving Adams College, I was back at my "second home" in the company of my wife. It was a joyous occasion for me and my wife although in almost every respect we were both strangers. The students were out of the college on a short Easter break.

Fortunately, the members of staff who received us were kind and hospitable. The acting rector of the college instructed the public relations officer, Mr Desmond Makhanya, to show us various places of interest. The institution had changed almost beyond recognition. Many splendid modern buildings had been constructed over the years, but I found them less inspiring than the old structures I had known as a student in the 1940s. For my wife, the short visit to Adams College was a joyful experience for which she had waited patiently from the time I married her

487

in December 1952. Before our chauffeur drove us back to Durban, we again called on the acting rector to bid him farewell. I informed him that the discipline and learning I experienced during my stay at Adams College was instrumental in shaping my future. I was proud that I was its former student. Margaret and I felt that our visit to Adams College was a huge success and worthwhile. We both looked forward to another visit to my "second home" one day.

Since our visit to Adams College in 2000, we now endeavour every year to visit one or two places of interest in various parts of the world on holiday. Although I retired a few years ago from active law practice, nevertheless many fellow citizens believe that I can still render service to our country from time to time. It is often difficult to refuse and, for this reason, going out of the country for holidays offers the best opportunity for real rest.

After our visit to Adams College, I wrote a letter to an intimate friend, Uche Mbanefo, about our experiences on that occasion. Uche Mbanefo at one time in the 1980s lived in Zambia with his family as the World Bank's resident representative. On a few occasions, he requested me to write papers for the World Bank's reports and publications on development issues. Over the years, I developed a friendship with him on the basis of mutual trust and respect. The fact that he was (and still is) a Nigerian citizen was inconsequential to me. We had much in common. That was the important factor. He retired recently from the World Bank. On 7 June 2000, he wrote a letter encouraging me to moderate my habit of work. It contained an encouraging message to me as follows:

> It was a very great pleasure to receive your letter of May 19 which arrived here about four days ago.

> I am very happy to read that you and my sister, Margaret, have found time to take an enjoyable vacation in Durban. That sounds more like retirement! I think (although I am not sure) it was William Wordsworth who wrote:

"What is this life, if, full of care,
We have no time to stand and stare?
No time to see when woods we pass;
Where squirrels hide their nests in grass?"

While you were finally redeeming yourself by taking a well-deserved vacation, I was, for the first time in my life, copying the one habit I have been trying to get you to give up, namely, OVERWORK!!!

In the last 8 months I have written four training courses in project financial management: three for the World Bank Institute (WBI), and one for the ILO's International Training Centre, in Turin, Italy. I have been delivering two of the WBI courses here in Washington every month (sometimes twice a month), since last December. In addition, I have, since last July, travelled on business to Uganda, Mozambique, South Africa, Eritrea, and Swaziland (at the end of March).

My plan is to slow down this hectic pace of activity during the rest of this year, and into the next. After all, I did not retire from the World Bank to work harder and be put under greater stress, but rather to do the exact opposite!!! I have been praying to the Almighty to grant me the strength of will to achieve a better balance between work and play. It is flattering to be offered more work in retirement than one was doing in active employment, but I also realize that one can be flattered into an early grave, if one is not careful!!! In the first place, I expect some of the work I have been doing to automatically disappear. For example, once you have written a good training course, you do not have to keep rewriting it every year, but rather to update it as and when necessary.

I have always accepted that overworking in retirement has little value to an individual. However, I also believe that complete idleness in retirement has its own hazards. In reality dangers to a person's life are ever-present when they indulge in excesses in whatever they do at any stage in life. I believe it is important always to strive to achieve, as Uche Mbanefo observed in the letter, "a better balance between work and play". Last year and this year, with holiday visits to Mombasa in Kenya, Kerala in India and London, accompanied by my wife on all occasions, I have made a good beginning in my efforts to achieve "a better balance between work and play" in retirement.

Uche Mbanefo quoted lines from a poem by William Wordsworth, an English poet, whose poems I enjoyed reading when I was a student at Adams College. He stated in simple lyrical language that life is meaningless if we cannot enjoy the beauty of nature around us due to preoccupation with material things. He had a profound influence on me.

Throughout my life, and even in the years I served the people of my country as a politician, faith in God was the anchor of my soul. I was always puzzled to note that there was so much in the world which seemed to contradict what I felt was the truth about God's love and acceptance of Him. I remembered that by my baptism as a Christian God's love should always be the starting point. If anyone tried to tempt me to do anything which contradicted my faith, then we had to part company for I had no other choice. Like many fellow countrymen and women, I have led a strenuous life of considerable stress and at times enormous risk to my life. I always held to my faith in a God of love and mercy. It is this conviction about God which has sustained and supported me throughout my struggles, in my distress and when it seemed that everything for which I have stood was likely to be lost.

As Margaret and I left Adams College after a short visit in April 2000, I remembered that it was this Christian institution which had strengthened my faith in God. At Adams College, I learnt that if a man has faith in Jesus Christ, he also has faith in God who sent Jesus and who was there in Jesus. I also learnt that when a man has complete faith – acceptance, surrender, trust – towards Jesus, he really has found God.

I shall never forget.

A P P E N D I X

I

Address to the Twenty Fifth Session of the General Assembly of the United Nations, 24 Sept. 1970.

Mr President, I wish, first of all, to associate my delegation with the sentiments of those who have already congratulated you on your election to the high office of president of this crucial and historic session of the General Assembly. Your credentials and personal attributes leave my delegation in no doubt that you are eminently qualified to guide the proceedings of this important session of the General Assembly. Mr President, you can count on the unstinting support and cooperation of my delegation to make your tenure of office a success.

Allow me also to pay tribute to your predecessor, Her Excellency Mrs Angie Brooks-Randolph of Liberia, who presided over the proceedings of the last session. The success which attended our last session is attributable, in no small measure, to her able and wise leadership. This illustrious daughter of Africa has set to rest the myth that statesmanship is the monopoly of men.

The secretary-general of the United Nations, U Thant, as always, deserves our gratitude, support and encouragement. We are indebted to him for his tireless efforts in the cause of peace and justice. His is a continuing service to mankind and we wish him well.

The United Nations is charged with the grave responsibility of maintaining international peace and security. To that end, the organization is expected to take effective measures for the prevention and removal of threats to the peace and for the suppression of acts of aggression or other breaches of the peace, and to bring about by peaceful means, and in conformity with the principles of justice and international law, adjustments or settlement of international disputes or situations likely to lead to a breach of the peace. The organization is also charged with the responsibility for fostering the development of friendly relations among nations, based on respect for the principle of equal rights and self-determination of peoples. Yet another function of this organization has to do with the promotion of international cooperation in solving international problems of an economic, social, cultural and humanitarian character, and encouragement of respect for human rights and fundamental freedoms for all without distinction as to race, sex, language or religion.

These are the lofty aims and objectives of the United Nations and all of us, whose countries are represented here today, have resolved to combine our efforts to make these noble objectives a living and tangible reality.

Yet it is a fact that many of us, for reasons best known to ourselves, have chosen to make a mockery of our obligations under the Charter. More often than not, we have adhered to the aims and purposes of the organization more in the breach than in the observance. The tension, the injustice and the exploitation of man by man which characterize the age we live in are, in large measure, a function of the refusal of member states to live up to their Charter obligations. So long as this attitude of mind on the part of member states remains unchanged, monstrous crimes against humanity will continue to be the order of the day in many parts of the world. The principle of self-determination of countries and peoples – a principle which this august body has reaffirmed time and again – will continue to be flouted with impunity in some of the countries represented here today.

The enemies of peace, freedom and justice will stop at nothing to achieve their sinister objectives. They are everywhere on the offensive and are determined, as never before, to undermine the efforts of this organization to build a world order in which respect for the rights of man becomes a concrete reality.

The denial of human rights to which I have alluded, exists in its crudest and ugliest forms and manifestations, as I hope to show, in Southern Rhodesia, South Africa, Namibia, Mozambique, Angola and Guinea (Bissau).

Southern Rhodesia continues to be Africa's running sore. The year under review has yielded no evidence that we are to any significant extent nearer to the resolution of the deadlock in that rebel colony. The measures which the international community has taken against Southern Rhodesia have so far proved hopelessly ineffective. Even Ian Smith himself and his cohorts have openly stated that the sanctions policy is nothing more than a mere inconvenience. The declaration of a so-called republic in Southern Rhodesia early this year is further evidence that the rebels intend to stick to their defiant posture.

As we assemble here today, the rebels are redoubling their efforts to turn back the clock of history. The course they have embarked upon promises nothing but continued enslavement of the black man in Zimbabwe. The most disturbing feature of the situation is that Britain, the administering authority, is doing next to nothing to bring the rebels to their knees.

The time has now come for us to admit that the measures we have so far taken against rebel Rhodesia have not produced the desired results.

In the face of rebel intransigence, the United Nations logical

493

course of action lies in the application of the relevant provisions of Chapter VII of the Charter. Half-hearted measures like the ones the organization has so far sponsored will continue to prove futile.

The situation in South Africa continues to be a grave threat to international peace and security. In that country, the high priests of racial bigotry have given no indication that they intend, even in the far-distant future, to allow the sixteen million oppressed and dispossessed people of both that country and Namibia to have a say in the affairs of their fatherlands. Countless resolutions have been passed by this assembly and other organs of the United Nations but there is still no evidence of a change of heart on the part of the descendants of the *Voortrekkers* in South Africa. World public opinion is ignored with impunity and every day that passes sees the tightening up of the fascist grip on every facet of South African life to ensure that the oppressed millions have no chance of effectively challenging the immoral and inhuman system under which they are forced to live. The pass laws, the Terrorism Act and related pieces of fascist legislation continue to be applied with a severity beyond description.

The country's overall defence expenditure continues to maintain an upward trend. The implications of this development are very clear. It is to ensure that the frontiers of injustice are secure – secure, that is, from the possibility of the ideas of freedom and human equality ever taking root in South Africa. One expects a government to increase its expenditure to defend the frontiers of freedom and justice but in South Africa the reverse is true. Vast sums of money are spent each year to defend and consolidate injustice and oppression.

That is the story of a country doing its utmost to cling stubbornly to antiquated and totally unacceptable norms of conduct in this latter part of the twentieth century. Zambia's posture vis-à-vis

South Africa reflects our well-known concern for the welfare of man. We have condemned and we shall continue to condemn the perpetrators of the evil policy of *apartheid* and racial arrogance. We condemn, in the strongest terms, the collusion of Western countries with the fascist regime of South Africa. The sale or intended sale of arms to South Africa by reactionary forces in Western Europe is a source of great concern to us. We therefore call on France, West Germany and Britain to refrain from this criminal act. The wider interests of freedom and justice in South Africa should take precedence over reasons of economic self-interest which currently dominate thinking in Western capitals.

As a faithful member of the United Nations and the Organization of African Unity, Zambia has supported and continues to support resolutions passed by the organs of these two bodies calling on member states to render moral and material support to the victims of *apartheid*. We are firmly committed to the just cause of the oppressed people of South Africa and Namibia.

The cost to Zambia of our opposition to *apartheid* is enormous, but we are determined to follow the course we have chosen because we believe it is the right course. Coexistence with the forces of evil in South Africa or anywhere is totally unacceptable to us. *Apartheid* is the very antithesis of what Zambia stands for both at home and abroad. We intend to remain true to our convictions.

In Mozambique, Angola and Guinea (Bissau) the exploitation of man by man, as is the case in rebel Rhodesia, South Africa and Namibia, is the order of the day. The victim, as always, is the innocent black man whose only crime – if it can be called a crime – is that he wants to have an unfettered enjoyment of his birthright. In attempt to justify their atrocities in Mozambique, Angola and Guinea (Bissau), the ruling circles in Lisbon have advanced a number of preposterous claims and arguments. One

495

such strange argument is that the territories they now control in Africa are overseas provinces of Portugal and form an integral part of one unitary state. As we have emphasized time and again, no act of a Portuguese dictator can make any part of Africa an integral part of Europe. Nor do we accept the contention that fascist Portugal has a civilizing and preordained mission in Africa. That is an insult to the dignity of the African continent, an insult we are not prepared to stomach.

The people of Portuguese-ruled territories in Africa and all freedom-loving people the world over do not subscribe to Lisbon's spurious arguments. It is therefore not surprising that the oppressed masses in those territories have sought, since the early sixties, to liberate themselves from the yoke of Portuguese colonialism by every means possible. Nationalist organizations in all those territories are waging a heroic and relentless struggle to achieve their freedom and independence.

Portugal, as is well known, has reacted to the nationalist challenge by increasing the striking power of its military machine. It is, with the overt support of its NATO allies, waging what can only be described as a brutal war to defend the fiction that Africa is part of the Iberian peninsula. Through Portugal's colonial wars and unholy crusades in Africa, Mozambique, Angola and Guinea (Bissau) have become more blood-drenched than the Roman Colosseum in the days of the Emperor Trajan.

The government and people of the Republic of Zambia have refused to adopt an ostrich-like attitude on the question of Portuguese colonialism. At the time of our independence in 1964, my president, Dr Kenneth D Kaunda, stated that Zambia's independence would be meaningless, so long as any part of the African continent remained under foreign domination. We have not deviated from this stand. Both here and at the Organization of African Unity, we have made it a point to sponsor and vote for resolutions calling on Portugal to grant independence to territories still under its barbaric rule.

The system of government prevailing in territories under Portuguese administration runs counter to the values we cherish in Zambia. The alien practice of the exploitation of man by man is completely unacceptable to independent Zambia. Zambia's role will continue to be one of firm and consistent opposition to Portugal until the territories of Mozambique, Angola and Guinea (Bissau) are free and independent.

One of the most heartening developments in the past year has been the appearance of the OAU Manifesto on Southern Africa. This historic document was adopted by the twenty fourth session of the General Assembly. Western spokesmen praised the document as "constructive", "thoughtful", "promising", "wise" and "humane". I should like to observe with deep regret that there has been a tendency to leave it there. This attitude is obviously not conducive to the peaceful settlement of the Southern African situation which we all desire. The response of the Western Powers to the manifesto should not be to heave a sigh of relief and slip back comfortably into inaction.

It is vital for all of us to recognize that the manifesto provides us with our last slim chance of preventing a racial holocaust in Southern Africa. Moreover, whether this opportunity is seized will depend more on the West than on Africa. The African states have done their part in extending the hand of friendship. It is up to the West now to grasp it eagerly and energetically.

The Middle East is one of the hotbeds of tension in the world today. In that part of the world, peace is a strange bedfellow. Since 1948 – over twenty years ago – the region has been the scene of repeated military clashes between Israel and its neighbouring Arab States. The last major encounter between the two sides took place in June 1967. Since then, sporadic fighting has been a characteristic feature of the region. The possibility of yet another major conflagration cannot be ruled out, notwithstanding the recent peace initiatives.

The involvement of the two super-powers in the conflict, though somewhat indirect, raises the ominous possibility of a nuclear exchange between the two giants over the issue. Such an exchange would have incalculable consequences for mankind as a whole. A nuclear war could very well result in the extinction of all forms of life on our planet. This is more than a theoretical possibility.

Zambia's stand on the tragedy – that is, the Middle East – has reflected our well-known desire for peace and justice in the world. We have condemned recourse to violence and have called on both sides to show restraint and to scrupulously observe Security Council resolutions on the issue. Cease-fire violations can only increase tension in the area and thus jeopardize the prospects of peace which we all desire.

It is the view of my delegation that there will be no lasting peace in the region, so long as the basic causes of the bickering between the two sides are not given serious attention. The injustice the Palestinian refugees have suffered is the main source of friction in the region. It is, therefore, our considered opinion that in any search for a lasting solution to the conflict, this fact should be taken into account.

For its part, Zambia will continue, as it has done in the past, to press for a negotiated settlement in accordance with the provisions of Security Council resolution 242 (1967) of 22 November 1967. We reiterate our firm opposition to the acquisition of territories by military conquest. We once again call on Israel to withdraw immediately from all Arab territories occupied after 5 June 1967.

The current situation does not augur well for peace and security in the area, and we can only hope that the parties to the dispute will appreciate the need to cooperate to the full with Ambassador Gunner Jarring, the secretary general's special representative, in his tireless efforts to restore peace to that troubled part of the world. It is not in the interest of peace for either side to refuse to be associated with current attempts to find a lasting solution to the conflict.

The intransigence and cynicism of those who have adopted a holier-than-thou attitude is the main stumbling block to the restoration of the lawful rights of the People's Republic of China in this organization. The most disturbing part of it all is that those same countries whose representatives have energetically resisted any move to have the People's Republic of China in this organization have chosen to remain silent on the need to get racist South Africa and fascist Portugal to honour their Charter obligations.

My delegation has never been impressed by the facile arguments employed by the opponents of the admission of the People's Republic of China to membership of the United Nations. So long as they support forces of evil in this organization we shall continue to question their right to block attempts to restore Peking's lawful rights. It is self-deception to cling to the notion that the People's Republic of China does not exist. China is a living reality, and there can be no doubt about that. Nor is it a wise policy to exclude that country from the dialogue of man. The fact of the matter is that, so long as we treat the People's Republic of China as an international outcast, we cannot expect that country to be of any great help in the solution of many of the problems confronting this organization today.

If we are really serious about peace, disarmament and related issues, we must take into account the need to enlist the support and cooperation of the People's Republic of China. My delegation will, as always, spare no effort to ensure that justice is done to the People's Republic of China, because it is bound to play an important role in the international scene.

One of the two super-powers – the United States of America – is fighting one of the smallest and poorest nations in South-East Asia. Vietnam, which is currently the subject of the inconclusive Paris peace talks, has never known peace since the turn of the last century.

The United States is in Vietnam, we are told, to prove to the enemy that aggression – whatever that means – does not pay. South Vietnam, it is emphasized by the self-appointed world policemen, must be saved from communist aggression, planned and directed, so the argument runs, from Hanoi and Peking. The ruling circles in Washington would have us believe that the Viet-Cong and their allies threaten the security of the United States. This, as everyone knows, is a pretext to justify their illegal presence in South-East Asia.

The conflict in Vietnam is basically a civil strife and my delegation feels very strongly that external forces have no right whatsoever to internationalise and complicate local conflict such as this one. The people of Vietnam should be left alone to fashion their destiny in the manner they deem fit.

We renew our call to the government of the United States of America to withdraw all its troops from Vietnam and to enable the people of that beleaguered country to determine their future free from foreign interference.

The crushing burden of armaments is one of the unresolved issues of our times. The world today is saturated with weapons of mass destruction. History has shown that stockpiles of weapons of war are not a sure guarantee for peace and security in the world. Weapons of war in the arsenals of nations can only serve to aggravate the already tense situation in the world.

It is the view of my delegation that the road to international peace and sanity calls for the adoption of measures designed to rid mankind of weapons of mass destruction. There can be no lasting peace in the world as long as the nuclear giants refuse to accede to our just demands to dismantle their deadly weapons. Our goal is general and complete disarmament. Half-hearted measures like the Treaty on the Non-Proliferation of Nuclear Weapons (resolution 2373 (XXII)) do not offer man a genuine sigh of relief.

One of the principal aims and objectives of the United Nations and its specialized agencies is, in the language of the Charter, "to promote social progress and better standards of life in larger freedom". That noble objective, however, has not been achieved by the United Nations. It is an indisputable fact that the gap between the rich and poor nations has been widening with the passage of time. The material condition of the majority of the people of this earth has not greatly improved since the signing of the Charter in San Francisco in 1945. If anything, their condition has deteriorated.

The failure of many international initiatives, including the First United Nations Development Decade, to achieve the goals of economic development is a matter of great concern to my delegation. As we prepare to launch the Second United Nations Development Decade, we should do well to ensure that we avoid the pitfalls of the first.

One of the obstacles to economic prosperity in many of our developing countries stems from existing discriminatory practices in international trade. We have drawn the attention of developed countries to the continued existence of discriminatory tariff arrangements, such as the General Agreement on Tariffs and Trade, which entrench and institutionalise unfair trade practices. We have called for the liberalization and restructuring of international trade agreements, but all our appeals have fallen on deaf ears.

The world cannot indefinitely remain half rich and half poor. Bold and imaginative steps should be taken to improve the lot of our people. Let me emphasize in no uncertain terms that, since the founding of the United Nations in San Francisco twenty-five years ago, the more developed nations have pursued a self-destructive policy of economic exploitation of the poor nations of the world; and yet, in the final analysis, their own interests and those of poor nations are closely interdependent. In the interests of the whole of humanity, in the interests of peace and security, we solemnly call on the more developed nations to adopt a positive and realistic approach to the problem of formulating practical guidelines for the Second United Nations Development Decade. Stable peace is not attainable so long as uneven distribution of the wealth of this earth continues to characterize relations among nations.

Finally, I wish to refer briefly to the Third Conference of Heads of State of Governments of Non-Aligned Countries, which my country had the great honour and privilege of hosting in Lusaka from 8 to 10 September.

That conference made very important decisions on the current international situation. The Lusaka Declaration on Peace, Independence, Development, Cooperation and Democratisation of International Relations which the conference issued, is an appeal to sanity, and we commend it to all those who share with us the view that peace is one and indivisible. The declaration defines the position of non-aligned countries on crucial issues such as *apartheid*, colonialism, disarmament and economic development and cooperation.

The fact that that this important conference has taken place has proved that the non-aligned movement is not a spent force as our detractors would have the world believe. The conference has demonstrated beyond doubt that non-alignment is now a firmly established and permanent feature of international relations. My head of state will, in the course of this session, come to New York to give the United Nations a full report on the decisions of that historic and epoch-making conference.

As we celebrate the twenty fifth anniversary of the founding of the United Nations, we should take stock of the critical issues which continue to bedevil our efforts to achieve the aims and objectives enshrined in the Charter of our organization.

The world of the twentieth century is sadly fearful and divided against itself. It is, therefore, incumbent upon us all to ensure that we remove the basic causes of the mutual suspicions and distrust which have placed humanity into hostile and apparently irreconcilable camps.

My delegation believes that the greatest challenge to all peace-loving men and women today in every part of the world is the task of providing international harmony, eliminating strife between man and man caused by religious differences, racial antagonism or ideological conflict. This, then, is the task that my delegation is committed to fulfil as we deliberate on various items on the agenda of this historic twenty fifth session of the General Assembly of the United Nations. We humbly and earnestly invite all the members to share with us this spirit of purposeful determination to make this session a turning point in man's quest for peace on earth and goodwill among men.

A P P E N D I X

II

Speech to the General Assembly of the SOS Children Village, Imst, Austria in 1998.

It would be premature today to attempt to make a balance sheet or inventory of what this General Assembly has achieved in its deliberations during the last two days. In spite of the limitation of time, it has been able to clarify important issues and to develop new ideas expressed in the reports of the secretary-general and the Supervisory Board. Messages which have been sent to this General Assembly from friendly governments have been quite supportive and encouraging.

Our country is being represented at this General Conference for the first time following the establishment of the SOS Children's Village of Zambia Trust only two years ago. Therefore, the representatives of our organization are attending this General Conference to interact as much as possible with our counterparts from countries where SOS Children's Villages have been in existence for many years. We are confident that from contacts with delegates representing long established Children's Villages we ourselves will be better equipped and properly motivated to serve the interests of disadvantaged children in our country who will enter the SOS Children's Village of Zambia from time to time.

Our organisation's programme for the development of the SOS Children's Village for Zambia a few kilometres only from the capital city, Lusaka, has now reached an advanced stage. Funds have been approved for the construction of the SOS Children's Village complex – thanks to the generosity of the head office administration of SOS-Kinderdorf International. Tenders were widely advertised and the response from local construction companies was good. The tender was awarded to a local company of good reputation which was the most competitive of all in terms of cost and time of completion. It is expected that about mid September this year a ceremony for laying the foundation stone will be held on site at which the government minister responsible for Sport, Youth and Child Development will officiate as guest of honour.

The government of Zambia has been recently quite supportive of our efforts to establish the SOS Children's Village of Zambia in the shortest time possible. The piece of land on which the SOS-Children's Village complex will be developed was freely given to our organization by the government. No difficulties have been encountered at all in obtaining from the government exemptions, concessions and other privileges and authorizations for our organization. On this basis, we believe that this healthy partnership between our government and SOS Children's Village of Zambia Board of Trustees will continue in future.

The Republic of Zambia is a country with a population of about ten million people. It lies across the heart of the interior plateau of Southern Africa surrounded by nine countries, namely Tanzania, the Democratic Republic of Congo, Angola, Botswana, Zimbabwe, Namibia, Mozambique and Malawi. It covers about three quarters of a million square kilometres. Roughly, it is the size of France, Hungary, Austria and Switzerland combined.

Zambia is endowed with rich minerals, including copper, gemstones and a wide variety of industrial mineral deposits. The country ranks among the top three producers in the world of quality emeralds. In addition, it has abundant water supply from four big rivers and inland lakes which make it potentially a source of cheap hydroelectric power for export to neighbouring countries. It has rich soils in most parts of the country on which practically all types of crops can be grown.

Notwithstanding its great potential for development it is unquestionably one of the world's poorest countries. And, at the same time, one of the most highly indebted countries in the world. Life expectancy has dropped considerably in recent years due, in part, to the HIV/Aids outbreak in Zambia just like in other parts of the world. Consequently, many parents die leaving young children without anyone to care for them. The difficult economic conditions make it difficult for the government to provide new homes for such orphaned children.

Therefore, there can be no doubt that on humanitarian grounds the establishment of the SOS Children's Village of Zambia will be a significant forward step in improving facilities for disadvantaged children. I and my colleagues on the Board of Trustees of the SOS Children's Village of Zambia will strive very hard to develop the new complex as a shining example of similar institutions established by SOS-Kinderdorf International worldwide.

Mr President, in conclusion, may I have the privilege to express on behalf of the Republic of Zambia our highest appreciation to all those who have made this session of the 16th Ordinary General Assembly of SOS-Kinderdorf International a success and to the government and people of Austria for their hospitality. In particular to you, Mr President, I submit our highest regards and respect for your wisdom and intellectual integrity in bringing this 16th Ordinary General Assembly to a meaningful end.

Index

507

Northern Rhodesia Commission, Office of; 111-13, 115
Northern Rural Constituency; 118, 130, 131-34, 142
Nyalugwe, Naphy; 331-32
Nyanga, Edward; 188-90
Nyirenda, Jameson; 12
Nyirenda, Wesley; 39, 396
Nyirongo, Jones; 246, 247

O

Oasis Forum; 444-45, 446, 450, 480
Oosthuizen, HJ; 301-02
Organisation of African Unity (OAU); 207, 232, 495, 497
O'Riordan Commission; 251

P

Parirenyatwa, Samuel; 33, 34
Patel, Solly; 402
Peru; 185, 193
Phillips, Professor; 293-95
Philport, Roy; 136
Phiri, Alport; 40-41, 42
Pike, Mary; 41-42
Post, The; 447-48, 449, 475, 478-80
Preferential Trade Area (PTA); 383, 409-20, 421, 424, 426, 427
President's Citizenship College; 137-38
PTA Bank. (See Eastern and Southern African Trade and Development Bank)
Public Works, Department of; 1, 4, 7, 9, 14
Puta, Robinson; 124

Q

Quirk, David Ffinlo; 376

R

Ramathe, ACJ; 14
Reed, James; 182-83

Rhodesia, see Southern Rhodesia.
Roads and Road Traffic Act; 362
Road Fund; 385
Roan Consolidated Mines; 289
Roan Selection Trust; 182-84
Roberts, Hedley; 64
Roberts, John; 142, 454
Robertson, Rev Maxwell; 40
Rowland, Tiny; 277-79
Rural Development, Ministry of; 224

S

Sakala, Acting Supreme Court Judge; 347
Sakala, Richard; 441
Sallah, AM; 424, 425
Sardanis, Andrew; 193, 269
Saunders, William; 385
Seal, RJ; 18
Shamwana, Edward; 177, 312, 318, 319, 324, 326, 330-31, 335, 341, 343, 351
Sharma, Beejay; 301, 437
Sharma, Dr Raj; 211, 226, 273, 279
Shaw, Joseph; 124
Sheikh, Gulam; 324, 325, 332
Shimba, Prof Lawrence; 456, 457, 464, 468, 475
Sichilongo, Lloyd; 279, 289
Sichone, Lucy; 457, 466
Silungwe, Annel; 270, 314, 322-23, 347
Simbyakula, Dr Ngosa; 407
Simuziya, Joshua; 324, 325, 332
Sirleaf, Ellen Johnson; 235, 237
Siwale, Donald; 50
Skinner, James; 454
Smallwood, Harry; 390
Snelson, Peter; 45, 62, 146, 157-59, 162-63, 167-69
Soko, Jasper; 226, 228, 230
Sokota, George; 261, 437
Sokota, Paskale; 50, 61

Wilker, Dr Karl H; 35, 38
Willombe, Abraham; 13, 17, 83
Willombe, Bevin; 310, 314, 316, 322,
    325-26, 329-30, 336, 337, 339,
    342, 344, 347
Willombe, Linda; 314
Wina, Arthur; 130-31, 135, 176, 280,
    426
Wina, Sikota; 55, 77, 135, 190, 256,
    271
Women for Change (WfC); 478
Wood, Anthony; 346-47, 348
Woodbridge, CT; 102
World Bank; 235, 270, 283, 293-94,
    296, 297-98, 362, 384-85, 413,
    488, 489

Y

Yamba, Dauti; 50
Young, Sir Hubert; 9

Z

Zaire (see also Congo); 185, 239,
    260, 312
Zamanglo Industrial Corporation Ltd;
    369-73
Zambia African National Congress;
    76, 109
Zambia Congress of Trade Unions;
    458
Zambia Confederation of Chambers
    of Commerce; 437, 438
Zambia Daily Mail; 342-44
Zambia Library Service; 157
Zambia National Commercial Bank;
    264, 267, 358, 360-61, 376, 379-
    81
Zambia Privatisation Agency (ZPA);
    370-73, 436-38
Zulu, Boniface; xiii
Zulu, Grey; 177-78, 331-32